Adventures in Good Cooking

Adventures in Good Cooking

Duncan Hines

Edited by Louis Hatchett

Foreword by Michael and Jane Stern

The University Press of Kentucky

Scholarly publisher for the Commonwealth, serving Bellarmine University, Berea College, Centre College of Kentucky, Eastern Kentucky University, The Filson Historical Society, Georgetown College, Kentucky Historical Society, Kentucky State University, Morehead State University, Murray State University, Northern Kentucky University, Transylvania University, University of Kentucky, University of Louisville, and Western Kentucky University.

Editorial and Sales Offices: The University Press of Kentucky
663 South Limestone Street, Lexington, Kentucky 40508-4008
www.kentuckypress.com

Previously published in 2002 by Mercer University Press

The Library of Congress has cataloged the 2002 edition of this book as follows:

Adventures in good eating and the art of carving in the home
Duncan Hines / edited by Louis B. Hatchett, Jr.
1st ed.
p. cm.
Originally published: 1933
With a new introduction
ISBN 0-86554-809-0 (hardcover: alk paper)
1. Cookery, American   I. Hatchett, Louis.   II. Title
TX715 .H7226 2002
641.5973-dc21
2002151133

ISBN 978-0-8131-4468-9 (pbk.: alk. paper)
ISBN 978-0-8131-4470-2 (pdf)
ISBN 978-0-8131-4469-6 (epub)

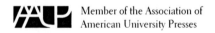

For Linda Priscilla

Foreword

As a restaurant reviewer, Duncan Hines earned fame for his integrity, for his high standards of cleanliness as well as cuisine, and for his unfailing ability to find wonderful things to eat. It was a natural next step that the author of *Adventures in Good Eating* should carry those standards into a cookbook: *Adventures in Good Cooking*. As he conceived it, this was not to be merely an all-purpose collection of workable recipes. It was to be a pantheon of extraordinary recipes from the finest kitchens in America. To get the recipes, Hines went to restaurants that had earned inclusion in his guidebook. Most of the chefs and owners he approached were so grateful for his recognition (which had invariably boosted their business) that they were only too happy to share the secrets for some of their best and best-known dishes.

In these pages you will find outstanding recipes indeed—none of them twenty-first-century trendy, but many of them timeless (Lindy's Cheesecake from New York), and others of them time-burnished relics that deserve enthusiastic revival (Ham Pie with Cheese Biscuit Top from the Anderson Hotel of Wabasha, Minnesota; Baked Indian Pudding from the Toll House of Whitman, Massachusetts). Browsing through the bonanza of more than seven hundred dishes, from the Waldorf Astoria's Brandied Grapefruit to Brennan's Bananas Foster, is like sitting down in a restaurant that presents you with an extensive, inviting menu. There is so much one craves to taste.

What amazes us is that every recipe we have tried from this book really works, exactly as written. Having authored several cookbooks using favorite restaurants' recipes, we have inevitably found ourselves rewriting and revising nearly everything the restaurants provided. As a rule, talented professional cooks are too good at what they do to pay close attention to precise measurements and exact times. They do it by feel and by taste. But Duncan Hines being Duncan Hines, you can be sure that each of the recipes he included passed muster in his own kitchen, presided over by his wife, or in the kitchen of a close and trusted relative. In addition to the recipes, the book is richly larded with savvy and fun marginalia ("Apple pie without rat cheese is minus the 'umpth.'"), and it includes extensive directions on "The Art of Carving in the Home."

As Roadfood explorers who consider ourselves deeply in debt to the pioneering work of Duncan Hines, we find the contents of this book especially alluring, because they so vividly reflect the interesting, regional, or unique meals Hines discovered in his travels and that he highlighted in his guidebook. Cooking from these pages is as close as you can come to actually exploring the culinary landscape along with the master. Here you will enjoy the sorts of extraordinary dishes that made eating on the road such a passion for Duncan Hines and a trip of delicious discovery for his millions of readers.

Michael and Jane Stern

Preface

As I was researching my biography of Duncan Hines (*Duncan Hines: The Man Behind the Cake Mix*), one of the items I had to examine was the last of a trio of books that Hines published in the latter half of the 1930s. In 1936 he self-published the first edition of his highly regarded *Adventures in Good Eating*, a guide to America's finest roadside restaurants. He followed that up in 1938 with *Lodging for a Night*, his guide to the nation's superior hotels and motels. And in 1939 he presented the non-traveling public with *Adventures in Good Cooking*, a collection of recipes that not only consisted of secret dishes from America's best restaurants of the time but also featured a number of delectable edibles from his family and friends.

I tried to acquire a copy of this book (this was before the Internet arrived on the scene), but finding one was difficult. When I interviewed people who owned a copy and requested to borrow it for further examination, they were reluctant to part with it. It was as if they were lending someone their soul. They were very possessive of it. The copies I had a chance to peruse were markedly worn and had been used extensively. They most definitely had not sat on a bookshelf collecting dust. The people I interviewed, all in their seventies and eighties, swore by the book's recipes. They swooned over its wonders, proclaiming it provided some of the most heavenly mouthfuls that had ever graced the human tongue.

Well, that got my attention. Instead of borrowing one of the cookbooks, I paid seventy-five dollars for a very good used copy. Once I examined it, I realized what all the fuss was about. These were extraordinarily good recipes. I concluded that today's public should have the opportunity to prepare, sample, and enjoy the same recipes that millions of others had savored a few generations earlier.

Most people have forgotten or have never been told that in the 1940s and 1950s, among American housewives, "Duncan Hines" was the most trusted name in the food industry. The name was synonymous with uncompromising quality, particularly in the realm of food.

From 1905 until 1938 Duncan Hines had been a salesman of printing wares and advertising specialties whose hobby was eating in roadside restaurants. But he wouldn't eat just anywhere. In that day and age, restaurants were not safe places in which to dine. Hundreds of Americans died as a result of unsanitary restaurant conditions; many others suffered severe stomach disorders after consuming squalid roadside fare. Eating in roadside restaurants in that day was a hit-or-miss affair. Sometimes you got lucky and had a wonderful meal; other times you did not. And if you were really unlucky, you went to the morgue. Especially in non-metropolitan areas, eating a meal away from home was always a risk and seldom a pleasure. As Duncan Hines crisscrossed the country as a salesman, whenever he dined in a restaurant that not only served excellent food but had a very clean kitchen in which to prepare it, he jotted down its name and location in a notebook and would visit it again next time he happened to be in town.

Even though this notebook expanded and contracted over the years, Hines soon acquired a reputation among his fellow salesmen as the man who knew where all the good restaurants were, ones in which it was safe to dine. Understandably, everyone in his profession wanted to dine in safety. But they were not the only ones interested in such matters. Honeymooners, vacationers, travelers of all sorts wanted to drive across the country with the assurance that they would arrive at their destinations unharmed; a fatal meal could ruin anyone's trip. As word of Hines's knowledge spread, they began calling and writing him, asking where was the best place to eat in certain cities.

For many years Hines managed this traffic in advice reasonably well. But in 1934 a Chicago newspaper wrote an article about his hobby of finding good restaurants, and from that point forward his life was never the same. People not only from Chicago but from distant cities began calling him with such frequency that he had to find a way to put a stop to it.

So when Christmas 1935 rolled around, he printed a list of 167 excellent restaurants he had visited throughout the nation and, along with his Christmas cards, sent them to over one thousand people with the hope that it would cut down on the number of letters and phone calls he had lately been receiving. Unfortunately, this action just accelerated the problem. The people to whom he had sent the list had, in turn, showed it to their friends, which generated an even heavier wave of requests. Hines tried to stop them by charging a dollar for it, but it stopped no one. Everyone, it seemed, wanted it. Finally, in exasperation, he put his notebook of restaurants into book form and self-published it in June 1936. Thus was born his restaurant guide *Adventures in Good Eating*.

The book had almost no advertising. Sales were generated strictly through word of mouth. People who tried it marveled at its accuracy for predicting enjoyable high-quality meals. Before that time, restaurant guides were nothing more than paid advertisements. Hines turned this practice on its head. He boldly announced that he would never accept outside advertisements, and he made it explicitly clear to everyone that he could not be bought. His standards for excellence were extremely high and rigorously uncompromising. When Hines said something was superb—regardless of what it was—everyone knew it was the best to be found. If he recommended it, his stamp of approval was all anyone needed to know.

By 1939 *Adventures in Good Eating* had caused many restaurants to celebrate Hines's arrival. Simply by word of mouth, his annual publication had driven most of the book-length advertisements masquerading as restaurant guides out of business. The public came to believe that if a restaurant wasn't included in Hines's guidebook, then it probably was not safe enough to dine in, and even if it was, its quality might be merely passable. For the most part, the restaurants listed in Hines's guidebook prospered; those that were not either struggled or failed. Hines had set a standard for the entire restaurant industry. Those who didn't live up to it the public left behind. Thus, with only the power of a book, Duncan Hines dragged the restaurant industry into the twentieth century.

Only those restaurants that could prepare their meals to Hines's satisfaction and that had sparkling clean kitchens that any guest could enter at any time could qualify for inclusion in his book. Restaurants that failed that test were barred from its pages. Hines arranged for a number of individuals—when he couldn't do it himself—to make surprise kitchen inspections to ensure that the institutions he recommended always remained above reproach. If he ever received a stream of complaints that a restaurant in one of his books had fallen down on the job, it was quickly removed from its pages, usually never to be seen again. And if that ever happened to a restaurant, it was not long before the restaurant closed.

This book, *Adventures in Good Cooking*, was inaugurated when a number of readers of his restaurant guide requested that he put together a cookbook of recipes drawn from the establishments he recommended. Hines realized that these culinary institutions would probably not divulge their most prized concoctions, but he surmised that they might be willing to part with one or two lesser, but no less delectable, ones. So as he traveled around the country, investigating new restaurants and inspecting old ones, he inquired about the possibilities. He was surprised at the response. In the eyes of the owners of the restaurants he recommended, Hines had done so much to elevate their businesses by providing them with a never-ending stream of customers that they gladly gave him a number of recipes for his proposed cookbook.

Hines collected the recipes, had them tested in his hometown of Bowling Green, Kentucky,[1] and published *Adventures in Good Cooking* in October 1939. After 1946 his third wife, Clara, helped him put out future editions of the cookbook. It is possible that there are some recipes in this volume that came from his first wife, Florence, and that he then put under his own name (since it was published after her death), but whether this is fact will never be known, as there is no evidence available to substantiate that assertion.

Along with the restaurant recipes were several dishes that originated with his immediate family members, including a few that he first tasted as a boy at his grandmother Duncan's house in the early 1880s. Several members of his family as well as numerous friends who shared his passion for culinary excellence also contributed to the book, and their recipes were just as high in quality and flavor as the ones from his recommended restaurants.

The cookbook was updated annually. From time to time some recipes were removed, but only because better ones were added. Over the next twenty-three years almost 250 new selections were added. The first edition had 466 recipes; that number climbed to 713 by 1960.

By the mid-1940s, whenever Duncan Hines recommended anything, Americans had become accustomed to paying attention to what he had to say. Yet no matter how famous he had become, he would not compromise his ideals to make a dollar. When he said he would not include restaurants in his guidebook if they did not continually upgrade their establishments in all manner of culinary and sanitary standards (and he then gave detailed instructions on precisely what he wanted), his listed restaurants complied with his wishes; there was too much money to lose in not currying his favor. Soon, even restaurants that were not included in his guidebook were forced to raise their standards or close. The public demanded it. In this way, by 1948 Duncan Hines had become the most important name in the American food industry.

In October 1949 Hines entered the food preparation business when he and entrepreneur Roy Park established Hines-Park Foods; within a few years their company was distributing over 250 different high-quality items with the Duncan Hines logo. When the Duncan Hines cake mixes were introduced in 1951, they quickly became the company's best-selling item.

In July 1953 Duncan Hines, then seventy-three, decided to sell his publishing business to Park, who continued to publish the guidebooks and the cookbook for several years under the auspices of the Duncan Hines Institute.

In August 1956 Procter and Gamble not only bought the Duncan Hines cake mix, it also bought the rights to the Duncan Hines name in all its incarnations. Within a few years, only Procter and Gamble's Duncan Hines mixes were available. For a time Hines's face was featured on the Procter and Gamble label. Duncan Hines died in 1959, and his face was removed from the label out of respect. Roy Park discontinued printing the guidebooks and the cookbook in 1962 and moved onto other entrepreneurial ventures. After several years had gone by, Duncan Hines, the man, had faded from public memory, and in time only his name on the cake mixes remained. Since 2003 Pinnacle Foods of the Philadelphia area has been distributing the Duncan Hines brand.

In this book's companion volume, *The Dessert Book*, I explain who some of the individuals were that contributed to that book and this one, but here I'd like to explore some of the institutions who gave us these remarkable recipes. What were the names of these restaurants, many of which are now long forgotten? What else did they serve besides the recipes mentioned in this volume? Did Mr. Hines leave behind many clues for people interested in such questions to pick up the scent? The best thing we can do to answer these questions is let Duncan Hines describe some of the restaurants from which these recipes came and let the reader's imagination take over. Since information about many of them can be found in my biography of Duncan Hines, let me concentrate on those not mentioned in that volume.

First and foremost of the restaurants is the Lowell Inn, which is still a wonderful hotel in which to dine and sleep, and which is located just west of the Minneapolis–St. Paul metropolitan area. Duncan Hines and his wife at the time, Florence, made this delightful discovery on September 4, 1937. Billed as "The Mount Vernon of the West," the Lowell Inn was located in a town of scarcely eight thousand people, then nineteen miles from the Twin Cities. "I'd heard much that was good about the Lowell Inn long before I published my first book," wrote Hines years later. "Because I was always on the lookout for good food and fine eating places, I wired Arthur Palmer, the proprietor, for a reservation. He wrote back immediately, saying that the bridal suite was all ready for us." When Hines and Florence arrived, they were staggered by the building's beauty. "Not only [was] the bridal suite" beautiful, Hines wrote, "but every room in the place had been redecorated and through it all could be seen the fine hand of a woman—a woman of extremely good taste." Because Hines was always attracted to people who took care in looking after the smallest details, he quickly got acquainted with the owner of that hand, Nelle Palmer, and her husband, Arthur. From them Hines learned the history of their business and their "fierce devotion to quality." As they related their story, Arthur and Nelle Palmer made a great impression on Duncan Hines, one that blossomed into a friendship that lasted for many years.

Nelle and Arthur Palmer were show business people who performed in theaters across the upper Midwest. They were married on Nelle's thirty-fourth birthday on June 27, 1927.[2] At the time of the marriage, Nelle was an actress in her family's troupe, and Arthur played on the piano. Toward the end of the 1920s the Palmers saw the popularity of vaudeville as America's preferred form of entertainment rapidly diminish—and their way of life vanish with it. A variety of coalescing factors brought an end to their days as traveling entertainers. Talking motion pictures, increased popularity of radio, and the effects of the country's economic depression during the 1929–1930 entertainment season all contributed to closing the door on their form of live entertainment. After a few months, the couple quickly saw that they would not be eating regularly if they continued in their line of work, so they looked for another, more steady, occupation.

They saw an opportunity when they spoke one day with one of Arthur Palmer's relatives. "Hotel management, as it happened, seemed to run in the Palmer family." Arthur L. Roberts, Arthur Palmer's uncle, was at the time perhaps the Northwest's best-known hotel owner; he operated fourteen hotels in Minnesota, Montana, North Dakota, and Wisconsin. In 1930 Roberts was in need of a new manager for the Lowell Inn, a fifty-room hotel in Stillwater. Built on the former site of a popular inn known as the Sawyer House, which had been razed in 1924, the hotel had not attracted many visitors since its construction. It had been designed in the image of a Southern Colonial mansion, highlighted by thirteen white, colon-

naded pillars gracing its façade. Despite a long succession of man-
agers since its opening in 1927, no one had been able to make the
enormous civic structure a commercial success. In Roberts's estima-
tion, Arthur and Nelle Palmer could do no worse than those before
them, so he asked the couple if they would be willing to manage his
hotel. Facing perhaps even worse consequences if they remained in
vaudeville, the Palmers "were willing to give it a try." They opened
the inn under their management on Christmas Day 1930.[3]

Once they settled into their new environment, the Palmers,
step by step, set about transforming the Lowell Inn into a hotel that
left its guests talking about it for days. What set the Palmers apart
from others who had run the Lowell Inn in the past was that they
brought with them a flair for showmanship. They decided that if
they were going to manage a hotel, it had to be special enough to
cause travelers to drive miles out of their way to experience and rec-
ommend it to others. They borrowed money to accomplish their
ends and made the most of what was lent to them. Their hotel did
not offer its guests merely simple furnishings, utensils, and food, as
their predecessors had done; rather, they furnished the hotel with
"creamy Irish linens of a delicate weave, the finest Spode china, silver knives, forks, and spoons, and lovely crystal glassware," to name
just a few items. It was something out of the ordinary. The Palmers'
efforts paid off handsomely. Soon the best kind of advertising—word
of mouth—caused Americans from across the country to make pil-
grimages to the Lowell Inn to see what delights it held in store.

But it was Duncan Hines's mention of the Lowell Inn in the
1939 editions of *Adventures in Good Eating* and *Lodging for a Night*
that really put it on the map as a coveted destination for travelers. In
his restaurant guide, Hines praised the institution the Palmers had
created, noting that "the Colonial Dining Room is furnished in au-
thentic Southern Colonial reproductions and antiques. In the Garden Room [the dining room], there is a hewn stone fountain which
pours forth sparkling spring water into an illuminated pool where
guests may catch brook trout, which are then fried for them." Hines
jovially stated that catching the fish was great fun, and that the best
part of fishing for them was that guests did not have to worry about

the game warden. Hines was also impressed with the Lowell Inn's main dining room and its "lovely arched ceiling," but he was especially drawn to the food served there. It was not just the hotel's salad that mesmerized him, it was also their recipes for chicken, steak, and lamb chop dinners. But the menu item that impressed him the most was the plate of hot rolls the inn served, the virtues of which he extolled in his book for decades to come. While the rolls were, in his opinion, the best to be found in America, his favorite dessert entrée at the Lowell Inn was its pecan pie, which was, Hines stated with an air of finality, "the best I have ever encountered." Another after-dinner entrée of which he was most fond was the Lowell Inn's blueberry pie, which he said was excellent "because the berries are shipped specially from South Carolina." The Lowell Inn remained a restaurant Hines swooned over until the day he died, and a number of its recipes are found in this book and its companion volume, *The Dessert Book*.

There were literally thousands of restaurants that Duncan Hines recommended, but only a fraction of their number ever made it to his cookbook. Here are a few more of their number that were not detailed in the biography, followed by Hines's comments about them:

- *Shadow Hill Tea Room, Hernando, Mississippi.* "Follow the arrows in the town for a really excellent old-fashioned Southern dinner. Motorists come again and again for their chicken, souffles, waffles, and *fried custard.*"
- *Christmas Tree Inn, Kingman, Arizona.* "One of the big and pleasant surprises of your trip here [will be] when you stop at Santa Claus Acres and dine with 'Mrs. Santa Claus.' . . . [They have] [p]erhaps the best rum pie you ever ate, chicken a la North Pole and lots other unusual things."
- *McLester Hotel, Tuscaloosa, Alabama.* [This is] "a comfortable, immaculate hotel which serves especially good food. Some of their dishes which stand out are honey glazed country ham, Southern fried chicken, shrimp McLester, thick steak stuffed with Roquefort cheese, black bottom, lemon, spiced nut and

fresh fruit pies, plenty of fresh vegetables, good salads, sandwiches, etc."
- *Frances Tea Room, Atlanta, Georgia.* [This is] "a third-floor
  tea room that has become very popular [1941] because of the
  quality of the food. . . . Tea room dinners comprise a choice
  of cocktail or soup, chicken, steak or filet mignon, two vegetables, salad and among their good desserts is the best peppermint candy I ever ate."
- *Anna Maud Cafeteria, Oklahoma City, Oklahoma.* "Few caf-
  eterias have enjoyed such a quick and continued success as
  this one. [Their] French onion soup and vegetable soup are
  unusually good, as well as hot breads, pies, cakes, and salads,
  but those with a he-man craving for meat [will] go for their
  roast beef, baked ham, [and] chicken pie. [They also have]
  Southern chicken, creole shrimp, baked (honest) hash and
  other meats, and the best spinach I have encountered in a long
  time."
- *Parker House, Boston, Massachusetts.* "Originators of Parker
  House roll[s] and famous from coast to coast for more than
  80 years [1952]. Specialties: Parker House rolls (of course),
  broiled tripe, baked lobster, broiled scrod, lobster stew, chocolate cream pie."
- *Headley Inn, Zanesville, Ohio.* "The meals are delicious—cottage cheese and homemade ice cream from their own dairy,
  jams and jellies along with chicken and steak."
- *Le Mirliton, New York, New York.* "Another delightful French
  restaurant where 'George' makes one of the best orange desserts I ever tasted. Try his boola soup (a combination of green
  turtle and green pea with whipped cream on top and browned
  in the oven); breast of guinea hen; Escallopine de Veau a la
  Stroganoff [is] one of the tastiest dishes in town, with an extraordinary sauce made of butter, real paprika, mushrooms,
  truffles, parsley, tomato paste, cream and brandy."
- *The Dinner Bell, Oakland, California.* "Once in a while you
  eat at a place where, when you push back your chair, you say to
  yourself: 'This is the kind of dinner I could enjoy every night.'
  And that is the kind of cooking turned out by Mrs. Elliott.

Whatever you order, and all of it is mighty good, don't omit the fresh coconut cream pie."

- *New Perry Hotel, Perry, Georgia.* "An outstanding place for exceptional Southern food. Nannette and Yates Green invite gourmets traveling in this vicinity to enjoy regional food from Georgia. Its country ham (when available), the freshly caught fish, peaches (in season) in pies and desserts, delicious pecan pie [are among some of their noted fare]. Other specialties: Southern fried chicken, chicken pie, Southern steak filets. Salad dressings are homemade, [as are] their rolls, cakes and pies." The New Perry Hotel is still serving delicious meals that are placed before diners on fine, white tablecloths, surrounded by lovely floral arrangements that grace the table, and immaculately-dressed, white-coated waiters attend to the gustatory desires of every diner. It remains a wonderful example of gracious Southern dining at its best.
- *Sanders Cafe and [Motel] Court, Corbin, Kentucky.* More than a decade before Colonel Harland Sanders hit the road selling Kentucky Fried Chicken franchises, he owned a successful restaurant, one that Duncan Hines recommended. It prospered until the early 1950s, when rerouting of the main road forced traffic to bypass Sanders's establishment, compelling him to try his luck in his now better-known realm. From 1939 to at least 1952, Hines's listing of Sanders's restaurant read: "A very good place to stop en route to Cumberland Falls and the Great Smokies. Continuous 24-hour service. Sizzling steaks, fried chicken, country ham, hot biscuits."
- *Hotel Anderson, Wabasha, Minnesota.* "They specialize in Pennsylvania Dutch dishes such as ham pot pie, chicken pot pie, special rolls, cream of peanut soup. [They have d]esserts such as apple dumplings, ice box pies and homemade ice cream."
- *Dolores Restaurant and Drive-In, Oklahoma City, Oklahoma.* "I enjoy eating here [1941], especially their steaks and Susi-Q potatoes and barbecued ribs. Pies and desserts you will long remember. [They have] the best biscuits I have found anywhere in America, made by Neal, a colored woman, who does not

use a recipe, but has a remarkable sense of feel, which tells her when the mixture is right—served twice a week. (I suggest you wire ahead requesting these remarkable biscuits). Their menu provides a variety of good salads and other things, and I hope you are fortunate enough to find Mr. and Mrs. Ralph A. Stephens there, so you may meet them personally."

- *Hody's, Los Angeles, California.* "An ample menu for the hungry man. [They have c]hicken pie along with other entrees, including their famous cheese cake."
- *The White Turkey Town House, New York, New York.* "Mr. and Mrs. Harry Davega are the owners, as they are of [the] White Turkey Inn at Danbury, Connecticut. Each of these restaurants provides a charming setting where you may enjoy quiet relaxation and delicious food. Specialties: French onion soup, chicken Maryland, chicken pie, roast turkey, chops, fresh vegetables, salad bowl and tempting desserts."
- *Villula Tea Garden, Seale, Alabama.* [The following information about this restaurant came from Duncan Hines's family]: "Two sisters ran this establishment. People came from miles around to eat there. Its reputation spread because it was just across the river from Fort Benning, where many people ate and delighted in devouring such prized specialties as Chicken Country Captain, which is chicken in a tomato sauce served over rice."

Now that you have become familiar with the story of Duncan Hines and the history and origins of his cookbook, I am sure you will enjoy this volume as you read, prepare, sample, and enjoy many of the delectable dishes included in it. Creating and tasting one concoction will no doubt guarantee the preparation of another. But beware. Some of these recipes are quite rich. The best way to approach them in these calorie-counting days is to adopt Duncan Hines's philosophy toward food and everything else: Have what you want, but want what you have.

Louis Hatchett

Notes

1. These tests were conducted mainly in the kitchens of his wife, Emelie, and his brother's daughter-in-law, Geraldine [Mrs. Hugh] Hines, who was originally from Nashville, Tennessee, and lived on Cabell Drive in Bowling Green, Kentucky.

2. Patricia Condon Johnston, "Nelle Palmer of Stillwater: Entertainer and Innkeeper," *Minnesota History* 48, no. 5 (Spring 1983): 207–208.

3. Johnston, "Nelle Palmer of Stillwater," 209.

Editorial Notes for the User of this Book

Recipe #22: The bean soup recipe is the recipe that Duncan Hines always used when he had a leftover country ham bone.

Recipe #87: "Lowell Inn French Dressing." In her private notes for this recipe, Clara Hines, the coeditor of this cookbook, added that the "salad herbs" listed at the bottom of this recipe should be "basil, chives, marjoram leaves, parsley, thyme and tarragon." In terms of proportion: the best guess is to use "a pinch of this and a pinch of that." She also wrote that one should sprinkle on top of this recipe "chopped Roquefort."

Recipe #125: "Fluffy Rolls." These were always served at the Hineses' dinners, especially at Christmas and Thanksgiving.

Recipe #384: "Peas Bonne Femme." In a copy of the cookbook, Clara Hines wrote in the margin to someone about this recipe: "Don't pay any attention to this. I am very much embarrassed over it, and was never allowed to serve it. I didn't know enough when I did this. I know now, and should you like to have my real recipe I will be happy to send it to you." After much examination of the recipe, it appears that Mrs. Hines did not use the last three ingredients: basil, tarragon, and fresh mint.

Recipe #449: "Spaghetti Sauce." In her own personal copy, Clara Hines scratched "sage leaves" and wrote above it "oregano," which may have just been her preference.

Introduction

This book is in answer to the oft-repeated requests of travelers who have visited so many of the places listed in *Adventures in Good Eating, Lodging for a Night,* and *Vacation Guide.* Having enjoyed the particular specialties for which many of these places are justly famous, they have eagerly sought an opportunity to try to prepare these same dishes in the intimate atmosphere of their own home kitchens. They are intrigued with the pleasant prospect of giving their own personal interpretation to some of these unusual specialties.

The editors are extremely gratified that so many places mentioned in The Duncan Hines books have consented to release their prized recipes for publication here.

It should hardly be necessary to remind the reader that all measurements must be made accurately, and oven temperatures observed closely; nor will the successful adventurer tolerate substitutes. Remember, practically all recipes written for restaurant use contemplate considerably larger quantities than is customary for family use, and it is a well-known fact that the amount of ingredients designated in quantity recipes cannot often be reduced proportionately and give the same results. Therefore, the reader is cautioned to mix reason and common sense with your measurements in undertaking to follow any quantity recipes contained herein.

There are many excellent cookbooks that have been especially prepared for the novice needing detailed advice.

No nation has a greater abundance of fresh eggs, butter, and cream than we have in America for use in cookery.

The heart and soul of any dish is its flavor. Therefore, the true disciple of Escoffier uses his seasonings and flavorings with discretion. Use your seasonings as an artist does his pigments. Some colors must be used with great restraint, and a "whisper" of garlic is usually more potent than a handful of herbs. It is genuine economy to use only the best and freshest spices and seasonings. Be sure that they are true to taste, for only in that way can you be assured of the same results every time. Quality ingredients combined with skillful preparation can usually be counted on to achieve the desired result.

The kitchen in the modern home is no longer the exclusive domain of the gentler sex, for there is an increasing number of men who enjoy displaying their culinary skill before their friends.

So, ladies—and gentlemen—let's go into the kitchen now and set forth on a new adventure in good cooking. May we have fun in the doing as well as the eating. Good luck!

DECLINE AND RISE OF HERBS

WHY the art of using herbs in domestic cookery, widely understood a century ago, fell into a decline, it is difficult to say. We know only that such a decline occurred, that it lasted many years, and that the American kitchen did not begin to recover from this blow until the end of prohibition brought a revival of interest in good home cookery.

The swing back to herb cookery was violent. Herbs broke into society. They went, as the saying goes, everywhere, too often crowding their way into pots where they didn't belong. Husbands and children began to complain that their food no longer tasted like food but only like herbs, herbs, herbs.

Get Acquainted

YET the fact remains that herbs properly used immeasurably enrich food flavors. With rare exceptions the herb you use should not itself be tasted, but should merely add a mysterious interest to the flavor of a dish. Charts and directions such as we offer here can be helpful in a general way, but with herbs as with wines, it is not enough to go by the book. To make the most of wines or herbs you must be familiar with the fragrance, flavor and potency of each kind, and must study its relationship to certain foods.

How to Do It

IF YOU grow herbs in your garden get acquainted with them one by one by chewing the raw leaves. Don't go too fast. When you have learned the flavor of a certain herb in your garden, take a pinch of the same herb in its dried form. Chew it. Think about it as a wine-lover thinks about his wine. With what food will it harmonize? Should the pinch or spoonful called for in a recipe be large or small? Or don't you like this herb at all?

Herbs vary in strength and flavor according to the conditions under which they are grown, or dried, or both. Find a brand of dried herbs you like and stick to it, sampling occasionally to make sure the herbs have not lost their strength.

To anyone who cares for what is fine in foods and flavors, the study of herbs is intensely interesting and rewarding.

SUPPLEMENTARY NOTES ON HERBS

"A LL GENERALIZATIONS are false, including this one," said an old-time wit. Generalizations about herbs are dangerous because the use of herbs depends so much on personal taste. The accompanying chart does not necessarily reflect our personal taste, nor does it pretend to be an encyclopedia of herbs and their uses. It is offered only as a guide to long established practice.

Here is a list of herbs not mentioned in the chart:

ANGELICA: Used as flavoring for rhubarb; to make herb tea; in jam; candied (the stalks)

BALM: Lemon scented balm is sometimes used in the broiling of meat and fish, and in salads. It is splendid in wine cups or punches.

BORAGE: With string beans, fennel; with green or cucumber salad. In claret cup, cider cup or fruit punch for its cucumber flavor.

BURNET: In green salad or as a flavoring for vinegar.

GERANIUM: To flavor icing for cakes. A sprig uncooked in a jar of crab apply jelly.

LOVAGE: With a tomato cocktail, in cream soups, stews, gravy, etc., for its strong celery flavor.

MUSTARD: The fresh leaves are sometimes used in salads, and the seeds in pickles.

NASTURTIUM: Fresh leaves in salads. Seeds placed in vinegar to flavor it should be removed.

OREGANO: Rubbed judiciously on raw steak before broiling it imparts a delicious flavor. It may be used effectively in marinade for roast beef or pot roast.

RUE: Fresh leaves in salads. In vegetable juice cocktail and in cheese sandwiches.

WOODRUFF: With wine cup and particularly with Mai Bowle.

SPECIAL NOTE ON SAGE: Don't let memories of unpleasant bread and sage stuffing for chicken cause you to bypass this fine herb. Experiment, but go easy.

BOUQUET GARNI: Tie in a small cloth bag a leek, a half carrot cut lengthwise, a sprig of celery, a few sprigs of parsley, a bit of thyme, two cloves and ¼ bayleaf.
Another version is a sprig of marjoram, ½ bayleaf, two sprigs of parsley, and two sprigs of thyme. Always take out bag before serving.

Herbs and spices should be kept in a container with tops on tight —not exposed to light or the heat on a shelf near the stove.

	ANISE *Annual*	BASIL *Annual*	BAY *Perennial*	CHERVIL *Annual*	CHIVES *Perennial*	DILL *Annual*	FENNEL *Perennial*	SWEET MARJORAM *Annual*
APPETIZERS		Fish Cocktails Tomato Juice		Stuffed Eggs	Stuffed Eggs	Fish Cocktails		
SOUPS		Turtle Tomato	Stock Fish Chowder Tomato	Spinach Chicken Asparagus Vichyssoise	Vichyssoise Bean Pea		Cream Soups	Almost Any Stock Soup
EGGS AND CHEESE		Omelets Other Egg Dishes		Any Egg Dish Any Cheese Dish	Omelet Cream Cheese Cottage Cheese	With Cheese in Sandwich	Stalk Raw with Bel Paese Omelets	Omelets Scrambled or Creamed Eggs
FISH		Court Bouillon Mackerel	Boiled Fish	Broiled Fish		Good With All Fish	Scandinavian Fish Dishes	
POULTRY				Broiled or Steamed Chicken Stuffings				Stuffings Duck
MEAT		Sausage Liver	Stews Pot Roasts With Liquid	With Butter on Filet Mignon	Hamburger Steak	Scandinavian Veal Broiled Chops		Stews Roasts Sausage Marinades
VEGETABLES	Sauerkraut	Tomato Spinach Peas Squash Turnip Onion	Cooked Tomatoes	Beets Celery Egg Plant Carrots	Potatoes Creamed Potatoes Peas	Parsnips Potatoes Egg Plant Beets	Stalk Cooked as Vegetable Lentils	Lima Beans Tomatoes Zucchini Spinach Potatoes Peas
SALADS	Beet or Carrot Salad	Tomato Lettuce Coleslaw Cauliflower		Potato Green Salad	Potato Tomato Coleslaw Lettuce	Cucumber Potato	Fresh Leaves in Salad	French Dressing Fresh Leaves in Salad
SAUCES		Maitre d'Hotel Tomato	Tomato Gravy Brown Sauce	Bearnaise All Sauces of Poultry or Fish Stock		Fish Sauces	Fish Sauces	Fish Sauce Gravy Brown Sauce
DESSERTS	Applesauce Confections						Apple Pie	
BEVERAGES	Herb Tea							
PICKLES		Sweet Pickles	Vinegar	Pickles Vinegar		Seeds in Pickles and Vinegar		

	MINT Perennial	PARSLEY Perennial	ROSEMARY Perennial	SAGE Perennial	SAVORY Annual	SORREL Perennial	TARRAGON Perennial	THYME Perennial
APPETIZERS	Melon Cup						Tomato or Fish Cocktail	
SOUPS		Almost Any Soup	Turtle	Almost Any Soup	Split Pea Lentil	Sorrel Soup	Tomato Potato	Almost Any Stock Soup
EGGS AND CHEESE		Omelets Scrambled Eggs	Special Egg Dishes	American Cheese	Scrambled Eggs Cottage or Cream Cheese	Creamed Eggs	Omelets Other Egg Dishes	With Cheese in Sandwich
FISH		In Sauces Marinades		Fish Chowder			Broiled Fish Salmon Broiled Lobster	Clam and Fish Chowders Fried Fish
POULTRY		Stuffings As Stuffing Fricassee Pies, Stews Steamed Chicken	Stuffings	Stuffings	Stuffings		Almost all Chicken Dishes	Stuffings
MEAT		Almost Any Type of Stew Marinades	Fresh or Dried on Roasting Lamb Veal and Pork Lamb Marinade	Roasts Stews Pork Especially	Roasts Stews Liver Sausage			Stews Roasts Marinades
VEGETABLES		Chopped on Carrots, Peas, Potatoes, Beans, etc.	Lima Beans Soy Beans Baked Beans Spinach	Cabbage Carrots	Beans Broccoli Cabbage Artichokes	With Spinach Cooked as Green	Cabbage Green Pepper Tomatoes Peas Mushrooms	Carrots Peas Onions Sweet Potatoes
SALADS		Mixed Green Vegetable Potato			In French Dressing for Tomatoes Beet Salad	Fresh Leaves in Salad	Tomato Mixed Green Vegetable French Dressing	Fresh Leaves in Salad
SAUCES	Mint Sauce for Lamb	All Stock Sauces Butter Vegetable		White Sauces for Vegetables	All Sauces of Poultry or Fish Stock		Tartar Bearnaise 1000 Island	Tomato Gravies Brown Sauces
DESSERTS	Fruit Cups Candied							
BEVERAGES	Iced Tea Juleps Cocktails Fruit Punch Mint Tea			Gin Drinks Herb Tea				Lemon Scented in Iced Tea and Fruit Drinks

RECOMMENDED TEMPERATURES

Simmering water	180 F	
Boiling water	212 F	
Boiled Icings	238 F—240 F	
Jellying Stage	218 F—222 F	
Very Slow Oven	250 F—275 F	
Slow Oven	300 F—325 F	
Moderate Oven	350 F—375 F	
Hot Oven	400 F—425 F	
Very Hot Oven	450 F—475 F	

DEEP FAT FRYING

Croquettes	370 F—380 F	4— 7 minutes
Fish	370 F—380 F	8—10 minutes
Fritters, Doughnuts, etc.	370 F—380 F	2— 5 minutes
Potatoes—raw	370 F—395 F	5— 8 minutes

BREADS, ETC.

Baking Powder Biscuits	450 F—475 F	12—15 minutes
Baking Powder Loaf Bread	375 F—400 F	50—60 minutes
Muffins	400 F—425 F	18—25 minutes
Yeast Bread	400 F	15 minutes then reduce to 375 for 30 to 45 minutes
Yeast Rolls	400 F—425 F	20—25 minutes
Cup Cakes	350 F—375 F	20—30 minutes
Layer Cake	375 F	25—35 minutes
Loaf Cake	350 F	45—60 minutes
Sponge Cake	325 F	40—60 minutes
Angel Food Cakes	325	60—75 minutes
Pie Shells	450 F	12—15 minutes
Double Crusted Pies	425 F or 450 F and reset to 350 F	15 minutes at 450 F and 35—45 minutes at 350 F

MEATS AND FOWL

Beef—Rolled Rib	rare	350 F—400 F	15—18 minutes to the pound
	medium	350 F—400 F	20—22 minutes to the pound
	well-done	350 F—400 F	23—26 minutes to the pound
Standing Rib	rare	350 F—400 F	12—15 minutes to the pound
	medium	350 F—400 F	18—20 minutes to the pound
	well-done	350 F—400 F	25—28 minutes to the pound
Fresh Ham		350 F	25—30 minutes to the pound
Leg of Lamb		350 F	28—30 minutes to the pound
Leg of Veal		350 F	28—30 minutes to the pound
Pork Loin		350 F	30—35 minutes to the pound
Chicken		450 F	20 minutes, then reduce to 300 F 25—28 minutes to the pound
Capon		450 F	20 minutes, then reduce to 300 F 18—22 minutes to the pound
Duck		475 F	20 minutes, then reduce to 350 F 18—20 minutes to the pound
Turkey		350 F	18—22 minutes to the pound

EQUIVALENT MEASURES AND WEIGHTS

A few grains = less than ⅛ teaspoon

3 teaspoons = 1 tablespoon
2 tablespoons = 1 oz. liquid or fat
4 tablespoons = ¼ cup
16 tablespoons = 1 cup
½ cup = 1 gill
4 gills = 1 pint
1 cup = 8 oz, or ½ lb. liquid or fat
16 ounces = 1 lb.
2 cups = 1 pint
1 pint = 1 lb. liquid or fat
4 cups = 1 quart
2 pints = 1 quart
4 quarts = 1 gallon
8 quarts = 1 peck
4 pecks = 1 bushel

1 dash = ¼ teaspoon
1 pony = ⅓ oz.
1 jigger = 1½ oz.
1 shell = 1½ oz.

1 wine glass = 4 oz. = 8 tablespoons = ½ cup
(This is a claret glass and is most commonly used
in the average home)

1 sherry glass = 3 oz. = 6 tablespoons = ⅓ cup
1 port glass = 2 oz. = 4 tablespoons = ¼ cup

Table silverware spoons do not correspond accurately
with the capacity of measuring spoons.

*There are four basic principles that should not be overlooked
in cooking any dish. Proper and accurate measurements; proper cooking temperature, proper length of cooking time and
proper time of serving.*

MEASURES OF CANNED FOOD CONTAINERS

Can Size	Approximate Cups Full	Can Size	Approximate Cups Full
8 ounces tall	1	No. 2	2½
No. 1 (Picnic)	1¼	No. 2 tall	3
No. 300	1⅔	No. 2½	3½
No. 1 tall (Western)	1¾	No. 3 tall	5¾
No. 303	2	No. 10	13
No. 303 tall	2⅔		

FOOD WEIGHTS AND MEASURES

This table is for approximate weights and measures of various foods and is intended as a handy compilation in estimating quantities. Courtesy of *Restaurant Management Magazine*, 222 East 42nd Street, New York City, N. Y.

Ingredient	Weights	Approximate Measures
Almonds (shelled, chopped)	1 oz.	¼ cup
Allspice (ground)	1 oz.	5 tablespoons
Allspice (whole)	1 oz	6 tablespoons
Apple (juice)	8 oz.	1 cup
Apples (dried)	1 lb.	5 cups
Apricots (dry)	1 lb.	3 cups
Apricots (soaked and cooked)	1 lb.	4 cups and juice
Asparagus (fresh) cut in 1-inch pcs.	1 lb.	2 cups
Baking powder	1 oz.	3 tablespoons
Bananas (mashed)	1 lb.	2 cups
Barley (pearl)	1 lb.	2 cups
Beans (dried)	1 lb.	2¼ cups
Beans (green or waxed, fresh) (cut in 1-inch pieces)	1 lb.	3 cups
Beans, lima (shelled, fresh)	1 lb.	2 cups
Beef (raw, ground)	1 lb.	2 cups
Beets (cooked, diced)	1 lb.	2½ cups
Bread	1 lb.	12 slices, ½-inch thick
Bread crumbs (dried, sifted)	4 oz.	1 cup
Butter	1 lb.	2 cups
Butter	1 oz.	2 tablespoons
Butter	Size of an egg	¼ cup
Cabbage (cooked)	1 lb.	2½ cups
Carrots (diced, raw)	1 lb.	3¼ cups
Carrots (diced fine, cooked)	5 1/3 oz.	1 cup
Cashew nuts	1 lb.	4 cups
Celery seed	1 oz.	4 tablespoons
Celery (minced)	1 stalk	1½ tablespoons
Celery salt	1 oz.	2 2/3 tablespoons
Cheese (cream)	1 lb.	2 cups
Cheese (cream, Philadelphia)	6 oz.	1 pkg.
Cheese (cubed)	1 lb.	2 2/3 cups
Cherries (candied)	1 lb.	3 cups
Chestnuts (in shell)	1 lb.	2 cups—meats
Chicken (cooked, cubed)	1 lb.	3 cups
Chili powder	1 oz.	4 tablespoons
Chocolate	1 lb.	16 squares
Chocolate (grated)	1 oz.	4 tablespoons
Chocolate (melted)	1 lb.	2 cups
Cider	8 oz.	1 cup
Cinnamon (ground)	1 oz.	4 tablespoons
Cinnamon (stick)	¾ oz.	4 (3-inches long)
Cloves (ground)	1 oz.	4 tablespoons
Cloves (whole)	1 oz.	6 tablespoons
Cocoa (ground)	1 oz.	4 tablespoons
Cocoanut (shredded)	1 lb.	6 cups
Coffee (ground fine)	1 lb.	5 cups
Corn (canned)	1 lb.	1¾ cups

Ingredient	Weights	Measures
Corn (fresh, cut off ear)	3 ears	1 cup
Cornmeal	1 lb.	3 cups
Cornstarch	1 oz.	3 tablespoons
Cracker crumbs	2½ oz.	1 cup
Crackers (graham, crushed)	1 cup	12 crackers
Cranberries	1 lb.	4 cups
Cranberry sauce (strained)	1 lb.	2 cups
Cream of Tartar	1 oz.	3 tablespoons
Cucumbers (diced)	1 lb.	2 cups
Currants (dried)	1 lb.	3 cups
Currants (dried)	10 oz	1 pkg.
Curry powder	1 oz.	4 2/3 tablespoons
Dates (pitted)	1 lb.	3 cups
Eggs (1 unbeaten)	1½ oz.	3 tablespoons
Eggs (whole)	1 cup	4 to 6 medium
Eggs (whites)—1 cup	8 oz.	8 to 10
Eggs (yolks)—1 cup	8 oz.	12 to 16
Figs (dried, cut-up)	1 lb.	2¾ cups
Filberts (shelled)	1 lb.	3½ cups
Fish (fresh, chopped)	1 lb.	2 cups
Anchovy Paste	3½ oz.	4 tablespoons
Caviar	1 oz.	2 tablespoons
Clams (minced)	7 oz.	1½ cups
Clam Chowder	11 oz.	1 cup
Crab	13 oz.	2½ cups
Lobster	12 oz.	1 2/3 to 2 cups
Oysters	4 oz.	1 cup
Salmon	8 oz.	1 cup
Sardines (in oil)	3½ oz.	18-25, tiny
Flour (bread, sifted)	1 lb.	4 cups
Flour (graham, sifted)	1 lb.	3½ to 3¾ cups
Flour (rye, sifted)	1 lb.	5½ cups
Flour (whole wheat)	1 lb.	3¾ cups
Flour (bread)	1 oz.	3 to 4 tablespoons
Flour (pastry, sifted)	4 oz.	1 cup
Flour (rice)	1 lb.	2 cups
Gelatine (granulated)	1 lb.	4 cups
Gelatine (prepared)	1 lb.	2½ cups
Ginger (ground)	1 oz.	6 tablespoons
Grapes (cut and seeded)	1 lb.	2 to 3 cups
Grapefruit juice	8 oz.	1 cup
Ham (cooked, diced)	1 lb.	2 2/3 cups
Ham (cooked, ground)	1 lb.	2 cups
Honey	11 oz	1 cup
Lard	8 oz.	1 cup
Lemons	1 lb.	3 to 5 lemons
Lemon juice	1 cup	4 to 5 lemons
Lemon rind	1 lemon	2 teaspoons
Macaroni (elbow)	1 lb.	3 cups
Mayonnaise	1 lb.	2 cups
Meat (chopped, cooked)	1 lb.	2 cups
Milk (condensed, sweetened)	11 oz.	1 cup
Milk (evaporated)	1 lb.	2 cups
Molasses	12 oz.	1 cup
Mixed spices	1 lb.	4 2/3 cups

Ingredient	*Weights*	*Measures*
Mushrooms (canned)	1 lb.	2 cups
Mustard (dried)	1 oz.	5 tablespoons
Mustard seed	1 oz.	3 1/3 tablespoons
Nutmeg (ground)	1 oz.	4 2/3 tablespoons
Oats (rolled, quick-cook)	2¾ oz.	1 cup
Oatmeal (quick-cook)	1 lb.	3 cups
Oils	1 lb.	2 cups
Olives (stuffed, chopped)	6½ oz.	1 cup
Onions (chopped)	1 lb.	2½ to 3 cups
Onions (large, minced)	1 onion	½ cup
Onions (medium, minced)	1 onion	5 tablespoons
Onions (small, minced)	1 onion	3 tablespoons
Onions (medium)	1 lb.	4 to 5
Orange (rind, grated)	½ oz.	2 tablespoons
Paprika	1 oz.	3¾ tablespoons
Parsley (chopped)	3 oz.	1 cup
Parsnips (cooked, sliced)	1 lb.	2½ cups
Peaches (dried)	1 lb.	3 cups
Peaches (fresh, sliced)	1 lb.	2 to 2½ cups
Peanuts (shelled, Jumbo)	1 lb.	3 cups
Peanut butter	1 lb.	1 2/3 cups
Peas (fresh in shells)	1 lb.	1 cup shelled
Peas (yellow, split)	1 lb.	2¼ cups
Pecans (shelled)	1 lb.	4 cups
Pepper (ground, black or white)	1 oz.	4 tablespoons
Peppercorns	1 oz.	6 tablespoons
Peppers (green, chopped)	4 oz.	1 cup
Pickles (chopped)	6 oz.	1 cup
Pineapple (canned, tidbits)	1 lb.	2 cups
Pineapple (canned, sliced, and diced)	3 slices	1 cup
Pineapple (candied)	1 lb.	7 rings
Pineapple (juice)	8 oz.	1 cup
Potatoes (cooked, diced)	1 lb.	2½ cups
Popcorn	1 lb.	3 cups
Prunes (cooked, pitted)	1 lb.	3 cups
Raisins (seedless)	1 lb.	3 cups
Raisins (seeded)	1 lb.	2 cups
Raisins (seedless)	5 1/3 oz.	1 cup
Rhubarb (edible part cooked)	1 lb.	2¼ cups
Rice	1 lb.	2 cups
Rutabagas (diced and cooked)	1 lb.	2 to 2½ cups
Rye Meal	2 1/3 oz.	1 cup
Sage (rubbed, packed)	2 oz.	1 cup
Salt	1 oz.	1¾ tablespoons
Soda	1 oz.	2½ tablespoons
Sauerkraut (packed)	1 lb.	3 cups
Scallops	1 lb.	20 medium
Shrimp	1 lb.	3¼ cups or 24 medium
Spinach (cooked)	1 lb.	2 cups
Squash (cooked, mashed)	1 lb.	2 cups
Strawberries (whole)	1 qt.	3½ cups
String beans (canned)	1 lb.	2 cups
Suet (chopped)	1 lb.	4 to 5 cups
Sugar, brown	1 lb.	3 cups

Ingredient	Weights	Measures
Sugar, confectioners	4½ oz.	1 cup
Sugar, granulated	1 lb.	2 cups
Sugar, powdered	6½ oz.	1 cup
Tapioca (minute)	1 lb.	2½ cups
Tapioca (pearl)	5 oz.	1 cup
Tea (dry)	2 oz.	1 cup
Tomatoes	1 lb.	4 medium
Tomatoes (cooked)	1 lb.	1¾ cups
Tomato juice	8 oz.	1 cup
Turnips (diced, raw)	1 lb.	2 cups
Vanilla	1 oz.	2 tablespoons
Vermicelli	8 oz.	2 cups
Vinegar	8 oz.	1 cup
Walnuts (English, shelled)	4 oz.	1 cup
Water	8 oz.	1 cup
Yeast	½ oz.	1 cake

SWEETENING VALUE OF SUGAR SUBSTITUTES
EQUIVALENTS OF 1 CUP SUGAR

¾ to 1 cup honey
1 cup brown sugar
1 cup maple sugar
1 cup maple syrup

1½ cups sorghum or molasses
1½ cups cane syrup
2 cups corn syrup

Cake and cookie recipes using 1 cup of sugar may be replaced with ½ *cup honey* and ¼ *cup sugar.*

YOU will find the recipes numbered rather than the pages, and credit for each one is given in the line immediately following the recipe.

Numbers in this book may be different from the same recipe in previous printings.

1. Artichoke Bottom Stuffed with Crab or Lobster

(Serves 1)

INGREDIENTS | DIRECTIONS

2½ oz. crab meat
or
½ lobster tail from a
1½ lb. lobster

Marinate in a little olive oil for 2 hours.

1 tablespoon tartar
sauce
1 dash of Tabasco sauce
1 teaspoon chopped
anchovies
1 teaspoon catsup

Mix together and add to crab meat or lobster.

1 fresh artichoke
bottom

Stuff with mixture, decorate with chopped
eggs (yolks and whites), slice of stuffed olive
and a spot of caviar.

Biltmore Hotel, Los Angeles, California

2. Canape Marquis

(Serves 4)

INGREDIENTS | DIRECTIONS

1 hard-boiled egg
½ green pepper
6 anchovy filets
1 peeled tomato
tuna fish, the weight
of an egg

Chop all together.

4 slices toasted sand-
wich bread
¼ lb. sweet butter

Cook slices of bread in butter until crisp on
both sides. Place on silver platter. Put chopped
ingredients flat on top of each piece of toast.

1 tablespoon of Rus-
sian dressing

Place ½ teaspoon of dressing on top of each
piece and garnish with several drops of
Worcestershire sauce. Serve immediately.

Restaurant Marguery, New York City, New York

3. Brandied Grapefruit

(Serves 6)

INGREDIENTS | DIRECTIONS

6 grapefruit halves
12 tablespoons light
brown sugar
6 tablespoons brandy

Remove seeds and cores from fruit halves.
Spread 2 tablespoons of sugar on top of each
half. Pour 1 tablespoon of brandy over each
and allow to marinate for ½ hour. Bake in
oven, 325°, until hot and bubbling. Serve immediately.

Waldorf Astoria, New York, New York

4. Grapefruit Burgundy   (Serves 6)

INGREDIENTS

1 cup fruit juice
½ cup sugar

¼ cup wine (either red or white)
6 grapefruit halves

DIRECTIONS

Simmer fruit juice and sugar until it becomes of medium thickness.

After syrup has cooled, add the wine. Cover top of half grapefruit with syrup and decorate with half a cherry or mint leaves.

Rustic Tea Room, Evergreen, Colorado

5. Golden Grapefruit   (Serves 1)

INGREDIENTS

½ grapefruit
1 tablespoon brown sugar
1 tablespoon sherry

DIRECTIONS

Core grapefruit and fill center with sugar and wine. Heat in 350 F. oven until sugar is melted.

Old Spinning Wheel Tea Room, Hinsdale, Illinois

6. Cheese Cigarettes   (Makes 60-70)

INGREDIENTS

1 pint very thick, rich cream sauce
½ lb. Parmesan cheese, grated
2 egg yolks beaten
¼ teaspoon cayenne pepper
salt to taste

DIRECTIONS

While cream sauce is still hot, mix other ingredients in order given. Place in covered bowl in refrigerator. When ready to use set out for about ½ hour to let paste soften for spreading. Slice very fresh bread into very thin slices, remove crusts and any hard places around edges. Spread each slice with cheese paste, and roll as a cigarette. Fry in deep hot fat, 375°, until brown and serve piping hot.

(Paste can be kept in the refrigerator for about a week if you do not wish to use the full amount at one time. The cigarettes can be made up the day before they are to be served if wrapped in aluminum foil or waxed paper and placed in refrigerator until ready to fry.)

La Cremaillere a la Campagne, Banksville, New York

> *One must enjoy what one is doing in order to be successful in any undertaking. Therefore, it follows that in order to be a good cook, one must love to cook.*

7. Cheese Johnnies   (Make as many as you wish)

INGREDIENTS

DIRECTIONS

thick bread slices
melted butter
grated Parmesan
cheese

Remove crusts from bread slices and cut into fingers. Dip into melted butter and cover completely with Parmesan cheese. Toast brown on both sides and serve hot with salads or as appetizers.

Vera Kirkpatrick, San Mateo, California

8. Hot Toasted Cheese Hors d'Oeuvres   (Serves 25)

INGREDIENTS

DIRECTIONS

2 cups grated cheese
1 egg beaten
10 dashes Tabasco sauce
1 teaspoon Worcester-
   shire Sauce
¼ teaspoon salt

Mix well with a fork.

2 loaves of bread

Remove crusts and cut in 1-inch squares. Place a spoonful of mixture on each piece.

1 lb. bacon

Top with thin strips of bacon. Toast in 450 F. oven until brown.

Cathryn's, Portland, Oregon

9. Cheese Roll   (Makes a roll about 12 or 14 inches long)

INGREDIENTS

DIRECTIONS

½ lb. aged cheddar
   cheese
1 small cake cream
   cheese
¼ lb. Roquefort cheese
2 tablespoons onion
   juice
¼ teaspoon tabasco or
   red pepper
1 teaspoon mayonnaise

Grate the cheddar cheese, mash and mix with it the other two cheeses. Add remainder of ingredients in order given, being sure to have thoroughly mixed. Form a long roll about two inches in diameter.

paprika

Sprinkle paprika on a sheet of waxed paper and roll the cheese roll in it so that it will have a slight coating of paprika. Roll up and place in refrigerator to chill thoroughly. When ready to serve, slice and serve on round crackers.

Mrs. Thomas A. Williams, Nashville, Tennessee

10. Cheese Spread

(Makes about a pint)

INGREDIENTS	DIRECTIONS
¼ lb. Roquefort ½ lb. sharp American cheese	Crumble into small pieces.
¼ lb. Camembert	Remove rind and add soft portion to other cheeses.
½ cup heavy cream Dash of cayenne	Stir cream into cheeses, add the cayenne. Cook the mixture in double boiler over boiling water, stirring constantly, until all cheese is melted. Strain into jars, seal, and place in refrigerator.

The cheese will be runny while hot, but when cool will be a good spreading consistency. Spread on crackers, it makes wonderful appetizers, or it may be used to stuff celery.

Mrs. Duncan Hines, Bowling Green, Kentucky

11. Mushroom Canapes

(Makes about 30 small canapes)

INGREDIENTS	DIRECTIONS
½ lb. fresh mushrooms 4 tablespoons butter	Peel and chop mushrooms. Do not use stems. Place in frying pan with butter, cook until soft over slow fire.
2 scant tablespoons flour salt and pepper	Add flour to above, season to taste. Cook again for a few minutes.
½ pint thin cream	Add to above, stirring constantly until it reaches consistency of a thick sauce. Place in refrigerator until ready to use, then spread on toasted rounds of bread.

Francis E. Fowler, Jr., Los Angeles, California

12. Oyster Canapes

(Serves 8)

INGREDIENTS	DIRECTIONS
1 quart oysters	Blanch and chop very fine.
1 tablespoon Hollandaise sauce	Mix with the oysters. Spread on pieces of toast.
3 tablespoons chopped parsley salt to taste	Sprinkle on top of each round of toast and put in 350 F. oven for 3 minutes.
1 teaspoon butter for each piece of toast	Serve hot.

La Louisiane, San Antonio, Texas

13. Onion Cake
(Serves 6)

INGREDIENTS

DIRECTIONS

Pastry:
  2 cups flour
  1 cup butter
    pinch sugar
    pinch salt
  4 tablespoons sweet
    milk

Mix all ingredients gently as you would regular pie pastry. Place in refrigerator until the dough handles easily. Roll out dough about 3/16 inch thick, put in 8-inch pie tin with straight sides, bake in preheated oven 350° until almost done—about 10 minutes.

FILLING:
  6 strips bacon

Dice fine and fry until crisp. Remove from fat and drain.

  4 large onions

Dice fine and fry in bacon fat gently until done but not brown. Drain off fat.

  2 whole eggs
  1 egg yolk
  ¾ cup sour cream
  1 teaspoon chopped
    chives
    salt and pepper to
    taste

Beat together eggs and egg yolk. Add to cooked onions with other ingredients and crisp bacon. Mix well and pour into pre-cooked pastry.

  ¼ teaspoon caraway
    seeds

Sprinkle on top of filling. Bake in a preheated oven 350-375° for 12-15 minutes. Serve immediately as appetizer.

Bismarck Hotel, Chicago, Illinois

You only get out of a meal what you put into its planning, preparation, and loving care in the cooking.

14. Broiled Oysters College Inn
(Makes 24 oysters)

INGREDIENTS

DIRECTIONS

  24 selected oysters
    salt and pepper
    flour
    butter

Salt and pepper oysters lightly, dredge with flour and broil on lightly buttered grill in 400° oven until crisp and brown on both sides.

  3 tablespoons melted
    butter
  2 teaspoons lemon juice
  2 tablespoons A-1 steak
    sauce
  1 tablespoon Worcester-
    shire sauce
  1 jigger sherry or
    Madeira wine

Combine these ingredients in sauce pan over low heat. Place freshly broiled oysters on hot plate and dress with hot sauce.

Serve immediately on frilled toothpicks.

Ye Old College Inn, Houston, Texas

15. Sausage Roll

INGREDIENTS

biscuit dough
sausage

DIRECTIONS

Roll biscuit dough in long, narrow strip ¼ inch thick. Be sure sausage is rather highly seasoned, salt, pepper, sage and tabasco may be added if desired. Spread sausage on dough about ½ inch thick. Roll up to make roll about 2 inches in diameter. Wrap in waxed paper and place in refrigerator until thoroughly chilled. Take out and slice in ½-inch slices, place on baking sheet and bake in preheated oven, 450°, until brown—about 10-15 minutes. Serve piping hot.

Mrs. Thomas A. Williams, Nashville, Tennessee

16. Jellied Tomato Canape   (Serves 8 to 12)

INGREDIENTS

1 tablespoon gelatin
¼ cup cold water

DIRECTIONS

Sprinkle gelatin over cold water and let soak for 5 minutes.

2 cups tomato juice
1 teaspoon powdered sugar
1 teaspoon salt

Heat and add to gelatin. Pour into individual molds and let set.

chicken livers— cooked.
salt and seasoning to taste

garnishes

Make a paste of these ingredients and with a small spoon scoop out the center of each mold. Fill the cavity with the liver paste. Melt the jelly removed from the centers over hot water and pour over the openings. Chill. Serve on rounds of crisp toast. Garnish with ½ deviled egg, decorated with sprig of parsley and dab of mayonnaise, 2 stuffed olives and sprigs of parsley.

Mrs. Louie M. Weathers, Elkton, Kentucky

17. Spiced Tomato Juice   (Serves 5 or 6)

INGREDIENTS

2 cups canned tomato juice
½ cup sugar
¼ teaspoon cinnamon
a pinch of nutmeg
8 whole cloves

DIRECTIONS

Simmer for fifteen minutes. Chill.

¼ cup lemon juice
1 cup cold water

Add just before serving.

The Carr House, Wolfeboro, New Hampshire

18. Spiced Orange Peel
(Makes 3 gallons)

INGREDIENTS

DIRECTIONS

12 quarts orange peel

Peel oranges carefully, so that no fruit is left on the rind. Cut rind into 2-inch lengths and measure until there are 12 qts. Soak overnight in cold water. Drain. Cover with water and bring to a boil, then discard water. Do this 3 times, cooking the rind until tender in third cooking. Drain.

5 quarts sugar
2 pints vinegar
1½ oz. whole cloves
1 pkg. stick cinnamon

Make a syrup and add the orange peel. This may seem a little thick, but after heating you will find it the right consistency. Cook slightly and bottle while hot, leaving cinnamon and cloves in the syrup. This same syrup may be used for spicing grapefruit peel, fresh pineapple, or tiny carrots if they are cooked previously in a little water then added to this syrup.

The Toll House, Whitman, Massachusetts

19. Fresh Rhubarb Juice
(Makes 2 quarts)

INGREDIENTS

DIRECTIONS

2½ lbs. fresh rhubarb
2 quarts of water

Cut rhubarb in 1-inch pieces and stew until soft. Strain and sieve.

1½ lbs. sugar
juice of 3 lemons

Add to above. Chill and serve. Amount of lemon juice may be increased or decreased according to taste.

Grace E. Smith's Restaurant, Toledo, Ohio

20. Shrimp Ernie
(Serves 6 or more)

INGREDIENTS

DIRECTIONS

2 lbs. raw shrimp

Remove shell and back vein and wash thoroughly.

1 pint salad oil
1 tablespoon salt
4 tablespoons catsup
1 teaspoon paprika
1 small pod garlic

Chop garlic fine and add to catsup, salt and paprika. Beat in the oil until well blended. Pour over shrimp and marinate overnight in refrigerator. When ready to serve, place shrimp on sides in shallow pan, pour over some of the sauce, broil under heat at 350° oven for about 8 minutes on each side. Do not put shrimp too near heat and do not over cook as that toughens them. They should be lightly browned on each side. Serve hot on frilled toothpicks. This also may be served as an entree.

Ye Old College Inn, Houston, Texas

21. Albondigo Soup   (Serves 8)

INGREDIENTS

DIRECTIONS

1 tablespoon bacon fat
½ cup chopped onion
1 can hominy drained
2 cups tomatoes
3 cups chicken or beef
  stock

In a heavy soup kettle, brown the onion and
hominy in the bacon fat. Add tomatoes and
stock to this and bring to a boil. If you do
not have stock, you may use canned bouillon.

½ lb. ground beef
¼ cup cornmeal
½ clove garlic, minced
½ teaspoon salt
1 egg
½ cup minced onion
  freshly ground black
  pepper

Mix together the ground beef, cornmeal,
minced garlic, onion, salt, pepper and beaten
egg. Form into tiny balls and drop in the
boiling soup. Lower heat and simmer for 1
hour.

Ruttger's Bay Lake Lodge, Deerwood, Minnesota

22. Bean Soup   (Serves 8)

INGREDIENTS

DIRECTIONS

2 cups California pea
  beans
2 qts. hot water
1 tablespoon sugar
1 onion—whole
2 small red (hot)
  peppers
⅓ stick butter
1 ham hock
2½ lbs. of bone and
  trimmings from bar-
  becued ham.

All ingredients go into pot at same time. Boil
slowly in covered pot for three hours or until
beans become soft, then boil hard for about
45 minutes or until soup becomes milky in
color. Watch carefully as beans burn easily
at this stage. Stir often. Add water to make
soup consistency you like. Salt and pepper to
taste.

This soup keeps 3 or 4 days in refrigerator.
Be sure it is absolutely cool before placing in
refrigerator in stone crock.

Mrs. R. A. Stephens, Los Angeles, California

23. Boola Soup   (Serves 6)

INGREDIENTS

DIRECTIONS

1 No. 2 can green
  turtle soup
1 No. 2 can green
  pea soup
  sherry to taste

Mix together, heat and pour into cups.

1 tablespoon whipped
  cream

Add to each cup and place under broiler
until a golden brown.

Le Mirliton, New York City, New York

24. Borsht

INGREDIENTS

2 lbs. small
  spareribs

2 cups shredded
  cabbage
1 cup shredded onion

2 cups julienne of
  beets (raw)
1 or 2 lumps Russian
  salt (citric acid
  crystals—to be used
  judiciously)
  salt and pepper

2 cups sour cream
  (real sour cream)

DIRECTIONS

Boil spareribs slowly in kettle with 2 qts. of water, salt and pepper, cook until tender.

Put cabbage and onions in a skillet with a little butter, braise but *do not* brown.

Drain juice of spareribs and combine with cabbage and onions and cook until tender.

The beets, raw peeled and sliced julienne style, must be cooked separately in just enough water to cover, until tender.

Combine all of the above including the meat, which should be cut small and the bones removed.

Add the sour cream to all of this and bring to a boil. If too thick add more stock or water. Serve in deep plates, with some sour cream on the side and whole rye wafers or rye bread sliced thin and buttered.

Minikahda Club, Minneapolis, Minnesota

25. Canadian Cheese Bisque
(Serves 8)

INGREDIENTS

2 tablespoons butter
2 tablespoons flour
½ lb. aged Cheddar
  cheese grated

1 qt. clear chicken
  broth
1 tablespoon carrot
1 tablespoon celery

⅛ teaspoon white pepper
½ teaspoon salt
½ teaspoon Worcestershire

1 tablespoon butter
1 tablespoon green
  pepper chopped

1 cup ale

DIRECTIONS

Blend flour and butter in pan until smooth. Add grated cheese and stir until smooth.

Chop vegetables finely and simmer in stock until tender. Add to above and whip until smooth.

Add to above.

Saute pepper in butter and add to above.

Warm slightly and add to above just before serving.

White Turkey Town House, New York, New York

26. Double Strength Beef Bouillon (10-12 persons)

INGREDIENTS

2 lbs. ground lean beef
1 large carrot
1 medium-sized onion
1 small stalk celery
5 eggs beaten
2 quarts hot beef stock

DIRECTIONS

Be sure that there is no fat on the beef. Put in stock pot. Cut carrot, onion, and celery into ½-inch cubes and add to ground beef. Stir in beaten eggs. Pour over this the hot beef stock and mix all together thoroughly. Put on moderate fire and let come to a boil.

Lower heat and simmer for three hours, stirring occasionally to keep beef and vegetables from settling to bottom of pot. Strain, and season with salt and tabasco sauce to taste. To obtain clear bouillon, only lean beef must be used.

Hotel Cleveland, Cleveland, Ohio

27. Chicken Velvet Soup (Serves 10 to 12)

INGREDIENTS

1 quart chicken stock
2 tablespoons cornstarch
2 tablespoons cold milk

½ cup cream 20%
½ cup cream 40%

4 egg yolks—beaten

speck curry powder
speck cayenne pepper
½ teaspoon salt
⅛ teaspoon white pepper
¼ teaspoon celery salt
1 teaspoon onion juice

DIRECTIONS

Combine stock with mixture of cornstarch and milk and boil for 10 minutes.

Add to above mixture and let come to a boil.

Pour mixture slowly over egg yolks, beating constantly. Put in double boiler.

Add to mixture and cook about 2 minutes.

Serve with whipped cream.

Grace E. Smith's Restaurant, Toledo, Ohio

28. Baked Chili Con Carne (Serves 6)

INGREDIENTS

1 lb. ground beef

1 cup condensed tomato soup
1 cup canned tomatoes
1 cup chopped onions
1 cup cubed celery

1 #2 can kidney beans
1 clove garlic—chopped
4 teaspoons chili powder

DIRECTIONS

Place in cold skillet over low heat and cook through but do not brown.

Combine with meat but do not cook.

Add to above mixture, place in casserole in 325° oven and bake for 2 to 2½ hours or until thoroughly done.

The Alcove, Mount Vernon, Ohio

29. Chili Con Carne (Serves 8)

INGREDIENTS

3 tablespoons bacon drippings
1/4 cup chopped onion
1 lb. ground beef

1 No. 2 1/2 size can of tomatoes
1 No. 2 size can kidney beans
1 quart of water
2 tablespoons chili powder
1 teaspoon salt
1/4 teaspoon cayenne pepper

DIRECTIONS

Melt drippings. Saute gently in the fat until tender. Add beef, stirring the mixture until the beef is cooked through. This takes about 3 minutes.

Add to the above and cook slowly over low heat for at least 4 hours. Stir frequently. More salt can be added to taste.

Mrs. Duncan Hines, Bowling Green, Kentucky

A good way to keep hot soups really hot is to use warm plates and serve from a heated tureen at the table.

30. Cream of Almond Soup (Serves 6)

INGREDIENTS

3 cups chicken stock
3 tablespoons chopped onion
6 stalks celery—cut fine

2 cups milk
1 cup cream

3 tablespoons butter—melted
3 tablespoons flour
1 teaspoon salt
pepper and Tabasco to taste

1/2 teaspoon almond flavoring (more if you like it)
6 tablespoons almonds —chopped

DIRECTIONS

Simmer until tender. Put through a sieve.

Scald and add to above.

Blend and slowly stir into the above.

Stir flavoring into the soup. Serve with spoon of whipped cream topped with chopped almonds.

The Mohawk, Old Forge, New York

31. Creme St. Germaine Pea Soup (Serves 6)

(This is my favorite cream soup)

INGREDIENTS	DIRECTIONS
3 cups fresh peas (shelled) 1½ cups water	Cook peas in double boiler and force through sieve. Or you may use 3 cups of frozen peas, or one No. 2 can of peas. (No extra water needed with canned peas.)
3 cups cream salt and pepper to taste	Put cream in pot and when hot, add puree of peas and seasoning. Cook 5 minutes, stirring vigorously.
3 egg yolks—beaten	Whip into the above. Remove from fire.
⅛ lb. butter	Add butter, blend with a fork and fold in until melted.

Mario Piccardi, Chicago, Illinois

32. Creme Senegalese Soup (Serves about 12)

INGREDIENTS	DIRECTIONS
1 fresh coconut 1 qt. milk	Grate coconut, scald milk and pour over grated coconut. Let stand for 1 hour and strain through a cloth.
1 small onion 1 small apple 2 oz. butter 2 heaping tablespoons flour 2 level tablespoons curry powder ½ teaspoon ginger pinch of mace 1 qt. chicken broth 2 bay leaves 1 sliced lime 1 tablespoon Indian chutney	In a heavy pot, melt the butter and add onion and apple which have been chopped. Cook 5 minutes but do not brown. Add dry ingredients and cook slowly about 5 minutes more. Add coconut milk and chicken broth, stir until smooth. Add bay leaves, lime and chutney. Cook slowly for about 30 min. Keep top skimmed off. Strain through sieve, and let cool thoroughly.
1 cup coffee cream 4 tablespoons breast of chicken diced 4 tablespoons mango diced salt to taste lime juice	Stir in cream, chicken and pieces of mango from bottle of chutney. Season with salt to taste and add a little lime juice. Serve very cold.

Tail o' the Cock, Los Angeles, California

33. Cream of Tomato Soup   (Serves 2)

INGREDIENTS

DIRECTIONS

1 cup very rich cream
sauce

Cream sauce should be very rich; the richer,
the better.

1 cup fresh tomatoes
1 tablespoon onion
juice
small piece of bay
leaf
pinch soda
salt and pepper to
taste
whipped cream

Peel and quarter fresh ripe tomatoes. Add bay
leaf and onion juice. Cook for about ten minutes slowly. Add tiny pinch of soda just as you
are taking off the fire. Combine tomatoes and
cream sauce, season to taste. Top each serving with a tablespoon of whipped cream.

(This is a cherished recipe handed down in the family of Nell Palmer.)

Lowell Inn, Stillwater, Minnesota

You might try adding Basil to your tomato soup.

34. Creole Okra Gumbo   (Serves 12 to 14)

INGREDIENTS

DIRECTIONS

3 lbs. okra

Wipe the okra with a damp cloth and cut
into round slices.

½ dozen crabs

Immerse crabs in boiling water for a few
seconds. Remove shells and quarter. Set aside in covered
pan until ready to use. Save shells.

2 lbs. fresh shrimp

Wash shrimp thoroughly, peel and set aside.
Save shells.

3 quarts of water

Put shells in pot and cover with water. Boil
for 30 minutes. You use this water for liquid for the gumbo.

1 cup of lard
salt and pepper to
taste
2 onions—minced

Heat lard, add okra, seasoning and onion.
Cook until okra is browned.

1 tablespoon tomato
paste
2 cloves of garlic—
minced

Add to okra and onion mixture, then add
crabs and brown for five minutes. Add the
water in which the shells were cooked and
boil for one hour.

small piece of bay
leaf
1 sprig of thyme
2 tablespoons parsley—
chopped fine
salt and pepper to
taste

Add the shrimp and other ingredients and let
simmer for 3 hours, stirring occasionally.

Serve with hot steaming rice.

Corinne Dunbar, New Orleans, Louisiana

35. Cream of Mushroom Soup (Serves 6 to 8)

INGREDIENTS | DIRECTIONS

¾ lb. fresh mushrooms
1 quart cold water

Wash and grind mushrooms without peeling or stemming. Soak ground mushrooms in cold water for 1 hour.

1 teaspoon onion juice

Add onion juice and slowly bring to boil. Boil 5 to 10 minutes. Strain through a fine sieve or cloth.

2 tablespoons butter
3 tablespoons flour

Make a paste and add to mushroom broth, stirring rapidly to blend. Bring mixture to boil and cook 5 to 7 minutes to get the flavor.

¾ cup cream
¼ cup milk

Heat the cream and milk and add to mixture just before serving.

1½ teaspoons salt
dash of white pepper

Add the seasoning last.

This is an excellent soup for the first course of a dinner, as it is like broth and not too rich. Serve with a spoonful of whipped cream.

Richards Treat Cafeteria, Minneapolis, Minnesota

36. Cream of Peanut Soup (Serves about 12)

INGREDIENTS | DIRECTIONS

¼ lb. butter
4 stalks celery—
chopped
1 onion—chopped

Braise celery and onion in butter over low heat.

2 tablespoons flour

Add to above and cook until well blended.

1 gallon chicken stock

Add to above and bring to boil.

1 lb. peanut butter

Stir into the above until well blended. Strain through cloth.

1 qt. light cream

Add to the above and serve.

Forest Hills Hotel, Augusta, Georgia

37. Cream of Tomato and Pea Soup (Serves 6)

INGREDIENTS | DIRECTIONS

2 cups cooked peas

Put through a sieve or electric blender to make a puree.

1 can tomato soup
2 cups cream

Add to pea puree and heat.

3 tablespoons sherry
seasoning to taste

Add to soup just before serving.

Twitchell Lake Inn, Big Moose, New York

38. Cream of Spinach Soup (Serves 6)

INGREDIENTS

½ pint cream
1 pint milk

⅓ cup butter
2 tablespoons flour
salt and pepper to taste

1 pkg. frozen spinach
1 small onion

DIRECTIONS

Heat together in double boiler.

Melt butter, stir in flour, salt and pepper until smooth. Add hot milk to this gradually and cook gently about 8 minutes.

Let spinach thaw out and run through food chopper along with the onion. Add to above and cook about 5 minutes stirring constantly.

Pendarvis House, Mineral Point, Wisconsin

39. Fish Bouillon (Serves 6)

INGREDIENTS

6 slices fish
salt to taste

1 onion—chopped
3 sprigs parsley—chopped
1 bay leaf
thyme to taste
salt and pepper and red pepper to taste
garlic to taste

1 cup claret wine
3 cups water

DIRECTIONS

Rub fish with salt and fry in hot fat. Remove from pan as slices brown.

Brown in the same pan and fat the fish was browned in.

Add just before returning fish to pan and let cook over slow fire for about 1 hour.
Strain before serving.

La Louisiane, San Antonio Texas

40. Fiske Suppe (Serves 6)

INGREDIENTS

1½ quarts fish stock
6 carrots
1 stalk celery

¼ cup butter
¼ cup flour

3 egg yolks beaten
1 cup cream
1 tablespoon sugar
1 tablespoon vinegar

2 cups scalded milk

DIRECTIONS

Dice vegetables and cook in fish stock until tender.

Blend and stir into the above mixture. Simmer ½ hour.

Mix together and pour into soup mixture.

Add to the mixture just before serving. Serve very hot.

Sundal Guest House, West Lebanon, Maine

41. Philadelphia Clam Chowder

(Serves 6 to 8)

INGREDIENTS	DIRECTIONS
1 medium onion 1 green pepper 2 leeks ½ cup celery 4 tablespoons butter	Dice vegetables and saute in butter.
3 tablespoons flour	Add to above mixture.
8 large clams—minced 2½ cups water	Scald clams with their juice and water. Gradually add this to the vegetable mixture and let come to a boil.
3 cups diced potatoes	Add to above and simmer for fifteen minutes.
2 large fresh tomatoes (or 1 small can)	Skin the fresh tomatoes and cut fine, or cut the canned tomato solids into small pieces. Add to mixture.
4 tablespoons catsup pinch black pepper pinch cayenne pinch marjoram pinch thyme 1 tablespoon parsley—chopped salt to taste	Add to mixture and bring to a boil. Serve.

Kuglers Restaurant, Philadelphia, Pennsylvania

Good food and the eating of it is not related to what any one person likes or dislikes, which is purely a personal matter, and good cooking is not related to the special type of cooking in any one country, but rather to the method of preparation.

42. Maine Clam Chowder

(Serves 6)

INGREDIENTS	DIRECTIONS
¼ lb. salt pork	Dice and saute until it will float.
2 onions medium size	Chop and add to salt pork and continue to cook 5 minutes.
1½ qts. fresh clam broth	Add to above, straining salt pork and onions if desired.
2 medium potatoes	Cube potatoes, add to above, cook 20 minutes.
1 pt. fresh clams	Chop clams in half, add to above, cook 5 minutes.
½ pt. milk ½ pt. cream	Add to above, bring to boil.
6 tablespoons butter salt and pepper	Add butter, and salt and pepper to taste.

The LaFayette, Portland, Maine, George M. Miller, Chef

43. Parker House Lobster Stew (Serves 4)

INGREDIENTS

¾ lb. cooked lobster meat—cubed
½ cup butter
½ cup sherry
pinch of paprika
salt and freshly ground black pepper to taste
1 pint heavy cream
1 pint milk
tablespoon sweet butter

DIRECTIONS

Melt butter in a pot and add lobster meat and saute until golden brown.

Add salt, pepper, paprika and sherry and let cook slowly for 5 minutes.

Add milk and cream and let come to boiling point. Remove from fire, add butter and serve at once.

Parker House, Boston, Massachusetts

44. Lentil Soup (Serves 10)

INGREDIENTS

2 slices bacon

1 carrot
3 or 4 slices turnip
1 onion
1 leek

3 quarts meat stock

1 lb. lentils
1 ham shank

3 to 4 potatoes

salt and pepper
dash of nutmeg

DIRECTIONS

Saute to extract fat.

Chop vegetables and cook in bacon fat until a light brown.

Add vegetables to this stock.

Wash and soak lentils overnight. Add these and shank to the above. Let simmer over low heat for 1½ hours.

Cube and add to above mixture. Cook until tender.

Season to taste and serve very hot with sliced frankfurters floating on top.

Wasum's Restaurant, Detroit, Michigan

Along with the advanced knowledge of vitamins and minerals improved cooking methods also have kept pace. To retain the important minerals and vitamins, vegetables especially should be cooked quickly and with as little water as possible, and regardless of what grandma told you, soda tends to destroy the vitamin content of cooked fruits and vegetables. A little vinegar or lemon juice added while these are cooking is said to aid materially in retaining these important elements.

45. Mushroom Soup

INGREDIENTS	DIRECTIONS
1 quart chicken broth 1 teaspoon onion juice ¼ lb. fresh mushrooms —ground	Simmer for 15 minutes.
¼ cup flour ¼ cup butter	Blend and work together. Gradually add the broth, stirring constantly.
½ cup cream	Add to mixture and let it boil up.
2 teaspoons lemon juice salt and white pepper and paprika, to taste whipped cream	Add to soup just before serving. Top with whipped cream.

Mrs. Louie M. Weathers, Elkton, Kentucky

46. Hungarian Gulyas Soup

INGREDIENTS	DIRECTIONS
½ lb. dried beef, cubed 2 lbs. onions, thinly sliced	Place in a saucepan with a small amount of water, cover and steam over low fire until onions are transparent.
2 lbs. lean beef 1 teaspoon pepper 2 teaspoons paprika 1 tablespoon butter	Cut beef in ½ inch cubes. Season and brown in butter in skillet over low fire. Add to onions and dried beef.
⅔ cup tomato paste (6½ oz. can)	Add to above and continue cooking until thoroughly blended.
½ cup red wine—dry	Add and simmer for a few minutes.
10 cups meat stock	Add meat stock and cook slowly until beef is tender. Let cook down so that soup is rather thick. Takes about 2½ to 3 hours.
2 teaspoons paprika 1 tablespoon minced garlic ½ teaspoon grated lemon rind 2 teaspoons chopped parsley 1 teaspoon caraway seed salt and pepper to taste	Remove from heat and add seasoning with salt and pepper to taste.

Kesseler's Weinrestaurant, Wiesbaden, Germany

47. Onion Soup

INGREDIENTS | DIRECTIONS

1 lb. onions
¼ lb. butter

Slice and cook until brown.

1 tablespoon flour

Sprinkle over onions and stir.

1½ quarts chicken stock
salt and pepper to taste
French bread
Parmesan cheese

Add stock slowly, stirring until smooth. Add seasoning and allow to stand several hours to improve the flavor. Serve with slice of French bread sprinkled with Parmesan cheese and toasted in oven the last moment. Serve extra cheese to be sprinkled over top at table.

Toll House, Whitman, Massachusetts

If the overfed were fed less and the underfed had enough, we would have no wars.

48. Philadelphia Pepper Pot

INGREDIENTS | DIRECTIONS

1 onion
1 green pepper
2 leeks
½ cup chopped celery
4 tablespoons butter

Dice vegetables and saute in butter.

3 tablespoons flour

Add to above mixture.

5 cups veal broth

Slowly add the veal broth and stir constantly.

¼ lb. cooked tripe—diced

Add tripe and let mixture come to a boil.

3 cups diced potatoes
pinch crushed black pepper
pinch cayenne pepper
pinch sweet marjoram
pinch thyme
1 tablespoon parsley—chopped
salt to taste

Add to mixture. Bring to a boil, then simmer 10 to 15 minutes. Serve hot.

Kuglers Restaurant, Philadelphia, Pennsylvania

Soup for breakfast is increasing in popularity with white collar workers. Cream of tomato, pea, celery soups and beef broth are among the most popular.

49. Pot Liquor

INGREDIENTS

½ lb. bacon or
1 average size ham
hock
¼ tsp. black pepper
½ small pod red
pepper

1 medium size head
cabbage
Water to cover 1 inch
and add water to
maintain original
volume of water

DIRECTIONS

Put black pepper on meat, add water and red
pepper, boil until meat is tender.

Take core out of cabbage. Cut in four pieces
and separate leaves. Cook at least an hour,
adding water as needed. Strain off pot liquor.
Serve in soup dish and dunk cornbread. Be
sure you do not dunk more than your mouth
will hold.

Charlie Grider, Bowling Green, Kentucky

*The best cooks I know are those who taste, taste, and taste
when cooking. This, no doubt, accounts for some particular
dish being so much better when prepared by one cook than
the same dish prepared by another cook.*

50. Poyster Soup

INGREDIENTS

1½ lbs. blackeyed peas

3 quarts unsalted
chicken broth
1 knuckle of smoked
ham

½ onion—diced
1 tablespoon butter

salt and pepper to
taste

¼ lb. butter

18 freshly opened juicy
oysters
2 tablespoons butter

DIRECTIONS

Soak in cold water for 2 hours. Drain.

Add to peas.

Saute and add to peas. Place over a low heat
and let simmer gently for 2 hours.

When done, force through a fine sieve and
add seasoning.

Put back on the stove and add the butter and
bring to just the boiling point, then remove
from fire.

Heat oysters in butter for not more than one
minute. Place 3 oysters in each plate and
pour soup over them and serve.

Stirrup-Cup Castle, Norwalk, Connecticut

51. Kalasoppa (A Fish Chowder)   (Serves 6)

INGREDIENTS

1 lb. fish filets
½ cup diced carrots
2 cups scallions
1 quart water
1 teaspoon salt
1 cup diced potatoes

2 tablespoons butter
2 tablespoons flour

1 cup cream

DIRECTIONS

Cook over low heat about 15 minutes until fish flakes. Remove the fish and continue boiling the liquid with potatoes added for about ½ hour. Strain—this should make about three cups of stock.

Melt butter and stir in flour. When well blended, add the stock and stir over low heat until mixture thickens.

Cut fish in cubes and add to sauce.

Add cream to mixture, along with strained vegetables. Reheat and serve. More salt or seasoning may be added to taste.

Mrs. Kuusamo, New York, New York

Peeling onions will cause you to shed tears unless you peel under running cold water. To remove unpleasant after odor, rub your hands with vinegar or salt.

52. Vegetable Soup   (Makes 2 qts. +)

INGREDIENTS

½ cup raw diced carrots
¼ cup raw diced green pepper
½ cup raw diced celery
¼ cup raw diced onion
½ cup raw chopped cabbage
½ cup raw diced potatoes
1 tablespoon salt

⅓ cup canned okra
⅓ cup canned corn
2 cups canned tomatoes

1 qt. beef stock
salt to taste

DIRECTIONS

Combine, barely cover with water and boil for about 15 minutes. Be sure not to let get mushy.

Add to the cooked vegetables and vegetable broth above. (Use fresh okra and corn if you have it.)

Beef stock should be good tasting and full flavored. Add to the vegetable mixture and let stand at least 1 hour before serving to absorb the vegetable flavors. Salt to taste. Reheat and serve.

The Maramor, Columbus, Ohio

53. Andalusian Cold Soup

INGREDIENTS	DIRECTIONS
2 egg yolks—boiled and put through sieve 2 tablespoons olive oil	Work into a smooth paste in a wooden salad bowl.
1 mild onion 1 clove garlic—crushed 1 lemon or 2 limes—juice 1½ teaspoons Worcestershire 1 dash tabasco 1 teaspoon dry mustard salt and pepper to taste	Chop onion fine. Mix all ingredients together and add to above.
1 quart tomato juice	Work into above.
1 sweet green pepper 1 small cucumber	Chop very fine. Add to above and stir briskly. Chill on ice for 3 hours.
2 egg whites—boiled cut in strips 2 tablespoons green pepper—chopped 1 lemon or lime—sliced thin 2 pimentos—cut in strips	Put some of each in bottom of soup bowl. Pour in the soup.
ice cubes	Add 2 to each bowl. Top with hot croutons, serve.

CROUTONS:

5 slices of thin bread melted butter grated cheese	Cut away all crust. Brush lightly with melted butter, sprinkle with cheese and toast in oven until brown.

Chas. H. Baker, Jr., Coconut Grove, Florida. Author of those exotic recipe books, "A Gentleman's Companion."

In recent years many real he-men have become interested in and developed into very good amateur cooks. For those of you who are thinking of taking it up, may I suggest that you learn the first kitchen rule—and that is to clean up as you go along.

54. Cream of the Garden Cold Soup   Serves 8)

INGREDIENTS

DIRECTIONS

1 lb. carrots, sliced thin
2 tablespoons butter
8 or 10 outside lettuce
    leaves

Put butter in heavy skillet, then carrots. Cover carrots with lettuce leaves, tucking them down close around the edge. Cover and cook slowly until carrots are half done.

1½ pints chicken broth
2 tablespoons un-
    cooked washed rice

Remove lettuce leaves and add broth and rice. Cover and cook slowly for one hour. Carrots and rice must be well done. Add water, if the mixture gets dry. Watch to prevent burning. Strain through a fine sieve, which should make 2½ cups. If you have more, put on stove and cook down, and if less, add water. Set aside to cool. After it is thoroughly chilled, skim fat from top.

1 cup milk
1 teaspoon chopped
    onion
2 large bay leaves
3 drops Tabasco sauce
⅛ teaspoon Worcester-
    shire
¼ teaspoon salt
⅟₁₆ teaspoon mace

Combine and heat to 196 degrees. Set aside for an hour or two to absorb the seasoning flavor. Strain. This should make 1 cup. Chill.

1½ pints cream

When the two mixtures above are chilled combine them with the cream. Taste. Sometimes carrots are not sweet enough and a pinch of sugar brings out the flavor. Keep very cold in earthenware bowl (NO METAL).

3 tablespoons chopped
    chives

Just before serving, stir from bottom, place in chilled cups and sprinkle with chives.

Note.—Poorly flavored carrots make poor soup. The time to serve this soup is when carrots are coming in fresh.

The Maramor, Columbus, Ohio

Some women rush to attend lectures on cooking, then hurry home and dish out leftovers, hurried up blah salads and such.

An old lady who was celebrating her hundredth birthday was being interviewed by a reporter who asked if there was any one thing to which she attributed her wonderful age. The old lady thought a moment and then answered, "Yes, I think there is—vittles."

55. Vichysoisse

INGREDIENTS

DIRECTIONS

2 tablespoons olive oil
5 strips bacon
½ clove garlic
3 medium sized onions
1 bunch of leeks—tops
1 teaspoon black pep-
per-corns

Chop onions and tops of leeks. Mix ingredients together and cook slowly—allowing to
simmer 10 minutes. (Save the bottoms of
leeks. See below.)

2 medium sized raw
potatoes

Slice potatoes thin and add to above. Simmer
for 10 minutes.

1 tablespoon flour

Add to above and stir well.

1 quart chicken stock
1 quart light cream

Add to above, bring to boil, then reduce heat
and simmer for 10 minutes. Strain through
colander but do not mash.

leeks
2 tablespoons butter
¾ cup chicken stock

dash Maggi sauce
dash Tabasco sauce
salt to taste

Chop finely the bottoms of the bunch of leeks.
Place with butter and stock in sauce pan
and simmer gently until leeks are tender.
Add to strained mixture while both are hot.
Add seasonings immediately and let cool.
When cold enough place in refrigerator.
Serve ice cold with chopped chives on top.
Also good served hot. If too thick, cream may
be added to desired consistency when ready to
serve.

The Hearthstone, Hartford, Connecticut

56. Split Pea Soup

INGREDIENTS

DIRECTIONS

2 quarts water
2 cups split peas
4 stalks celery
2 carrots
1 onion
¼ teaspoon thyme
1 pinch cayenne pepper
1 bay leaf
salt and pepper to
taste

Put all ingredients in soup pot, bring to boil
and let cook for 20 minutes at high heat. Reduce heat and simmer until peas are done.
Strain through colander.

Andersen's Valley Inn, Buellton, California

> *In my recipe library I have about 600 cook books. One of my
> favorites is "The Gold Cook Book," written by a master chef,
> the late Louis P. De Gouy, published in 1947 by Greenberg,
> New York.*

57. Avocado Salad

INGREDIENTS

1 pkg. lime gelatin
2 cups boiling water
1 avocado
1 pkg. cream cheese
½ cup mayonnaise
¼ cup celery–cut fine
½ green pepper–
  chopped
a few drops of onion
  juice
1 pinch of salt

DIRECTIONS

Dissolve gelatin in hot water.

Mash avocado and cheese. Mix all ingredients together.

When gelatin is nearly set, add these ingredients and place in a shallow pan until completely set. Cut in squares for serving, or it could be poured into individual molds.

The Anna Maude, Oklahoma City, Oklahoma

58. Avocado Grapefruit Salad

INGREDIENTS

1 scant cup grapefruit
  juice
1 package lime gelatin
1 ripe avocado
1 package of cream
  cheese
¼ teaspoon Accent
½ teaspoon celery juice
1 scant cup mayonnaise
¼ teaspoon salt

1 cup grapefruit
  sections

DIRECTIONS

Heat grapefruit juice and dissolve gelatin in it. Let cool until almost ready to jell.

Peel avocado and put in small bowl of electric mixer. Blend with cream cheese thoroughly. Add the remaining ingredients and blend well. Stir in the gelatin mixture.

Drain grapefruit well and place in mold. Pour mixture over the grapefruit and place in the refrigerator to set.

Stage Coach Inn, Salado, Texas

59. Coleslaw with Sour Cream Dressing

INGREDIENTS

3½ lbs. cabbage

2 tablespoons salt
2 tablespoons sugar
2 tablespoons vinegar
2 tablespoons lemon
  juice
½ onion—grated
1 pint thick sour cream

DIRECTIONS

Cabbage should be crispy. Shred edible portion very fine, and dry as much as possible. Set in refrigerator to chill.

Put dry ingredients in a bowl. Stir in vinegar, lemon juice and grated onion. Stir in sour cream until mixture is thoroughly blended. Just before serving, pour over chilled cabbage and toss lightly until the cabbage and dressing are thoroughly mixed. Serve at once.

Jane Davies Restaurant, New York City, New York

60. Dressing for Cabbage Salad

(Serves 4)

INGREDIENTS

cabbage

1 tablespoon
mayonnaise
¼ pimento
¼ green pepper
1 teaspoon celery seed
½ lemon—juice only
1 teaspoon sugar
½ tablespoon vinegar
pinch pepper and salt

DIRECTIONS

Grate sufficient cabbage to serve 4 persons.

Chop pimento and green pepper finely. Mix mayonnaise with all other ingredients. Stir into cabbage, let marinate in refrigerator for half an hour and serve on lettuce leaf.

James Shouse, President, Crosley Broadcasting Corp., Cincinnati, Ohio.

61. Cole Slaw

(Serves 4)

INGREDIENTS

6 cups shredded
cabbage
½ bell pepper
2 small white onions
2 stalks celery

DRESSING:

3 eggs
½ cup vinegar
1 teaspoon mustard
½ teaspoon salt
¾ cup sugar
¼ teaspoon freshly
ground black pepper
2 rounded tablespoons
butter

DIRECTIONS

In a large salad bowl, place cabbage, chop fine the pepper, onions and celery and add to cabbage and toss all together. Place in refrigerator to crisp until ready to use.

Beat eggs, add sugar, then add vinegar, butter and seasonings. Cook in double boiler until thick. Cool and place in covered jar in refrigerator. When ready to use, thin amount desired with cream. What is left will keep for a couple of weeks in the refrigerator.

Mrs. Edmund Singmaster, Philadelphia, Pennsylvania

62. Beets Vinaigrette

(Serves 4)

INGREDIENTS

1 16 oz. can shoestring
beets
2 tablespoons pickle
relish
2 tablespoons chives
½ cup celery

½ teaspoon dry mustard
½ teaspoon sugar
½ teaspoon salt
⅛ teaspoon pepper
1 clove garlic, crushed
3 tablespoons vinegar
3 tablespoons salad oil

DIRECTIONS

Drain beets well and put in bowl. Chop celery and chives, combine with relish and add to beets. Toss together to mix.

Combine dry ingredients, add crushed garlic, and vinegar to dissolve. Stir well. Add oil and blend well. Pour over beet mixture, toss with a fork, chill and serve on lettuce or romaine.

Duncan Hines Test Kitchen, Ithaca, New York

63. Cranberry Salad (Serves 14)

INGREDIENTS

DIRECTIONS

1 cup water
2 cups sugar

Boil until syrupy.

1 quart cranberries

Add to syrup and cook until they burst. Remove from fire and let stand covered for 10 minutes. Remove cover and cook another 5 minutes. Chill.

2 cups marshmallows
2 apples–diced
3 bananas–sliced
3 cups orange sections
½ cup pecans

Add to cooled cranberries and thoroughly chill.

University Dining Service, Iowa City, Iowa

64. Dutch Cucumber Salad (Serves 4)

INGREDIENTS

DIRECTIONS

3 large crisp cucumbers
1 large sweet onion
3 cups granulated sugar

Slice cucumbers and onions very thin. Pour sugar over and mix well. Chill for 3 hours in the refrigerator.

¼ cup white vinegar
salt
freshly ground
pepper

Pour juice off above mixture. Add vinegar and salt and pepper. Chill a few more minutes, drain all liquid off and serve in lettuce cups.

Amsterdam House, Phoenix, Arizona

65. Molded Cucumber Salad (Serves 6 to 8)

INGREDIENTS

DIRECTIONS

1 pint package of Jello
1 cup hot water

Pour water over gelatin, stir until dissolved and let stand until beginning to set.

1 cup ground cucumber
½ cup mayonnaise
1 tablespoon grated
onion
salt and red pepper
to taste

Add to above and mix well. Pour into individual salad molds and let stand until set. Serve on lettuce with mayonnaise. More or less onion juice may be used depending upon your taste.

Elizabeth Parker's Restaurant, Richmond, Indiana

The preparation of food is equally as important as good cooking.

66. Finnish Salad (Serves 4)

INGREDIENTS

1 cup left-over meat or
  ham
½ cup raw apple
½ cup cooked carrots

1 cup cooked peas

2 tablespoons mayon-
  naise
½ cup whipping cream
1 teaspoon prepared
  mustard
  juice of 1 lemon or
  sweet pickle juice
1 tablespoon chili
  sauce

DIRECTIONS

Cut opposite ingredients in match-stick size
strips.

Mix with the above.

Mix all together and pour over meat mixture.

Shape on a salad bowl and serve.

Mrs. Kuusamo, New York, New York

67. Frozen Cottage Cheese Salad (Serves 12)

INGREDIENTS

1 pint cottage cheese
½ teaspoon salt
¼ teaspoon white
  pepper
1 teaspoon sugar
2 tablespoons grated
  onion
½ cup mayonnaise

½ cup whipping cream
½ lb. blanched almonds
1 small bottle stuffed
  olives

DIRECTIONS

Mix together cottage cheese, seasonings and
mayonnaise.

Whip cream and fold in. Then add whole
blanched almonds and whole stuffed olives.
Pack in quart size cardboard cylinder container. Freeze. When ready to serve, peel
off container, slice ½ inch thick and
serve on lettuce and a tomato slice. Top with mayonnaise and sprinkle with paprika.

Mrs. Duncan Hines, Bowling Green, Kentucky

*Some men have an idea that women spend too much time
"fussin' with food," yet they keep on trying to please the beast
and educate him to enjoy something more than meat, potatoes,
and gravy.*

*Hot or cold sandwiches should be served as soon as made.
Crusts should not be trimmed off unless requested.*

68. Frozen Fruit Salad (Serves 8)

INGREDIENTS

1 tablespoon butter
2 egg yolks—beaten

1 heaping tablespoon
flour
1 heaping tablespoon
sugar
½ teaspoon mustard
½ teaspoon salt
½ teaspoon cayenne
½ teaspoon paprika

½ cup vinegar
⅔ cup milk

1 cup whipped cream

peaches, bananas,
white cherries,
pineapple chunks or
any fruit desired.

DIRECTIONS

Melt butter in saucepan and add egg yolks slowly.

Mix dry ingredients together and stir into above. Stir and blend until smooth.

Add vinegar and then milk. Stir until smooth. Put back on heat and cook over low heat, stirring constantly until thick. Remove from heat and beat for several minutes. Set aside to cool.

When sauce is cool, add whipped cream.

Prepare enough fruits to almost fill your refrigerator tray. Pour sauce over them and mix thoroughly. Place in refrigerator and let freeze. Serve on lettuce with mayonnaise.

Mrs. Duncan Hines, Bowling Green, Kentucky

69. Frozen Fruit Salad (Serves 8)

INGREDIENTS

4 egg yolks
4 tablespoons vinegar
4 tablespoons sugar

½ lb. marshmallows

1 cup crushed pine-
apple
1 cup canned peaches
1 cup white cherries
½ lb. whole blanched
almonds
1 pint cream—whipped

FRUIT DRESSING:

2 eggs
¼ cup pineapple juice
¾ cup lemon juice
⅓ cup sugar

DIRECTIONS

Beat egg yolks well, add sugar and vinegar. Cook in double boiler until thick.

Add to above and stir constantly until dissolved. Cool.

Drain fruit thoroughly. Add to above along with nuts. Fold in whipped cream and freeze. Serve with fruit dressing.

Beat eggs well and add other ingredients. Cook in double boiler until thick. Cool and thin with cream to desired consistency.

Johnson's Restaurant, Monessen, Pennsylvania

70. Grenadine Salad

(Serves 8 or more)

INGREDIENTS

3 tablespoons gelatin
⅝ cup cold water
1 cup boiling pineapple syrup
½ cup lemon juice
1⅞ cup grenadine
½ cup orange juice
2 grapefruit

DIRECTIONS

Soak gelatin in water and dissolve in pineapple syrup. Let cool. Add lemon juice, orange juice and grenadine to above and refrigerate.
Peel grapefruit and separate into sections. When gelatin is partially congealed, add grapefruit and mold in a 1½ qt. ring mold.

GRENADINE DRESSING:

1 egg
1 tablespoon sugar
¼ teaspoon dry mustard
¼ teaspoon salt
1 tablespoon vinegar
1 tablespoon lemon juice
2 tablespoons grenadine
½ cup whipping cream

Beat egg. Mix dry ingredients together. Add to egg, mix well and add rest of ingredients except cream, and cook in double boiler until thick. Let cool and when cold, add cream beaten stiff.

The Farm Kitchen, Baraboo, Wisconsin

"It takes four persons to make a salad—a spendthrift for the oil, a miser for the vinegar, a counselor for the salt, and a madman to stir them up."

An Old Spanish Proverb

71. Gingerale Aspic Salad

(Serves 6)

INGREDIENTS

1 tablespoon gelatin
2 tablespoons cold water
¼ cup heated gingerale

¼ cup lemon juice
1½ cups gingerale

½ cup seedless grapes
¼ cup celery–chopped
½ cup crushed pineapple
½ cup chopped preserved ginger

DIRECTIONS

Soak gelatin in cold water for 5 minutes, then dissolve in gingerale.

Stir into above, and put in refrigerator to set.

When gelatin begins to set, add the ingredients and put back in refrigerator to set.

Serve on lettuce with mayonnaise to which whipped cream has been added.

The Carr House, Wolfeboro, New Hampshire

One way of improving fresh vegetable juices is to whip them with milk.

72. Ginger Pineapple Salad (Serves 3)

INGREDIENTS

6 slices pineapple
1 3½ oz. package
  cream cheese
4 tablespoons shredded
  crystalized ginger
2 tablespoons light
  cream

DIRECTIONS

Spread half of pineapple sections with cream cheese blended with ginger and cream. Top sandwich fashion with the remaining pineapple sections. Serve on shredded lettuce with French dressing.

Overbook Town Shop, Scranton, Pennsylvania

73. Pineapple Salad (Serves 6)

INGREDIENTS

1 cup crushed
  pineapple
½ lemon–juice
¼ cup sugar

DIRECTIONS

Heat.

1 tablespoon gelatin
½ cup cold water

Soak and add to hot mixture. Let cool.

1 cup grated cheese
½ cup whipped cream

When mixture begins to congeal add these ingredients. Serve with pine-dressing.

PINE DRESSING:

½ cup mayonnaise
1 tablespoon pineapple
  juice

Thin the mayonnaise.

1 tablespoon pimento–
  chopped
1 stalk celery–cut fine
1 tablespoon crushed
  pineapple

Fold into mayonnaise.

Tick Tock Tea Room, Los Angeles, California

74. Jellied Cherry Sherry Salad (Serves 20)

INGREDIENTS

1 cup wild cherry gelatin
1½ cups boiling water

DIRECTIONS

Dissolve gelatin in water.

2 cups juice from
  canned cherries
½ cup sherry wine

Add to gelatin and stir.

3 Bing black cherries
3 Royal Anne cherries
3 pecan halves

Place these ingredients in each individual mold and fill with liquid. Put in refrigerator to set.

Devon Gables Tea Room, Bloomfield Hills, Detroit, Michigan

75. "My Salad" (Called this by Mr. Edgar Guest)

(Serves 6)

INGREDIENTS

2 heads lettuce
(large)
1 head chicory or
romaine

6 oz. julienned chicken
or turkey
4 oz. Roquefort cheese
—crumbled
½ teaspoon celery salt
1 cup Thousand Island
dressing
2 tablespoons Tarragon
vinegar

6 hard boiled eggs

DIRECTIONS

Pull lettuce apart in small pieces and cut chicory very fine.

Mix opposite ingredients with the lettuce and chicory and serve in 6 bowls lined with leaves of lettuce.

Garnish top of each salad with 4 quarters of egg. Serve at once.

Wrigley Building Restaurant, Chicago, Illinois

76. Stuffed Avocado Salad

(Serves 4)

INGREDIENTS

1 large avocado
2 oz. cream cheese
2 tablespoons avocado
pulp
1 tablespoons cream
4 stuffed olives
2 tablespoons pecans
1 teaspoon onion juice
1 tablespoon lemon
juice
¼ teaspoon salt

DIRECTIONS

Slice avocado in half lengthwise and remove seed. Scoop out cavity to make somewhat larger. Measure 2 tablespoons pulp and add to cream cheese. Add cream, onion and lemon juice, blend well. Chop olives and nuts finely and stir into mixture with salt. Fill avocado halves with mixture and put back together, fastening with a toothpick. Wrap in waxed paper and chill for about an hour. When ready to serve, peel and cut in slices crosswise. Serve on lettuce with French dressing.

Mrs. Duncan Hines, Bowling Green, Kentucky

All fresh greens and vegetables used for salads should be kept clean and cold and crisp before mixing and serving.

When you use sliced cucumber for salad, put in cold water for an hour or two. Then it will be as crisp as it should be.

77. Blushing Pear Salad   (Serves 6)

INGREDIENTS

DIRECTIONS

12 canned pear halves
½ lb. cinnamon candy
drops

Heat juice from pears to boiling point. Add cinnamon candy. When dissolved, pour the syrup over the pears and let stand until the pears are a bright red. Take pears out of syrup and drain.

6 ounces cream cheese
4 tablespoons cream

Blend together to a creamy consistency.

6 lettuce cups
6 sprigs water cress

Place 2 pear halves in each lettuce cup and fill with creamed cheese. Garnish with sprigs of water cress.

Hotel Roanoke, Roanoke, Virginia

78. Potato Salad   (Serves 6)

INGREDIENTS

DIRECTIONS

6 large potatoes

Boil in skins until done but still firm. Let get cold, then peel, quarter and slice thin.

¼ large onion
½ green pepper
1 stalk celery
¼ cup sweet mixed pickles or water-melon pickle

Put all through a medium food chopper. Mix with sliced potatoes.

¼ teaspoon celery seed
¼ teaspoon Worcester-shire sauce
1½ teaspoon parsley
1½ teaspoon pimento
½ teaspoon prepared French mustard
salt and pepper to taste

Chop parsley and pimento. Add all opposite ingredients to above.

½ cup mayonnaise

6 hard-boiled eggs

Add to above and toss all together. Place in refrigerator overnight. Serve on crisp lettuce and garnish with hard-boiled eggs, quartered.

Monticello Hotel, Norfolk, Virginia

In mixing green salads, first rub your wooden bowl with garlic, then put in your lettuce, endive, watercress or what have you, and shortly before the salad is to be served pour on the dressing and toss with fork and spoon.

79. Shower Salad (Serves 12)

INGREDIENTS

2 packages strawberry gelatin
2 cups boiling water
1 No. 2 can crushed pineapple

4 tart apples–cubed
1 pinch of salt

½ pint whipping cream –whipped

DIRECTIONS

Dissolve gelatin in boiling water.

Drain the juice off the pineapple and add enough cold water to make 2 cups liquid. Add to gelatin and let get very cold.

Mix the apples and pineapple and add to gelatin.

Fold in whipped cream and pour into molds.

When firm serve on lettuce leaves with mayonnaise and a Maraschino cherry.

Park View Inn, Berkeley Springs, West Virginia

80. Salade Biltmore (Serves 10 to 12)

INGREDIENTS

3 or 4 heads of lettuce
4 bunches of watercress
1 quart special dressing

SPECIAL DRESSING:

1 quart tart French Dressing (omit paprika)
½ pint grapefruit juice
½ pint sliced radishes
½ pint parsley– chopped fine
½ cup scallions– sliced fine
½ cup carrots–diced
salt to taste

DIRECTIONS

Cut each head crosswise into 3 or 4 slices about 1 inch thick. Place sprays of watercress on top. Serve special dressing on the side.

Mix well and serve.

Hotel Biltmore, Los Angeles. California

> *Some serve the salad as a separate course, but I believe it should be served before the entree unless the salad is the principal dish.*
>
> *A little lemon juice adds greatly to the flavor of salads.*

81. Stuffed Lettuce (Serves 4 to 6)

INGREDIENTS | DIRECTIONS

1 package cream cheese
2 tablespoons Roquefort
2 tablespoons raw carrot–chopped fine
1 tablespoon green pepper chopped fine
2 tablespoons raw tomato–chopped fine
1 teaspoon onion juice
salt to taste

Blend these ingredients.

1 head of lettuce

Hollow out the lettuce and stuff with the mixture. Wrap in waxed paper and place in refrigerator until ready to serve. Slice in desired thickness.

Mrs. Louie M. Weathers, Elkton, Kentucky

82. Lettuce—Smothered (Serves 6)

INGREDIENTS | DIRECTIONS

1 head lettuce

Procure lettuce before it heads. Chop fine.

3 young onion heads and tops—chopped fine
1 teaspoon sugar
salt to taste

Mix with the lettuce.

2 tablespoons vinegar

Pour over the ingredients.

5 slices of bacon—cut in strips

Fry crisply and put over lettuce and pour hot drippings over all. Toss and serve immediately.

Nu-Wray Hotel, Burnsville, North Carolina

In order to have a salad which will appeal to the eye and to the appetite, it is necessary first of all that the ingredients should be of first quality. Then the ingredients should be of the freshest and those that are to be cooked, should be well cooked.

Dressing should not be added to the salad until the last minutes, because oil causes lettuce to wilt.

83. Snow Cap Salad (Serves 8)

INGREDIENTS	DIRECTIONS
1 package lime gelatin juice from can spiced grapes.	Prepare according to instructions using the juice from can of spiced grapes with added water to make two cups liquid.
½ cup cottage cheese	Pack 1 tablespoon of cheese in bottom of each of 8 individual gelatin molds. Pour in just as much gelatin as the cheese will absorb and refrigerate until firm.
1 cup spiced grapes ½ cup chopped nuts	When remaining portion of gelatin is beginning to thicken, fold in grapes and nuts. Fill molds with this mixture and chill until firm. Unmold on lettuce leaves and serve with Russian dressing or mayonnaise.

Duncan Hines, Bowling Green, Kentucky

84. Raw Spinach Salad (Serves 6)

INGREDIENTS	DIRECTIONS
1 lb. spinach	Wash well to remove sand.
1 teaspoon baking soda	Add to water in which spinach is washed. Drain well and cut into strips 1 inch wide.
2 tablespoons olive oil 1 tablespoon lemon juice	Season spinach.
1 hard boiled egg— chopped	When ready to serve, add to spinach. Garnish with tomato and asparagus, and top all with dressing.

DRESSING:

| |
--- | ---
2 eggs
½ teaspoon dry mustard
1 teaspoon salt
½ teaspoon paprika
½ cup tomato catsup
1 tablespoon sugar
1 teaspoon Worcestershire sauce | Rub bowl with a clove of garlic. Mix opposite ingredients together and stir into a smooth paste.
1 pint oil | Add to paste slowly.
½ cup vinegar | Add to dressing alternately with the oil. Beat in electric mixer to a thick dressing.
2/3 cup warm water | Add to dressing slowly. Keep in a cool place, and use as needed.

Omar Khayyam's, San Francisco, California

Salad is supposed to be served cold on cold plates. If the plates are not cold, I pass up the salad.

85. Tomato Aspic Buffet Mold   (Serves 6 to 8)

INGREDIENTS

DIRECTIONS

3 cups tomato juice
¼ cup lemon juice
3 bay leaves
½ cup brown sugar
1 medium sized onion
   whole cloves
½ teaspoon salt

Stick whole cloves into onion until it is covered. Combine with tomato juice and other ingredients. Bring to a boil and let boil for 5 minutes. Strain.

2 envelopes gelatin
¾ cup cold water

Dissolved unflavored gelatin in water and add to hot tomato mixture. Pour into ring mold and chill until set. When ready to serve unmold on nest of endive on a salad plate at least three inches larger than the mold.

2 cups cottage cheese
½ cup mayonnaise
1 tablespoon chopped chives
1 tablespoon chopped parsley
salt to taste

Mix all ingredients together until well blended. Form 6 or 8 tiny balls of the cheese mixture and place around the ring mold. Fill the center with the remainder of cheese and serve with mayonnaise or thousand island dressing.

The Corner Cupboard, Grand Lake, Colorado

86. Anchovy Dressing   (Serves 8 to 12)

INGREDIENTS

DIRECTIONS

1 cup French Dressing
2 tablespoons anchovy paste

Blend the anchovy paste with the French Dressing, beating thoroughly. If you really go for anchovy flavor, more paste may be added to the French Dressing.

Duncan Hines, Bowling Green, Kentucky

87. Lowell Inn French Dressing

INGREDIENTS

DIRECTIONS

¼ cup sugar
1 teaspoon salt
½ cup catsup
½ cup vinegar
1 cup olive oil
   garlic
   grated onion
   salad herbs

In a quart jar place salt and sugar, add vinegar and catsup and stir to dissolve. Beat in oil and finally add grated onion, crushed garlic, and herbs to taste. Herbs are optional, but add fine flavor.
Let stand in jar in refrigerator at least 24 hours before using. Shake well before serving on tossed green salads.

Lowell Inn, Stillwater, Minnesota

88. Dressing for Avocado Cocktail (Makes 1 cup)

INGREDIENTS

3 tablespoons cream
2 tablespoons catsup
1 tablespoon lemon juice
6 drops Tabasco sauce
¼ teaspoon salt

½ cup mayonnaise

DIRECTIONS

Blend together.

Mix well with above.

This dressing may also be used on sea food cocktails.

Mrs. W. B. Taylor, Bowling Green, Kentucky

89. Celery Seed French Dressing (Makes 1½ cups)

INGREDIENTS

½ cup sugar
½ cup vinegar
⅛ teaspoon salt
⅛ teaspoon dry mustard
1 teaspoon paprika
1 tablespoon grated onion

1 cup oil
1 teaspoon celery seed

DIRECTIONS

Mix all ingredients together. Bring to boil and let simmer for 5 minutes, stirring all the time. Remove from fire.

Add oil slowly to above, stirring all the time. Add celery seed. Chill. Delicious with fruit salad.

Anderson Hotel, Wabasha, Minnesota

90. Chef's Special Salad Dressing (Makes 1 quart)

INGREDIENTS

1½ cups chili sauce
¼ cup celery—finely chopped
¼ cup sour pickles chopped
2 cups mayonnaise
1 teaspoon lemon juice
½ teaspoon Worcestershire sauce
1 teaspoon horseradish

DIRECTIONS

Put all ingredients into a bowl and mix together until well blended.

Do not put in refrigerator, but it will keep indefinitely in a cool place.

Excellent dressing for any seafood salad.

The Fishermen's Grotto, San Francisco, California

Grow chives and parsley in flower pots for use throughout the year. Remove stems, wash, drain, put in covered dish in refrigerator to insure crispness.

91. Cranberry Dressing (Makes about 1 quart)

INGREDIENTS

⅔ cup sugar
1 teaspoon salt
1 teaspoon dry mustard
½ cup vinegar

1 teaspoon onion juice
1 cup oil

1 orange
1 cup cranberries
½ cup sugar

DIRECTIONS

Combine dry ingredients, mix with vinegar to dissolve.

Combine with above and beat until well blended.

Wash and cut orange into segments, removing seeds. Grind with cranberries. Stir in sugar and blend with oil mixture.

This is delicious over fresh pear or banana salad. Put in covered jar. Will keep in cool place until used up. Stir well before each serving.

Cromer's Restaurant, Flint, Michigan

92. Cream Salad Dressing (Makes 1½ cups)

INGREDIENTS

1 tablespoon butter
1 tablespoon flour
1 cup milk

2 eggs
1 tablespoon salt
pinch white pepper
2 tablespoons sugar

1½ teaspoons dry mustard
½ cup vinegar

DIRECTIONS

In top of double boiler, melt butter, stir in flour until smooth. Gradually add milk and cook until thick.

Beat together eggs, seasonings and sugar.

Add to egg mixture and stir into sauce. Cook until the consistency of a soft custard. Whip with an egg beater while cooling.

1820 House, Plymouth, New Hampshire

93. French Dressing (Serves 8)

INGREDIENTS

12 tablespoons olive oil
2 tablespoons malt vinegar
2 tablespoons tarragon vinegar
½ teaspoon salt
¼ teaspoon freshly ground black peppercorns or whole pepper

DIRECTIONS

Dissolve salt in vinegar, add pepper and stir well, then whip in the olive oil—shake before using.

If ground pepper, such as is bought in cans is used, a little more would be necessary, because the pepper when freshly ground is considerably hotter or stronger. (If paprika is used, it turns the dressing a sort of pinkish or reddish tinge, or if sugar is used to mellow the vinegar, it is not a French Dressing.)

The only ingredients to go into genuine French Dressing are oil, vinegar, salt and pepper.

Wrigley Building Restaurant, Chicago, Illinois

Some home cooks add a suspicion of curry to French Dressing.

94. Fruit Salad Dressing

(Serves 6 to 8)

INGREDIENTS

2 eggs–beaten
½ cup honey
juice of 1 lemon

½ pint whipping cream
–whipped

DIRECTIONS

Place in double boiler and cook until thick, stirring constantly. Remove from heat and allow to cool.

When ready to serve, add whipped cream. Crushed pineapple may also be added to this dressing.

Mrs. C. H. Welch, Tucson, Arizona

95. Green Goddess Salad Dressing

(Makes 1 quart)

INGREDIENTS

8 to 10 filets of anchovies
1 piece of young onion
2 sprigs parsley
1 pinch tarragon leaves

3 cups mayonnaise
1 tablespoon tarragon vinegar
1 bunch chives

romaine
escarole
chicory

DIRECTIONS

Chop these very fine.

Chop chives fine, combine with mayonnaise and vinegar. Mix with above ingredients.

Cut and toss in bowl that has been rubbed with a piece of garlic. Add the dressing and toss all together and serve.

The Palace Hotel, San Francisco, California

96. Mayonnaise

(1 pint)

INGREDIENTS

1 whole egg
1 teaspoon salt
½ teaspoon freshly ground black pepper
1 teaspoon sugar
1 teaspoon dry mustard
2 tablespoons wine vinegar
1 pint olive oil

DIRECTIONS

Put all ingredients except the olive oil in the bowl of your electric mixer. Beat at high speed for 1 minute or until they are thoroughly blended. Start pouring in the oil, allowing only a very little bit to go in at a time. Continue pouring a small amount of oil and beating at high speed until all of the oil has been beaten into egg mixture. Store in covered container in refrigerator.

Mrs. Duncan Hines, Bowling Green, Kentucky

Too many people, men especially, crave only meat, bread, potatoes and gravy. They overlook the importance of the mineral salts contained in salads which act as a digestant.

97. Roquefort Dressing

(Serves 8 to 12)

INGREDIENTS

1 cup French Dressing
4 tablespoons Roque-
fort cheese

DIRECTIONS

Crumble the Roquefort cheese and beat into the French Dressing, blending thoroughly.

If desired, more Roquefort may be added. This dressing may be kept a reasonable length of time in the refrigerator by storing in a small covered container. Be sure to beat well before using each time as the cheese will go to the bottom of the container after standing for a time.

Mrs. Duncan Hines, Bowling Green, Kentucky

98. Russian Dressing

(Makes 1 cup+)

INGREDIENTS

¾ cup of mayonnaise
4 tablespoons of good
chili sauce
2 tablespoons chopped
pimientos (canned)
1 teaspoon chopped
chives

DIRECTIONS

Add chili sauce, pimientos and chives to mayonnaise.

Stir well and serve very cold.

Another Version:

Place 1 to 2 ounces of good whole grain caviar on top and in center of 1 cup of mayonnaise at table. *Do not stir caviar into mayonnaise;* the whole grain fresh caviar is best if it can be obtained.

Wrigley Building Restaurant, Chicago, Illinois

99. Salad Dressing

(Makes 1 pint)

INGREDIENTS

1 cup salad oil
⅓ cup tomato catsup
⅓ cup vinegar
⅓ cup honey
1 teaspoon
Worcestershire sauce
pinch ground cloves
1 small onion—grated

DIRECTIONS

Mix all ingredients together, stirring all the while.

Columbia Gorge Hotel, Hood River, Oregon

Vegetables grown below the surface of the soil contain valuable mineral salts in the skins.

100. Special Salad Dressing (Serves 6)

INGREDIENTS

½ teaspoon salt
½ teaspoon celery salt
½ teaspoon dry
mustard
¼ teaspoon pepper–
freshly ground
¼ teaspoon sugar
12 anchovy filets–
chopped fine
1 clove garlic–minced

½ pint vinegar

½ teaspoon Worcestershire sauce

½ pint olive oil

DIRECTIONS

Blend these ingredients in a bowl.

Add to mixture a little at a time to make a paste and continue stirring until all the vinegar is blended.

Stir into the mixture.

Gradually stir into the mixture. Shake well before using.

Duncan Hines, Bowling Green, Kentucky

101. Tartar Sauce (Makes 1 cup)

INGREDIENTS

⅓ cup good mayonnaise
1 tablespoon chopped
capers
1 tablespoon chopped
gherkins
1 tablespoon chopped
chives
1 tablespoon chopped
parsley
1 tablespoon chopped
dill pickles

DIRECTIONS

After capers, gherkins, dills, chives and parsley are chopped, they should be wrung out in a clean cloth and then added to the mayonnaise. By wringing these out, the mayonnaise will be tart, will not curdle and will be of a desired consistency—in other words, it will not be sloppy. Oftentimes, when capers, gherkins, or other sour pickled items that are used in the making of Tartar Sauce, are added to the mayonnaise without wringing, they have a tendency to curdle it.

Sour pickles and green olives can be substituted for capers and gherkins, if above ingredients are not available.

Wrigley Building Restaurant, Chicago, Illinois

Cut out the core of head lettuce, wash under cold water faucet, drain, place in covered dish, put in refrigerator, and use the leaves as needed. The leaves will stay fresh and crisp.

102. Banana Bread

(1 loaf)

INGREDIENTS

½ cup butter
1 cup sugar

2 eggs

3 bananas

2 cups flour
1 teaspoon salt
1 teaspoon soda

8 dates
1 cup pecans

DIRECTIONS

Cream well together.

Beat eggs well and fold into above.

Scrape and mash bananas and add to above.

Sift dry ingredients together and add to above, beating in quickly.

Chop dates and pecans and flour lightly. Add to above. Turn into greased loaf pan and let stand 20 minutes. Bake in 350° oven for 50 minutes.

The House by the Road, Ashburn, Georgia

103. Bishop's Bread

(Makes one 8-inch square)

INGREDIENTS

1¼ cups flour
½ teaspoon cinnamon
1 teaspoon salt
1 cup brown sugar
¼ cup butter

1 teaspoon baking powder
¼ teaspoon soda
1 egg—well beaten
½ cup sour cream

DIRECTIONS

Mix together all ingredients and crumble evenly. Take out ¼ cup of the crumbs.

Add baking powder and soda to the above mixture and mix well. Combine egg with sour cream and add to mixture. Beat batter well and pour into greased 8-inch cake pan, sprinkle with reserve crumbs and pat down. Bake for 35 minutes in 350° oven. This is good hot or cold.

Duncan Hines, Bowling Green, Kentucky

104. Cinnamon Bread

(Makes one 9-inch square)

INGREDIENTS

2 egg whites–beaten
½ cup milk

½ cup butter
1 cup sugar
2 egg yolks–beaten

1¼ cups cake flour
2½ teaspoons baking powder
1 teaspoon cinnamon

1 tablespoon butter–melted

DIRECTIONS

Mix together.

Cream butter and sugar, add egg yolks and stir in above mixture.

Sift together and add to the above mixture. Pour into 9-inch square pan which has been greased and floured.

Bake in 300 F. oven for 30 minutes. When done pour melted butter over top and sprinkle with mixture of sugar and cinnamon.

Mrs. W. B. Taylor, Bowling Green, Kentucky

105. Garlic Toast: Hard Rolls or French Bread

INGREDIENTS

1 small clove garlic

⅓ cup butter
salt to taste

grated Parmesan
cheese

DIRECTIONS

Crush.

Heat gently and add garlic. Let stand overnight.

Slice rolls or bread, brush sides with garlic,
butter, sprinkle with grated cheese. Place
under broiler until browned. Serve hot.

Green Gables, Phoenix, Arizona

106. Graham Bread (Hot)   (Serves 12 to 15)

INGREDIENTS

1 egg
1 cup milk
¼ cup sugar
¼ cup shortening

1 cup flour
1 cup graham flour
1 teaspoon salt
3 teaspoons baking
powder

DIRECTIONS

Beat together quickly.

Sift together and mix into the above. Pour in
buttered 9-inch square pan and bake in 325 F.
to 350 F. oven for 20 to 30 minutes. Cut in
squares and serve hot with butter.

Marshlands Inn, Sackville, N. B., Canada

107. Jonnycakes   (Makes about 30 small cakes)

INGREDIENTS

1 qt. R. I. Jonnycake
meal
2 level teaspoons salt
4 level teaspoons sugar
1½ qts. boiling water
½ pt. milk

DIRECTIONS

Sift together the Jonnycake meal, salt, and
sugar. Add gradually the boiling water, stirring constantly, then the milk. Beat well. Drop
on hot griddle, well greased with lard (or
drippings or other fat) from a large tablespoon. Turn when well-browned, being sure
to keep the griddle well-greased. Serve piping
hot.

The Kingston Inn, Kingston, Rhode Island

*Breads containing so-called roughage are considered the most
healthful.*

*A few grains of salt added to cooked food will enhance the
sweetening of the sugar which it contains.*

108. Orange Bread

(Makes 1 loaf)

INGREDIENTS

1 orange—juice
enough boiling water
to make 1 cup

1 orange rind—grated
1 cup pitted dates
½ cup pecans

2 tablespoons melted
butter
1 egg
1 teaspoon vanilla

2 cups flour
1 teaspoon baking
powder
½ teaspoon salt
½ teaspoon soda
¾ cup sugar

DIRECTIONS

Do not strain juice. Put juice and water in mixing bowl.

Chop dates and pecans. Combine with orange rind and stir into liquid.

Blend these ingredients together and add to above mixture.

Sift together and fold into mixture.

Bake in well greased bread pan in 350 F. oven for 1 hour, then reduce heat to 300 F. and bake for 30 minutes longer.

This makes a delicious moist bread that keeps fresh a long time.

Mrs. Alonzo Newton Benn, Chicago, Illinois

109. Cromer's Orange Bread

(Makes 1 loaf)

INGREDIENTS

4 large California
oranges
water to cover
½ teaspoon soda

1½ cups granulated
sugar

2½ cups flour
1 teaspoon salt
3 teaspoons baking
powder
½ cup nut meats
2 eggs
½ cup milk
2 tablespoons butter

DIRECTIONS

Wash oranges. With a sharp knife, peel the thin outer layer of the orange skin, taking care not to get any of the bitter white part beneath. Cut peel into small pieces and place in saucepan, add soda and cover with water. Bring to boil and let cook for 15 minutes. Drain and rinse thoroughly with cold water.

Add sugar to orange peel, stir well and let cook slowly until peel is candied and transparent. It will take 15 to 20 minutes. Peel should be moist and syrupy.

Sift flour, measure and sift again with salt and baking powder. Mix nutmeats lightly with flour. Beat eggs and combine with milk and stir into flour mixture. Stir in melted butter and combine all with orange peel and syrup. Dough should be quite stiff. Pour into greased loaf pan and bake in 300° oven for 1 hour.

Cromer's Restaurant, Flint, Michigan

110. Orange Bread

(Makes 1 loaf)

INGREDIENTS

DIRECTIONS

2 cups flour
2 teaspoons baking powder
½ cup sugar
¼ teaspoon salt

Sift these ingredients together.

1 cup candied orange peel—cut in pieces

Add to the above.

1 egg—beaten
1 cup of milk

Combine egg and milk. Stir well into the dry ingredients. Put in pan and sprinkle with sugar. Let stand for 20 minutes before baking. Bake in 325 F. oven for 30 minutes.

Grace E. Smith's Restaurant, Toledo, Ohio

111. Orange Date Bread

(Makes 1 loaf)

INGREDIENTS

DIRECTIONS

1 cup sugar
2 tablespoons butter

Cream.

1 egg

Stir into above and beat hard.

1 cup dates chopped fine
½ cup orange juice
1 orange rind—grated
1 teaspoon soda
⅓ cup hot water

Mix together in a bowl and when cool, add to above.

2 cups flour—sifted
1 teaspoon salt
1 teaspoon baking powder

Sift together and add to above.

½ cup broken nuts

Add to above and stir well. Pour in bread pans and bake in 350 F. oven for 1 hour.

Meredith Inn, Meredith, New York

112. Short Bread

INGREDIENTS

DIRECTIONS

1 lb. soft butter
6 cups flour
1½ cups sugar
1 egg

Cut butter into flour and sugar until like coarse sand as for a pie crust. Add egg. blend well. Roll or knead into large cakes about ½-inch thick and cut with a cookie cutter. Bake in a 300° oven for 20 to 30 minutes.

Mrs. David Donald, Pittsfield, Massachusetts

113. Fruit Loaf

INGREDIENTS

¼ cup shortening
¼ cup butter
2 teaspoons salt
½ cup sugar
1⅓ cup boiling water

2 yeast cakes
¼ cup lukewarm water
1 tablespoon sugar

6 cups flour
1 teaspoon allspice
¼ teaspoon nutmeg

¼ cup currants
¼ cup raisins
¼ cup citron—chopped
¼ cup candied orange
    and lemon peel—
    chopped
½ cup nuts

DIRECTIONS

Pour boiling water over these ingredients and let cool.

Soften yeast in water and add sugar. Add to above when it is cool.

Sift together and add one half of the amount to the above.

Add fruit and nuts to above and then remainder of flour mixture. Knead well—or you may mix it on an electric mixer. Let rise over night. In the morning knead again, divide in two portions and put in two greased loaf pans. Let rise to double in bulk. Bake in preheated oven, 325°, for 1 hour or until done. Remove from pans and brush with melted butter.

Mrs. Duncan Hines, Bowling Green, Kentucky

114. Butter Horn Rolls

INGREDIENTS

¾ cup butter
½ cup sugar

1 yeast cake
1 cup scalded milk

4 cups flour
1½ teaspoon salt

3 eggs beaten

DIRECTIONS

Cream butter and sugar together.

Mix yeast to a paste with the cooled milk. Blend into butter and sugar.

Sift salt with flour and stir or beat into mixture.

Stir the eggs into the dough. Let rise until doubled. Put the dough on a well-floured towel or canvas. Use a wide spatula to fold the dough over. Continue folding over until it can be handled easily, then knead lightly. Spread top of dough with butter and cover tightly. Set in refrigerator overnight. Roll out the size of a large pie and cut in 6 or 8 pieces. Grease top with butter and then roll. Let get very light and bake in 425° oven for 15 minutes. The sponge will keep 3 to 5 days in the refrigerator.

Duncan Hines, Bowling Green, Kentucky

Soft bread cuts more easily with a slightly heated bread knife.

115. Swiss Pear Bread
(6 to 8 loaves)

INGREDIENTS

DIRECTIONS

1 lb. dried prunes
1 lb. dried pears

Cook separately, drain. (Save juice for sponge and put through meat grinder.)

½ lb. raisins
½ lb. currants
½ lb. citron
½ lb. orange peel
½ lb. lemon peel
1 tablespoon cinnamon
½ teaspoon cloves
½ oz. anise

Mix together and add to the above.

SPONGE:

4 cups fruit juice
½ lb. yeast
1 tablespoon salt
1½ cups sugar
2 tablespoons butter
6 to 8 cups flour
1 wineglass brandy

Knead until dough is stiff and does not stick to board, working in the above mixture. Let stand overnight. Put into loaves and let rise about 2 hours. Bake 15 minutes in 450 F. oven until brown. Turn heat down to 350 F. and bake another hour.

Lowell Inn, Stillwater, Minnesota

When using butter for sandwiches, it may be whipped—you may add whipped cream—1 cup to 1 pound butter and add for zest—l e m o n juice—onion juice—tarragon—garlic—thyme— mustard or what have you, but use them sparingly.

116. Biscuits
(Makes approx. 48 biscuits 2 inches in diameter)

INGREDIENTS

DIRECTIONS

4 cups flour
½ teaspoon salt
3 tablespoons baking powder

Sift dry ingredients together.

2 tablespoons butter
⅓ cup shortening
1⅓ cup buttermilk

Work butter and shortening into flour and add buttermilk. Do not work too much, and knead very lightly on floured board just enough to make a smooth dough. Place in refrigerator until ready to use. Then roll out on floured board to ½ inch thickness, cut with 2-inch cutter, place in greased pan and bake in preheated oven, 450°, for 10-12 minutes. You do not need to bake all the biscuits at one time, but only as needed. Dough will keep in covered bowl in refrigerator for a couple of days.

John Marshall Hotel, Richmond, Virginia

117. Butterscotch Rolls (Makes about 50)

INGREDIENTS

DIRECTIONS

2¼ cups milk
½ cup butter or shortening

Scald milk and melt the shortening in it as it cools.

2 yeast cakes
¼ cup sugar

Mix together until the yeast liquefies. When the milk is lukewarm, pour over yeast mixture.

2 eggs

Beat well and add to the above mixture.

7 cups flour
1 teaspoon salt.

Blend and beat into the mixture, until it is a soft dough. Sprinkle with flour and pat into a ball in the mixing bowl. Cover and set in ice box until 3 hours before using.

1 cup brown sugar
½ cup butter

Mix together. Grease muffin tins heavily and drop a spoonful of sugar and butter mixture into each tin.

melted butter
cinnamon

Roll dough into oblong shape about ¼ inch thick and spread with melted butter and cover with cinnamon. Roll into a long roll and cut in 1 inch thick pieces. Place in muffin tin and let rise in warm room 2 or 3 hours until double in bulk.

Bake in 375° F. oven about 25 minutes, using care not to burn sugar. Before taking them out of oven have a large flat pan ready and turn the tin over immediately on this. Lift and let sugar run on rolls.

Iron Gate Inn, Washington, D. C.

118. Buttermilk Rolls (Makes 24)

INGREDIENTS

DIRECTIONS

2 cups buttermilk
1 yeast cake

Have buttermilk at room temperature. Add yeast and allow it to soften.

½ teaspoon soda
2 tablespoons sugar
2 teaspoons salt
4 cups flour
2 tablespoons shortening

Mix these ingredients using only a part of the flour. Beat well into yeast mixture, then add balance of the flour, until the dough forms a stiff ball. Knead quickly until smooth. Roll out to ¾ inch thickness and cut with biscuit cutter. Place in a greased bread pan. Let rise in a warm place for 1 hour. Bake in 450 F. oven for 15 minutes. When done, brush over lightly with milk sweetened with a little sugar.

Marshlands Inn, Sackville, N. B., Canada

119. Miniature Cinnamon Rolls

INGREDIENTS

1 tablespoon butter
3 tablespoons brown sugar

small amount of yeast dough
melted butter

2 tablespoons sugar
¼ teaspoon cinnamon

DIRECTIONS

Dot bottom of baking pan with butter. Cover evenly with the sugar.

Roll out dough to about ⅛ inch thick in long, narrow strips and brush with melted butter.

Mix together and sprinkle over dough. Roll and cut in pieces ½ inch thick. Place cut side up in baking pan 6x6 inches and allow to rise. Rolls should be not more than an inch in diameter.

Bake in 400 F. oven for 10 to 12 minutes. After baking, brush the top of rolls with melted butter and turn upside down to remove rolls from pan. Serve hot.

These cinnamon rolls are outstanding and I hope those you make turn out as well.

Mrs. Bessie Crane Hise, Chagrin Falls, Ohio

120. Banana Dutch Coffee Cake   (Serves 6 or 8)

INGREDIENTS

1 cup sifted flour
1¼ teaspoons baking powder
½ teaspoon salt
2 tablespoons sugar

¼ cup shortening

1 egg well beaten
3 tablespoons milk

3 bananas (firm)
2 tablespoons butter— melted

2 tablespoons sugar
¼ teaspoon cinnamon
1 teaspoon grated orange rind

DIRECTIONS

Sift together.

Cut shortening into the above.

Mix together and stir into flour mixture. The dough should be stiff. Turn into a well-greased baking pan.

Peel bananas and slice into ½-inch diagonal pieces. Cover dough with bananas. Brush butter over the bananas.

Mix together and sprinkle over the bananas. Bake in 350 F. oven about 35 minutes. Serve hot for breakfast or as dessert with whipped cream or lemon hard sauce.

Home Economics Department, Fruit Dispatch Company, New York City

121. Coffee Cake

(Serves 8)

INGREDIENTS

1 cup sugar
5 tablespoons butter

1 egg

½ cup milk
½ cup cream
1 teaspoon vanilla

2 cups flour
½ teaspoon salt
2 teaspoons baking powder

1 cup walnuts chopped
⅓ cup sugar
½ teaspoon cinnamon

DIRECTIONS

Cream together.

Beat well and add to above.

Blend into above mixture.

Sift together, add to above, and beat well.

Pour mixture in shallow pan about 1 inch deep.

Sprinkle top with sugar, cinnamon, then nuts. Sprinkle more sugar and dot with butter. Bake in 350 F. oven for 30 minutes until done.

Sidney Hoedemaker, Los Angeles, California

122. Deluxe Coffee Cake

(Makes one 10-inch tube cake)

INGREDIENTS

¾ cup butter
1½ cups sugar
3 eggs

3 cups flour
pinch of salt
3 teaspoons baking powder
1 cup sweet milk
rind of one lemon— grated
2 tablespoons lemon juice
chopped pecans
powdered sugar

DIRECTIONS

Cream butter and sugar together. Add eggs one at a time and beat well.

Sift flour and measure. Add salt and baking powder and sift again. Add milk and flour alternately to above mixture. Mix well. Add lemon rind and juice. Grease 10-inch tube pan with butter, sprinkle with flour and cover bottom thickly with pecans. Pour batter into pan and bake at 350° for 50 to 60 minutes. Turn over and cover nut topping with powdered sugar.

Mrs. Gorden Pilkington, St. Louis, Missouri

The connoisseur will tell you that you can never experience the true flavor of coffee when you add sugar and cream.

123. Sally Lunn

(Makes one 9-inch tube)

INGREDIENTS	DIRECTIONS
½ cup butter 1 tablespoon sugar ½ teaspoon salt	Cream together.
2 eggs	Beat eggs and add to above and beat well.
1 yeast cake 1 cup milk 3 cups flour	Heat milk to lukewarm and dissolve yeast in it. Add to above. Add flour, mix thoroughly, pour into buttered tube pan. Let rise 1½ hours or until doubled in bulk. Bake in 350° F. oven 45-50 minutes. Serve hot with butter.

Althaea, Lewisburg, West Virginia

124. Orange Rolls

(Makes 36 rolls)

INGREDIENTS	DIRECTIONS
1 cup hot water 1 teaspoon salt 1½ tablespoons shortening ¼ cup sugar	Combine these ingredients.
1 yeast cake 2 tablespoons warm water	Dissolve and add when the above mixture is lukewarm.
1 egg—beaten 2 cups of flour	Add to the mixture. Beat well.
2 to 2½ cups flour	Stir into the mixture and knead until elastic. Grease top of the dough and let rise. Cut down and roll out in long strip about 1 inch thick.
½ cup butter—melted	Spread on dough.
2 orange rinds—grated 2 cups sugar	Mix together and spread on the dough. Roll and cut in 1-inch slices.
	Put into greased muffin tins and let rise. Bake in 425 F. oven for 12 to 15 minutes.

Quaker Bonnet, Buffalo, New York

There is no true economy in "substitutes."

My advice to an amateur cook in adding seasonings is taste and test as you go along.

125. Fluffy Rolls

(Makes 40 or 50 rolls)

INGREDIENTS	DIRECTIONS
1 cup shortening ¾ cup sugar	Cream and blend together.
1 cup boiling water	Add to the above and let cool until lukewarm
2 eggs—beaten	Add to mixture.
2 yeast cakes 1 cup lukewarm water	Dissolve, and add to the mixture.
7½ to 8 cups flour 1 teaspoon salt	Sift together and add 4 cups to the mixture and blend thoroughly until the dough is smooth. Then gradually add the balance of the flour.
2 tablespoons melted butter	Place the dough in a greased bowl, brush with melted butter and cover the bowl tightly with waxed paper and place in the refrigerator. Use as needed. When made into rolls, let the dough rise for 2 hours before baking. Bake in 450 F. oven for 15 to 20 minutes.

Mrs. Louie M. Weathers, Elkton, Kentucky

126. "Hush Puppies"   (Makes approximately 100 small pones)

In the days of our Southern forefathers the whole family, including the dogs, participated in the "fish fry." While the grown folks were engaged in frying the "big catch," something had to be devised to keep the children and dogs from under foot, so the "hush puppies" were originated. This was a tidbit of corn meal, etc., fried along with the fish (or chicken, etc.) and tossed to the waiting children and dogs as an appeasing gesture—hence the name "Hush Puppies."

INGREDIENTS	DIRECTIONS
3 cups corn meal 1 teaspoon salt ½ teaspoon black pepper 1 large mild yellow onion chopped fine	Mix together.
1 egg 4 tablespoons cooking oil	Stir into above.
1½ teaspoons baking powder	Add to mixture.
sweet milk	Stir in enough to hold the mixture together. Shape into small finger-size pones and fry in skillet with fish.

Old Southern Tea Room, Vicksburg, Mississippi

127. Corn Muffins
(Makes 14 or 16 muffins)

INGREDIENTS	DIRECTIONS
1 pint white corn meal 1 teaspoon salt	Sift together.
1 pint boiling water	Pour over corn meal and mix together.
1 cup cold milk	Pour immediately after addition of boiling water to prevent corn meal from lumping.
2 eggs	Add to mixture and beat well.
4 teaspoons baking powder 1 tablespoon melted butter	Add to mixture. Pour into greased and floured individual glass molds and bake in 475 to 500 F. oven for 30 minutes.

McDonald Tea Room, Gallatin, Missouri

128. Corn Pones
(Makes 12 servings)

INGREDIENTS	DIRECTIONS
2 cups corn meal (must be water ground) 1 teaspoon salt 1 tablespoon fat (half lard, half butter) 1 cup of milk	Form by hand into ovals 1x3 inches and pat on top with fingers. (True Virginia Corn Pones always have the imprint of three fingers on them.) Bake in 400 F. oven until a rich brown or about 25 minutes. Serve very hot.

Forest Tavern, Natural Bridge, Virginia

129. Corn Pocket Rolls
(Serves 6)

INGREDIENTS	DIRECTIONS
1½ cups flour ½ cup corn meal 2 tablespoons baking powder ½ teaspoon salt 2 tablespoons sugar	Mix these ingredients together.
1 egg—beaten ¾ cup sour cream	Combine egg and cream and mix with dry ingredients. Put on floured board and roll out rather thin.
1 tablespoon melted butter	Brush dough with butter and cut in rounds and fold in half. Bake in 350 F. oven 12 to 15 minutes.

Old Spinning Wheel Tea Room, Hinsdale, Illinois

130. Cornbread Truett

(Serves 8 to 10)

INGREDIENTS

DIRECTIONS

⅜ cup butter or shortening
½ cup sugar
2 cups corn meal
1¼ teaspoons salt

Cream butter or shortening. Add sugar and blend. Stir in meal and salt.

2½ cups boiled rice

Work in lightly.

2 eggs beaten
2 cups milk

Mix together and add to mixture.

1 cup flour
6 teaspoons baking powder

Sift together and add to mixture. Pour in buttered pan and bake in 375 F. oven for 30 to 35 minutes.

Vera Kirkpatrick, San Mateo, California

South of the Mason-Dixon line, don't you dare put sugar in cornbread or the night riders may meet up with you some dark night.

131. Corn Meal Puffs

(Serves 6)

INGREDIENTS

DIRECTIONS

5 tablespoons white corn meal

Scalded with enough boiling water to make mixture, but not too soft.

4 egg whites—beaten
1 teaspoon salt

When corn meal has cooled to a lukewarm temperature, fold in egg whites and drop from spoon onto baking sheet and bake in 300° F. oven for 20-30 minutes.

Old Spinning Wheel Tea Room, Hinsdale, Illinois

132. Corn Sticks

(Makes 12)

INGREDIENTS

DIRECTIONS

¾ cup sifted meal
½ cup sifted flour
1 teaspoon sugar
½ teaspoon salt
1½ teaspoons baking powder

Mix all together.

¾ cup buttermilk plus 2 tablespoons
⅛ teaspoon soda
1 egg beaten
¼ cup melted shortening

Combine buttermilk and soda and stir into dry ingredients and add beaten egg. Lastly add shortening. Have your oven preheated to 425° and grease corn stick pan and put in oven to let get hot. Pour batter into pan and bake for 15 minutes or until done.

Frances Virginia Tea Room, Atlanta, Georgia

133. Spoon Bread (Serves 10)

INGREDIENTS | DIRECTIONS

1½ cups water — Bring to boil.

1½ cups water-ground corn meal

1⅓ teaspoons salt
1 teaspoon sugar — Mix together and scald with boiling water.

⅛ lb. butter—melted — Add to mixture.

5 eggs—beaten
2 cups milk — Beat eggs and add milk to eggs. Add to above.

1 tablespoon baking powder — Add and stir to get an even mixture. Pour into greased baking pan. Bake in preheated oven, 350° 30 to 40 minutes.

Hotel Roanoke, Roanoke, Virginia

134. Apple Muffins (Makes 12 muffins)

INGREDIENTS | DIRECTIONS

1 cup cake flour — Sift dry ingredients together twice.
1 cup all-purpose flour
1 tablespoon baking powder
3½ tablespoons sugar
⅛ teaspoon salt

1 egg — Beat egg and combine with milk. Add to dry
1 cup milk — ingredients and mix thoroughly. Add chopped
1 cup chopped apples — apples and butter. Fill muffin tins ¾ full and
4 tablespoons melted butter — sprinkle the top with a little sugar and cinnamon. Bake at 400° F. for 20 to 25 minutes.

Success of this recipe depends upon mixing and getting into oven in as short a time as possible.

Peckett's on-Sugar-Hill, Franconia, New Hampshire

135. Gingerbread Muffins (Makes 12 or more)

INGREDIENTS | DIRECTIONS

1 cup butter — Mix together.
1 cup sugar
1 cup molasses
1 cup boiling water

2½ cups flour — Sift together and add to the above. Mix well.
2½ teaspoons soda
1 teaspoon salt
1 teaspoon cinnamon
1 teaspoon ginger

2 eggs—beaten — Add to mixture. Pour into greased muffin tins and bake in 350 F. oven for 30 to 40 minutes.

Cock O' The Walk, Oakland, California

136. Graham Muffins (Makes 12 muffins)

INGREDIENTS

2 eggs

¾ cup milk
½ cup molasses
(with a pinch of
soda)

1¼ cups graham flour

¾ cup white flour
1 teaspoon salt
3 teaspoons baking
powder

3 tablespoons butter—
melted

½ cup dates, or raisins
and nuts may be
added

DIRECTIONS

Beat well.

Mix into the eggs

Sift into the above and stir.

Sift together and add to the above mixture.

Stir into the above mixture.

Optional.
Bake in hot greased muffin pan in 400 F. oven
for 30 minutes.

Mrs. A. J. Arnold, Cleveland, Ohio

137. Graham Nut Muffins (Makes 14 or 16 muffins)

INGREDIENTS

1 cup graham flour
¾ cup flour
¼ cup sugar
1 teaspoon salt
2 eggs well beaten
3 tablespoons
shortening
5 teaspoons baking
powder
½ cup nut meats
½ cup raisins
1 cup sweet milk

DIRECTIONS

Mix dry ingredients. Add nuts and raisins.
Add milk. Stir quickly and spoon into small
greased muffin rings. Bake in 400° oven for
about 20 minutes.

Hearthstone House, Winnetka, Illinois

*Should you make the mistake of letting your muffins get done
too soon while you continue to sweat and stew with the balance
of the meal, just loosen and tilt them in the pan but please, for
peace in the world, keep them warm.*

*To keep butter from burning in your skillet, add a little
cooking oil.*

138. Maple Muffins

(Makes 8 muffins)

INGREDIENTS

1 egg
¼ cup milk

1¾ cups flour
2½ teaspoons baking
   powder
¼ teaspoon salt
½ cup maple syrup
¼ cup melted butter

DIRECTIONS

Beat egg lightly, add milk and beat together.

Sift together dry ingredients. Stir into milk and egg a little at a time. alternating with syrup. Fold butter into mixture. Bake in buttered floured muffin pan in 325 F. oven for about 25 minutes.

Maple Cabin, St. Johnsbury, Vermont

139. Oatmeal Muffins

(Makes 12 large or 16 medium muffins)

INGREDIENTS

1 cup quick cooking
  oats
1 cup buttermilk

DIRECTIONS

Soak the oats in the buttermilk for 1 hour or longer.

1 large egg

Beat and add to above.

½ cup brown sugar
  (generous)

Add to above.

1 cup bread flour
1 teaspoon salt
1 teaspoon baking
  powder
½ teaspoon soda

Mix dry ingredients together and sift. Add to above mixture.

⅓ cup shortening
  melted

Add to above, mixing well.
Do not beat too much. Place in muffin pans and bake at 400° for 20 minutes.

Mrs. Elsie Smythe, Bowling Green, Kentucky

Cornbread, biscuit and baked potatoes should be served as quickly as possible after being taken from the oven.

Rye bread retains its flavor longer than white bread and does not mold so quickly.

140. Potato Flour Muffins   (Makes 8 muffins)

INGREDIENTS	DIRECTIONS

5 egg whites—beaten	Beat into egg whites until stiff but not dry
2½ teaspoons sugar	
½ teaspoon salt	
2½ tablespoons ice water	Add gradually to the above.
5 egg yolks—beaten slightly	Add to mixture.
1 cup potato flour	Sift together and add to mixture. Mix thoroughly and place in greased muffin tins immediately. Bake in 400 F. oven for 20 minutes. Best results obtained when an electric mixer is used.
2 teaspoons baking powder	

Marshall Field & Company, Chicago, Illinois

141. Spiced Pecan Muffins   (Makes 16 muffins)

INGREDIENTS	DIRECTIONS

2 cups flour	Sift dry ingredients together.
3 teaspoons baking powder	
½ teaspoon nutmeg	
½ teaspoon cinnamon	
¼ teaspoon ground cloves	
¼ cup sugar	
½ teaspoon salt	
½ cup pecans—chopped	Stir in nuts.
1 cup milk	Mix milk and egg and stir into mixture.
1 egg—beaten	
¼ cup melted shortening	Add the shortening. Pour into greased muffin pans and bake in 425 F. oven for 25 minutes.

The Carr House, Wolfeboro, New Hampshire

Somewhere I have said that some men are funny. Well, that goes for some gals too. Just imagine a man having only a stale doughnut and coffee for breakfast, or a finger sandwich smeared with blah mayonnaise and sliced cucumbers and tea for lunch.

The color of an egg shell does not add or detract from the goodness of fresh eggs.

142. White Muffins (Makes 12)

INGREDIENTS | DIRECTIONS

¼ cup butter
¼ cup shortening
¼ cup sugar

Cream.

1 egg—beaten
1½ cup milk

Mix together and add to the above.

2⅓ cups flour
5 teaspoons baking powder
¼ teaspoon salt

Sift together and add to the above. Do not mix the dough too much. Bake 20 minutes in 400° F. oven.

½ cup dates, raisins or fresh blueberries may be added

Optional.

¼ cup grated cheese

Optional.

Myron Green Restaurant, Kansas City, Missouri

143. Cheese Biscuits (Makes about 24)

INGREDIENTS | DIRECTIONS

¼ lb. butter
¼ lb. very sharp cheese

Cream butter.
Grate cheese, work in and cream with butter.

¼ lb. flour

Work flour into above.
Roll out ½ inch thick and cut with cutter 1¼ to 1½ inches in diameter. Bake from 12 to 15 minutes in 450 F. oven. Place ½ pecan on each and brush with powdered sugar.

Mrs. Earle Forbes, Versailles, Kentucky

144. Cheese Straws (Makes 48)

INGREDIENTS | DIRECTIONS

1 cup grated cheese
½ cup butter
1 cup flour
½ teaspoon baking powder
1 pinch red pepper
½ teaspoon paprika
1 teaspoon curry powder (optional)
1 egg yolk
2 tablespoons milk or water

Mix and knead well. Roll thin and cut in strips. Bake in 375 F. oven for 15 minutes.

Mrs. Otto J. Sieplein, Miami, Florida

145. Sally Lunn Muffins (Makes 24 medium-sized muffins)

INGREDIENTS

DIRECTIONS

1 yeast cake
1 tablespoon sugar
¼ teaspoon salt

Crumble yeast in bowl, sprinkle sugar and salt over yeast to dissolve.

1 pint milk
½ cup butter
4 eggs

Scald milk, add butter and let melt. Beat eggs and when milk is cool, mix with eggs. Add to yeast mixture.

1 quart flour

Stir in flour and mix well. Let rise until light. Beat well and spoon into greased muffin tins. Fill ⅔ full and let rise again. Bake in 375° oven for about 20 minutes.

Mrs. Duncan Hines, Bowling Green, Kentucky

146. French Toast (Serves 4 to 6)

INGREDIENTS

DIRECTIONS

6 eggs
2 cups milk
6 tablespoons sugar
2 teaspoons vanilla

Beat eggs well, add milk, sugar and vanilla.

12 to 14 slices bread
butter

Slice bread in ¾-inch slices. (Bread should be 2 or 3 days old.) Remove crusts from slices and dip in egg mixture. Melt butter in heavy skillet and brown slices on both sides.

½ cup sugar
½ teaspoon cinnamon

Combine sugar and cinnamon. Sprinkle over slices. Place in broiler and caramelize on top. Serve with maple syrup or tart jelly.

Mrs. Duncan Hines, Bowling Green, Kentucky

You must know your temperatures. Know the time to put on whatever you are cooking and know when to take it off.

There are about 1.000 different brands of coffee marketed in the United States. You should have no difficulty in securing a satisfying blend. If you enjoy coffee with sufficient authority, use enough. Longer brewing does not add strength, only ruins the aroma and flavor.

147. Beaten Biscuits

(Makes 3 to 4 dozen)

INGREDIENTS

DIRECTIONS

4 cups sifted flour
1 teaspoon salt
1 teaspoon sugar
1 teaspoon baking
powder

Sift together.

½ cup shortening

Blend with above.

¼ cup cream and
enough milk to make
a fairly stiff dough

Add to above and blend.

Roll in beaten biscuit roller until dough blisters and pops. Cut in small squares or with round cutter. Prick with fork dipped in flour. Bake in 450° F. oven for 10 to 15 minutes. Then turn down to 375 F. for 25 to 30 minutes, or until done.

Do not open door for first 10 minutes of baking. If not brown enough when done place under broiler until a very delicate brown.

Duncan Hines, Bowling Green, Kentucky

Biscuit placed in baking pan one inch apart when cooked should have crust all around, but you who do not like crust all around, jam the biscuit close together.

148. Sour Cream Gingerbread

(Serves 6)

INGREDIENTS

DIRECTIONS

1 cup flour
¼ teaspoon salt
¼ cup sugar
½ teaspoon soda
1½ teaspoons ginger
1 teaspoon cinnamon
½ teaspoon cloves
⅔ cup thick sour cream
3 tablespoons butter
¼ cup dark molasses
1 egg

Mix and sift all dry ingredients in mixing bowl. Heat cream, remove from heat and add butter and stir until melted. Add molasses. Beat egg and pour into it the other ingredients gradually, beating constantly. Add this to dry ingredients, mixing only enough to make a smooth batter. Pour into a buttered 8-inch square cake pan, and bake in 350° F. oven for 25 to 30 minutes or until done. Serve hot with whipped cream or hot buttered rum sauce.

Althaea, Lewisburg, West Virginia

149. Warm Gingerbread with Honey Butter
(Serves 6 to 8)

INGREDIENTS

½ cup molasses
½ cup sugar
½ cup melted shortening
½ cup sour milk
1 egg—well beaten
½ teaspoon soda
1 cup flour plus
1 tablespoon
½ teaspoon ginger
2 tablespoon cinnamon

¼ lb. butter
¾ cup strained honey

DIRECTIONS

Mix ingredients in order given. Sift soda and spices with flour. Pour into greased 8-inch pan and bake in 350° oven about 35 minutes.

Soften butter at room temperature. Place in electric mixer and slowly add strained honey, beat until consistency of whipped cream. Serve on squares of warm gingerbread.

Homestead Dinners, Inc., Fillmore, Indiana

150. Gingerbread
(Makes one 13x9x3 inch cake)

INGREDIENTS

1 cup boiling water
1 cup shortening

1 cup brown sugar
1 cup molasses
3 eggs—beaten

3 cups flour
1 teaspoon baking powder
1 teaspoon soda
1 teaspoon salt
1½ teaspoons ginger
1½ teaspoons cinnamon

DIRECTIONS

Pour water over shortening.

Add to the above.

Sift together and add to the mixture. Beat with an egg beater until smooth. Pour batter into greased and floured cake pan. Bake in 350 F. oven for 30 to 40 minutes.

Houghtaling's Woahink Lake Resort, Glenada, Oregon

Who doesn't like good gingerbread? If you prefer to eat it hot try it with a pat of butter and a little port or sherry wine. Better still, a teaspoonful of peach or apple brandy. And if you want the open admiration of your club members try splitting and toasting cold gingerbread and serving it at your next tea.

151. Popovers

INGREDIENTS

2 eggs
2 cups flour—sifted
2 cups thin milk

DIRECTIONS

Beat eggs hard until thick and light in color. Add milk and flour and blend into a smooth batter. Half fill well-greased muffin pans and bake in 400 F. oven for 10 or 12 minutes, or until they have raised ½ inch above the top of pan. Lower temperature to 350° and continue baking for about 30 minutes until they are nice and brown.

Santa Maria Inn, Santa Maria, California

152. Orange Toast
(Makes 6 slices toast)

INGREDIENTS

2 tablespoons orange juice
1 orange rind—grated
½ cup sugar
⅛ teaspoon cinnamon
6 slices buttered toast

DIRECTIONS

Spread this mixture on buttered toast and put in oven or under the broiler for 2 or 3 minutes.

The Nut Tree, Vacaville, California

153. Orange Toast
(For 12 slices toast)

INGREDIENTS

½ cup orange rind— grated
1 cup sugar
1 tablespoon orange juice

DIRECTIONS

Mix together and spread on buttered toast. Put in oven a few minutes until heated.

Grace E. Smith's Restaurant, Toledo, Ohio

154. Guacamole (Mexican Sandwich Spread)
(Makes about 2 cups)

INGREDIENTS

3 ripe tomatoes—peeled
1 onion
1 avocado pear
salt and fresh ground pepper to taste

DIRECTIONS

Grind and mix ingredients together to form a paste consistency.

These same ingredients may be used as a salad or for hors d'oeuvres, in which case, ingredients should be cut in pieces. Serve with melba or a thin toast.

Mrs. Douglas Broadhurst, Redwood City, California

155. Cooked Dressing for Sandwich Spread

(Makes about 1 pint)

INGREDIENTS	DIRECTIONS
1 cup sour—very thick —cream	Put into a double boiler and mix together.
⅓ cup milk	
⅓ cup vinegar	
3 egg yolks	
1 tablespoon flour	Blend together and add to the above mixture.
2½ tablespoons sugar	Let cook until it gets thick.
1 teaspoon salt	
1 teaspoon dry mustard	
½ teaspoon celery seed	
grated onion to taste	This may be added if desired.

This is a delicious dressing; can be used with ground odds and ends of baked ham leftovers, hock or butt-end, as a sandwich spread.

Note: When the ground ham is placed in the refrigerator, it should be put in an uncovered container as it will quickly mold if covered. To be mixed with the dressing as needed.

Duncan Hines, Bowling Green, Kentucky

156. Egg Bread Chicken Sandwich

(Serves about 6)

INGREDIENTS

DIRECTIONS

BREAD:

1 pint corn meal	Combine cornmeal, soda, and baking powder. Add buttermilk and eggs, thin with a little sweet milk if necessary. Add salt and melted butter, bake in greased loaf pan in 400° oven for 20 minutes or until done. Cut in squares.
½ teaspoon soda	
1 cup buttermilk	
2 eggs—beaten	
1 teaspoon baking powder	
6 tablespoons melted shortening	
1 teaspoon salt	
1 thick slice cooked breast of chicken for a sandwich	Split a square of bread, butter both sides. Place chicken on one side, cover with other slice and top with sauce.

SAUCE:

2 tablespoons onion— minced	Brown until a light golden color.
2 tablespoons celery— minced	
½ cup butter	
4 tablespoons flour	Add to the above and cook until it thickens.
1½ pints strong chicken broth	
¾ cup cream	
salt and pepper to taste	

Mrs. C. H. Welch, Tucson, Arizona

157. Batter Cakes
(Makes about 30 small cakes)

INGREDIENTS | DIRECTIONS

3 egg yolks—beaten
¼ cup maple syrup
1⅛ cups milk

Mix well.

3 cups cake flour
2 tablespoons baking
  powder
1½ teaspoons salt
1⅛ cups milk

Sift dry ingredients together. Add to mixture, alternately with the milk. Beat well.

¼ cup melted shorten-
  ing

Should not be hot when added to mixture. This mixture will be very thin when first made, but should be allowed to stand for 30 minutes before using, to thicken. Make cakes on a griddle that has been rubbed over with a piece of salt pork.

Williamsburg Inn, Williamsburg, Virginia

158. Buckwheat Cakes
(Makes about 20 cakes)

INGREDIENTS | DIRECTIONS

2 cups buckwheat flour
¾ cup flour
1 teaspoon salt
2 cups buttermilk

Make a batter and let stand overnight in a cool place.

1 teaspoon soda
  little warm water

Dissolve in water and when ready to fry cakes, add to batter. Add enough buttermilk so that batter will pour off spoon onto hot griddle. Use piece salt pork to grease griddle. Make cakes and serve with maple syrup.

Marshlands Inn, Sackville, N. B., Canada

159. Corn Pancakes
(Serves 6)

INGREDIENTS | DIRECTIONS

2 eggs—well beaten
1 cup milk

Mix together.

¼ cup sugar
2 teaspoons baking
  powder
1 cup flour
1 teaspoon salt

Sift together and add to the above.

1 cup corn (fresh or
  canned)

Add to mixture.

⅓ cup shortening

Add to mixture and stir well. Bake on hot griddle and serve very hot.

Sundal Guest House, West Lebanon, Maine

160. Pancakes for Two (Makes 10 medium-sized cakes)

INGREDIENTS	DIRECTIONS
1 cup flour 1 teaspoon baking powder ¼ teaspoon salt 1 tablespoon sugar	Sift together.
1 egg ⅔ cup sweet milk 1 tablespoon melted butter	Beat the egg and combine with milk. Add to dry ingredients and add the melted butter. Bake on hot griddle.

Mrs. E. E. Forbes, Versailles, Kentucky

> *To season your new waffle or griddle iron before using to avoid the necessity of greasing, brush clean when cold, then with unsalted fat and heat to baking temperature and let cool. When you bake waffles or cakes, throw the first out the door to your friend dog, the balance should make kids and grown-ups smile provided you have plenty of butter and good sweets to go with them.*

161. Flapjacks
(Makes about 24 flapjacks 8 to 10 inches in diameter)

INGREDIENTS	DIRECTIONS
1 can condensed cream	Weaken with water to ⅔ quart. If sweet buttermilk is available, use ⅔ quart instead of condensed cream and water.
⅔ teaspoon soda pinch of salt flour	Stir in sufficient flour to make a thin batter. Add the soda and beat like the devil until the batter comes up. Use a piece of salt pork rind to grease the griddle.

John M. Bush, Negaunee, Michigan

Flapjacks constitute one of the staple items in the daily menu of lumberjacks, who are noted for their robust appetites. The cook in the larger camps accumulates a stockpile of 1,000 before starting to serve the meal. The reason for such a reserve is that the "jacks" eat with such rapidity when they do start, that the cook could not keep up with them if he did not have the jump on them. They have been clocked, and it is from 10 to 15 minutes from the time they enter the dining room until the first one emerges. They would all be out in 30 minutes. In addition to the flapjacks, they consume large quantities of bacon, ham, eggs and quarts of coffee. Flapjacks get their name from the fact that when a cake is cooked on one side, the cook loosen it with a knife and with a dexterous twist of the wrist he tosses the cake into the air, catching it on the turn.

162. Buttermilk Corn Cakes

(Serves 4)

INGREDIENTS

DIRECTIONS

1 cup flour
1½ teaspoons salt
1 teaspoon soda
1 teaspoon baking powder

Sift together.

1 cup coarse yellow cornmeal

Add to above.

2 eggs, well beaten
2 cups buttermilk

Add to above. Bake on hot, lightly greased griddle. Serve with honey or syrup and plenty of butter.

Duncan Hines Test Kitchen, Ithaca, New York

163. Corn Meal and Rice Griddle Cakes

(Makes about 20)

INGREDIENTS

DIRECTIONS

½ cup corn meal
½ cup flour
½ teaspoon soda
1 teaspoon salt

Mix and sift.

2 egg yolks—beaten
1 cup sour milk
1 cup cold cooked rice

Mix up together and add to dry ingredients.

2 egg whites—beaten

Fold in egg whites. Fry on hot griddle.

Serve with maple syrup.

Sawyer Tavern, Keene, New Hampshire

GRIDDLE CAKES, HOT CAKES, ETC.

If you use a baking griddle which requires greasing, there is nothing better than bacon rind—but sparingly. Do not let your griddle get too hot or smoking. Pour on just enough batter to make a cake the size of a saucer, unless you prefer the Paul Bunyan size.

Turn the cakes only once—you will know when to do this as the cakes start to make small bubbles. The second side requires only half as long to cook.

164. Buttermilk Hot Cakes

(Makes about 20)

INGREDIENTS

DIRECTIONS

2 eggs
2 cups buttermilk
1 teaspoon soda
2 cups flour
1 teaspoon baking powder
½ teaspoon salt
2 teaspoons melted shortening

Beat the eggs and add buttermilk and soda and beat again slightly.

Sift dry ingredients together, add to above and beat well. Add shortening and bake on greased hot griddle.

Umpqua Hotel, Roseburg, Oregon

165. German Pancake

(Makes about 6 thin cakes)

INGREDIENTS

DIRECTIONS

3 eggs—beaten
½ teaspoon salt
½ cup flour

Beat eggs very light. Add salt and flour, beating all the time.

½ cup milk

Add and beat constantly.

2 tablespoons butter

Spread bottom and sides of 10-inch cold frying pan with butter. Pour in the batter. Put in 450 F. oven and bake 20 to 25 minutes, gradually reducing the heat. Place on a hot plate and serve with lemon juice, cinnamon, sugar, and hot applesauce.

Roy C. Neuhaus, Evanston, Illinois

166. German Potato Pancakes

(Serves 10)

INGREDIENTS

DIRECTIONS

3 lbs. raw potatoes

Grate and drain off water.

5 tablespoons flour
3/5 tablespoon salt
4 eggs
6 slices diced bacon (if desired)

Add to potatoes and mix well. Have pan hot with about ¼ inch shortening and drop mixture from a spoon. Fry on both sides until a golden brown. Dry on a napkin and serve with applesauce or maple syrup. Also good with pot roast, duck or goose.

Wasum's Restaurant, Detroit, Michigan

"Get 'em while they're hot!" This cry could well be brought to the dinner table because hot foods should be served while they still are hot, and throwing the rule into reverse, cold foods should be served cold.

167. Potato Pancakes (Serves 8)

INGREDIENTS

DIRECTIONS

4 large potatoes—grated
2 eggs—beaten
1 tablespoon flour
1 onion—grated
(optional)
salt and pepper to
taste

Mix thoroughly.

Bake on a hot griddle. Bacon greased griddle
is the best.

Viola A. Brehmer, Elmwood, Fond du Lac, Wisconsin

168. Special Hot Cakes (Serves 8)

INGREDIENTS

DIRECTIONS

2 cups flour
1 cup corn meal
1 teaspoon salt
½ teaspoon soda
4 teaspoons baking
powder

Sift together.

1 cup whole wheat flour
1 cup bran flakes

Add to the above.

2 eggs—beaten
1 quart buttermilk

Beat together and mix with the dry ingredients. Thin with a little sweet milk to desired
consistency. Bake on ungreased griddle slowly,
allowing 2 minutes for each side of cake.

Big Sur Lodge, Big Sur, California

169. Rye Hot Cakes (Makes about 30)

INGREDIENTS

DIRECTIONS

1½ cups white flour
1 cup rye flour
½ teaspoon salt
1½ tablespoons sugar
2 teaspoons baking
powder

Sift together.

2½ cups buttermilk

Slowly add to the above and beat thoroughly.

3 eggs

Add one at a time and beat in each one hard.

1½ tablespoons butter

Melt and stir into above.

1 teaspoon soda
1 tablespoon hot water

Mix together and add to the batter. Make
cakes on medium hot griddle and serve with
maple syrup.

Thomsons Lodge, Vida, Oregon

170. Wheat Cakes (Serves 6)

INGREDIENTS

2 egg yolks
2 cups milk
2 cups flour
1 tablespoon sugar
1 teaspoon salt
4 tablespoons melted butter
2 teaspoons baking powder

2 egg whites—beaten

DIRECTIONS

Beat all together with an egg beater until a smooth batter.

(If sour milk or buttermilk is used, substitute soda for baking powder and do not separate eggs. If sour cream is used, put in only 2 tablespoons.)

Fold in egg whites.

Mrs. Voigt F. Mashek, Chicago, Illinois

171. Waffles (Makes about 6)

INGREDIENTS

2 egg yolks
1 cup milk
1½ cups cake flour—sifted
2 teaspoons sugar
1 teaspoon salt
¼ cup butter—melted

2 egg whites—beaten stiff
2 teaspoons baking powder

DIRECTIONS

Stir to a smooth batter.

Fold in eggs and baking powder. Stir lightly.
Bake on a hot greased waffle iron, until brown.

The House by the Road, Ashburn, Georgia

172. Banana Suzettes (Makes 16)

INGREDIENTS

2 tablespoons flour
2 egg yolks beaten
4 tablespoons cream
2 bananas
2 egg whites

NEW ENGLAND SAUCE:

1 cup sugar
1 tablespoon cornstarch
1 teaspoon vinegar
2 cups water
2 tablespoons butter

DIRECTIONS

Dice bananas in ¼-inch slices. Beat egg whites very stiff. Mix ingredients in order given. Fry golden brown in butter. Suzettes should be size of silver dollar. Serve with New England Sauce.

Mix ingredients together in saucepan. Simmer over low heat for about 50 minutes until transparent and the consistency of thin custard.

Silver Grille, The Higbee Company, Cleveland, Ohio

173. French Pancakes or Crepes Suzette with Southern Comfort Sauce (Makes 5 to 6 cakes)

INGREDIENTS

DIRECTIONS

3 eggs—beaten
1 cup milk
⅓ cup water

Mix together.

1 cup flour
¼ teaspoon baking
powder
½ teaspoon salt
3 tablespoons sugar

Sift together and add to mixture.

The batter should be very thin. Take about ½ cup to a griddle. Turn carefully and brown on the other side. When done, put on a dinner plate, sprinkle with powdered sugar and jelly and roll.

1 jigger Southern
Comfort to a cake

Heat, pour over pancake and light with a match.

Mr. Francis E. Fowler, Jr., Los Angeles, California

174. Minced Clam Souffle (Serves 12)

INGREDIENTS

DIRECTIONS

6 tablespoons butter
3 tablespoons onion—
chopped
½ green pepper—
chopped

Saute until a light brown color.

5 tablespoons flour

Blend into above.

2 cups milk
clam juice from 2
cans

Mix liquids and slowly add to mixture, stirring until smooth. Bring to a boil and remove from the fire.

6 egg yolks—beaten
2 7 oz. cans clams—
minced
2 pimentos—cut fine
2 teaspoons
Worcestershire sauce
salt and pepper to
taste

Stir into mixture.

6 egg whites—beaten

Fold into mixture. Pour into individual casseroles.

buttered bread
crumbs
grated cheese

Top casseroles with a little of each and place in pan of hot water and bake in 325 F. oven for 30 minutes.
A small piece of garlic may be used, but care should be taken as it is easily ruined.

Cafe Del Rey Moro, San Diego, California

175. Baked Clams au Gratin (Serves 6 to 8)

INGREDIENTS

2 cups coarsely ground clams
2 eggs
½ cup grated cheese
1 teaspoon salt
½ teaspoon white pepper

DIRECTIONS

Mix all these ingredients together. Set aside until needed.

¼ lb. butter
3 strips diced bacon
⅓ cup chopped celery, green pepper, and green onion

3 tablespoons flour

1 pint boiling milk

Braise in a pan, but do not brown.

Add the flour and cook well.

Gradually add the boiling milk and let cook until thick. Stir in the first mixture and place in buttered dish, sprinkle with grated cheese, melted butter and dust with paprika and bake in 350 F. oven for 10 to 15 minutes. (Clam shells or individual molds may also be used.) Serve immediately, piping hot.
If clams are not available, shrimp, crab, or lobster may be used, adding 3 or 4 oz. of dry sherry wine.

Plessas Tavern, Pismo Beach, California

176. Crab Custard en Casserole (Serves 6)

INGREDIENTS

4 tablespoons butter
1 teaspoon grated onion

DIRECTIONS

Cook in top of double boiler, but do not brown.

4 tablespoons flour
salt and pepper to taste

Blend and add to the above. Cook and stir until smooth.

4 cups milk
½ cup cream
1 dash of Tabasco sauce
1 teaspoon A-1 sauce

Blend and add to mixture slowly, stirring constantly until thick. Strain. Cover and keep hot.

4 eggs—beaten
1 tablespoon sherry

Blend and add to above sauce.

3 cups crab meat

Into individual (pint size) casseroles, put ½ cup crab meat. Pour sauce over each.

½ cup buttered bread crumbs

Sprinkle over each casserole. Bake in 325 F. oven for 1 hour, or until a silver knife comes out clean.

Valley Green Lodge, Orick, California

177. Deviled Crab

(Serves 6)

INGREDIENTS

DIRECTIONS

1 tablespoon butter
2 tablespoons flour
⅔ cup white stock
2 egg yolks—beaten
salt and pepper to
taste

Make a cream sauce. Chill for 2 hours.

1 cup chopped crab
meat
1 cup chopped
mushrooms
2 tablespoons sherry
wine
1 teaspoon chopped parsley
salt and pepper to taste

Blend together and mix into sauce.

6 crab shell backs

Fill shells with mixture.

5 tablespoons bread
crumbs
4 tablespoons melted
butter

Mix together and sprinkle over top.
Bake in 400 F. oven for 10 to 12 minutes.

Tarpon Inn, Port Aransas, Texas

178. Crab and Spaghetti

(Serves 5 or 6)

INGREDIENTS

DIRECTIONS

½ cup chopped onions
1 teaspoon chopped
garlic
1 teaspoon chopped
parsley
1 teaspoon chopped
celery
¼ cup olive oil

Braise vegetables in oil, until a golden brown.

1 cup solid pack
tomatoes
1 cup tomato sauce
1½ cups water
2 teaspoons salt
1 teaspoon black
pepper
½ teaspoon paprika

Mix together and add to the above ingredients and let simmer for 1 hour.

1 lb. fresh crab meat
¼ cup sherry wine

Add and simmer for a few minutes.

1 lb. spaghetti
grated cheese to
taste

Cook and drain spaghetti. Put on platter and pour sauce over it and mix well. Sprinkle with cheese. Serve immediately.

Fishermen's Grotto, San Francisco, California

179. Deviled Crab   (Serves 8)

INGREDIENTS

1 stalk celery
½ large onion
2 tablespoons butter

6 cooked crabs or
2 6½ oz. cans crab
    meat
6 eggs
½ cup bread crumbs
1 tablespoon poultry
    seasoning
salt
red pepper

DIRECTIONS

Melt butter in sauce pan, add celery and onion which have been ground and cook slightly.

Add shredded crab meat and mix thoroughly. Beat eggs and stir into mixture with remainder of ingredients. Season to taste and mix thoroughly. Place in crab shells, brush with melted butter and bake for 15 minutes in 400° F. oven.

Pier 21, Houston, Texas

180. Crab Stew   (Serves 4)

INGREDIENTS

4 tablespoons butter
3 tablespoons flour
1 piece red pepper to
    taste

2 cups milk

½ cup cream
3 tablespoons
    Worcestershire sauce
1 teaspoon celery salt

4 cups shredded crab
    meat
segments of lemon

4 tablespoons sherry

DIRECTIONS

Cream together until smooth. Cook in double boiler.

Gradually add to mixture and cook slowly until thick.

Blend these ingredients and add to mixture.

Add to sauce and keep hot in double boiler. Do not boil.

At the last moment add the wine and serve.

This recipe is given as a one dish meal. If used as an entering soup, use less crab meat so the consistency of the finished dish meets the requirements of the server.

Dr. T. J. LeBlanc, Cincinnati, Ohio

Many cooks ruin fish by using too high temperature and overcooking, resulting in loss of flavor and fish so dried out it is a distinct disappointment.

181. Crab Meat Souffle a la Rene (Serves 6)

INGREDIENTS	DIRECTIONS
3 tablespoons butter 4 tablespoons flour ¼ teaspoon salt pepper to taste 1 cup milk	Make a white sauce and let cool.
3 egg yolks	Stir into sauce.
1 cup cooked crab meat —flaked 1 teaspoon lemon juice	Mix with the sauce.
3 egg whites—beaten	Fold into mixture. Place in baking dish and bake in 350 F. oven for 40 minutes, or until a silver knife comes out clean when thrust into center. Served with a tossed salad and dessert, this makes an ideal luncheon.

Phil Libby, Radio Food Commentator, Chicago, Illinois

182. Fish Balls (Serves 4 to 6)

INGREDIENTS	DIRECTIONS
1 cup codfish	Use a dry, boneless brand and let soak overnight in cold water. Drain and cover with fresh water and let boil about 10 minutes. Then pull apart.
2 cups mashed potatoes	Mix with fish.
2 egg yolks 3 tablespoons butter ¼ teaspoon pepper	Add to mixture and stir well. Drop from a spoon into hot fat and fry until brown.

Mrs. Kenneth Campbell, Salem, New Jersey

Doctors refer to certain sections of our country as goiter belts. Iodine is the natural substance in our diet which prevents goiter. Fish from salt water and many other delicious sea foods contain nature's supply of iodine and generally speaking, the farther from the sea coast one lives the less of this will be found in the soil and water. Ordinary table salt with iodine added, known as Iodized salt, is a good source of this mineral and may be used on the table and in cooking.

183. Fish Mousse (Serves 6)

INGREDIENTS | DIRECTIONS

2 lbs. raw fish
1 onion

Be sure that all bones are removed from fish. Put through food chopper with the onion three times.

3 teaspoons salt
1 tablespoon melted butter
2 eggs—well beaten

Combine.

1 cup milk

Add to above and beat until fluffy. Add to fish mixture. Place in buttered mold and then place mold in pan of water. Bake in 350° oven for ½ hour, or until done.

SAUCE:

2 tablespoons butter

Melt in sauce pan or double boiler.

2 tablespoons flour
¼ teaspoon salt
⅛ teaspoon freshly ground black pepper

Mix dry ingredients together. Add gradually to melted butter, blending well. Be sure there are no lumps.

1 cup sweet milk

Warm milk slightly and add to above gradually. stirring constantly to avoid lumping. Bring sauce to a boil and cook for 2 minutes.

½ of 4 oz. bottle stuffed olives
½ cup blanched almonds

Chop olives and cut almonds crosswise. Add to whitesauce. If a ring mold is used, put sauce in center. Otherwise, serve on top of fish.

The fish and onion can be ground in advance and kept in refrigerator until ready to use.

Mrs. Wallace Rigby, Larchmont, New York

184. Lobster a la Newburg (Serves 6)

INGREDIENTS | DIRECTIONS

6 tablespoons butter
3 cups fresh cooked lobster—diced

Melt butter in double boiler. Add lobster and cook directly over low heat for 3 minutes.

2 tablespoons sherry
1 dash paprika
1 dash nutmeg

Add to the above and put over hot water.

6 egg yolks—beaten
1½ cups cream

Blend eggs and cream and add to mixture. gradually. Cook until smooth and thick.

toast points

Serve at once on toast points.

For a Lobster Thermidor, this mixture may be returned to lobster shells, sprinkled with fine buttered bread crumbs and put under low broiler heat to brown.

Jordan Pond House, Seal Harbor, Maine

185. Seafood Newburg

(Serves 2)

INGREDIENTS | DIRECTIONS

2 Littleneck clams
¼ cup lobster meat
¼ cup crab flakes
¼ cup shrimp
1 dash paprika
2 tablespoons butter

Saute for a few minutes.

1 tablespoon sherry wine

Add to mixture and toss over the fire for a few minutes more.

¾ cup cream

Add to mixture and let come to a boil.

3 egg yolks—beaten
¼ cup cream

Blend together and add to mixture, stirring constantly until thick. (Do not allow to boil, after eggs are in.) Remove from the fire.

1 tablespoon lemon juice
salt and pepper to taste
2 tablespoons butter

Stir into mixture and serve hot on toast or in a chafing dish.

Marjorie Mills, Boston, Massachusetts

186. Lobster Thermidor

(Serves 6)

INGREDIENTS | DIRECTIONS

2 fresh boiled lobsters

Cut in one-inch pieces.

2 tablespoons butter
2 medium size truffles
salt, pepper, cayenne to taste

Slice truffles thin and chop fine. Put in saucepan, add lobster meat and cook slowly for 3 minutes.

1 glass Madeira wine

Add to mixture and cook until wine reduces.

1 cup cream
3 egg yolks

Beat yolks in cream with a fork. Put in double boiler and cook slowly until thick. Stir sauce slowly into the lobster mixture and allow to heat thoroughly, but DO NOT BOIL. Pour into a tureen and serve very hot.

Waldorf-Astoria Hotel, New York City

America is blest with having a large variety of fine fish along the coastal waters and inland regions and yet, generally speaking, we do not know many ways of preparing them; merely fry, boil and broil it and squirt a dash of lemon or tomato sauce and let it go at that. What a delightful change it is to bring forth a delectable dish of poached fish. Nine out of ten persons will order a broiled whitefish, but when it is poached in wine and served with an egg sauce, it is indeed a welcome change.

187. Baked Scallops

(Serves 12)

INGREDIENTS

DIRECTIONS

36 scallops
12 shells

Put 3 scallops in each shell (deep side of shell is best) . Sprinkle with salt.

3 cups bread crumbs

Cover scallops.

¾ cup butter

Dot top of scallops.

¾ cup cream—
1 tablespoon to each
shell

Add to scallops.

pepper to taste

Add to scallops. Bake in 400 F. oven for 10 minutes. Serve immediately. Decorate with parsley and serve with tartar sauce.

Hackmatack Inn, Chester, N. S., Canada

188. Baked Scallops

(Serves 4)

INGREDIENTS

DIRECTIONS

1 pint of cape scallops
1 pint white wine

Boil scallops in wine until tender and cut in quarters.

6 fresh mushrooms
2 tablespoons butter
2 or 3 finely chopped
shallots
1 tablespoon finely
chopped parsley
salt and pepper
1 tablespoon flour
1 cup liquid in which
scallops were cooked
6 tablespoons cream

Slice mushrooms and saute them in butter with shallots and parsley, and seasonings. Cook very lightly and then blend in flour. To this add very slowly, stirring constantly, the liquid in which the scallops were cooked and the cream. When well blended, add scallops, put in shells, sprinkle with bread crumbs, dot with butter and place under broiler, 400-425°, until golden brown.

Hotel Sam Peck, Little Rock, Arkansas

189. Shrimp de Jonge

(Serves 4)

INGREDIENTS

DIRECTIONS

¼ cup butter

Melt.

2 cloves garlic
chopped fine
½ cup bread crumbs

Add to butter.

1 lb. fresh cooked
shrimp

Mix with the above and fry until a golden brown. Serve with hot fluffy rice.

Duncan Hines, Bowling Green, Kentucky

190. To Cook Fresh Shrimp

Not more than two pounds of shrimp should be cooked at a time. In this way you get even heat penetration and the shrimp can be cooked at a lower temperature.

Before cooking, clean shrimp by removing shell and tail, remove vein in back and wash out all signs of spinal or entrail tract in cold water. Split shrimp down the back, but do not cut in two.

In a pot heat water enough to cover shrimp to 200° to 205°. Season water with a tablespoon of salt and 2 tablespoons of pickling spices from which the red pepper has been removed. The spices should be tied in a small piece of cheese cloth. Place shrimp in wire basket and when water has reached required temperature, immerse shrimp. When water comes back to temperature, allow shrimp to simmer for approximately 4 minutes.

When time is up, lift the shrimp out and take one shrimp, break it open, and if it is still glassy inside, it is not done. Immerse shrimp again for a few minutes until the glassiness disappears. Do not overcook and do not bring shrimp to a boil as this will toughen them. Immediately upon removing from pot, plunge into cold water and chill.

Barnacle Bill's Galley, Erie, Pennsylvania

191. Fried Rice with Shrimp   (Serves 10)

INGREDIENTS	DIRECTIONS
2 tablespoons peanut oil or butter 1 large onion, finely chopped	Place oil or butter in frying pan and heat over low heat. Fry onion gently and cook until tender but not brown.
1 cup finely diced celery ½ cup mushrooms, chopped 1 lb. cooked shrimp	Add to above and cook for about 5 minutes.
4 cups cooked rice 3 tablespoons soya sauce 1 teaspoon salt	Add to the above and mix well. Let cook for a few minutes.
4 eggs	Beat eggs well and add to above and stir well. Cook a couple of minutes until the eggs are done.

Trader Vic, Oakland, California

192. Oysters a la Carnival (Serves 12)

INGREDIENTS

DIRECTIONS

50 oysters

Chop and let drain.

3 onions—minced
1 clove of garlic—
minced
1 shallot
1 bay leaf
1 sprig of thyme
1 tablespoon shortening

Put in iron skillet and fry until onions are a light brown color. Add the oysters.

1 cup toasted bread
crumbs

Moisten with water from the oysters and add to mixture. Fry for about 30 minutes, or until the oysters have stopped drawing water.

¼ cup butter

Add to mixture and let it cook until the butter is melted.

1 doz. oyster shells

½ cup bread crumbs
¼ cup butter

Boil and scrub shells, then fill with mixture. Sprinkle with dry toasted bread crumbs and dots of butter. When ready to serve, put in 425 F. oven for a few minutes until thoroughly heated and serve at once.

This recipe by Mary Bell, an old family cook for Corinne Dunbar, New Orleans, Louisiana

193. Baked Oysters Cremaillere

INGREDIENTS

DIRECTIONS

12 oysters
1 oz. dry white wine

Remove from shells and cook in wine for 2 minutes. Remove oysters from juice and let the juice reduce.

1 cup heavy cream
1 tablespoon cream
sauce

Add to juice and cook until it thickens.

1 tablespoon cooked
spinach
1 shallot
2 mushrooms
1 branch estragon
(Tarragon)

Add to the oysters and chop all together finely. Cook for 5 minutes, and add to sauce.

season to taste

Add to oyster mixture.

2 egg yolks beaten

Stir into the mixture and fill the oyster shells. Bake for 5 minutes and serve with a slice of lemon.

La Cremaillere a la Campagne, Banksville, New York

194.   Baked Oysters, Emerson   (Serves 2)

INGREDIENTS

12 oysters in shell

12 tablespoons cocktail
   sauce
   fresh white bread
   crumbs

12 teaspoons shallots
2 slices bacon
   butter
   salt and freshly
   ground black pepper

DIRECTIONS

Shuck oysters into a bowl. Wash the deep shell in cold water and make certain all sand and dirt are removed. Put shells in pan with rock salt underneath so shells will not tilt.

Put 1 tablespoon sauce in each shell. Lightly pat the raw oysters in bread crumbs and lay on top of sauce in each shell.

Chop shallots fine. (Onion and parsley may be substituted.) Put 1 teaspoon on each oyster. Chop bacon fine and put some on each oyster and top with small piece of fresh butter. Season slightly. Bake in 400° oven from 7 to 10 minutes. If they are not browned in this time, place under broiler until they are. Garnish with lemon and parsley and place small piece of fresh butter on top of each oyster and let it melt. Serve at once.

The Emerson Hotel, Baltimore, Maryland

195.   Minced Oysters   (Serves 15)

INGREDIENTS

1 small loaf bread

1 qt. oysters
4 eggs, beaten
¼ lb. butter
¼ teaspoon red pepper
1 teaspoon pepper
1 teaspoon mustard
   dash nutmeg
2 teaspoons salt

DIRECTIONS

Toast slices of bread and when cold roll into crumbs.

Place butter in sauce pan and let melt. Chop oysters coarsely, put in butter and stir in beaten eggs. When oysters start to bubble, add seasonings and bread crumbs, reserving some of the crumbs for topping oysters. Fill shells, top with bread crumbs and more butter. Bake in 400° oven until brown.

Villula Tea Garden, Seale, Alabama

Meals at home become more interesting with the artful use of herbs and other seasonings, but do not overdo them.

196. Scalloped Oysters   (Serves 4)

INGREDIENTS

1 pint oysters

3 cups bread crumbs
¾ cup melted butter
salt and pepper

DIRECTIONS

Drain off juice.

Remove crusts from slices of bread and grate coarsely. Allow to dry out slightly. In a buttered casserole place 1 cup bread crumbs. Then a layer of ½ the oysters, ¼ cup butter, salt and pepper. Next a layer of 1 cup bread crumbs, the remainder of the oysters, ¼ cup melted butter, salt and pepper. Next layer 1 cup bread crumbs, ¼ cup butter and salt and pepper. When you have finished you should have three layers of crumbs, two of oysters. Bake in preheated oven at 425° for 15-20 minutes.

Mrs. Roy Morningstar, Bowling Green, Kentucky

FRYING OYSTERS

Select large ones and they must be fresh. The old fellows will not hold together. Lay on a soft cloth, sprinkle with seasoned corn meal, do not handle more than necessary.

197. Codfish a la Metolius

INGREDIENTS

Codfish

1 small piece butter
1 cup olive oil
a little garlic

DIRECTIONS

Soak overnight.

Put in saucepan and melt over a very slow fire. Shred codfish and stir into sauce pan.

From time to time add more olive oil drop by drop. Also add a small piece of butter and a few drops of milk. Stir all the time until the mixture becomes a paste, like very rich mashed potatoes. The quality depends upon the stirring movement which must always be in the same direction. Stir gently and continuously.

Mr. John Gallois, San Francisco, California

For flavoring all kinds of fish, meats and vegetables, nothing excels good fresh butter.

Do not overcook smoked fish or it will lose some of its natural flavor. Remember it has already been partially cooked once.

If you must use a large fish, remove the excess fat along the back which may contain too much oil.

198. Shrimp Mull
(Serves 8 to 10)

INGREDIENTS

DIRECTIONS

½ cup diced white bacon
½ cup chopped onion
½ cup butter

Brown together in frying pan.
Transfer to heavy kettle.

1 quart water
1 can tomatoes
½ cup tomato soup
½ cup diced white
  bacon
½ cup chopped onion
1 clove garlic, sliced
½ lemon, sliced

Put opposite ingredients in heavy kettle over low heat, and add above mixture.

½ cup chopped celery
½ teaspoon celery seed
8 drops Tabasco
1 cup tomato catsup
1 tablespoon Worcester-
  shire sauce
⅛ teaspoon allspice
⅛ teaspoon curry
  powder

Add opposite ingredients. Let come to boil and cook gently for about two hours. Should be reduced somewhat.

2½ lbs. raw shrimp

Peel, clean and wash thoroughly. Add to above and let simmer for about an hour. Sauce should be rather thick by that time.

½ cup sherry
½ cup butter
¼ cup cracker crumbs

Add sherry, butter and cracker crumbs and stir well. Let simmer for about 10 more minutes then serve over flaky rice.

The Deck, Brunswick, Georgia

This dish was concocted on the Georgia Coast by plantation owners, prior to the war of 1860. As far as we know, this is the only place in the world serving it.

Heat tends to destroy vegetable mineral matter which is so essential in body-building. This is done by boiling too long in too much water.

Something I have never figured out is why most of the food we like best is not good for us.

199. Baked Shrimp and Noodles (Serves 6)

INGREDIENTS

3 cups noodles

2½ cups milk
2 tablespoons butter
1 tablespoon flour
¼ cup cream
salt and pepper to
taste
1 lb. cooked shrimp

DIRECTIONS

Cook, wash, and drain.

Combine and cook into a well blended smooth sauce.

In a buttered casserole put a layer of noodles, then white sauce, then shrimp, until the dish is filled. Top with cracker crumbs and dots of butter. Bake in 350 F. oven, until the crumbs are well browned.

Allenwood, Burlington, Vermont

200. Shrimp Supreme (1 portion)

INGREDIENTS

6 raw jumbo shrimp

3 strips bacon

1 egg
flour

DIRECTIONS

Peel, but leave the tail on. Open back and clean. Wash thoroughly. Sprinkle each with salt, white pepper, and a little lemon juice.
Cut each strip in two pieces. Wrap each shrimp in strip of bacon pinning with toothpick to hold.
Beat whole egg until frothy. Dip each shrimp in egg, then lightly in flour. Fry in deep fat, 300° for ten minutes. Serve either plain or with sauce.

Columbia Restaurant, Tampa, Florida

201. Scampi (Serves 2)

INGREDIENTS

1 pound fresh or frozen
shrimp

¼ lb. butter
¾ cup olive oil
3 cloves garlic
1 teaspoon basil
½ cup sherry

DIRECTIONS

Split shrimp, place in pan, salt and brush with olive oil. Broil for 2 minutes in 350° oven.

Place butter in saucepan and let brown lightly. Add olive oil, and garlic which has been finely chopped. Add basil and sherry, let simmer for 5 minutes. Place over shrimp and broil, basting until golden brown. (About 15 minutes.) Eat with French bread and dunk bread in sauce.

The Springs, New Ashford, Massachusetts

202. Poached Whitefish with Egg Sauce (Serves 4)

INGREDIENTS

DIRECTIONS

Cold water (amount depending on size of pan and fish)
1 or 2 pieces of thyme (not too much)
½ lemon—sliced
1 raw carrot
2 grains black pepper
½ tablespoon salt
½ teaspoon wine or vinegar
(if you boned the fish, put the bones in also)

Have a shallow oval-shaped pan 1½ to 2 inches deep with a loose-perforated inner bottom on which to lay the fish. Combine opposite ingredients in pan and bring to a boil.

1 whitefish—about 4 lbs.

Put fish in hot liquid and reduce the flame. Let simmer slowly until fish is done (time depends on kind and size of fish), about 18 minutes.

EGG SAUCE:

1 cup cream
2 hard-boiled eggs— chopped fine
salt and pepper to taste
3 teaspoons of water in which fish was cooked

Mix together and bring to a boil. Remove from heat.

1 egg yolk—well beaten

Add to sauce.

3 twigs parsley— chopped

Add to the sauce and serve.

Mario Piccardi, Chicago, Illinois

203. Special Creamed Wall-eyed Pike (Serves 4)

INGREDIENTS

DIRECTIONS

About ⅓ cup cream for 2 to 4 pike 1½ lbs. each

Salt and pepper, put in shallow pan with plenty of butter, little water, bake. About 15 minutes before done pour cream over them. Do not cover at any time and serve as soon as taken from oven.

Remember: In baking fish it must be strictly fresh or it will fall to pieces.

Lake Breeze Resort, Three Lakes, Wisconsin

204. Lincklaen Famous Fish Balls   (Makes 36 small balls)

INGREDIENTS

DIRECTIONS

½ lb. salt codfish—cut
  in pieces
1 quart raw potatoes—
  diced
2 quarts cold water

Cover with cold water and soak overnight.
Pour off half the water and add hot water.
Boil until the potatoes are done, drain and
mash thoroughly.

4 tablespoons butter
  black pepper to taste
2 eggs—beaten

Stir into mixture. Flour the hands and roll
into small round balls. Fry in a good grade
of hot lard. Serve with bacon curls and tartar
sauce.

Lincklaen House, Cazenovia, New York

*Fresh fish should be kept very cold, some almost to the point of
freezing, unless it is to be cooked immediately. Many expert
"fish eaters" say that the average person is likely to miss the full
flavor by putting too many sauces and flavors on it before eating.
Some fish are best broiled quickly and served while still hot.*

205. Poached Fish with Oysters   (Serves 4)

INGREDIENTS

DIRECTIONS

1 pint oysters

Drain the oysters.

2 tablespoons catsup

Heat oyster liquor in an enamel pan with
catsup.

1 lb. halibut steak

Remove skin and brush underside with melted
butter. Put in hot oyster liquor and cover
tightly. Reduce heat to under boiling and
cook 20 to 30 minutes until the fish is done.

3 tablespoons butter
3 tablespoons flour
½ teaspoon salt
¼ teaspoon pepper
1 cup cream

Blend butter, flour, salt and pepper in a
small sauce pan.
Gradually add cream and stir until it boils.

2 hard-cooked eggs

Put the cooked fish on a platter and pour
the cream sauce into the liquor. Stir well together and add the oysters. Cook until the
gills separate and pour over the fish. Garnish with sliced hard-cooked egg and lemon
slices.

Sawyer Tavern, Keene, New Hampshire

206. Danish Fish Pudding (Serves 10 to 12)

INGREDIENTS | DIRECTIONS

1½ lbs. fish pulp

To be either flounder, halibut, or red snapper. Scrape into a pulp.

4 egg yolks

Add to pulp, one at a time. Stir in well.

1 thick slice of bread (remove crusts)
1½ cups milk

Soak bread in milk and add. to mixture.

¼ lb. butter
3 teaspoons salt
½ teaspoon pepper
1 teaspoon. nutmeg

Add to mixture and stir well.

4 egg whites—beaten

Fold into mixture. Pour into a 2-quart mold that has been greased and crumbed and boil 3 hours.

Serve with drawn butter, lime juice, and parsley, or with sauce.

SAUCE:

1 pint fresh shrimps
1 lb. fresh mushrooms
½ lb. butter

Chop shrimps and mushrooms and saute in butter.

½ pint cream
¾ tablespoon cornstarch
1 teaspoon salt
½ teaspoon pepper

Make a smooth paste of these ingredients. Put all together into a double boiler and cook until smooth and done. With this sauce, the recipe will serve 12 to 15.

La Chaumiere, Palm Beach, Florida

207. Fried Fish

INGREDIENTS | DIRECTIONS

fish neatly prepared and dipped in milk canned preferred as it adheres to fish better
whole eggs beaten lightly
fine cracker meal
cooking oil

Quantities depend upon how many servings you desire.

Dip fish in pan of milk, then into eggs, next, into cracker meal. This method seals up fish, keeping oil out and retaining flavor.

Use heavy iron skillet with about ½-inch of good cooking oil. Have oil good and hot but not smoking. This will quickly form a crust on fish, resulting in a nice golden brown. Turn fish over. Time of cooking depends upon thickness of fish.

No need to butter after cooking.

Bennett's Sea Food Grotto, Santa Monica, California

208. Golden Creamed Fish   (Serves 4)

INGREDIENTS	DIRECTIONS
1 onion—chopped 12 peppercorns (whole black pepper spice) 1 sprig of chopped parsley 1 cup water	Boil for 5 minutes.
2 lbs. fish (sand-pike, fresh cod, whitefish, lake trout, etc.)	Cut into 4 pieces. Add to the above sauce and simmer gently for about 5 minutes, until the fish is cooked.
salt to taste	Season the fish.
1 tablespoon flour 6 tablespoons cold milk	Blend together and add to the fish. Simmer gently for a few minutes.
½ cup cream	Add to the fish and heat, but do not boil.
2 egg yolks—beaten	Beat in earthen bowl from which fish will be served until a nice lemon color. Slowly add the hot fish and sauce. Serve with boiled potatoes.

Mrs. A. E. R. Peterka, Cleveland, Ohio

209. Sea Bass with Almond Butter

INGREDIENTS	DIRECTIONS
1 sea bass	Remove fillets from fish and bones.
salt to taste 2 tablespoons butter	Season fillets.
2 tablespoons olive oil	Saturate fillets and broil over slow heat. Do not brown.
fresh boiled Parisienne potatoes 1 tablespoon chopped parsley	Dress on a large platter. Surround with potatoes and parsley.
1 tablespoon grated almonds—browned in butter 1 dash lemon juice	Cover surface of fish. Decorate with whole parsley and lemon, cut fancy.

Hotel St. Regis, New York City

Be sure to buy fish with bright clear protruding eyes. If the fish is not fresh the eyes will be dull and sunken.

210. Salmon Balls Deluxe (Serves 4)

INGREDIENTS

1 No. 2 can salmon
1 raw egg
4 small green onions
⅛ cup walnuts
12 salt crackers rolled
 fine

DIRECTIONS

Remove bones and skin from salmon and break up with fork. Stir in beaten egg. Chop onions and walnuts very fine and add to salmon. Stir in crackers until the salmon will hold together. Roll into balls about the size of golf balls. Drop into deep hot fat, about 350°, and let fry for about 5 minutes. Makes about 20 balls.

Roberta Linn, Los Angeles, California

211. Salmon Loaf with Curry Sauce (Serves 4)

INGREDIENTS

1 1 lb. can salmon
1 cup milk
1 cup fine bread crumbs
1 egg, slightly beaten
2 tablespoons chopped
 parsley
2 tablespoons chopped
 onion
2 teaspoons lemon
 juice
¼ teaspoon salt
 dash of pepper

DIRECTIONS

Drain salmon, remove bone and skin and break into flakes. Combine all ingredients. Place in greased loaf pan or casserole. Bake in 375° oven for 25 to 30 minutes or until loaf is set in center. Remove from oven, cool 5 minutes in pan. Turn out on heated serving platter. Serve with hot curry sauce.

CURRY SAUCE:

1 tablespoon butter
1 tablespoon onion

Melt butter in saucepan. Chop onion and saute in butter until golden brown.

1 10½ oz. can cream of
 celery or cream of
 mushroom soup
¼ teaspoon curry
 powder

Blend soup into above and add curry powder. You may add more curry powder if you like. Heat thoroughly and serve immediately over salmon.

Mrs. Duncan Hines, Bowling Green, Kentucky

So you think you know how to broil a fish? If the fish sticks to the grill or breaks when you try to turn it or take it up, then you didn't let the grill get hot enough to begin with; and a pretty good thing to remember is that the smaller the fish the hotter the grill should be. Large pieces of fish naturally take longer to cook and may be started with less heat. But in any event—do not overcook. Remember, you learn by experience.

212. Corn Beef and Cabbage a la House of Murphy

A Whole Brisket:

A whole brisket cooks better and holds the flavor, and has less shrinkage. While a small family will not use this much Corn Beef at one sitting, cold Corn Beef is delicious. Corn Beef Hash is an excellent breakfast or supper dish—then, too, slices of Corn Beef fried with eggs Country Style, should wind up the matter.

COOKED CORN BEEF will keep in modern refrigeration two weeks.

INGREDIENTS	DIRECTIONS
1 whole brisket (about 8 lbs.)	Place brisket in pot, cover well with cold water, bring to a boil, turn heat low, let simmer 30 minutes. Drain water off, cover again with fresh cold water, add cabbage hearts, celery, parsley, onions, one small head of garlic. Put on stove, let come to a boil, then simmer until done. This should take about five hours.
1 large head cabbage	Set the pot off the stove, allow the Corn Beef to cool in its own liquid. When ready to serve, cut off from the brisket as much as needed and set on stove to warm. Take as much stock as you need to cover the cabbage, this should be strained—bring to a boil, add a pinch of soda, and cabbage. Cook 15 minutes——SERVE.

THE HOUSE OF MURPHY serves boiled potatoes with this noted dish.

You may also add whole onions, whole carrots, whole turnips and whole beets to the dinner.

House of Murphy, Los Angeles, California

213. Turkey Hash   (Serves 6)

INGREDIENTS	DIRECTIONS
6 cups turkey	Cut into pieces about 3/8 inch size.
3 cups cream 6 tablespoons butter	Add to above and cook until cream thickens.
Fresh-ground, whole black pepper salt	Season to taste. There is nothing here to destroy the delicate turkey flavor.

Mrs. Roy B. Morningstar, Bowling Green, Kentucky

214. Red Flannel Hash (Serves 8 to 10)

INGREDIENTS	DIRECTIONS
2 lbs. corned beef	Selected corned beef, well boiled, diced ($\frac{2}{3}$ part lean, $\frac{1}{3}$ part fat).
$\frac{1}{2}$ medium onion	Dice.
3 baked potatoes	Also dice the inside of freshly baked potatoes.
fat from corned beef	Brown the onion with little fat from the corned beef, add the corned beef, also the potatoes. Bake in 350 F. oven for 15 minutes.
1 cup beets (diced)	Add diced red beets.
seasoning	Season to taste.
2 tablespoons butter	Arrange in the pan in form of an omelette. Finish by browning well; using little butter on top.

Hotel Waldorf-Astoria, New York City

Beef is the juiciest of all roasts, its juice the tastiest. When simply seasoned with very little water added, it is mighty good.

215. Cornish Pasty (Makes 6 individual pasties)

INGREDIENTS	DIRECTIONS
4½ cups flour 3¼ teaspoons salt 1 cup shortening ⅜ cup finely chopped beef kidney suet	Blend lard with dry ingredients using pastry mixer or fork.
1 to 1¼ cups cold water	Add to above and mix well. Place in refrigerator to chill.
FILLING: 7 cups sirloin steak cut in ¾-inch cubes ¾ cup finely chopped beef kidney suet 2¼ cups sliced onions 6 cups potatoes quartered and sliced 1 teaspoon black pepper 3¼ teaspoons salt	Mix all ingredients together adding salt last. Divide crust equally. For each pasty roll portion on floured board to a disk 9 inches in diameter. Place 1/6 of filling on half crust disk. Moisten edge with water and fold over to make tight bond. Crimp with rope twist or fork. Place on shallow edged cookie tin or pan and put in pre-heated oven of 375°. Bake for 30 minutes, reduce heat to 300° and bake for 45 minutes more. Pasties are best when served right from the oven.

Pendarvis House, Mineral Point, Wisconsin

216. Carbonnade (Serves 4)

INGREDIENTS

4 ounces beef suet
2 pounds round steak
   or sliced sirloin tips
5 medium-sized onions
   —sliced
   salt and pepper

1 bottle beer
1½ tablespoons butter

DIRECTIONS

Render fat from suet over low heat. Cut beef in 2- or 3-inch squares and brown in hot fat. Remove meat from pan. Brown onions in fat, then drain. In a casserole arrange a layer of browned meat and a layer of onions, repeating with alternate layers of meat and onions until all are used. Season with salt and pepper to taste.

To the drippings in which meat and onions have been browned, add beer and stir until well mixed, then add butter. Pour the mixture of drippings, beer and butter over the meat and onions. Cover casserole and bake slowly in 300° oven for about 3 hours. If you use sirloin tips 2 hours may be enough. Serve with hot boiled potatoes.

This recipe is printed here through the courtesy of Sunset Magazine.
George Ayrault, San Francisco, California

217. Steak and Kidney Pudding (Serves 6 to 8)

INGREDIENTS

1 cup grated or
   chopped suet
2 cups flour
1 teaspoon baking
   powder
1 pinch of salt
   enough cold water to
   make a stiff paste

2 lbs. round steak
1 ox kidney

¼ cup flour
1 teaspoon salt
1 pinch of mace
1 pinch of pepper

½ cup cold water

DIRECTIONS

Make a stiff paste. Roll out thin and line a pudding dish. Leave enough dough for a top on the pudding.

Cut into 2-inch squares.

Mix these ingredients together and dip the pieces of meat and kidney into it and place in the lined pudding dish.

Pour over the meat and put on top crust. Join crusts together by pinching all around. Steam for 3½ hours. Serve in the same dish it was baked in, using a linen serviette wrapped around the outside. Never use onion in this pudding.

The Elk, Comox Bay, Vancouver Island, B. C., Canada

218. English Steak and Kidney Pie   (Serves 12)

INGREDIENTS

DIRECTIONS

3 lbs. round steak—
diced
1 onion—chopped
2 tablespoons butter

Saute until brown.

1 lb. lamb kidneys
diced

Parboil and add to the above mixture.

1 lb. fresh mushrooms
salt and pepper to
taste
2 tablespoons butter

Saute until done. Add to the above mixture
and let simmer until the steak is tender.

2 tablespoons flour

Thicken the mixture and let stand to cool.

Put all ingredients in a half-lined baking dish
and cover with a rich pastry. Glaze top of
pie with white of egg and a little milk. Bake
in 350 F. oven for 30 minutes. Serve with
fresh horse-radish sauce.

San Ysidro Ranch, Montecito, Santa Barbara, California

*Whipped cream has its place. Ripe olives have theirs. Pickles
are nice. But let's be reasonable.*

219. Cuban Beefsteak Bigarade   (Serves 8)

INGREDIENTS

DIRECTIONS

8 pieces of steak
½-inch thick

Have your butcher pound steak quite thin.

8 to 10 limes or lem-
ons

Cut in half and squeeze and rub peel into
steaks.

3 or 4 garlic cloves—
crushed

Spread a little on each piece of meat. Salt
lightly and place in layers in a bowl, squeez-
ing juice over each piece of meat as you
stack it in the bowl. Marinate for 2 hours.

3 tablespoons olive oil

Brush each piece of meat with oil just before
cooking over a hot fire.

salt and pepper to
taste
butter

Season and butter. Serve piping hot.

*Chas. H. Baker, Jr., Coconut Grove, Florida. Author of "A Gentleman's
Companion," books of exotic recipes.*

220. Roast Prime Ribs of Beef (Serves 6 to 8)

In selecting beef, remember, to be top quality, the lean must be well flecked with fat. Have the backbone sawed off by your butcher. Leave the ribs on as they add their flavor to the meat as well as enhance the flavor of the gravy. White fat indicates corn-fed beef, yellow fat indicates grass-fed beef.

INGREDIENTS

8 lb. rib roast
salt and pepper

GRAVY:

Juice from the cooked roast
salt and pepper to taste
flour

DIRECTIONS

Wipe meat with damp (not wet) cloth. Salt and pepper well on both sides. Place on rack in roasting pan in pre-heated oven. See cooking temperature on page x.

Place the juice from the meat in a sauce pan over heat on top of the stove. If there is not enough juice, water may be added shortly before the roast is done. Dissolve 1 tablespoon of flour in a little water mixing thoroughly. Pour into the liquid in the sauce pan, stirring constantly to avoid lumps. A little more flour and water may be added to make gravy the desired consistency if necessary. It is important to cook the gravy long enough to have the flour well done.

Duncan Hines, Bowling Green, Kentucky

221. Pot Roast (Serves 10)

INGREDIENTS

5 lbs. beef—chuck or rump
1 quart of water
1½ teaspoons mixed spices
1 tablespoon salt
1 tablespoon sugar
1 stalk celery—diced
2 onions—sliced
1 teaspoon pepper
½ teaspoon curry powder

2 tablespoons butter—melted
2 tablespoons flour

DIRECTIONS

Put beef in large earthenware crock. Mix other ingredients together and pour over beef. Let stand in mixture for 24 hours. Remove and sear in 425° F. oven for 20 minutes. Pour the spiced liquid over the meat, cover and bake in 300° F. to 325° F. oven for 2 or 3 hours until tender. Remove meat.

Mix together and add to gravy. Cook until thick. Strain and pour over the meat. Serve with noodles or pineapple fritters.

Parry Lodge, Kanab, Utah

222. Cock 'n Bull's Yorkshire Pudding   (Serves 8)

INGREDIENTS	DIRECTIONS
6 eggs	Beat until thick and light.
1 cup all purpose flour ½ teaspoon salt	Sift flour and add salt, sift again. Add to eggs and mix well.
1 cup rich milk	Add milk gradually and beat for 3 minutes.

It would be well to use an electric mixer for this as the beating is necessary so that the pudding will puff well. Prepare in time to pour into pan 45 minutes before beef has finished roasting. Remove beef from roasting pan. Pour off all fat except ⅓ cup. Tip pan to grease sides well. With pan spitting hot, pour in pudding to a depth of ½ inch. Set beef on "horse" or roast rack over the pudding so that the meat juice will drip down over pudding. Return at once to 425° oven and bake for 15 minutes. Reduce heat to 375° and continue cooking for another 30 minutes.

If desired, the pudding can be cooked in individual muffin pans. Use heavy iron ones if you should have them. To each cup add 1 tablespoon of meat drippings coating sides and bottom well. Heat very hot, until spitting hot, fill each cup half full of pudding batter and bake as directed. Less time will be required for the second baking time—about 20 minutes. Serve at once.

Cock 'n Bull, Los Angeles, California

Do not salt meat until ready to cook. Salt tends to draw out the juices.

Buy ground meats in small quantities. If stored in refrigerator, wrap in wax paper, leave ends open.

An intelligent, accommodating butcher is a prize jewel. If you can find one like this, don't hesitate to ask him questions for fear of showing your ignorance about meats. He has spent years learning about them and you will be surprised to find how much it pleases him when you ask his advice; and no doubt you'll get better meat, too.

Hickory-smoked salt will give added flavor to steaks or chops if put on just before they have finished broiling.

223. Chop Suey

INGREDIENTS

8 onions—sliced
1 green pepper—sliced
4 tablespoons butter

1 lb. veal
1 lb. round steak
¼ lb. pork

1 can mushrooms
1 can chop suey sprouts
and vegetables

2 stalks celery
2 fresh tomatoes—ripe
1 tablespoon catsup
1 tablespoon
Worcestershire sauce
3 tablespoons LaSoy
sauce
1 dash red pepper

SAUCE:

mushroom and sprout
and vegetable juice
3 tablespoons bean
molasses
3 tablespoons flour

1 can chop suey noodles

DIRECTIONS

Saute in Dutch oven.

Cut in small pieces or grind up. Add to the above, stirring constantly until most of the juice from the meat disappears.

Strain off the juice and add to the meat mixture. Save juices.

Chop celery into ½ inch pieces. Chop tomatoes. Add to mixture and stir. Cover and let simmer 10 minutes, stirring often. When celery is tender add sauce.

Blend together and mix well. Pour over the other ingredients. Place in 400 F. oven for 10 minutes.

Serve with heated crisp noodles over top. Steamed rice balls, a stuffed tomato salad of cucumbers, celery, onions, green pepper, and hard cooked eggs and the chop suey, make a delicious quick meal.

Charlot C. Moore, Henderson, Kentucky

224. Marinated Steak

INGREDIENTS

2½ lbs. boneless sirloin
strip steak

1 cup dry red wine
½ cup olive oil
2 cloves garlic—
crushed
½ teaspoon salt freshly
ground black pepper
1 teaspoon MSG
(Accent)

DIRECTIONS

If steak is frozen let thaw out in marinade overnight.

Combine opposite ingredients and marinate steak in sauce for 6 hours, turning every hour. Broil. Take fat from broiler and put in a sauce pan with sufficient flour to absorb fat. Add remaining marinade to make gravy.

Jerry Ransohoff, Cincinnati, Ohio

225. Broiled Steak

*My special favorite is topgrade corn-fed (U. S. inspected) beef
—aged 4 or 5 weeks in cooler. I prefer a sirloin strip 2½ inches
thick—about 2 lbs. in weight. Porterhouse, T-bones, and other
cuts are good too.*

Steak	Do not wash—wipe with damp cloth. Rub with salt, black pepper. If you desire, you may also use English mustard.
Temperature	Rub your grid with suet—this prevents sticking. Preheat oven 15 minutes at high temperature. Place steak 5 inches below flame.
Broiling Time	Sear quickly on both sides to prevent loss of natural juices. You may turn your steak two or more times. For a 2½ inch steak—15 minutes more or less for each side should be sufficient. A steak less thick requires less time, and place closer to flame. Again, rare or medium requires less time than well-done.
Butter	Do not add butter over steak until it is through cooking. Serve hot.

Green Gables, Phoenix, Arizona

*A splendid sauce for steaks can be made by working into butter:
salt, fresh ground black pepper, lemon juice, and chopped
parsley.*

226. Swiss Steak

INGREDIENTS

DIRECTIONS

2 lbs. round steak
2 teaspoons salt
½ teaspoon black pepper
flour

Trim the edges of the steak and slit in a few places to prevent the edges of the steak from curling. Season one side with ½ of the salt and pepper and pound into the steak as much flour as it will take. Turn the steak over and repeat.

¼ cup shortening or bacon drippings

Put into a Dutch oven and let melt. Sear the steak quickly on both sides.

1 large onion
1 #2½ can of tomatoes
1 cup of water
2 bay leaves
¼ teaspoon marjoram

Slice onion over the steak. Add the tomatoes and water. Add the bay leaves and marjoram. Cover tightly and simmer over a low flame for 2 hours or until steak is tender. If the gravy gets too thick, more water may be added.

Mrs. Duncan Hines, Bowling Green, Kentucky

227. Stroganoff

(Serves 4)

INGREDIENTS

1½ lbs. round steak
⅛ lb. butter
    salt and pepper

¾ lb. fresh mushrooms
⅛ lb. butter
1 onion—minced

½ cup consomme
1 tablespoon vinegar
½ pt. sour cream
    season to taste

DIRECTIONS

Cut steak in strips, removing fat and gristle. The strips should be small and thin. Season and dust lightly with flour. Saute in buttei.

Saute in another pan. Do not let get too brown.

Add to mushrooms and boil up once. Add steak, cover and barely simmer for 30 minutes or until steak is tender. Serve with rice and buttered Melba toast.

Duncan Hines, Bowling Green, Kentucky

228. Beef Stroganoff

(Serves 10)

INGREDIENTS

4 lbs. lean beef—top round, butt or tenderloin, sliced into very small thin slices, *cut across grain. This is very important.*
1 lb. fresh mushrooms sliced fine
2 cups stock or water
2 cups sour cream (real sour cream, purchased as such)
1 tablespoon paprika
    season to taste

DIRECTIONS

Into a stainless steel pan or tinned copper pan put a little butter and start the meat to saute, season, cook long enough till juice has cooked away. Add mushrooms, let cook till slightly browned, add about two cups of stock or water, cover and place in 350° oven, cook until tender. Take out and drain the juice, add the paprika and all the sour cream.

Bring to a boil and thicken with a little butter and flour made into a pellet to make it a thin consistency cream sauce. Put your meat back, bring to a boil, serve in a chafing dish with rye toast.

Minikahda Club, Minneapolis, Minnesota

Good meats are relatively expensive items of food purchases and should be handled carefully before cooking. You may scrape or wipe off a piece of meat before putting it in the refrigerator but certainly you should not wash it with water. Store it in the coldest part of your refrigerator, covered with wax paper if you prefer but never tightly. Bacterial growth is prevented on the surface of meat when the cold air can get to it. Many meats which have been cooked may be covered because this is the best method of storing to prevent excessive drying out in the refrigerator.

229. Roast Beef Tenderloin   (Serves 10)

INGREDIENTS

3 lbs. beef tenderloin

salt and pepper to taste

1 carrot—chopped
1 slice of bacon
1 bay leaf
2 whole cloves
1 pinch of allspice

MUSHROOM SAUCE:

¼ can mushrooms
1 tablespoon lemon juice

Pilot Butte Inn, Bend, Oregon

DIRECTIONS

Lard with bits of bacon.

Rub into meat.

Put into pan with meat, cover and bake in 450 F. oven for 30 minutes, basting often. Serve with mushroom sauce.

Add to the brown gravy.

230. Sauerbraten   (Serves 6 to 8)

INGREDIENTS

4 lbs. beef—rump, chuck or sirloin
1 cup vinegar
3 cups water
1 onion—cut in slices
10 peppercorns
3 tablespoons whole mixed spices
¼ cup salt
1 sliced carrot

2½ tablespoons shortening

¼ cup sugar—white or brown

½ cup flour
2 gingersnaps
½ cup red wine

DIRECTIONS

Mix vinegar, water, onions, spices, salt and carrots, Pickle meat in this brine for 3 to 4 days, turn once in a while—save brine for making gravy later.

Grease heavy roasting pan with shortening and roast meat in 300° heat for about 2 hours or until meat is brown on both sides and almost done.

Sprinkle sugar over meat and roast for 5 to 10 minutes more turning meat while roasting until sugar is dissolved and meat is nice and brown.

Add flour and gingersnaps to brine meat was pickled in, mix well and pour over meat. Roast meat for ½ hour more or until gravy is creamy and thick—take out meat, stir wine into gravy and then remove grease from gravy and strain.

(Note: During roasting, if meat looks too dry, baste with the pickling brine.) Potato dumplings or noodles are good with this roast.

Mader's Restaurant, Milwaukee, Wisconsin

231. Tongue with Tomato Sauce   (Serves 6 to 8)

INGREDIENTS

DIRECTIONS

1 fresh beef tongue

Boil slowly until tender, or about 3 hours.
Peel and put into a baking dish.

1 can tomatoes
1 white mild onion—
  sliced
1½ cups vinegar
1 cup of stock from
  the tongue
⅓ cup sugar
¼ cup butter
½ teaspoon cinnamon
⅛ teaspoon allspice
¼ teaspoon cloves
1 teaspoon salt

Mix these ingredients and pour over tongue.
Bake in 300° F. oven for three hours.

Serve with baked or mashed potatoes.

Pelican Cafe, Klamath Falls, Oregon

232. Eliza Gallois Ox Tail Recipe   (Serves 4 to 6)

INGREDIENTS

DIRECTIONS

1 ox tail

Cut in 3-inch pieces.

1 large onion sliced
1 carrot
1 celery
1 bay leaf
2 cloves
2 teeth of garlic
1 bunch parsley

Add to above and roast in hot oven for 30
minutes.

2 qts. cold water
  or stock

Add to above and boil 3 to 4 hours until
well cooked. Cool.

DEVILED MUSTARD FOR OX TAIL:

2 soup spoons English
  mustard
1 soup spoon Worces-
  tershire
1 soup spoon cold
  water
2 soup spoons melted
  butter

Mix into a thick sauce. Brush sauce over ox
tail, roll in bread crumbs and broil.

This recipe comes from my good friend, Mr. John Gallois, San Francisco

*Juice which drips from meat in cooking is termed natural
gravy, yet many gourmets call it sauce. In either case, if your
taste dictates, you may add different or more seasoning than
was used in cooking the meat.*

233. Tamale Pie
(Serves 6 to 8)

INGREDIENTS

DIRECTIONS

½ cup olive oil
1 onion—chopped
1 clove garlic

Cook until onions are tenderized.

1 green pepper—
chopped
1 lb. round steak—
ground
¼ lb. ground pork

Add to the above and brown the meat.

1 can tomatoes (2½
size)
½ cup ripe olives—
pitted
2 chili peppers—cut
fine salt and pepper
and cayenne to taste

Add to the mixture and cook slowly for 1 hour. Add a little water from time to time, if it is a little dry.

½ cup grated cheese
2 tablespoons corn meal
1 teaspoon chili powder

When the mixture is soft and mushy, add these ingredients. Stir in well and cook for just a few minutes longer. The mixture should be the consistency of baked hash.

1 cup corn meal
3 cups water
ripe olives

Make a corn meal mush. Place the meat mixture in a pan and cover with corn meal mush. Garnish with ripe olives.

Hody's, Los Angeles, California

The ingredients and directions of a recipe should be followed accurately. The minute you start improvising you end up with a different dish.

234. Berzola Fooroun (Baked Lamb Chops)
(Serves 4)

INGREDIENTS

DIRECTIONS

8 thick loin chops

Set in open baking pan.

2 large tomatoes—
quartered
2 large onions—sliced
1/3 cup parsley—chopped
1 tablespoon salt and
pepper to taste
½ teaspoon paprika
1 teaspoon oregano
2 cups water

Mix together and put over the lamb chops.

Cover with the water and bake in 375° F. oven for 45 minutes. Then turn the chops and bake for another 30 minutes. The juice is served as gravy.

Omar Khayyam's, San Francisco, California

235. Individual Lamb Roasts with Dressing
(Serves 6)

INGREDIENTS

6 six ounce slices of breast of lamb, after it has been boned and trimmed, about ¾ inch thick

DRESSING:

¼ cup chopped onion
¼ cup chopped celery
2 fresh mushrooms—chopped
1 tablespoon butter

¾ cup soft diced bread
1 teaspoon salt
1 teaspoon poultry seasoning

½ lb. chopped carrots and celery—cut fine
3 onions—chopped

2 cups of stock

DIRECTIONS

Spread each slice of lamb with dressing, roll and fasten with a tooth pick.

Saute for about 20 minutes.

Add to the above mixture. Spread on the slices of lamb.

Place in bottom of a roaster and lay the lamb rolls on top. Brown in 350 F. oven for 10 minutes. Turn the rolls and brown the other side.

Add to the browned rolls. Cover roaster, turn the oven down to 300 F. and bake for 1½ hours. Additional stock may be added if necessary.

Jane Davies, New York, New York

236. Turlu Dolma (Lamb, Stuffed Tomatoes, Peppers and Squash)
(Serves 4)

INGREDIENTS

1 lb. lamb shoulder—ground
½ cup rice—washed
½ lb. onions—chopped
½ small can tomato puree or 1 large chopped tomato
3 teaspoons parsley—chopped
1½ teaspoons salt
¼ teaspoon pepper
a few leaves of fresh mint (optional)

4 tomatoes
4 peppers
4 squash—preferably zucchini

DIRECTIONS

Mix all ingredients together.

Stuff with the above mixture. Place in a baking pan and partly cover with water.

Cover the pan and cook on top of stove for 1 hour, or in a 375 F. oven for 1 hour.

Serve 1 of each to a person. The sauce will serve as gravy.

Omar Khayyam's, San Francisco, California

237. Lamb Hawaii

INGREDIENTS

DIRECTIONS

6 lb. boned leg of lamb

Brush with lemon juice and let stand 2 hours. Then stuff the bone cavity with the following dressing.

DRESSING:

½ clove garlic—crushed
1 tablespoon onion—scraped
2 tablespoons parsley—chopped
½ teaspoon ginger
salt and pepper to taste
2 tablespoons melted butter
2 cups toasted bread crumbs

Toss in a pan for 5 minutes.

1 cup fresh pineapple
1 tablespoon brown sugar
(If canned pineapple is used, do not add sugar)

Mix together and toss into the dressing.

salt and pepper and a little ginger

Stuff the bone cavity and sew it up neatly. Season the outside of the meat.

3 tablespoons melted butter
pineapple juice

Flow on the meat and sear in 425 F. oven. Reduce heat to 350, cover and baste every 10 minutes with pineapple juice. Serve with pan gravy.

Chas. H. Baker, Jr., Coconut Grove, Florida. Author of "A Gentleman's Companion," two delightful volumes of exotic recipes.

238. Lamb Chop

INGREDIENTS

DIRECTIONS

1 lamb chop—2 inches thick

Broil on one side.

1 tablespoon minced chicken spread

Spread on cooked side of chop. Lay in pan, raw side down and bake in 325 F. oven for 30 minutes.

Serve with rich chicken gravy.

Pilot Butte Inn, Bend, Oregon

239. Lamb Roast
(Serves 8 to 10)

INGREDIENTS

1 leg of lamb
salt and small
amount of cayenne
pepper—to taste

1 bottle tomato catsup
1 cup vinegar
1 clove garlic
1 cup water

DIRECTIONS

Rub lamb well with salt and cayenne pepper.

Pour over the roast and bake in 350 F. oven
for 1½ to 2 hours. Add water as needed to
keep the gravy at the right consistency.

Thicken the gravy with flour before serving it
desired.

Mrs. C. H. Welch, Tucson, Arizona

240. Curried Lamb Pie
(Serves 6)

INGREDIENTS

1 teaspoon curry
powder
1 tablespoon chopped
parsley
pie crust

2 medium sized
potatoes
1 large onion
2 carrots

3 cups cubed cooked
lamb
2 cups lamb gravy
salt and freshly
ground black pepper
¼ cup grated American
cheese

DIRECTIONS

To your favorite pie crust recipe, add the
curry powder and parsley as you mix it.

Dice vegetables and parboil lightly in small
amount of water for 5 minutes.

Mix vegetables with lamb, lamb gravy and
seasonings to taste. Pour into deep casserole
and cover with pie crust. Sprinkle with cheese
and bake in 375° oven for 45 minutes.

Paint Pony Lodge, Show Low, Arizona

*Fuel foods are those which contain a greater number of calories.
The amount necessary depends upon the amount of exercise
a person takes in work or play. Athletes and active workers
need more calories than the man who sits at a desk all day
and gets his exercise from the sport pages of the afternoon
paper.*

241. Baked Slice of Ham (Serves 4)

INGREDIENTS

DIRECTIONS

1 slice of ham an inch or more thick

Cut off the fat and put fat through a grinder. Spread it over the slice of ham.

2 tablespoons brown sugar
1 teaspoon dry mustard

Sprinkle over the top of the fat and place in pan about half covered with water. Bake in 350° oven for 1 hour or until tender.

Miss Katharine Little, Chicago, Illinois

242. Hickory Smoked Ham

INGREDIENTS

DIRECTIONS

1 ham

Soak in enough cold water to cover the ham overnight. Use fresh water, when starting to cook. Scrub ham. Put a false bottom in the pan so the water can circulate around the ham, place skin side down in pan and cover with cold water.

6 medium onions
2 cups brown sugar
1 pint cider vinegar or cooking wine
2 bay leaves

Add to the ham, cover the boiler and let SIMMER—(DO NOT BOIL) 20 to 25 minutes to the pound. You will know the ham is done, when the small bone at the hock end can be twisted out. When done, let the ham cool in this mixture, then remove the skin, cut off some of the fat, score, and put in whole cloves (optional).

24 whole cloves

¾ cups brown sugar
1 cup bread crumbs
2 teaspoons dry mustard
1 teaspoon ground cloves

Mix together and pat on the ham while it is still moist. Bake in a hot oven (400 F.) until glazed or brown. To serve, slice thinner than commercial type of hams.

FOR FRYING THIS TYPE OF HAM

Cut slices thinner than commercial type of hams. Fry on each side and remove from pan. Let grease get very hot, add ¼ teaspoon sugar and about 4 tablespoons water. Put ham back in gravy, cover the pan and cook a few minutes. Should you desire the gravy to be redder than it is, add paprika.

Duncan Hines, Bowling Green, Kentucky

When you have to scrape the sauce off the meat what you find under it is not always worth the effort.

243. Hot Baked Ham with Raisin Sauce

INGREDIENTS	DIRECTIONS
1 12- to 14-lb. ham enough hot water to cover	Bring to a boil and let simmer 20 minutes to the pound. When done, remove from the water and skin. Score, by cutting through the fat diagonally.
½ cup vinegar 2 cups brown sugar 2 tablespoons dry mustard	Make a paste and spread evenly over the surface, fatty side up. Bake uncovered in 350 F. oven for 15 minutes, until nicely browned. To serve, slice and cover with raisin sauce.

RAISIN SAUCE:

1 lb. puffed seeded raisins 2 cups brown sugar 3 pints water	Cook together for about 30 minutes, until raisins are soft.
2 tablespoons cornstarch 1 tablespoon cold water	Mix together and add to raisins.
1 lemon—juice	Add to mixture; and bring to a boil.

Park View Inn, Berkeley Springs, West Virginia

244. Sugar Ham

INGREDIENTS	DIRECTIONS
1 12-lb ham enough water to cover	Boil the ham until tender. Remove from water and remove skin.
¾ lb. brown sugar	Cover ham.
½ cup prepared mustard ½ cup water	Mix together and pour over the ham. Bake in 425 F. oven for 15 minutes.

SAUCE:

3 lbs. sugar 1 pint water	Let come to a boil.
1¼ cups red cinnamon candies	Add to above and cook until they are dissolved.
½ cup raisins	These are optional and can be omitted. If desired, add to sauce. Let cool.
½ cup sherry	When cooled add to sauce. Cut the cooled ham in ¼-inch slices and heat in sauce. Best results are obtained when the ham is allowed to cool for 24 hours before serving.

Mrs. Bessie Crane Hise, Chagrin Falls, Ohio

245. Ham Pie with Cheese Biscuit Top (Serves 6)

INGREDIENTS

1 cup sliced cooked
  carrots
1 cup diced cooked
  potatoes
1½ cups chopped, cooked
  ham
1½ cups medium thick
  white sauce

CHEESE BISCUITS:

2 cups sifted flour
1 teaspoon salt
4 teaspoons baking
  powder
⅓ cup shortening
¾ cup sweet milk
½ cup grated sharp
  cheese

DIRECTIONS

Arrange layers of carrots, potatoes and ham
in buttered casserole. Pour over all the white
sauce. Cover top with as many cheese biscuits as will fit. Bake in pre-heated oven, 400°,
for about 30 minutes.

Sift together dry ingredients. Cut in shortening. Add milk to make soft dough. Knead
slightly on floured board until smooth. Roll
out into strip about ¼ inch thick and 6 inches
wide. Sprinkle dough with cheese and roll like
jelly roll. Cut off pieces 1 inch thick. The
cheese biscuits not used on the casserole above
may be placed on a greased baking sheet and
baked in a hot oven, 450°, for 20-25 minutes.

Anderson Hotel, Wabasha, Minnesota

246. Ham and Noodle Casserole (Serves 4 to 6)

INGREDIENTS

1 6 oz. package broad
  noodles
2 cups chicken stock
2 cups sweet milk

2 tablespoons flour
2 tablespoons butter
2 cups broth
  salt and freshly
  ground black pepper
  to taste

1 cup finely chopped
  cooked ham
½ cup chopped celery
½ cup green pepper
¼ to ½ cup heavy
  cream
  bread crumbs
  butter
¼ cup grated Parmesan
  cheese

DIRECTIONS

Mix milk and chicken stock together and bring
to boil in large kettle. Add noodles and let
cook for about 8 to 10 minutes. Do not let
get soft and mushy. Lift noodles out of liquid
with slotted spoon. Measure liquid left—
should have at least 2 cups for package of
noodles.

Blend together butter and flour. Heat the
broth and stir in butter and flour. Season
carefully, taking care not to get too much
salt, because of ham. Cook until thick.

When broth is thick add ham and vegetables,
mix with noodles and place in heavily greased
casserole. Correct seasoning to taste. Pour
heavy cream over mixture, top with bread
crumbs, dot with butter and sprinkle with
grated Parmesan cheese. Bake for about 30
minutes in 375° oven or until crumbs are
nicely browned.

Mrs. Duncan Hines, Bowling Green, Kentucky

247. Baked Ham Loaf in Pineapple-Raisin Sauce
(Serves 4)

INGREDIENTS

¾ lb. smoked ham,
  ground
¾ lb. lean fresh pork,
  ground
¼ cup finely chopped
  bread crumbs
½ teaspoon dry mustard
2 eggs
½ cup tomato juice
½ cup milk

DIRECTIONS

Grind pork and ham together and mix all other ingredients into the meat thoroughly. Turn into a greased loaf pan. Bake at 350° for one hour. Pour pineapple-raisin sauce over all and return to oven for 30 minutes.

PINEAPPLE-RAISIN SAUCE:

4 tablespoons pineapple
  juice
½ cup raisins
1 tablespoon lemon
  juice
  grated rind of 1
  lemon
½ teaspoon ginger
1 teaspoon prepared
  mustard
¼ cup currant jelly

Combine ingredients in a saucepan. Stir over low heat until jelly melts. Pour over ham loaf.

Hotel Fort Hayes, Columbus, Ohio

In spite of vastly increased nutritional education there still remains a certain amount of confusion in the minds of some people, particularly the older generation. A humorous example of this attitude was recently voiced to me by a seventy-six year-old Irishman by the name of Lafferty. He had just recently been fitted with new glasses and in two months' time had tried to catch up on two years' reading. One conclusion at which he had arrived prompted this very earnest and serious statement.

"Mr. Hines, you are supposed to know everything about eating and I don't doubt that you do but I want to tell you that I am too old to start any of these new ideas about what I eat. I've been reading about vitamins, minerals, proteins, calories and carbohydrates and I have come to the conclusion that these are for the younger generation. Just give me a big, juicy beefsteak with Irish potatoes, cornfield beans, turnip greens, egg bread and buttermilk and you can have all your vitamins, minerals and other new-fangled things to eat."

I haven't decided yet whether the old man was kidding me but after a good hearty laugh I got to thinking that one of the modern slang phrases would have been appropriate, namely: "I believe you've got something there."

248. Ham Shortcake (Serves 6)

INGREDIENTS

4 tablespoons butter
4 tablespoons flour
2 cups sweet milk
2 teaspoons dry mustard
2 cups cubed cooked ham
2 tablespoons Worcestershire sauce
4 tablespoons finely chopped pimiento
2 tablespoons finely chopped parsley
salt and freshly ground black pepper to taste

DIRECTIONS

Melt butter in saucepan. Combine flour and mustard and stir in butter until smooth. Add milk and cook gently until smooth and thick —about 10 minutes. Add ham, pimiento, parsley and seasonings and stir to mix thoroughly. Keep hot. If it gets too thick, add a little more milk.

4 cups grated raw potato
3 eggs, well beaten
¼ teaspoon baking powder
2 teaspoons salt
3 tablespoons grated onion
4 tablespoons flour
bacon drippings

Mix potatoes with other ingredients in order given, with exception of bacon drippings which are put in iron skillet and heated. When hot, drop large spoonfuls of batter in fat and cook until brown on both sides. For each "Shortcake," one potato cake, a layer of ham sauce, another cake and finish with more sauce. This is wonderful if made with Kentucky hickory-smoked ham.

Mrs. Duncan Hines, Bowling Green, Kentucky

Ham is good morning, noon or night. There are countless ways to cook it.

249. Ham in Cream (Serves 6)

INGREDIENTS

4 tablespoons butter
2 small onions
½ lb. fresh mushrooms

DIRECTIONS

Melt butter in saucepan. Chop onions and brown until golden in butter. Wash and slice mushrooms, add to onions and brown lightly.

2 cups cooked ham

Cube ham, add to above and cook for a few minutes until ham is warmed through.

2 tablespoons flour
2 cups sour cream

Sprinkle flour over above mixture and blend well. Add cream and simmer until thick. Serve on toast, rice pilaff or noodles.

Mrs. Duncan Hines, Bowling Green, Kentucky

250. Selection and Initial Preparation of Sweetbreads

Veal sweetbreads are tender and white or slightly pink. Those which are reddish and tough under pressure of the fingers are from steers and not so desirable.

Let stand in cold water an hour, then plunge into boiling water to which 1 tablespoon lemon juice or vinegar and 1 teaspoon salt have been added for each quart of water. Simmer gently for 20 minutes. Drain and chill quickly and thoroughly in cold water. Carefully remove fat, tubes, and membranes without damaging the tissues.

Split them in half if they are thick. Dry with towel and keep covered in refrigerator for later use in any or all sweetbread recipes.

251. Sweetbreads Supreme   (Serves 8 to 12)

INGREDIENTS	DIRECTIONS
1½ cups cooked sweetbreads	To cook sweetbreads. Let stand for 1 hour in cold water. Cook slowly in boiling salted water for 20 minutes, adding the vinegar. Blanch in cold water.
2 tablespoons vinegar to each quart of water used	
4 eggs—slightly beaten	Mix with sweetbreads.
2 cups cream salt and pepper to taste	Add to sweetbreads and place in buttered molds. Bake in pan of water in 350 F. oven for about 20 minutes, or until firm.
individual slices of tenderized ham— lightly browned	Serve on ham slices and cover with a cream sauce.
CREAM SAUCE: 2 tablespoons butter	Melt.
2 tablespoons flour ¼ teaspoon salt a few grains of pepper ⅓ cup minced pimento	Blend into the butter, making a smooth paste.
1 cup milk	Add slowly to the paste and stir until the sauce thickens. Boil 3 minutes.

The Farm Kitchen, Baraboo, Wisconsin

252. Broiled Sweetbreads a la Reich   (Serves 4)

INGREDIENTS

8 halves sweetbreads
¼ cup flour
½ teaspoon Accent
½ teaspoon salt

½ cup melted butter
paprika
4 thin toast squares
4 teaspoons capers
1 tablespoon Tarragon
vinegar
1 teaspoon Worcester-
shire sauce
parsley

DIRECTIONS

Prepare sweetbreads according to Recipe No. 250. Sift flour and seasonings together and dredge sweetbreads with this.

Place sweetbreads in flat pan, pour butter over them and dust with paprika. Broil in 350° oven until golden brown on both sides. Place sweetbreads on toast squares, sprinkle ½ teaspoon capers over each half. Blend the vinegar and Worcestershire sauce with the browned butter in the pan and pour over each serving.

Blosser's Restaurant, Logan, Ohio

In buying meats, watch the color. It should be clear and rather bright, not purplish or dull.

253. Sweetbreads Braise, Financiere   (Serves 1)

INGREDIENTS

1 pair sweetbreads
4 tablespoons salt

whole spice and salt
—to taste

3 tablespoons butter

1 jigger or more white
wine

½ cup fresh mushrooms
¼ cup olives
¼ cup shallots
3 tablespoons butter

1 jigger or more white
wine

Fines Herbes and
butter—to taste

DIRECTIONS

Add enough cold water to cover sweetbreads and let stand for 12 hours. Wash thoroughly.

Parboil in enough water to cover with these ingredients for about 5 minutes. Dry off and place in a roasting pan.

Saute for about 10 minutes, or until brown.

Add to sweetbreads and bake in 350 F. oven for 30 minutes.

Dice and place in a separate pan and cook until the mushrooms are done.

Add this, and sauce from the sweetbreads.

Mix sweetbreads and mushrooms together and add seasoning just before serving.

The Monument Inn, Bennington, Vermont

254. Creamed Kidneys (Serves 4)

INGREDIENTS

DIRECTIONS

1 lb. veal kidneys—
sliced thin
4 tablespoons butter
salt and pepper to
taste

Saute quickly on both sides.

1½ cups thin white
sauce
4 tablespoons red wine
½ tablespoon
horse-radish
a dash of cayenne
pepper

While the white sauce is still hot, add the
other ingredients and mix into the kidneys.

Serve on toast.

Mrs. Edwin P. Morrow, Frankfort, Kentucky

255. Roast Pig

INGREDIENTS

DIRECTIONS

1 six weeks old pig

Scrub pig thoroughly with stiff brush removing
any remaining hairs from ears and nostrils.
Remove eyes. Dry thoroughly. Rub well inside
with mixture of salt, ground fresh black
pepper, thyme, paprika and a suggestion of
bay leaf.

DRESSING:

4 cups bread crumbs
½ teaspoon cayenne
pepper
2 teaspoons powdered
sage
2½ cups good stock
salt to taste

Mix dry ingredients to bread crumbs and add
stock.

4 hard boiled eggs

Chop and add to above.

1½ cup chopped onions
1½ cup chopped celery
3 tablespoons chopped
parsley
¼ lb. butter

Saute in butter until tender but not too
brown. Add to the above. Stuff pig. Sew up
carefully. Place corncob in mouth and truss
both fore and hind legs forward. Bake in
moderate oven for about 3 hours, basting frequently. Serve on large platter garnished with
water cress and sweet potato puffs baked in
orange cups. Replace corncob with red apple.
Place uncooked cranberry in each eye.

McLester Hotel, Tuscaloosa, Alabama

256. Sausage and Cabbage au Gratin (Serves 6)

INGREDIENTS	DIRECTIONS
1 small head of cabbage	Chop coarsely and cook in boiling water with salt, until tender. Season with salt and pepper.
½ lb. pork sausage in bulk	Fry out the sausage and drain off fat.
3 tablespoons sausage fat 3 tablespoons flour 1 cup milk 2 cups cabbage liquor	Put fat in saucepan, add flour, stirring until blended. Gradually add milk and cabbage liquor, stirring and cooking for about 5 minutes.
⅓ cup grated American cheese ½ cup cracker crumbs ½ teaspoon salt	Grease a casserole, place layer of cooked cabbage, then one of sausage. Pour over white sauce; sprinkle with cheese then with cracker crumbs. Repeat this procedure until all the mixture is in the pan. Bake at 350° for 35 minutes until crumbs are golden brown.

The Baron Steuben Hotel, Corning, New York

257. Barbecued Spareribs (Serves 5 or 6)

INGREDIENTS	DIRECTIONS
3 lbs. spareribs	Cut the spareribs into portions of three bones each, and salt them.
1 cup vinegar 1 clove garlic (cut fine, and mashed) 2 tablespoons Worcestershire sauce ½ teaspoon Tabasco 1 tablespoon sugar ½ cup catsup 1 teaspoon salt 1 teaspoon dry mustard	Combine ingredients and simmer for about 10 minutes. Brush the spareribs with the sauce and place them in pre-heated broiler. Cook 30-35 minutes, brushing the spareribs with the sauce and turning them every ten minutes. This is an excellent sauce for any barbecued meat.

Herman A. Groth, Aubrey, Moore & Wallace, Inc., Chicago, Illinois

With the exception of chicken and pork, most vegetables and meats are over-cooked.

Pork is not easily digested; therefore, it should be thoroughly cooked before serving. However, many other meats and vegetables should not be cooked to excess.

258. Baked Canadian Bacon (Serves 6 to 8)

INGREDIENTS

DIRECTIONS

1 strip Canadian bacon
3 or 4 pounds
1⅓ cups brown sugar
¾ cups water
¾ cup Burgundy wine
1 teaspoon cloves

Dot bacon with cloves—cover with brown sugar, put in roasting pan and add liquid. Bake in 350° oven for 2 hours or until very tender. Baste every 15 or 20 minutes. Serve with sauce.

SAUCE:

1 10 oz. jar apple or
current jelly
1 tablespoon vinegar
1 teaspoon prepared
mustard
½ teaspoon ground
cloves

Combine and heat until jelly melts. Serve with bacon. This is also good with apple or banana fritters.

Mrs. C. H. Welch, Tucson, Arizona

259. Fresh Pork Sausage

INGREDIENTS

DIRECTIONS

10 lbs. lean meat
3 lbs. fat meat

Use shoulder and trimmings from loin and sides of dressed pig.

2 teaspoons cayenne
pepper
3 teaspoons sugar
5 teaspoons salt
4 teaspoons freshly
ground black pepper
1 teaspoon finely
minced bay leaf
1 teaspoon finely
minced sprig thyme
3 teaspoons powdered
sage

Dice meat. Sprinkle with blended seasonings, then grind, first with coarse meat chopper. Then put through grinder again using fine chopper. Pack in earthenware crock. Cover with wax paper. Keep at temperature of 34 degrees until consumed. Form into patties lightly. Do not press tightly. Cook slowly at 300°. Pour off fat as it accumulates. Lay on absorbent paper to get rid of excess grease.

McLester Hotel, Tuscaloosa, Alabama

Have you ever tried a few drops of Worchestershire sauce on bacon before broiling? It does things to it.

When cooking link sausages, if you will place a little water— 2 or 3 tablespoons—in the frying pan, cover and cook until water is evaporated over low heat, then remove cover, increase heat and brown, they will not burst.

260. Johnnie Mazotta (Serves 4)

INGREDIENTS

DIRECTIONS

1 6-oz. package broad noodles

Cook noodles in boiling water 12 minutes. Put in colander and let cold water run over them. Drain. Put into a buttered baking dish.

¾ lb. pork shoulder—ground
2 cloves garlic minced fine
1 onion—cut fine

Fry together until pork is done. Drain off the grease. Add to noodles.

1 can condensed tomato soup
½ lb. cheese—grated (hold out enough to sprinkle on top)
1 teaspoon sugar
½ cup water
salt and pepper to taste

Mix all ingredients together in baking dish. Dot plentifully with butter and sprinkle top with cheese.

Bake in 350 F. oven for about 30 minutes.

Mrs. Mathew Jackson, Chicago, Illinois

To avoid toughness, cook pork slowly and it must be well done.

261. Philadelphia Scrapple (Two 2-lb. pans)

INGREDIENTS

DIRECTIONS

2½ lbs. fresh pork shoulder
2 quarts cold water
1 teaspoon salt
½ teaspoon black pepper

Simmer slowly for 2 hours adding seasoning when nearly done. Remove meat from stock and shred with a fork. The longer the meat fibers the better. Strain stock and let 2 cups cool. Should have 5 cups left, which continue to boil.

2¼ cups white corn meal
¾ cup flour
4 teaspoons summer savory
1 teaspoon salt
½ teaspoon black pepper

Blend these ingredients. Add 2 cups of cooled stock slowly, stirring constantly to prevent lumping. This will make a paste. Slowly add this to boiling stock and keep stirring. Add shredded meat and cook slowly 2 hours, constantly stirring to prevent burning. More seasoning can be added to suit taste. When done put in *enamel* pans; when cold, slice thin and fry on dry griddle until browned on each side. Can be served with maple syrup.

Duncan Hines, Bowling Green, Kentucky

262. Philadelphia Scrapple (About 2 pans 8x4x4)

INGREDIENTS

DIRECTIONS

1 pig's head

Cook slowly in boiling water to barely cover until meat comes off bones. Remove meat from stock and let meat and stock cool.

2 lbs. corn meal to every 3 lbs. of meat

Weigh meat after removed from bones. Remove fat from stock and strain. Bring stock to boil and slowly add corn meal. Cook to a mush, adding hot water to thin a little, if necessary.

½ tablespoon salt
¼ teaspoon black pepper
1 teaspoon onion juice

Mix this into each pound of meat. Add to mush and cook in double boiler for 1 hour. Place in pans and when ready to serve, cut in ¼-inch slices and brown in a little fat. Serve piping hot.

Waldorf-Astoria Hotel, New York City, New York

263. Koenigsberger Klopse (Serves 8)

INGREDIENTS

DIRECTIONS

3 slices white bread
½ cup milk

Remove crusts and soak in milk.

1 pound pork—ground
1 pound veal—ground
1 egg
salt and pepper to taste

Mix well with the above and form small balls.

½ gallon water
2 tablespoons vinegar
1 teaspoon mixed spices

Bring water to a boil and add meat balls. Turn down fire and simmer for 15 minutes.

SAUCE:

4 tablespoons butter
4 tablespoons flour

Put in a pan and blend.

3 or 4 cups stock from meat balls
1 tablespoon capers

Add stock to the above slowly, making a thick rich sauce. Cook for ten minutes. Pour sauce over Klopse, add capers and let simmer for about 10 minutes. Serve with boiled potatoes.

Wasum's Restaurant, Detroit, Michigan

Pig's feet, if properly cooked, have a flavor which makes up for the many bones encountered.

264. Baked Savory Pork Chops

(Serves 6)

INGREDIENTS

6 pork chops—1½
inches thick
salt and pepper to
taste
6 slices lemon
6 teaspoons brown
sugar
1 cup catsup
1 cup water

DIRECTIONS

In a deep baking pan place the pork chops and sprinkle with salt and pepper. On each chop place a slice of lemon and a teaspoon brown sugar. Mix together the cup of catsup and water and pour around the chops until they are just covered. Bake in 350° oven for 1 hour or until tender and well done.

Damon's, Cleveland, Ohio

265. Pork Chops Baked in Sour Cream

(Serves 4)

INGREDIENTS

4 pork loin chops
2 inches thick, salt
and pepper to taste
4 tablespoons butter
4 cloves

1 tablespoon sugar
2 tablespoons vinegar
½ cup water
½ cup sour cream
1 bay leaf

DIRECTIONS

Melt butter in frying pan. Season chops and dredge in flour. Brown in butter. Insert a clove in each and arrange in baking dish or Dutch oven.

Add opposite ingredients to drippings in frying pan, bring to a boil and pour over meat. Cover and bake in 350° oven for 1½ hours.

Duncan Hines, Bowling Green, Kentucky

266. Stuffed Pork Chops

(Serves 6)

INGREDIENTS

6 large lean pork chops
salt and pepper to
taste

12 tablespoons uncooked
rice
6 slices tomatoes
6 slices onion
6 rings of green pepper

DIRECTIONS

Wash chops. Place in heavy pan with enough water to almost cover. Salt and pepper. Cover with tight lid and cook over low heat for 20 minutes.

Wash rice. Place 2 tablespoons of rice on each chop. Then place vegetables on top of rice in order given. Add enough water to almost cover rice. Cover and cook for 30 minutes or until chops are well done.

Sunset Farm, Whittier, North Carolina

Ladies: Do not over-spend today. Money won't go out of style tomorrow.

267. Pork Chops with Spiced Pears (Serves 4)

INGREDIENTS

4 thick loin chops

¾ cup pear juice
¼ cup brown sugar

No. 2½ can spiced
pears
flour
parsley

DIRECTIONS

Season and pan fry until brown and tender.
Remove to hot serving dishes.

Pour off all but 2 tablespoons of fat, add
juice and sugar and cook to a syrup.

Dust drained pears with flour and brown in
hot fat and juice. Arrange on plate with chops.
Garnish with parsley.

Duncan Hines Test Kitchens, Ithaca, New York

268. Pork Chops, Spanish (Serves 6)

INGREDIENTS

6 loin pork chops 1½
inches thick
1 tablespoon fat

2 onions—sliced thin
1 green pepper—
chopped
1 small can pimento—
with juice
½ can tomatoes
½ teaspoon
Worcestershire sauce
salt and pepper to
taste

1 cup rice—measured
and then cooked.

DIRECTIONS

Brown the pork chops in a pan and place in
a casserole.

On top of the chops place ingredients in
layers in order given.

Place cooked rice over all and simmer on top
of stove for 2 hours, or cover and place in
300 F. to 325 F. oven and bake for 2 hours.
When ready to serve, lift each chop out with
a spatula, leaving the rice on top of each chop.

Hotel Leopold, Bellingham, Washington

*Hamburgers containing pork require longer cooking, but do not
press the patties tightly, just enough to hold together, or they
will be tough.*

*Meats are perishable foods. All fresh cured and cooked meats
must be kept in a cold refrigerator and used as soon as possible
if you wish to enjoy the original fine flavor.*

269. Lihahyytelo (Jellied Meat Mold) (Serves 8)

INGREDIENTS

1 lb. fresh pork
1 lb. veal

2 carrots—sliced—
cooked
3 small onions
1 sprig dill
1 stalk celery cut fine
salt and pepper to
taste
1 hard-boiled egg

1 pkg. gelatin
½ cup cold water

1 pint liquid from
cooked meat

DIRECTIONS

Cover with water and cook slowly until tender.

On the bottom of the mold, place the sliced carrots, onions, hard-boiled egg and chopped celery.

Dissolve gelatin.

Add to gelatin and bring to boil. Place meat in mold and pour gelatin mixture over it and set aside to cool. Serve with tomato, dill and cucumber garnish.

Mrs. Kuusamo, New York, New York

Do not serve strong flavored vegetables with veal. They tend to cover up the delicate flavor of the veal.

270. Veal Chops Cooked in Wine (Serves 4)

INGREDIENTS

4 veal chops with
kidney at least 2
inches or more thick
⅛ lb. butter
3 tablespons flour

1 cup white wine

¼ lb. fresh mushrooms
—chopped
1 grated onion
⅛ lb. butter

DIRECTIONS

Dip chops lightly in flour and saute in butter until a golden brown. Remove chops and place in a casserole.

Add wine to drippings the chops were cooked in and simmer until syrupy. Pour over the chops.

Saute slowly for 5 minutes. Pour around the chops. Cover the baking dish with buttered heavy paper tied tight and bake in 375 F. oven for 30 minutes.

Duncan Hines, Bowling Green, Kentucky

Veal has a delicate flavor. Do not overcome it by cooking with vegetables of strong flavor. If a roast of veal, chop, or stew, added fat helps, such as pork fat, bacon or butter but in cooking veal, be sure it is thoroughly cooked.

271. Veal-Pork Roast

(Serves 10)

INGREDIENTS

DIRECTIONS

3 to 5 lbs. veal shoulder
3 to 5 lbs. pork shoulder or loin

Have the butcher bone both pieces of meat and roll and tie it together, having the pork fat outside.

3 tablespoons flour
salt and pepper to taste

Roll the roast in dry ingredients and place in roasting pan, veal side down.

1 cup of water

Add to roast and cover. Bake in 300 F. to 325 F. oven for 4 hours. Remove the cover and brown the top under the broiler for 15 to 20 minutes before serving. Remove strings and serve with applesauce or fresh sliced mangoes.

Mrs. Otto J. Sieplein, Miami, Florida

272. Veal a la Dunton

(Serves 6-8)

INGREDIENTS

DIRECTIONS

2 lbs. veal—from the leg

Brown veal over a hot fire using just a little fat in the pan. When brown, turn fire low, add water to cover, cook very slowly covered for about 1½ hours. Let cool and cut into cubes.

2 cups white sauce
1 can mushrooms— 4 oz.
2 tablespoons chopped pimiento or
2 tablespoons chopped green pepper

Add mushroom juice and any liquid from the meat to the white sauce. Green pepper or pimiento are optional. Put veal in buttered baking dish with mushrooms, pour sauce over it, cover with crushed corn flakes. Place in medium oven, 350°, and heat through.

Dunton's Cafeteria, Dallas, Texas

273. Veal in Sour Cream

(Serves 2)

INGREDIENTS

DIRECTIONS

1 lb. of leg of veal cut in slices ½ in. thick
salt and pepper
flour
3 tablespoons butter

Melt butter in sauce pan. Sprinkle salt and pepper over veal slices, dredge with flour and saute in butter until brown on both sides.

1 pint sour cream

Pour over veal and simmer until tender. Serve with noodles.

Plentywood Farm, Bensenville, Illinois

274. Veal Scaloppini a la Vanessi   (Serves 4)

INGREDIENTS

3 lbs. veal
6 tablespoons butter
2 tablespoons olive oil

4 medium green onions
1 lb. fresh mushrooms
2 cloves garlic minced
salt and freshly
ground black pepper
pinch of rosemary
1 table glass of Marsala
wine
pinch of parsley

DIRECTIONS

Cut veal in 2-inch squares and pound ¼ inch thick. Dip in flour and put in hot frying pan with olive oil and butter. Brown on both sides.

Chop onions fine and slice mushrooms. Add to veal along with rosemary and salt and pepper to taste. Let all brown gently and then add wine and a pinch of chopped parsley. Let simmer for about 5 minutes and serve with decoration of peas and cottage fried potatoes.

Vanessi's Restaurant, San Francisco, California

275. Veal Cutlet Parmigiana   (Serves 4)

INGREDIENTS

1½ lb. veal cutlet
½ inch thick
1 egg—beaten
bread crumbs
butter
tomato sauce
Mozzarella cheese

DIRECTIONS

Flatten cutlet very thin, flour on both sides, dip into beaten egg, then bread well. Saute in butter until brown. Over the top of each cutlet put a spoonful of tomato sauce and a slice of cheese. Bake in a 375° oven until the cheese is melted and serve.

Giovanni Restaurant, New York, New York

276. Roast Veal and Kidney with Rice

INGREDIENTS

5 lbs. veal—see that the kidney and suet are left in
salt and pepper to taste

1 cup washed rice

DIRECTIONS

Season the meat. Sprinkle the bottom of the roaster with a little flour. Put the meat on top of this and place in 400 F. oven until the flour browns. Reduce the oven to 300 F. Add a small amount of water, cover the pan and bake 2⅓ to 3 hours, basting frequently and adding water as needed.

Add to the roast and cook for 1 hour. Add only a little water at a time as it is needed. The juices should be dark brown, which will make the rice a rich brown color when done and the water has been absorbed. Serve the meat on a platter surrounded with the rice. A tossed salad, julienne green beans or peas and a light dessert make an excellent dinner.

Mrs. H. A. Resener, Huntington, West Virginia

277. Braised Veal au Vin Blanc (Serves 2)

INGREDIENTS

4 medium sized carrots
4 medium sized onions
3 tablespoons butter

2 lbs. loin of veal
1 bay leaf
salt and pepper to taste
½ bottle of white wine

DIRECTIONS

Peel and slice carrots and onions. Melt butter in heavy cast iron Dutch oven and saute vegetables for 2 minutes. Set aside.

Brown veal on all sides, turning with two wooden spoons to keep from puncturing the meat. Season and add the bay leaf. Pour wine over meat, cover and place in 350° oven. Cook for two hours or until tender. Remove meat and place in warm oven. Strain liquid and boil briskly to reduce. If not enough liquid add a little beef stock or bouillon cube dissolved in hot water. Puree some of the vegetables and stir into liquid. If gravy is not thick enough stir in a little cornstarch which has been dissolved in water and cook until gravy clarifies. A good accompaniment is a dish of noodles freshly boiled and then drained and sauted in butter.

Mrs. Duncan Hines, Bowling Green, Kentucky

278. Chicken Livers Saute a la Marsala (Serves 4)

INGREDIENTS

4 tablespoons butter
1 lb. chicken livers
salt and pepper
flour

1 pod garlic
3 tablespoons parsley
1½ cups chicken stock

½ cup Marsala wine

DIRECTIONS

Melt butter in skillet. Season chicken livers, roll in flour and brown over low heat.

Chop garlic and parsley fine and add to chicken livers along with chicken stock. Let simmer for about 15 minutes.

Add to above and let cook for about 5 minutes. If sauce is thin, thicken with a little arrowroot or cornstarch. Serve on rice, toast, waffles or an omelet.

Mrs. Duncan Hines, Bowling Green, Kentucky

CAN YOU TELL THE DIFFERENCE WHEN SELECTING A TURKEY

Tom turkeys have a thinner breast, larger drum stick and are almost as tender as a hen turkey. In markets, tom turkeys sell twelve to fifteen cents per pound less than hens, although there is little difference in taste when either is served after correct cooking.

279. Arroz Con Pollo   (Serves 4)

INGREDIENTS

1 3-lb. chicken
½ cup olive oil

garlic to taste
1 medium onion
3 medium green pep-
pers

2 fresh tomatoes

bit of red pepper
2 cups long grain rice
4 cups chicken broth
5 grains saffron

8 tablespoons fresh
cooked peas
8-12 slices pimientos
4 teaspoons chopped
parsley

DIRECTIONS

Wash and disjoint chicken. Saute in oil until
golden brown.

Chop all fine and add to chicken. Let cook
gently until brown.

Peel and cut small. Add to above and cook
2 more minutes.

Add to mixture and place in 400° oven. Cook
for 15 minutes.

Take above from oven and decorate top with
these ingredients. Cover and let stand for 10
minutes before serving. The most important
thing about cooking this dish is to be sure to
cook it in an earthenware casserole and
after the rice is in, to use a wooden spoon and
go all around the edges without taking out
the spoon so as not to break up the rice. Do not put the spoon in the center
and stir the chicken and rice, but go around the edge and work to the center
gradually.

El Chico, New York, New York

280. Breast of Chicken   (Serves 6)

INGREDIENTS

3 two and half pound
chickens— (use fillets)
3 pieces larding pork
3 tablespoons butter

SAUCE:

2 tablespoons butter
2 shallots—chopped
6 large mushrooms—
sliced thin
1 sliced truffle

2 tablespoons sherry
wine
2 tablespoons white
wine

½ cup cream
salt and cayenne
pepper to taste

DIRECTIONS

Remove skin and lard. Place in buttered
sautoir and bake in 400 F. oven until a golden
brown. Place on heart-shaped pieces of toast,
fried in butter and spread with pate de fois
gras. Dress on a round platter.

Fry lightly in the sautoir.

Moisten mixture with wine.

Add to mixture and cook until sauce is thick
Season mixture and serve with chicken.

Hotel St. Regis, New York, New York

281. Chicken Adobo (Serves 6)

INGREDIENTS

2 3½ lb. chickens

1 cup tarragon vinegar
1 cup sharp white wine
½ cup olive oil
6 cloves garlic
3 bay leaves
1 tablespoon pepper-
  corns
1 tablespoon salt or to
  taste
1 tablespoon soy sauce

DIRECTIONS

Disjoint chickens, using only the good pieces. Make stock out of neck, backs and wing tips.

Combine all of these ingredients. Place chicken pieces in large bowl and pour over the liquid mixture. Let marinate at least 4 hours but overnight is better.

When ready to cook, remove chicken from liquid, flour very lightly, and saute in butter or fat until browned. Place in an open roaster with the strained liquid around it, oven bake gently at 350° for about 45 minutes or 1 hour—when tender but not falling from the bones. Serve with fried rice or white rice boiled in the chicken stock made from the bony pieces. The sauce remaining in the pan can be served separately—thicken very, very slightly with fecula (potato flour).

For a really gala dish, sauteed fresh mushrooms are sometimes added.

Ramor Oaks, Atherton, California

282. Baked Chicken in White Wine (Serves 4 to 6)

INGREDIENTS

1 3 lb. broiler
1 stalk celery
  salt and pepper to
  taste

¾ stick of butter
1 teaspoon olive oil

¾ cup flour
  salt and pepper

½ cup chicken stock
¾ cup dry white wine

DIRECTIONS

Cut in pieces for frying. Put neck, wingtips and giblets in saucepan, add a stalk of celery and salt and pepper. Cover with water and simmer until tender to make ½ cup of stock.

Melt butter in skillet, add olive oil to keep butter from burning.

Salt and pepper chicken, roll in flour. Saute in butter until golden brown. Place in casserole.

Pour opposite ingredients over chicken. Bake in 375 F. degree oven for 1 hour or until tender.

Mrs. Duncan Hines, Bowling Green, Kentucky

> The hardest dish to sidestep is some-
> thing "I made especially for you."

283. Chicken a la King on Swiss Fondue
(Serves 8 to 12)

INGREDIENTS

DIRECTIONS

3 tablespoons butter
5 tablespoons flour
1 cup chicken stock
1 cup cream
1 teaspoon salt
¼ teaspoon paprika

Make a cream sauce.

2 cups cooked chicken
—diced
1 cup chopped
mushrooms
⅓ cup ripe olives—cut
2 tablespoons pimentos
—chopped
1 teaspoon lemon juice

Put into the sauce and heat for 5 minutes.

2 egg yolks—beaten
2 tablespoons milk

Beat together and add to above mixture. Stir
and cook slowly for 2 minutes.

FONDUE:

2 cups milk—scalded
2 cups stale soft bread
crumbs
½ lb. sharp cheese cut
in bits
2 tablespoons butter
1 teaspoon salt

Mix all these ingredients together.

6 egg yolks—beaten

Add to the above mixture.

6 egg whites—beaten

Cut and fold into mixture. Pour into buttered
baking dish. Bake in 350° F. oven for 20
minutes. Cut hot fondue in 2-inch squares,
partly covered with Chicken a la King.
Garnish with parsley and paprika.

The Barclay House, Oregon City, Oregon

*Some roast chickens have a blah flavor. Try rubbing with a
little mustard, ginger, and salt before roasting.*

*When recipes call for a can of food, consult "Measures of
Canned Food Containers" on page xi which indicates the
approximate number of cups.*

284. Chicken a la King

(Serves 5 to 6)

INGREDIENTS

DIRECTIONS

1 cup heavy cream
1 cup milk

Mix together and heat in a double boiler.

¾ cup chicken fat

Melt and add to the above.

⅛ lb. butter
½ cup flour
2 teaspoons salt
⅛ teaspoon pepper

In another double boiler, melt butter and whisk in flour and seasonings. Add the cream mixture, whisking continually, until smooth and well-blended.

¼ cup pimento
1 cup fresh mushrooms

Dice pimiento and mushrooms and add to mixture. Let stand for 1 hour.

2½ cups cooked chicken—diced

Add to sauce and heat for serving.

Hartwell Farm, Lincoln, Massachusetts

285. Baked Chicken Bird and Bottle

(Serves 6)

INGREDIENTS

DIRECTIONS

3 broiler chickens—split in half
3 teaspoons butter
½ cup water

Place chickens in pan with skin side up. Place ½ teaspoon butter on top of each half of chicken. Add water to pan and bake in oven 375° for 20 minutes.

14 or 1 cup medium-sized oysters
3 tablespoons green bell pepper
2 tablespoons celery
2 tablespoons onion
1 clove garlic
3 tablespoons parsley
1 teaspoon salt
½ teaspoon freshly ground black pepper
¼ teaspoon cayenne
5 tablespoons butter
1 cup bread crumbs
½ cup oyster juice

Chop and drain oysters, reserving juice. Chop garlic finely and mash. Chop vegetables and saute in butter with the oysters and garlic and seasonings. When tender, remove from pan and add bread crumbs and oyster juice. When chickens have cooked 20 minutes, remove from oven, turn over and fill cavity with a heaping spoonful of dressing. Sprinkle with more bread crumbs and a teaspoon melted butter. Place back in oven for 15 minutes. Garnish with cranberry or lingonberry preserves.

The Bird and Bottle Inn, Garrison, New York

A whole chicken keeps better than one which has been disjointed. Wash thoroughly inside and out, dry, cover loosely with waxed paper and store in the cold part of the refrigerator.

286. Chicken Dumplings (Serves 4)

INGREDIENTS

DIRECTIONS

1½ cups pastry flour
¾ teaspoon salt
1½ tablespoons baking powder

Mix together and sift well.

1 tablespoon butter
¾ cup milk

Work butter into the above flour mixture. Just before ready to drop into the broth (not more than a minute or two), pour the milk in a hole in the center of the flour mixture and mix up together very quickly and lightly. Use a folding motion, not a stirring or beating motion, or you will collapse the air cells caused by the action of the baking powder.

2 qts. chicken broth
½ cup chicken fat

Be sure broth is nicely flavored and not too salty; combine broth and chicken fat. Allow to boil rapidly in wide stew pan. Place rounded tablespoons full of the dumpling mixture in the broth to make one layer only. Do not crowd.

Broth should be boiling, but should not be in violent motion or it will break up the dumplings.

Work as quickly as possible and place a lid on the kettle so that the part of the dumpling that rises up away from the broth will be subjected to extreme heat within about 20 seconds after placing in the broth.

After about two minutes, remove the lid and turn the dumplings over lightly and quickly. Do not fool with them or you will break them up; do it with one stroke; this takes a deft, quick hand. Never let the boiling cease during the whole time. Cook for five to eight minutes longer with lid on (seven to ten minutes in all for cooking)

Remove dumplings and thicken broth left for gravy if desired.

If this recipe is followed accurately, dumplings will never be heavy or doughy. They will be light as a feather and can even be reheated for another meal without getting heavy or unpalatable. But you must follow the recipe carefully for results.

The Maramor, Columbus, Ohio

Dumplings served in the gravy become soggy. Serve the gravy on the side.

Cooked poultry meat should be eaten promptly. Leftover should be stored in cold part of refrigerator.

287. Breast of Chicken   (Serves 2)

INGREDIENTS

2 chicken breasts—
   cooked
1 cup light cream
salt and pepper
¼ teaspoon paprika
butter

DIRECTIONS

Remove bone. Place breasts in a shallow casserole, add salt and pepper and cream. Dot with butter and sprinkle with paprika. Bake in slow oven 300°, for 30 minutes or until cream thickens. Baste occasionally.

Iron Gate Inn, Washington D. C.

288. Chicken Pie   (Serves 6)

INGREDIENTS

1 large chicken
¼ lb. salt pork
salt to taste

DIRECTIONS

Place in large pot with a lid, cover with water and simmer until tender. Cool. Remove skin and bones from chicken and cut in large pieces. Simmer broth down to about half in volume to make strong.

2 tablespoons butter
2 tablespoons flour
1½ cups broth
salt and pepper to
   taste

Melt butter and stir in flour. Cook until crumbly. Add broth slowly, stirring constantly. Cook until it thickens. Season to taste.
Roll light biscuit dough 1½ inches thick and line greased baking dish. Fill with chicken and gravy. Bake in 400° oven until crust is done, about 15 minutes. Roll a circle of dough to fit top of baking dish, place on greased cooky sheet and bake separately. When both are done, place on top of chicken. (When baked separately like this, the crust is always crisp and perfect.) This is an old family recipe.

Old Hundred, Southbury, Connecticut

Foods which are naturally high in vitamins should be cooked with special care. The preparation of such foods, the length of time and method of cooking determine the amount of these important vitamins which you will get.

In making milk gravy from the drippings of ham, steak, chops, or fowl to which flour is added for thickening, be sure to cook long enough for the flour to become thoroughly done. If a rich milk is used, you should use half water.

289. Chicken a la Stroh   (Serves 2)

INGREDIENTS

DIRECTIONS

1 chicken cooked
2 calves sweetbreads
2 tablespoons flour
3 tablespoons butter

Bone and dice chicken. Dice sweetbreads. Roll chicken and sweetbreads in flour and brown in butter.

2 artichoke bottoms

Cut in quarters and add to the above.

3 oz. sherry wine

Add to mixture and let boil until the liquid is reduced to ⅓ its original contents.

½ pint cream

Add to above and let simmer for 15 minutes

2 sausages

Fry and add to the above.

seasoning to taste

Put all ingredients in a casserole.

6 pieces of corn meal mush

Cut in diamond shape and top the casserole.

6 ripe stuffed olives

Place in casserole as a decoration.

Clift Hotel, San Francisco, California

Culinary laws are no more fixed than chemistry.

290. Rogers Special Casserole Chicken   (Serves 2)

INGREDIENTS

DIRECTIONS

1 2½-lb. chicken
1 tablespoon flour
3 tablespoons butter
salt and pepper to taste

Disjoint chicken, roll in flour and saute in butter until brown, cover and cook for 10 minutes. Put in casserole.

4 lbs. spinach

Cook about 5 minutes, drain dry, chop fine, season and make a ring around chicken.

1 onion—chopped fine
½ clove garlic

Saute in pan chicken was cooked in. Let brown.

1 qt. sour cream

Pour over onions and let bubble. Pour over chicken and spinach. Put cover on casserole and bake for 20 minutes in 350 F. oven.

This delightful dish was served us at the Minikahda Club.

R. H. Hirmke, Minneapolis, Minnesota

291.   Chicken Blintz (Serves 8)

INGREDIENTS

½ medium-sized hen

4 tablespoons chicken
fat or butter
1 tablespoon chopped
green onions
4 tablespoons flour
2 cups chicken stock

1 teaspoon chopped
pimiento
1 teaspoon Worcester-
shire sauce
1 tablespoon lemon
juice
1 teaspoon chopped
parsley
salt and pepper to
taste
1 wine glass Burgundy

DIRECTIONS

Boil until tender, remove from bones and chop
fine.

Saute onions in fat until tender. Add flour and
let brown. Add chicken stock to make brown
sauce. This is the basic sauce.

Add to sauce above, with chopped chicken,
cook until sauce is very thick. Let cool. Take
pie crust which is not too short, roll thin, cut
in circles 5 inches in diameter. Place tablespoon chicken filling in center, fold over and
crimp edges. Fry in deep fat, 325°, about 4
minutes until light brown. Serve with rich
brown sauce.

BROWN SAUCE:

Make the basic sauce as in paragraph 2 above, and to this add a 2-oz. can
of sliced mushrooms and a wine glass of Burgundy wine.

Ye Old College Inn, Houston, Texas

292.   Chicken in Sour Cream (Serves 4)

INGREDIENTS

1 3½ lb. chicken
flour
¼ lb. butter
salt
pepper

½ cup white wine
(Sauterne or Graves)

1 to 2 tablespoons
finely cut chives
1 to 2 tablespoons
finely cut parsley
1 to 1½ cup sour
cream

DIRECTIONS

Disjoint. Dust lightly with flour. Fry at low
heat in butter until golden brown. Salt and
pepper each piece lightly. Place chicken and
drippings in casserole.

Add to above. Cover and tilt lid slightly so
some steam can escape. Place in 325° oven.
Baste frequently with wine and butter. Let
cook about 30 minutes or until chicken is
tender.

Add to above. Heat carefully, but do not allow to boil, until cream thickens slightly.

Col. and Mrs. S. P. Meek, Delray Beach, Florida

293. Chicken Saute a la Vanessi   (Serves 4)

INGREDIENTS

2 frying chickens
2½ lbs. each
¼ cup Italian olive oil

2 cloves garlic
pinch rosemary

2 medium onions
3 small bell peppers
1½ lbs. fresh mushrooms
1 teaspoon parsley finely chopped
¼ cup dry sauterne

DIRECTIONS

Disjoint chicken and roll in flour. Heat oil in heavy iron skillet and brown chicken on both sides.

Chop garlic and rosemary and add to chicken while cooking. Remove chicken from pan when brown.

Chop onions, peppers, mushrooms and cook in skillet until golden brown. Return chicken to skillet, sprinkle with parsley, add the wine, cover and simmer for 20 minutes. Season to taste and serve.

Vanessi's Restaurant, San Francisco, California

Whenever you have chicken, put the neck, wing tips, gizzard and backs in a pot. Add a little salt, a small onion, some celery tops, and a few peppercorns, barely cover with cold water and simmer for about an hour or until chicken flesh is falling from bones. Strain into a freezer jar and place in your freeze box. You will then always have chicken stock on hand when it is needed.

294. Sauteed Chicken   (Serves 4)

INGREDIENTS

1 3½ to 4 pound chicken
2 tablespoons butter

5 slices bacon

½ pound fresh or 1 can mushrooms
1 onion—sliced
¼ green pepper—sliced

1 cup cold water
2 tablespoons flour

DIRECTIONS

Cut in pieces and brown in skillet.

Cut in pieces and brown.

Saute to a golden brown. Season to taste.

Mix to a smooth paste. Put chicken in heavy covered skillet, cover with other ingredients.

Pour flour mixture over all, add a little water, cover and simmer slowly 1½ hours. Serve with fluffy mashed potatoes.

Vera H. Smith, Chicago, Illinois

295. Oven Broiled Chicken (Serves 6)

INGREDIENTS	DIRECTIONS
3 spring chickens	Cut in quarters, removing the backs and necks. Use these undesirable pieces with the livers and gizzards to make a cup of stock.
1½ teaspoons salt	Salt each piece separately and place in small covered roasting pan, skin side down.
½ cup butter	Dot generously with butter.
	Bake until brown, turn and brown other side, putting bottom pieces on top and browning all evenly. Keep covered to retain moisture. Bake for 1 to 1½ hours. When chicken is browned, remove to another pan to keep hot.
2 tablespoons flour	Add to butter in roaster and brown. Add the stock and make gravy.
	Serve at once. Put gravy in gravy boat.

High Hampton, Cashiers, North Carolina

If you want your fried chicken to be crisp when done, never put a cover on your frying pan while the chicken is cooking.

296. Country-Fried Chicken (Serves 4)

INGREDIENTS	DIRECTIONS
1 spring chicken— 2¾ lbs.	Dress and joint chicken the day before it is to be used. Put joints in cold salt water for at least an hour, then put in refrigerator.
2 tablespoons flour	Roll each piece in flour.
⅓ butter ⅔ lard	Fry slowly until brown.
salt and pepper to taste	Season after the pieces are in the skillet. When the chicken is brown put in roaster and pour a little water and melted butter over

it, cover and steam in 300 F. oven for 1 to 1½ hours. Add a little more water to keep the pieces from getting too dry.
Add to a lightly browned (not too thin) cream gravy all the scrapings from the skillet and roaster.

Mr. John T. McCutcheon (Chicago Tribune); recipe given to him by Mary Fletcher, a cook on George Ade's farm in Indiana

297. Chicken Creole

(Serves 4 to 6)

INGREDIENTS

1 No. 2 can tomatoes
1 tablespoon butter

1 teaspoon salt
few grains pepper
¼ teaspoon cayenne

1 sprig fresh thyme or
¼ teaspoon dried thyme
1 tablespoon parsley
1 bay leaf
3 small cloves garlic

¼ cup olive oil
3½ lb. frying chicken

1 tablespoon butter
1 tablespoon flour
6 chopped shallots or
½ cup minced onion
5 tablespoons chopped
green pepper
½ cup white wine

DIRECTIONS

Simmer tomatoes and butter in saucepan for about 10 minutes.

Add to above and simmer 10 minutes.

Mince parsley and garlic. Add seasonings to above and simmer 15 minutes or until sauce is thick.

Disjoint chicken, wipe pieces with clean damp cloth. Saute in olive oil, brown on both sides.

Melt butter in saucepan, add flour, blend well and brown slightly. Add onions, pepper and let brown slightly. Add wine and stir constantly until slightly thickened. Add to tomato sauce and pour over chicken. Cover and simmer 45 minutes or until tender. If desired place chicken on hot cooked rice and garnish with avocado slices and parsley.

Antoine's Restaurant, New Orleans, Louisiana

298. Chicken Fricassee

(Serves 6)

INGREDIENTS

1 chicken—5 lbs.
1 quart boiling water
1 onion
4 stalks or stems of
celery

2 teaspoons salt
6 or 7 carrots

4 to 6 tablespoons
chicken fat
4 to 6 tablespoons
flour

2 cups cooked rice

DIRECTIONS

Put in large kettle, cover and bring to a boil, then simmer gently for 30 minutes.

Add to above and continue simmering for about 2 hours. Remove fowl and carrots, keep hot. Strain stock, remove all fat and measure stock. There should be 2 or 3 cups.

(Should be 2 tablespoons of each for each cup of broth.) Blend these ingredients over a low flame, add the stock and stir until thick and smooth. Add more seasoning, if necessary.

Remove skin from fowl and take meat off the bones. Arrange pieces in center of platter, place carrots around chicken and outside of that place a ring of rice. Pour a little gravy over the chicken and carrots and serve the rest in a gravy boat.

Waldorf-Astoria Hotel, New York, New York

299. Chicken Country Captain   (Serves 6)

INGREDIENTS

4 chicken breasts
4 legs
4 thighs
4 wings
½ cup garlic oil

1 chopped onion
1 green pepper sliced

1 No. 2½ can tomatoes
2 teaspoons parsley
1 teaspoon curry
½ teaspoon thyme
pinch cayenne pepper

½ cup raisins
½ cup toasted almonds

DIRECTIONS

Season chicken with salt, pepper, paprika and flour by shaking in a bag. Heat garlic oil in frying pan and brown chicken quickly on both sides, turning so that it is golden brown and not dark. Remove to roaster, cover and put in 325° oven.

Cook onion and pepper in drippings until limp but not brown.

Chop fresh parsley and add to onions and pepper, along with other ingredients. Cook gently for about 5 minutes until blended. Pour over chicken. Rinse out frying pan with ½ cup water so that all of the scrapings are included. Cover chicken and bake for 45 minutes. Remove chicken to warm platter.

Add raisins to the sauce, pour over the chicken and garnish with almonds.
Serve with fluffy rice.

Mildred Williams, Food Editor, Richmond News Leader, Richmond, Virginia

300. Chicken Macaroni   (Serves 18)

INGREDIENTS

1 chicken—5 lbs.
1 bay leaf
1 onion
1 bunch celery tops
salt and pepper to taste

1 cup chicken fat or butter
¾ cup flour

5 cups chicken broth
1 cup milk

1 cup celery—cut fine
1 large can mushrooms
1 7 or 8 oz. can tomato sauce
1 can pimentos chopped
2 cloves garlic—cut fine

⅔ lb. large macaroni

1 lb. grated American cheese

DIRECTIONS

Simmer slowly until the chicken is tender. Remove meat from bones and cut into large pieces. Strain stock to use in sauce.

Melt butter and add flour.

Slowly add to the above and cook until thick.

Add to sauce, mix thoroughly.

Add the chicken to the sauce and let stand for at least 1 hour.

Blanch the macaroni and add to the above.

Cover with cheese and bake in 350° F. oven for 45 minutes.

Mrs. Elsie Smythe, Bowling Green, Kentucky

301. Chicken a la Waleski   (Serves 2)

INGREDIENTS

1 chicken—spring—
  disjointed
1 can chicken broth
1 carrot—sliced
1 onion—sliced
2 tablespoons chopped
  parsley
1 pinch thyme
1 bay leaf
1 whole clove
2 peppercorns
2 tablespoons butter

SAUCE:

3 tablespoons butter
2 tablespoons flour

1 cup chicken broth
½ cup dry white wine

1 egg yolk
2 tablespoons cream

½ lb. mushrooms
2 tablespoons butter

1 lemon—juice

DIRECTIONS

Simmer gently for 30 minutes or until tender.
Drain and save the broth. Dry the chicken on
a cloth.

Brown the chicken.

Blend and let cook 5 minutes.

Gradually add to the above stirring into a
smooth sauce, bring to a boil and remove fat
and strain through a sieve. Let the sauce simmer and reduce.

Add to the sauce.

Saute until light brown. Place browned
chicken in serving dish, place mushrooms all
around, cover with a little gravy.

Pour over all. Serve excess gravy in a gravy
boat.

L'Omelette, Los Altos, California

302. Chicken Lucrecio   (Serves 4)

INGREDIENTS

4 lb. chicken

8 tablespoons flour
1 tablespoon salt
2 tablespoons chili
  powder
½ cup olive oil
1 toe garlic—chopped
  fine
1 teaspoon camino seeds
  —chopped fine

1 tablespoon butter

2 tablespoons shredded
  almonds

DIRECTIONS

Disjoint.
Blend these ingredients and roll the chicken
in it.

Fry chicken in oil until a golden brown.
Add to chicken as it is browning.

After the chicken is browned, cover with
water and let simmer for 3 hours. Remove
the chicken from the sauce. Strain the sauce.

Add to the sauce while stirring and pour over
the chicken.

Brown in butter and top the chicken.

La Fonda, Sante Fe, New Mexico

303. Le Coq au Vin Antoine (Serves 4)

INGREDIENTS   DIRECTIONS

2 chickens, 2 lbs. each	Separate breasts and legs. Season, salt and pepper, roll in flour and place in saucepan with hot butter. Brown on both sides.
6 mushrooms 8 small white onions 1 slice salt pork—diced	Add to the chicken, cover and let cook slowly for 15 minutes. Drain out all fat.
1 pint good red wine ½ pint brown gravy "bouquet garni"	Add to the ingredients and let cook for 15 minutes. Season to taste and serve.

La Cremaillere a la Campagne, Banksville, New York

304. Chicken Stew (Yields 2 quarts)

INGREDIENTS   DIRECTIONS

1 six-lb. hen	Prepare hen for stewing. When tender, let cool enough to pick meat off bones. Cut in cubes with scissors.
2½ cups cooked, diced potatoes 1 cup cooked, diced carrots ½ cup cooked, green peas 4 cups chicken gravy salt and pepper to taste	Add to the chicken gravy, together with potatoes, carrots and green peas. Serve in casserole topped with very small baked tea biscuits on top of stew.

Myron Green, Kansas City, Missouri

305. Chicken with Rice (Serves 4 to 6)

INGREDIENTS   DIRECTIONS

4 lb. chicken	Cut into pieces.
1 onion—minced 1 tablespoon parsley 2 whole cloves 2 tablespoons butter	Braise with chicken for a few minutes.
1 cup tomato sauce 2 cups soup stock salt and pepper to taste	Add to mixture and let simmer until done. Serve with cooked rice.

Pilot Butte Inn, Bend, Oregon

306. Creme De Volaille

INGREDIENTS

1 spring chicken
2 lbs. pork
1 lb. salt pork

1 lb. butter
6 eggs
1 pint milk
1 onion—chopped
1 tablespoon parsley—
   chopped
crumbs from inside a
loaf of bread

DIRECTIONS

Put through a meat grinder.

Mix all together and add to meat mixture.

Place in individual molds and steam for 3 hours.

salt and pepper to taste

mace to taste
nutmeg to taste

Virginia Duvall Greenhow, Frankfort, Kentucky

307. South Seas Curry

INGREDIENTS

1 5 lb. hen
1 carrot
2 stalks celery
1 onion
1 teaspoon salt

1 qt. sweet milk
1 fresh coconut, grated

¼ lb. butter
1 large onion
2 green peppers
4 cloves garlic

4 tablespoons freshly
   grated coconut
3 tablespoons curry
   powder
3 tablespoons
   arrowroot
1 teaspoon cinnamon
6 cardamom seeds
½ teaspoon ginger
½ teaspoon turmeric
½ teaspoon nutmeg
¼ teaspoon cloves
1 ground red chili
   pepper
1 ground green chili
   pepper
2 limes—juice
   milk which has been
   drained from the
   coconut

DIRECTIONS

Put hen and vegetables in pot, cover with cold water and simmer until tender. Remove meat from bones, cut into bite sized pieces and set aside.

Scald milk and pour over coconut. Let stand 1 hour, then strain through cloth and squeeze until dry. Set aside milk and discard dry meat.

Chop vegetables and garlic finely. Melt butter in heavy pot and saute slowly until brown.

Mix all together in a bowl and add to vegetables in pot. Mix thoroughly and then add, very slowly, the quart of coconut milk above, stirring constantly. Let simmer for 20 minutes. Add chicken and simmer for another 20 minutes. Salt to taste and serve with fluffy rice and condiments. Caution should be used in adding chili peppers or you may omit them entirely.

Condiments should consist of side dishes of grated coconut, currants, chopped nuts, chutney, chopped crisp bacon.

Mrs. Duncan Hines, Bowling Green, Kentucky

308. Curry Sauce   (Serves 6)

INGREDIENTS

¼ cup butter
½ cup finely chopped onion
1 cup finely chopped apple

5 tablespoons flour
1 tablespoon curry powder

1 quart chicken stock

2 tablespoons lemon juice
the grated rind of ½ lemon
2 tablespoons jelly
salt to taste
2 cups cooked fresh shrimp, chicken, lobster, crabmeat, or lamb

shredded coconut
currants
chutney
salted almonds
peanuts
crisp chopped bacon

DIRECTIONS

Place butter in heavy sauce pan and add onion and apple. Carefully cook until it is a very delicate color.

Blend together and add to above.

Add to above very gradually stirring all the while. Bring to a boil and then reduce heat to simmer for 30 minutes. Strain.

Add to strained sauce.
Season to taste with salt and add 2 cups of any one of these seafoods, meat or fowl. Serve over flaky rice.

Small bowls of any or all of these ingredients may be served as an accompaniment of the curry.

The Country Kitchen, Littleton, Colorado

309. Curried Chicken   (Serves 4)

INGREDIENTS

1 3½ lb. chicken—disjointed
1 onion—sliced

1 teaspoon salt
2 tomatoes or 1 cup of canned tomatoes

2 tablespoons curry powder

DIRECTIONS

Brown the onion in some of the chicken fat. Add the chicken.

Add to chicken and cover with water. Simmer for 1 hour.

Add to chicken and cook until the chicken is tender. Keep covered with water. Remove chicken. Bone and cut in small pieces. Make a gravy of the stock. Add the meat which is taken off the bones. Serve on hot rice.

Quaker Bonnet, Buffalo, New York

310. Curry

INGREDIENTS

DIRECTIONS

3 cups lean meat

Pork, lamb, veal, or chicken leftovers—cut in ½-inch dices. Shrimp may also be used. Saute until a golden brown.

1½ cups chopped celery, including the tops
1 onion—chopped fine
2 tablespoons butter

¾ cup beef or chicken broth
2 tablespoons flour

Make into a gravy and add to celery and onion combination.

¼ teaspoon curry powder
3 dashes Tabasco sauce
2 tablespoons butter

Add to mixture and taste. If more curry is desired it may be added. Blend thoroughly by stirring smoothly. Add the meat and let simmer. Salt to taste. If necessary, put in double boiler. If it becomes too dry by evaporation, add boiling water to bring back volume. Serve heaped in center of warmed plate surrounded by a ring of boiled rice and garnish with parsley.

Dr. T. J. LeBlanc, Cincinnati, Ohio

311. Curry of Sea Food Rizotto

INGREDIENTS

DIRECTIONS

1 onion—cut fine
1 apple—cut fine
1 tablespoon butter

Saute.

2 tablespoons curry powder
1 cup cocoanut milk
1 tablespoon shredded cocoanut

Blend together and add to the above.

½ lb. fresh lobster
½ lb. crab meat—fresh
½ lb. shrimp
½ lb. scallops—fresh
½ lb. oysters—fresh

Parboil first and then cut in large pieces. (Save the stock.) Add to the curry sauce and bring to a boil.

1 jigger white wine
3 tablespoons cream
3 tablespoons butter

Add to the above mixture. Serve with rizotto.

RIZOTTO:

1 tablespoon chopped onion
2 tablespoons butter

Saute.

3 cups washed rice celery salt, Maggi sauce and salt—to taste
5 cups consomme or stock sea food was boiled in

Add to the onion, to rice and seasonings and place on warming shelf to dry. When the mixture is very dry, add liquid and bring to a boil. Bake in 350 F. oven for 15 minutes.

Monument Inn, Bennington, Vermont

312. Indian Curry   (Makes about 3 pints sauce)

INGREDIENTS	DIRECTIONS

1 onion—sliced
3 slices of bacon

Cook until brown.

1 quart chicken stock

Add to the above and as it comes to a boil add:—

4 teaspoons curry powder
2 tablespoons milk

Mix these together and add to above and let boil for 20 minutes. Strain, and return to the fire.

1 apple—chopped
1 cup fresh cocoanut—grated
½ cup cream

Add to the mixture and thicken to the consistency of heavy cream.

cooked chicken, cold meat, or hard boiled eggs

Add whatever base desired and serve with cooked rice and condiments.

Casa de Manana, La Jolla, California

Cooking with wine, expert chefs advise using white wine with white meat and red wine with red meat. My advice to beginners in cookery—taste and taste as you go along. You cannot approximate the exotic results too quickly. Taste and again taste as you proceed.

---

313. Breast of Guinea Hen au Sherry   (Serves 2)

INGREDIENTS	DIRECTIONS

2 breasts of hen
4 mushrooms sliced
2 tablespoons butter

Brown on each side in a sauce pan. Add mushrooms. Cover the pan and cook in oven 400° F. for 10 minutes.

steamed wild rice

Remove guinea and put on a cooking pan over a layer of steamed wild rice.

Sherry wine (whisky glass)
1 cup heavy cream

In a sauce pan cook wine and cream two minutes.

1 egg yolk—beaten

Add egg yolk to cream and wine, but don't let it boil any more, it should thicken the sauce.

Pour sauce over the breast and brown under broiler before serving. Of course, the seasoning is according to taste. Can be spread with grated cheese before browning.

La Cremaillere a la Campagne, Banksville, New York

314. Roast Mallard (Serves 2)

INGREDIENTS

1 wild mallard duck

1 whole onion
1 tablespoon vinegar
1 stalk celery—cut in
long pieces

1 apple—sliced
1 stalk of celery—cut

2 slices salt pork
salt and pepper to
taste

½ cup olive oil
3 tablespoons butter

DIRECTIONS

Wash and dry.

Put opposite ingredients inside the duck, set in a covered pan in a cold place overnight. This is for the purpose of eliminating all fishy flavor and should be removed and discarded next day.

Stuff the duck and discard after it is roasted Seldom are wild ducks cooked in this manner, stuffed with dressing.

Lay diagonally across the breast of the duck and season.

Put in small roaster and be certain it is very hot before putting in the duck. Roast in a 500 F. oven for 15 to 20 minutes, basting every 4 to 5 minutes. My favorite accompaniment is wild rice and cranberry relish.

Duncan Hines, Bowling Green, Kentucky

315. Roast Duckling en Casserole (Serves 4)

INGREDIENTS

1 duck—4 lbs.
salt and pepper to
taste
3 tablespoons oil or lard

1 onion—diced
1 carrot—sliced
1 stalk celery
1 bay leaf
1 pinch thyme

6 small pearl onions
3 oz. melted butter

3 slices bacon—minced

1½ lbs. shelled peas
½ heart of lettuce—
shredded
½ teaspoon salt
1 teaspoon sugar
2 cups water

¼ cup butter

DIRECTIONS

Season duck and place in roasting pan, in a 400° F. oven until it browns, basting every 10 or 15 minutes.

Add to the duck and let simmer in 325 F. oven for 45 minutes to 1 hour. Remove the duck and make a gravy. Quarter the duck and place on a platter.

Let brown.

Add to onions and simmer for 5 minutes.

Add to mixture. Cover with oiled paper or a tight lid and cook for 30 to 35 minutes. Remove from the fire.

Fold into the mixture, and circle the duck with peas. Pour gravy over the duck.

Applesauce may be served with this dish.

El Prado, San Francisco, California

316. Sour Cream Quail

(Serves 6)

INGREDIENTS

DIRECTIONS

6 pieces salt pork
6 quail
3 tablespoons butter

Wrap pork around quail and fasten with toothpick. Fry in butter, turning from side to side until brown.

12 juniper berries—
crushed
1 cup boiling water

Mix together in a pot and put in the quail. Simmer for 1½ to 2 hours. Add water from time to time if necessary.

salt and pepper to
taste

Put on the quail.

1 pint sour cream (to
be 5 or 6 days old)

Pour over quail and boil well for 30 minutes.

If the cream curdles, add a teaspoon of hot water slowly until the cream becomes smooth.

Huntington Hotel, Pasadena, California

When roasting a turkey, baste every 15 minutes. If liquid evaporates, add butter, stock, or wine.

317. Quail

(Serves 6)

INGREDIENTS

DIRECTIONS

6 quail
1 tablespoon flour
salt and pepper to
taste

Dredge the birds lightly.

½ cup butter
1 tablespoon lard

Heat as much as possible without scorching. Add the birds and brown fast to seal in the juices. Keep turning.

1 cup boiling water

Lower temperature and add to birds, cover the pan and cook until tender. Add water as needed until ready to brown the breasts. After the water is gone, place breasts side down in butter and brown over low heat on top of stove. Take the birds out and make the gravy.

1 tablespoon flour

Stir into the butter.

1 to 1¼ cups water

Add to flour mixture and scrape all the brown coating off the roaster into the gravy. Stir and cook until thick.

Duncan Hines, Bowling Green, Kentucky

318. Sliced Turkey, John Paffrath

(Serves 1)

INGREDIENTS	DIRECTIONS
1 cluster boiled broccoli	Place in oblong casserole that has been well buttered.
1 tablespoon melted butter 1 tablespoon grated cheese	Sprinkle over broccoli.
2⅔ tablespoons sherry	Douse broccoli.
4 thin slices white meat of turkey	Arrange over the broccoli.
1 tablespoon grated cheese 2⅔ tablespoons sherry	Sprinkle over the turkey.
1 cup cream sauce 2 egg yolks salt and pepper to taste	Beat these ingredients together.
1 tablespoon whipped cream	Fold into sauce, and pour over the turkey so it is completely covered.
1 tablespoon grated cheese 2⅔ tablespoons sherry	Put over the top and bake in 350 F. oven for 12 minutes until a golden brown and slightly souffled.

Divan Parisien, New York City

In stuffing a turkey, be sure that the neck is cut off close to the shoulder. Stand the turkey on end, and drop the stuffing in by the spoonsful. Do not pack in tightly or the stuffing will be soggy and tough. Fill the breast cavity in the same manner. Truss up the openings with skewers and string so that no liquid can penetrate the body cavity during the roasting. The result will be a delightful dry, light stuffing.

319. Pheasant

(Serves 2)

INGREDIENTS	DIRECTIONS
1 pheasant 3 tablespoons butter 1 pint thick cream 3 tablespoons sherry salt and pepper to taste	Disjoint pheasant, discarding backs and wings. Season with salt and pepper and brown lightly in butter in saucepan. Place pheasant in pressure cooker with ⅛ cup water and cook at 15 lbs. pressure for 15 minutes or until tender. Remove from pressure cooker to saucepan, cover with cream, add sherry and let simmer until cream is thick. Serve with wild rice.

Mrs. Duncan Hines, Bowling Green, Kentucky

320. Supreme of Turkey Filet with Virginia Ham
(Serves 6)

INGREDIENTS

6 turkey filets
6 tablespoons butter
1 shallot
1 clove garlic

½ cup light port
½ cup dry white wine
liqueur glass of brandy
liqueur glass of cherry brandy

1 cup heavy cream
2 egg yolks

6 pieces of toast
6 slices broiled Virginia ham

DIRECTIONS

Melt butter in sauce pan and brown filets with the shallot and garlic. (If you do not have the filets, chicken breasts will be a good substitute.)

Add to above and let come to a boil. Light with a match and shake pan until flame dies. Allow sauce to simmer down to about half. When done, remove pieces of turkey.

Add to sauce above and let cook until thick, stirring with a wire whisk to prevent lumps.

On each plate place a piece of toast, a slice of ham and on that a turkey filet. Remove garlic and shallot from sauce and pour over ham and turkey. Serve under glass.

Blackstone Hotel, Omaha, Nebraska

321. Breast of Turkey and Ham, Mary Christine
(Serves 4)

INGREDIENTS

4 slices of ham

4 slices breast of turkey

2 cups turkey stock
1 stalk celery—cut
1 onion—chopped
salt and pepper to taste

1 tablespoon butter

1 teaspoon cornstarch
1 tablespoon cold water

½ lb. fresh mushrooms
1 tablespoon butter

2 tablespoons sherry wine

DIRECTIONS

Place in bottom of a buttered casserole.

Place over the ham.

Boil down to reduce to a strong stock. Strain through a cloth.

Melt.

Dissolve and add to the butter. Stir until smooth and add to the stock.

Cut in pieces and saute in butter. Add to sauce.

Add to sauce and pour over the ham and turkey in the casserole. Cook in 350 F. oven just long enough to heat all and serve.

Normandy Inn, Carmel, California

322. Huntington Special Steak (Serves 10)

INGREDIENTS

2 lbs. cooked breast of turkey
1 lb. cooked veal

salt and pepper to taste
1 pinch of nutmeg
3 egg whites—beaten

½ cup whipped cream

3 tablespoons butter

DIRECTIONS

Put through a meat grinder several times to be sure it is ground fine.

Add to the above.

Add enough whipped cream to the mixture to mold into balls. The patties should weigh about 5 or 6 ounces each.

Melt and saute patties.

Serve with creamed mushroom sauce. Put the sauce on the plate first then the patty on top.

Supreme sauce may also be used, in which case, put a whole mushroom on top of the patty and serve under glass.

Huntington Hotel, Pasadena, California

A word to dinner givers. PLEASE have ashtrays larger than thimbles.

323. Turkey and Almond Loaf (Serves 4)

INGREDIENTS

¾ cup medium thick white sauce
1 egg
1 tablespoon grated onion
1 tablespoon chopped parsley
¼ teaspoon salt
⅛ teaspoon pepper
¼ teaspoon celery salt
½ cup soft white bread crumbs
½ cup blanched almonds
2 cups finely chopped cooked turkey

DIRECTIONS

Beat egg lightly, add white sauce and other ingredients in order given. Almonds should be chopped. Mix until well blended. Shape into loaves in buttered pans or buttered souffle cups. Bake in hot water at 325° about 30 minutes.

L. S. Ayres Tea Room, Indianapolis, Indiana

324. Turkey Filling

INGREDIENTS	DIRECTIONS
1 loaf bread	Let dry slightly. Cut or break into small cubes, crust and all.
6 white onions—sliced ½ cup parsley 1 cup celery ¼ lb. butter	Saute until thoroughly browned. Add the bread and stir until thoroughly blended.
2 eggs—beaten	Stir into mixture.
1 teaspoon salt 1 teaspoon thyme (if desired) ¼ teaspoon pepper	Blend together and stir into mixture. Set aside to cool. Fill the fowl and roast breast side down.

Mrs. Edmund H. Singmaster, Philadelphia, Pennsylvania

Do not pack the fowl stuffing in the bird tightly.

325. Turkey Filling

INGREDIENTS	DIRECTIONS
1¼ lbs. French bread	Buy the long loaf of French bread. Cut in half lengthwise, put in warm oven and brown lightly. Grate crust and all.
2½ teaspoons salt 1½ teaspoons pepper 3 teaspoons sage—crushed 1¼ teaspoons poultry seasoning 1 teaspoon celery salt	Mix together and add to grated bread, blending thoroughly.
1¾ to 2 cups butter	Melt in a large pan.
4 onions—cut fine 1 cup celery hearts—cut fine 1 lb. chestnuts—cooked, blanched, and quartered	Add to the butter, and when onions are a little done add the bread, stirring all together. Brown the bread slightly.
½ cup cream	Add to mixture. Stuff the turkey, but do not pack, if you want a light dressing. Rub the turkey with butter and flour and season well with the same dry seasonings that were used in the dressing.

Gertrude Chaffin Wellman, Cleveland, Ohio

326. Asparagus Souffle

(Serves 12)

INGREDIENTS	DIRECTIONS
1 quart asparagus	Cut in ¼-inch pieces and cook.
8 tablespoons butter	Make cream sauce.
⅞ cup flour	
1 cup milk	
1 cup asparagus water	
1½ tablespoons salt	
⅓ teaspoon pepper	
9 egg yolks	Beat until thick and add to sauce, and mix with asparagus.
9 egg whites—beaten stiff	Fold in above mixture. Pour into greased baking dish and place in hot water bath and bake in 350 F. oven for 1 hour, or until a fork inserted in center comes out clean. Serve with cheese sauce.

CHEESE SAUCE:

4 tablespoons butter	Melt butter, add flour and cook 5 minutes.
½ cup flour	
3 cups milk	Heat milk and gradually add to above and cook until smooth—15 to 20 minutes.
½ teaspoon salt	Add and stir until the cheese is melted.
speck of pepper	
8 tablespoons snappy cheese	

Grace E. Smith's Restaurant, Toledo, Ohio

327. Cheese Souffle

(Serves 6)

INGREDIENTS	DIRECTIONS
4 tablespoons butter— melted	Blend together.
4 tablespoons flour	
1⅓ cups milk	Slowly add to the above. Cook until a creamy sauce.
1 cup cheese—cut fine	Add to the mixture, and then remove from the stove.
½ teaspoon salt	
½ teaspoon baking powder	
¼ teaspoon paprika	
¼ teaspoon celery salt	
4 egg yolks	Add to the mixture and beat 2 minutes.
1 tablespoon parsley— chopped	Add parsley and pimento after egg yolks are beaten in.
1 tablespoon pimento— chopped	
4 egg whites—beaten	Fold into mixture. Pour into buttered baking dish and bake in pan of hot water 50 minutes.

Mrs. Louie M. Weathers, Elkton, Kentucky

328. Cheese Souffle

(Serves 6)

INGREDIENTS

DIRECTIONS

8 square soda crackers
1¾ cup milk

Put in pan 3 inches deep and let stand in refrigerator 3 or 4 hours. Mash crackers thoroughly.

3 egg yolks—beaten
¾ lb. grated cheese
dash of Tabasco

Mix well with crackers and let stand until ready to heat and serve.

3 egg whites—beaten
stiff but not dry

Fold into mixture and bake for about 30 minutes in oven that has been preheated and turned down to 300 F. Turn up temperature and brown for 2 minutes.

Shadow Hill Tea Room, Hernando, Mississippi

329. Eggplant Souffle

(Serves 8 to 10)

INGREDIENTS

DIRECTIONS

1 eggplant—large

Peel and cut in small chunks. Boil in clear water until tender. Drain well by pressing lightly in colander.

4 eggs
1 cup cream
¼ cup melted butter
salt to taste

Thoroughly mix and beat in with eggplant, using a potato masher. Bake in pyrex dish in 350° F. oven for 30 minutes, or until it puffs up like a sponge cake. Serve very hot.

William Jack Latta, Goshen, Indiana

330. Boulghour Pilaff (Cracked Wheat)

INGREDIENTS

DIRECTIONS

¼ lb. butter—melted
3 cups Boulghour
(cracked wheat)

Braise for 5 minutes.

1 onion—chopped
1 tablespoon butter

Fry on the side and add to the boulghour.

6 cups clear broth
salt and pepper to
taste

Add to mixture, stir well, cover the pot and bake in 350 F. oven for 30 minutes.

Take out, mix well, cover and bake for another 10 minutes.

Also very good used as a turkey, duck, or chicken dressing.

Omar Khayyam's, San Francisco, California

331. Souffle of Summer Squash (Serves 6)

INGREDIENTS

2½ to 3 cupfuls cooked
   squash
1 teaspoon minced
   onion
1 cup rich, thick white
   sauce
2 eggs beaten separately
1 tablespoon sugar
   salt to taste
   black pepper

DIRECTIONS

Blend all together, pour into buttered baking dish, bake 30 minutes in moderate oven, until set.

If squash is selected of even size, and carefully scooped from shells, the mixture can be baked in the shells, making a most attractive serving.

Chanticleer Lodge, Lookout Mountain, Tennessee

The modern serve-yourself groceries have brought personal marketing back into popularity. Particularly is this true in shopping for fresh fruits and vegetables. Go to market on Friday instead of Saturday and avoid the crowds. Try to get there early and get these at their freshest, because the longer they are handled the less vitamins they retain. Wash them thoroughly and place them in the proper compartment in the refrigerator.

332. Sweet Potato Souffle (Serves 8)

INGREDIENTS

6 sweet potatoes,
   medium size

2 egg yolks—beaten
½ cup milk

½ cup sugar
½ cup raisins
1 teaspoon nutmeg
3 tablespoons melted
   butter

2 egg whites—beaten
4 tablespoons sugar
1 teaspoon lemon juice
   or orange juice

DIRECTIONS

Peel and boil in salted water, until tender. Put through a potato ricer and mash thoroughly.

Mix together.

Add to egg mixture and stir in mashed potatoes. Put in buttered casserole and bake in 350 F. oven for about 30 minutes, or until light brown on top and bottom.

Make a meringue and place on top and put under broiler a few minutes to brown.

The House by the Road, Ashburn, Georgia

When possible, cook vegetables and fruits in their "jackets" as most of the food value is contained in these skins.

333.   Spinach Souffle   (Serves 14)

INGREDIENTS	DIRECTIONS
2½ cups spinach—cooked, and drained dry	Press through a colander.
¼ teaspoon salt dash pepper	Add to spinach.
1 quart of milk	Heat until steaming.
5 eggs—beaten	Whip until frothy and add slowly to hot milk. Add milk and egg mixture to spinach and pour into buttered baking dish or individual cups. Bake in 300 F. oven for 30 minutes.
1 cup sliced mushrooms 2 tablespoons butter	Saute in butter and put some on top of each serving.

Fallen Leaf Lodge, Lake Tahoe, California

334.   Spinach Souffle   (Serves 5 to 6)

INGREDIENTS	DIRECTIONS
2 tablespoons butter 2 tablespoons flour ½ cup milk ¾ cup cooked spinach, chopped fine	Make cream sauce. Add spinach.
½ cup grated cheese 3 egg yolks—beaten ½ teaspoon salt pepper to taste	Add to sauce and mix with spinach.
3 egg whites—beaten	Fold in mixture, Pour in buttered pan and set in hot water in 350 F. oven and bake for 30 minutes. Let stand a few minutes after taking it out of oven.

Mrs. R. T Cooksey, Madison, Wisconsin

335.   Apple Sauce   (Serves 8)

INGREDIENTS	DIRECTIONS
8 medium apples—tart ¼ cup water	Peel and cut in large pieces. Cook and drain and put in bowl.
½ cup sugar 1 teaspoon butter 1 teaspoon nutmeg	Add to apples.
1 dozen marshmallows	Put apples in baking dish and cover with marshmallows. Stick in oven until brown.

The House by the Road, Ashburn, Georgia

336. Apple Casserole (Serves 6)

INGREDIENTS

6 big Northern Spy or
Morgan apples

¼ cup sugar
2 tablespoons butter

DIRECTIONS

Wash, pare, quarter and core. Pack quarters close together in open casserole.

Sprinkle with sugar and dot with butter.

Bake in 350 F. to 375 F. oven until tender and brown—about 30 to 40 minutes.

These are sent bubbling to the table and eaten as a vegetable.

High Hampton, Cashiers, North Carolina

337. Fried Apples (Serves 8)

INGREDIENTS

6 to 8 winesap apples

½ cup water

4 tablespoons bacon
drippings
⅜ cup sugar

DIRECTIONS

Core (peel or not as desired), slice in ½-inch slices, like the sections of an orange.

Add to apples and cook in covered frying pan until almost tender. Remove the cover and let the water evaporate.

Add to apples and fry until a deep golden brown and candied. Turn frequently while browning.

Duncan Hines, Bowling Green, Kentucky

338. Baked Beans (Serves 4)

INGREDIENTS

1 lb. dry small beans
5 dry white onions—
sliced thin

1 cup brown sugar
2 tablespoons dry
mustard
¼ lb. bacon, cut in 2-
inch pieces
½ bottle catsup

DIRECTIONS

Soak beans and sliced onion in cold water overnight. Pour off water and add fresh water to cover and boil slowly until the beans are done.

Place alternate layers of beans, onions, sugar, mustard, bacon, and catsup spread over all until the casserole is filled. Top generously with sugar and bake in 350 F. oven until a crusty brown.

Reheating almost improves the flavor.

Mrs. Edmund H. Singmaster, Philadelphia, Pennsylvania

339. Quick Oven Baked Beans (Serves 3)

INGREDIENTS

1 can baked beans
1 onion—chopped
2 tablespoons syrup
1½ teaspoons dry mustard
2 tablespoons chili sauce
2 strips bacon

DIRECTIONS

Drain most of the juice from the beans.
Mix all ingredients thoroughly and place in casserole.
Garnish top of beans with bacon strips and bake for 40 minutes in 425° oven.

Mrs. Duncan Hines, Bowling Green, Kentucky

340. Spanish Beanpot (Serves 6)

INGREDIENTS

2 #2 cans red kidney beans
2 tablespoons bacon fat
1 clove garlic—minced
¼ teaspoon thyme
¼ teaspoon rosemary
1 small bay leaf
¼ teaspoon cloves
1 tablespoon dry mustard
¼ teaspoon black pepper
2 tablespoons wine vinegar
½ cup watermelon pickle juice or juice from pickled peaches
1 large onion, chopped
4 strips bacon

DIRECTIONS

Drain juice from beans and place in beanpot.
Mix all ingredients except bacon strips together and pour over beans. Stir until well blended. Top with bacon strips, bake in 375° oven for 1 hour covered. Remove top, run under broiler flame until bacon is crisp.

Mrs. Duncan Hines, Bowling Green, Kentucky

Learn to know your herbs, spices and seasonings. They will enhance the natural flavor. Do not overseason, be cautious in their use.

As I have said before, eye appeal adds much to the enjoyment of our food. Just think how drab and uninteresting looking would be our meals if we did not have the glowing colors of the vegetables—the gold of carrots, warm reds of tomatoes and beets, and the cool greens of lettuce, peas and beans.

341. Beets in Sour Cream (Serves 3)

INGREDIENTS

2 tablespoons butter
1 tablespoon flour
3 tablespoons vinegar
2 tablespoons sugar
salt and freshly
ground black pepper
½ cup thick sour cream

DIRECTIONS

Melt butter, add flour, mix well and let saute for about 5 minutes. Add remainder of ingredients, and let cook very slowly for about 5 more minutes, stirring constantly.

1 16 oz. can whole midget beets
¼ teaspoon dill seeds

Add beets, sprinkle with dill seeds, heat thoroughly and serve at once.

Mrs. Duncan Hines, Bowling Green, Kentucky

342. Black-eye Peas (Serves 4)

INGREDIENTS

2 strips bacon

DIRECTIONS

Fry until crisp. Remove and drain.

1 cup chopped onions
1 cup chopped green pepper
1 cup chopped celery

Fry in bacon fat until tender.

1 No. 2 can tomatoes
1 tablespoon sugar
1 large bay leaf
⅛ teaspoon basil
salt and freshly
ground black pepper
to taste

Add to above and stir well. Simmer for 5 minutes.

1 pkg. frozen black-eye peas

Add to above without defrosting peas. Cook slowly for about 30 minutes or until liquid is cooked away.

From a friend in Atlanta, Georgia.

343. Broccoli Ring (Serves 6)

INGREDIENTS

2 cups cooked broccoli

DIRECTIONS

Chop fine. Line ring mold with waxed paper and place broccoli around it.

1 cup mayonnaise
1 tablespoon butter— melted
1 tablespoon flour
3 eggs, beaten light
½ pint cream
½ teaspoon salt

Mix all ingredients thoroughly together. Pour over broccoli. Set mold in water and bake in preheated oven 350° for about 30 minutes.

The Derings, Green Lake, Wisconsin

344. Brussels Sprouts with Chestnuts   (Serves 4)

INGREDIENTS | DIRECTIONS

1 lb. chestnuts — Cook 15 minutes in boiling water. Plunge in cold water and peel.

1 lb. Brussels sprouts — Drop into boiling salted water and cook until tender—about 8 minutes.

1 cup rich cream sauce — Drain sprouts and combine with chestnuts. Over this pour cream sauce. Green beans or spinach may be used in place of sprouts.

Mrs. K's Toll House Tavern, Silver Spring, Maryland

345. Little Cabbages and Kings   (Serves 6)

INGREDIENTS | DIRECTIONS

1 qt. Brussels sprouts — Clean sprouts and soak in cold water for a few minutes and drain. Have two pots of boiling water on stove, each containing a quart of water. In one put 1 teaspoon soda. To other add 1 teaspoon salt. Cook sprouts in soda water for 3 minutes uncovered. Drain and finish cooking in salt water uncovered. Drain and keep hot.

1 cup sweet milk
1 tablespoon butter
1 tablespoon flour
½ teaspoon salt
1 tablespoon lemon juice
mace to taste
½ cup blanched almonds slit lengthwise

Scald milk. Melt butter and blend in flour. Add scalded milk, blend well and cook over low heat for 8 minutes. Beat smooth, add salt, lemon juice, mace and almonds. Cover sprouts with sauce and serve hot.

The Spinning Wheel, Redding Ridge, Connecticut

346. Deviled Brussels Sprouts   (Serves 4)

INGREDIENTS | DIRECTIONS

1 qt. brussels sprouts — Wash, remove outer leaves and cook in a small amount of boiling salted water until barely tender. Takes less than ten minutes for they should be a little crisp and not cooked to a pulp.

⅔ stick of butter
2 tablespoons prepared mustard
1 teaspoon Worcestershire sauce
½ teaspoon salt
¼ teaspoon cayenne pepper

Melt butter and blend in seasonings. Pour hot over cooked drained sprouts.

Mrs. Duncan Hines, Bowling Green, Kentucky

347. Cabbage in Sour Cream (Serves 4)

INGREDIENTS

1 stick of butter
½ cup green pepper chopped
6 cups shredded cabbage
½ cup sour cream
2 teaspoons sugar
salt and freshly ground black pepper
½ teaspoon caraway seed

DIRECTIONS

Melt butter in saucepan, add green pepper and saute over low heat for 3 or 4 minutes.

Add cabbage, stir well and saute in covered pan for about 15 minutes. Add cream and season to taste. Cook for a few more minutes. Serve at once.

This method will aid in preventing cabbage aroma from spreading throughout the house.

Mrs. Duncan Hines, Bowling Green, Kentucky

348. Scalloped Cabbage (Serves 4)

INGREDIENTS

1 small head cabbage

3 tablespoons butter or chicken fat
3 tablespoons flour
½ teaspoon salt
1 cup warm milk

coarsely shredded cheddar cheese

DIRECTIONS

Chop cabbage coarsely. Wash, drain and cook in boiling salted water for 7 minutes.

Melt butter or chicken fat, stir in flour and salt until well blended. Add warm milk slowly, stirring constantly. Cook about 10 minutes.

In a greased casserole, place layer of cabbage, cover with white sauce, then a generous layer of cheese.

Repeat until casserole is filled, having layer of cheese on top. Brown lightly in 375° oven.

The Hearth Tea Room, Lawrence, Kansas

349. Cauliflower Vinaigrette (Serves approximately 4)

INGREDIENTS

1 head cauliflower

FRENCH DRESSING:

2 tablespoons malt vinegar
2 tablespoons tarragon vinegar
1 pod garlic
½ teaspoon salt
¼ teaspoon freshly ground black pepper
12 tablespoons olive oil
finely chopped parsley

DIRECTIONS

Wash thoroughly and let cook gently until tender. Be careful not to overcook. Drain well.

Blend together vinegars, salt and pepper. Crush garlic and add. Stir in olive oil. Pour over cauliflower and sprinkle with chopped parsely. This dish can be served cold as an appetizer or hot as a vegetable. If served hot, heat dressing before pouring over hot cauliflower.

Mrs. Duncan Hines, Bowling Green, Kentucky

350. Sweet and Sour Carrots (Serves 4)

INGREDIENTS

1 large bunch carrots
2 tablespoons olive or peanut oil
½ cup sweet-sour sauce
½ green pepper

DIRECTIONS

Scrape carrots and cut into ¼-inch slices. Heat oil in saucepan with a tight fitting cover, add carrots, stir and cover. Cook about 8 minutes. Stir in sweet-sour sauce. Cut green pepper into thin strips and stir into carrots. Cook over low heat only until the pepper becomes a bright green. Serve at once.

SWEET-SOUR SAUCE:

¼ cup sugar
1½ teaspoons corn starch
¼ cup vinegar
¼ cup water
pinch salt

Mix sugar and cornstarch in small saucepan. Stir in vinegar to dissolve, add water. Cook over direct heat until it clears. Add salt and pour sauce over carrots.

Mrs. Duncan Hines, Bowling Green, Kentucky

351. Red Cabbage (Serves 8 to 10)

INGREDIENTS

1 medium head red cabbage
1 medium sweet onion
2 large apples

DIRECTIONS

Wash and remove outer leaves of cabbage. Remove core and slice. Peel and slice onion. Peel and quarter apples. Toss all together.

1 large tablespoon bacon fat

Add to cabbage mixture.

1 teaspoon salt
½ cup sugar
1 cup vinegar
1½ cup water
1 bay leaf
2 whole allspice
2 cloves (heads removed)
6 peppercorns

Add to cabbage mixture. Simmer 1½ hours covered. Thicken slightly with small amount of cornstarch. This is excellent reheated. Fine with wild game of any kind.

Lowell Inn, Stillwater, Minnesota

When cooking carrots, tomatoes or peas, add a teaspoon of sugar to enhance their natural flavor. Then season as your taste desires, but go easy on herbs and spices.

352. Blushing Cauliflower

(Serves 6)

INGREDIENTS

1 large cauliflower
1 tablespoon salt

DIRECTIONS

Place cauliflower upside down in cold water. Sprinkle with salt and let stand 30 minutes. Place in boiling water and cook until just tender. Time will vary from 10 to 20 minutes. Drain and place on platter and cover with tomato sauce.

TOMATO SAUCE:

2 tablespoons butter
1 tablespoon minced onion

Melt butter and cook onion.

1 teaspoon curry powder
1 tablespoon cold water
¼ teaspoon salt

Blend and add to butter and onion.

1 cup tomato soup (condensed)
few drops condiment sauce

Add to above mixture and let simmer slowly for 10 minutes.

Valley View Inn, Hot Springs, Virginia

353. Julienne Carrots

(Serves 3)

INGREDIENTS

6 good-sized carrots cooked with skins on

DIRECTIONS

Cook until tender. Skin and slice in lengthwise strips. Put in baking dish.

½ cup water
1 cup brown sugar
4 tablespoons butter

Cook until syrupy. Pour over carrots and bake in 350 F. oven for 20 minutes, until candied.

Sunset Farm, Whittier, North Carolina

354. Carrot and Rice Casserole Dish

(Serves 6)

INGREDIENTS

1 cup ground raw carrots
1 tablespoon grated onion

DIRECTIONS

Bring to a boil and drain.

1 cup grated cheese
1 egg—beaten
1 cup cooked rice
salt and pepper to taste

Combine with carrot and onion. Place in buttered casserole and dot with butter. Place in pan of hot water and bake in 400 F. oven for 40 minutes.

Serve with sauce of creamed dried beef, peas or mushrooms, or any rich cream sauce.

H. M. Carruth, Cleveland, Ohio

355. East Indian Carrot Pudding (Serves 4)

INGREDIENTS

3 cups grated fresh carrots
1½ cups grated onion
2 tablespoons finely chopped chives
1 teaspoon sugar
½ teaspoon salt
½ teaspoon salt
¼ teaspoon curry powder
2 tablespoons melted butter
¼ cup chicken bouillon

DIRECTIONS

Mix all ingredients together well. Place in casserole. Cover and bake in 350° oven for about 35 minutes.

Mrs. Duncan Hines, Bowling Green, Kentucky

356. Carrot Loaf (Serves 4)

INGREDIENTS

1 bunch carrots

3 small eggs—beaten
1 teaspoon sugar
1 teaspoon salt
2 teaspoons melted butter

1 teaspoon cornstarch
little cold water
1⅛ cups cream

DIRECTIONS

Cover carrots with water and cook until tender. Cool slightly and put through a food chopper or sieve.

Add eggs to carrot mixture. Add opposite ingredients to above mixture.

Make a paste and add to mixture. Stir in cream and mix well. Place in buttered baking dish and set in pan of hot water. Bake at 350° for 45 minutes.

Williamsburg Inn, Williamsburg, Virginia

357. Braised Celery

INGREDIENTS

clean celery, trim and cut into halves lengthwise

chicken broth or bouillon

SAUCE:

DIRECTIONS

Steam for ten minutes. Fold and lay on bed of fine sliced onions and carrots in shallow baking pan.

Cover with broth or bouillon and braise in oven until tender. (About 20 minutes.)

Take some fine chopped onion, slowly fry in butter to a golden brown. Reduce with red wine and add good thick brown gravy, cook slowly to blend.

Take celery out of pan and place into baking dish. Pour sauce over it. Sprinkle with Parmesan and bake until cheese is melted.

Minikahda Club, Minneapolis, Minnesota

358. Carrot Mold

INGREDIENTS

DIRECTIONS

3 bunches carrots — Cook and mash.

½ cup cream
½ cup cracker crumbs
3 tablespoons butter
5 egg yolks—beaten
salt to taste

Add to carrots.

5 egg whites—beaten — Fold into mixture. Place in buttered ring mold form pan, setting pan in hot water for 30 minutes in 350 F. oven. Turn mold out on flat plate and fill center with peas, arranging a row of mushrooms around the outside of the ring. (Fresh lima beans, green beans, spinach, or any other vegetable may be used in the center.) Cover center vegetable with cream sauce.

Mrs. C. H. Welch, Tucson, Arizona

359. Corn Creole

INGREDIENTS

DIRECTIONS

3 tablespoons butter
3 tablespoons green pepper
1 tablespoon onion

Mince onion and green pepper.
Melt butter in heavy skillet and add vegetables.
Saute over low heat until lightly browned.

2 cups whole kernel corn
1 tablespoon pimiento
¼ teaspoon salt
¼ teaspoon sugar
⅛ teaspoon paprika
2 tablespoons cream

Chop pimiento and add with corn, seasonings and cream to above. Cook slowly, covered for about 5 to 10 minutes. (Corn may be either fresh, frozen or canned. If canned corn is used, drain before adding to skillet. Canned corn needs less cooking time than fresh or frozen.)

Mrs. Duncan Hines, Bowling Green, Kentucky

360. Corn Pie

INGREDIENTS

DIRECTIONS

3 strips of bacon — Lay bacon in bottom and sides of baking dish.

1 cup bread crumbs
1 cup tomatoes—sliced
½ cup green peppers—sliced
1 teaspoon salt
1 teaspoon sugar
2 tablespoons butter
2 cups uncooked corn

Fill up dish with these ingredients, alternating layers. See that a lot of uncooked corn is in the center. The top layer to be of corn. Top with bread crumbs, and dot with butter. Bake in 350 F. oven until done.

Grated cheese may also be used on top if desired.

Mrs. W. B. Taylor, Bowling Green, Kentucky

361. Crisp Corn Patties (Serves 4)

INGREDIENTS

2½ cups fresh corn or 1 No. 2 can fancy cream-style corn

2 eggs
2 tablespoons flour
1 tablespoon sugar
¼ teaspoon salt

DIRECTIONS

If fresh corn is used, cut in thin layers from the top of the kernels and scrape the cob, to extract the corn milk.

Beat eggs and dry ingredients together until smooth and add to above. Drop by spoonful into a hot skillet containing a small amount of butter. Fry until edges are crisp. Turn and brown on other side. Serve immediately with fried ham or sausage. If corn is starchy and too thick, add a little milk to make it the consistency of cream so that patties will be thin.

Duncan Hines Test Kitchen, Ithaca, New York

362. Fried Corn (Serves 4 to 6)

INGREDIENTS

8 ears tender corn

8 strips bacon

1 cup of milk, cream or water
salt and pepper to taste

DIRECTIONS

Cut close to outer edge, cutting twice around ear. Scrape the ear to remove all the milk.

Render to make ½ cup fresh bacon drippings. Have skillet very hot, add drippings and corn. Let the corn crust, but not burn. Stir constantly for five minutes, until thick.

Add to corn, cover and let simmer for 15 minutes or until thick.

Charlot C. Moore, Henderson, Kentucky

363. Corn Pudding (Serves 6)

INGREDIENTS

1 No. 2 can cream style corn
½ teaspoon salt
1 teaspoon sugar
2 tablespoons butter

2 eggs beaten well
1 cup milk

DIRECTIONS

Stir all together.

Mix together and stir into corn mixture.

Pour into greased baking dish and bake in 300 degree oven for about 25 minutes or until done.

Nu-Wray Hotel, Burnsville, North Carolina

When sweet corn is at its best, try dropping the whole ear into deep fat, 300°, and frying for 3 minutes.

364. Deep South "Cawn Puddin" (Serves 6)

INGREDIENTS

1 #2 can cream style corn
¾ quart whole milk
6 eggs
2 tablespoons sugar
pinch salt
2 tablespoons corn starch

DIRECTIONS

Mix all ingredients, beating eggs before adding. Mix corn starch with enough cold water to make smooth paste before adding to corn. Pour into greased casserole. Bake in 300° oven for 30 minutes or until the consistency of custard.

Old Southern Tea Room, Vicksburg, Mississippi

Boiled vegetables are more wholesome if cooked quickly.

365. Corn Saute (Serves 1)

INGREDIENTS

Fresh corn

DIRECTIONS

Husk corn, drop whole ears into boiling water. Let come to boil again and cook from 4-5 minutes. Cool immediately by submerging in cold water. When cold, cut kernels from cob by splitting down center of each row, then cutting and scraping from cob. Measure cut-off kernels.

1 cup corn
½ cup cream
½ teaspoon sugar
½ teaspoon salt and pepper mixed

To each cup of corn kernels add proportion of other ingredients as given. Mix all well together, bring to boil. Reduce heat and let simmer until thick (takes just a few minutes), stirring constantly to prevent burning or sticking.

Beau Sejour, Bethpage, Long Island, New York

366. Succotash (Serves 1)

INGREDIENTS

¼ cup baby green lima beans
pinch of soda
pinch of salt
1 cup corn saute

DIRECTIONS

Boil lima beans, soda, and salt together until tender. Drain and add to prepared corn saute (recipe given above), and mix well together.

Beau Sejour, Bethpage, Long Island, New York

I do not add salt to boiling water or sweet milk in which I cook fresh sweet corn. Just a bit of sugar. When it comes off ready to eat, I add butter and salt but by all the edicts from those who think they know, do not husk corn until ready to cook.

367. Aubergine Pont Neuf

(Serves 4)

INGREDIENTS

1 large eggplant
1 egg beaten
flour
bread crumbs

DIRECTIONS

Peel eggplant and cut into strips as for French frying. Roll in flour, dip in beaten egg and then roll in bread crumbs. Fry in deep hot fat 350° until brown, about 8 minutes.

Voisin, New York, New York

368. Baked Eggplant

(Serves 4 to 6)

INGREDIENTS

1 medium sized
eggplant
cracker crumbs
melted butter
chopped pecans
1½ cups very light cream

DIRECTIONS

Cut egg plant into inch thick slices and peel. Butter shallow baking plan, and place slices of eggplant in side by side. Butter tops with melted butter and cover with crumbs and pecans. Pour cream around slices and bake in 350° oven for 35 to 45 minutes until done and slightly browned.

Twitchell Lake Inn, Twitchell Lake, New York

369. Baked Stuffed Eggplant

(Serves 4)

INGREDIENTS

1 eggplant

DIRECTIONS

Select nice, large, firm eggplant. Slice off top and scoop out inside, leaving enough so that eggplant will retain its shape when boiled in salt water for about 10 minutes. Boil part scooped out in salt water until tender. Pour off water and mash well.

1 green pepper
1 medium-sized onion
3 pieces of celery
3 tablespoons butter

Chop vegetables well and saute gently in butter until tender. Add mashed eggplant. Cook for about 5 minutes.

1 hard-boiled egg
3 cooked chicken livers
1 raw egg—beaten
2 tablespoons cracker
crumbs
pinch cayenne
salt and freshly
ground black pepper
to taste

Grate the hard-boiled egg and chop the chicken livers. Add to above with rest of ingredients in order given. Fill eggplant shell with mixture, sprinkle top with cracker crumbs and bits of butter. Bake in 375° oven until top is nice and brown. Serve on platter and garnish with parsley.

Hotel Sam Peck, Little Rock, Arkansas

370. Deviled Eggplant
(Serves 6)

INGREDIENTS | DIRECTIONS

⅓ cup onions
⅓ cup green peppers
1 tablespoon butter

Chop onions and peppers finely and saute until tender in the butter.

1 quart cooked eggplant
⅓ cup diced pimientos

In a large mixing bowl combine eggplant, pimientos and sauteed onions and peppers.

4 eggs
2 cups sweet milk
1 teaspoon sugar
1½ teaspoons salt
freshly ground black pepper

Beat eggs and combine with milk, sugar, salt and pepper. Add to above mixture.

2 cups bread crumbs
½ cup melted butter
2 teaspoons baking powder

Fold in bread crumbs, add butter and baking powder. Combine well and pour in greased casserole. Top with a little melted butter and sprinkle with paprika. Bake in 350° oven for 20 to 30 minutes.

The Frances Virginia Tea Room, Atlanta, Georgia

Do not buy eggplants or squash unless they are free from blemishes and are hefty, even though they are small.

371. Guinea Squash Pie
(Serves 6)

INGREDIENTS | DIRECTIONS

1 eggplant—medium size

Peel and boil eggplant in salted water. When done drain and mash.

3 slices toasted bread
little milk

Soak bread until soft. Mix with mashed eggplant.

2 eggs—beaten slightly

Add to above mixture.

1 onion—chopped
3 tablespoons of melted butter
1 teaspoon salt
pepper to taste

Blend in with mixture and put in buttered casserole.

2 tablespoons cream

Put over top and bake in 350 F. oven for 25 minutes until a golden brown.

The House by the Road, Ashburn, Georgia

To remove skins from tomatoes, put in hot water or hold over flame. Remove skins, place in refrigerator to become firm for slicing, etc.

In any dish the flavor greatly enhances the eye appeal.

372. Eggplant Supreme (Serves 6)

INGREDIENTS   DIRECTIONS

1 large eggplant   Peel and slice thin. Boil until tender in salted water. Drain well and mash.

2 tablespoons butter Mix in with mashed eggplant.

1 ten oz. can whole clams Mince the clams. Save juice.

1 cup cracker crumbs
3 tablespoons butter Butter individual ramekins or a casserole. Put in a layer of eggplant, a layer of clams, a layer of cracker crumbs and dots of butter.

½ cup milk
clam juice
salt to taste Blend together and pour over mixture and bake in 350 F. oven for 30 minutes.

Christmas Tree Inn, Kingman, Arizona

373. Scalloped Eggplant (Serves 6)

INGREDIENTS   DIRECTIONS

2 cups cooked eggplant Peel eggplant, cube and boil in salted water until tender. Drain.

¼ cup white sauce
¼ cup grated cheese
1 teaspoon chopped onion
½ cup canned tomatoes Place layer of eggplant in bottom of buttered baking dish, then alternate layers with sauce, cheese, onion and tomatoes. Have the top layer of eggplant. Cover with buttered bread crumbs and bake in 350 F. oven for 20 to 30 minutes.

The Anna Maude, Oklahoma City, Oklahoma

374. Luncheon Tophats (Serves 6)

INGREDIENTS   DIRECTIONS

6 ½-inch slices of egg plant
1 cup cracker crumbs
½ cup cream Peel the slices of eggplant. Dip in crumbs, then in cream, then in crumbs again. Fry in butter until golden brown. Place in baking dish.

6 slices mild raw onion
6 thick slices tomato
6 thin slices of cheddar cheese
salt and pepper On top of each slice of eggplant stack a slice of each of these ingredients in the order given. Bake in 350° pre-heated oven for 25 minutes. Serve at once.

Vera Kirkpatrick, San Mateo, California

375. Baked Acorn Squash

INGREDIENTS

Dark green squash

DIRECTIONS

Do not use yellow ones. Allow ½ squash per person. Cut squash in half and remove seeds. Place cut side down in ½ inch of water in flat pan. Bake 45 minutes in 350° oven or until tender. Turn cut side up and place 1 tablespoon of brown sugar hard sauce in center.

BROWN SUGAR HARD SAUCE:

⅓ cup butter
⅔ cup brown sugar
1 tablespoon rum

Cream butter and add brown sugar. Add rum a drop at a time.

Plentywood Farm, Bensenville, Illinois

376. Stuffed Acorn Squash   (Serves 3)

INGREDIENTS

1 acorn squash—1½ lbs.

¼ cup bread crumbs
¼ cup thick cream
2 tablespoons butter
salt and pepper to taste

DIRECTIONS

Wash thoroughly and place in oven 325°. Bake for 1½ hours or until done.

Split squash in two, scoop out seeds and discard, then scoop out the meat. Mash with fork, add butter, bread crumbs, cream and seasoning. Mix well and replace in one of the shells. Sprinkle with more bread crumbs, top with dots of butter, and place in 450° oven until brown. Serve in shell.

Mrs. Duncan Hines, Bowling Green, Kentucky

377. Green Squash   (Serves 6)

INGREDIENTS

6 green squash cubed
1 clove mashed garlic
1 tablespoon chopped onion
2 green peppers— chopped fine
3 tablespoons butter

¾ cup milk
1 cup kernel corn
2 teaspoons salt
½ cup grated cheese

DIRECTIONS

Fry slowly until tender, stirring constantly.

Add to the above and cook slowly ten minutes.

Dona Eloisa Delgado De Stewart, Santa Fe, New Mexico

Keep on hand only small quantities of perishable food unless stored in deep freeze.

378. Squash en Casserole

(Serves 2)

INGREDIENTS

1 lb. summer squash
2 small onions
½ teaspoon salt
¼ teaspoon pepper
¼ teaspoon sugar

1 tablespoon butter
¼ cup heavy cream
3 tablespoons grated
Parmesan cheese

DIRECTIONS

Wash and slice squash with skin on. Chop onions. Place both in saucepan with seasoning, barely cover with cold water and bring to boil. Cook until both onions and squash are tender. Remove from heat and drain well.

Mix butter and cream with squash, add more salt and pepper if desired. Place in buttered casserole, sprinkle top with grated cheese, place in pre-heated oven, 400°, until brown.

Mrs. Duncan Hines, Bowling Green, Kentucky

379. Zucchini Saute

(Serves 2)

INGREDIENTS

1 lb. zucchini squash

4 tablespoons olive oil
1 teaspoon chopped
onion
1 teaspoon chopped
green pepper
salt, pepper, pinch of
sugar

DIRECTIONS

Wash and without peeling cut into ½ inch slices.

Heat oil in skillet, add onion and pepper and saute gently until soft. Add zucchini and cook gently, turning and stirring frequently. Cook until tender or slightly brown. Add seasonings and serve immediately.

Headley Inn, Zanesville, Ohio

380. Fried Yellow Squash

(Serves 4)

INGREDIENTS

2 lbs. yellow squash
4 medium onions
2 tablespoons flour
2 tablespoons corn
meal
salt and pepper to
taste

6 tablespoons butter

DIRECTIONS

Peel onions, wash and slice squash with skin on. Mix flour, corn meal, salt and pepper and sprinkle vegetables.

Melt in frying pan over low heat. Add above vegetables and saute until golden brown.

Sunset Farm, Whittier, N. C.

Vegetables should be cooked in the least amount of water in the shortest possible time. Never overcook.

381. Hubbard Squash in Cream (Serves 4)

INGREDIENTS

DIRECTIONS

1 qt. squash
3 tablespoons sugar
salt and black pepper

Peel and slice thinly. Place in well buttered baking dish. Sprinkle with sugar, salt and pepper to taste.

1 cup heavy cream
½ teaspoon cinnamon

Pour cream over squash, sprinkle with cinnamon and bake in 300° oven for about 2 hours or until tender.

Mrs. Duncan Hines, Bowling Green, Kentucky

382. Oven Baked Peas (Serves 6)

INGREDIENTS

DIRECTIONS

2 tablespoons butter
2 tablespoons flour
1¼ cups milk

Melt butter in heavy pan, add flour and mix, add heated milk slowly and stir until smooth.

¼ cup mushrooms
¼ cup pimientos
⅛ teaspoon Worcestershire sauce
½ cup grated American cheese

Cut mushrooms and pimientos in small pieces and add to sauce. Add Worcestershire and cheese to sauce and cook until thick and smooth.

1 No. 2 can peas

Drain peas and add to sauce. Pour into buttered casserole.

1 tablespoon butter
⅛ cup bread crumbs

Melt butter in skillet, add bread crumbs and stir. Sprinkle over top of casserole and bake in 350° F. oven for 30 minutes.

Fort Hayes Hotel, Columbus, Ohio

383. Garden Peas Francaise (Serves 8 to 10)

INGREDIENTS

DIRECTIONS

½ head lettuce
4 or 5 small white onions finely chopped
1 teaspoon sugar
¼ cup chicken stock
2 qts. shelled peas
1 tablespoon butter
salt and pepper to taste

Shred lettuce and place with other ingredients in heavy pot. Cover closely and cook gently for 45 minutes, shaking pan frequently.

Villa Chartier, San Mateo, California

384. Peas Bonne Femme (Serves 4)

INGREDIENTS

1 pkg. frozen peas
2 tablespoons butter

2 cups shredded lettuce
¼ cup chopped onion
1 teaspoon salt
¼ teaspoon freshly
  ground black pepper
pinch sweet basil
pinch tarragon
pinch fresh mint

DIRECTIONS

Melt butter in saucepan, add peas and cook very slowly until peas defrost. Do not add water.

Add lettuce, onion, salt and pepper. Any one of the three herbs will give you that little extra something in the taste. Mix lightly, cover with a tight fitting lid and let steam for 5 minutes. Serve at once.

Mrs. Duncan Hines, Bowling Green, Kentucky

385. Frozen Peas, Chinese Style (4 to 5 servings)

INGREDIENTS

½ cup soya or peanut
  oil
1 medium-sized onion
3 stalks celery
8 small water chestnuts
1 pint frozen peas

½ teaspoon sugar
½ teaspoon Accent
1 cup chicken broth or
  2 chicken bouillon
  cubes dissolved in 1
  cup water

1 teaspoon cornstarch
3 tablespoons water

DIRECTIONS

Slice onion and water chestnuts. Chop celery. Saute vegetables in oil for 10 minutes only.

Add to above mixture and cook 5 minutes longer.

Dissolve cornstarch in water and add to above, cook a few minutes to thicken. Do not over cook as vegetables should be crisp.

Marion Flexner, Louisville, Kentucky

GREEN ASPARAGUS

Cut off the butts, use for soup. Scrape the stalks, stand upright tied in a bunch, tips above boiling salted water. In about fifteen minutes they should be tender.

Save your celery leaves for flavoring soups.

386. Baked Stuffed Green Peppers (Serves 6)

INGREDIENTS

DIRECTIONS

½ cup chopped onions
2 tablespoons butter

Saute onions until light brown.

1 cup tomato puree
1½ teaspoons sugar
¾ teaspoon salt
⅛ teaspoon pepper

Add to above and simmer for 10 minutes.

5 tablespoons raw rice
1 cup water

Wash rice in cold water, simmer 20 minutes
until light and fluffy.

½ lb. ground beef

Combine beef with all above ingredients.

6 green peppers

Wash, clean and parboil for 5 minutes. Fill
with above stuffing, bake in buttered pan for
1 hour at 350° F. Serve with tomato sauce.

The Doll House, Salt Lake City, Utah

387. Latvian Style Baked Onions (Serves 4)

INGREDIENTS

DIRECTIONS

5 large onions
2 tablespoons bacon
  drippings or butter
½ cup toasted bread
  crumbs
½ cup grated mild
  cheese
  salt and freshly
  ground black pepper
  to taste

Slice onions medium thick and saute in large
iron skillet until faintly brown. Put in baking
dish, cover with bread crumbs, baste with a
little melted butter, sprinkle with cheese and
bake in 350° oven until brown, about 15 to 20
minutes.

Allison's Wells, Way, Mississippi

388. Scalloped Cucumbers and Onions (Serves 6)

INGREDIENTS

DIRECTIONS

2 8-inch cucumbers
4 Spanish onions

Pare cucumbers and cut in thin slices. Cut
onions in thin slices.

4 tablespoons flour
salt and pepper to
taste

Alternate cucumbers and onions in baking
dish. Sprinkle each layer with flour and salt
and pepper.

2 cups ketchup or chili
sauce

Pour over all.

2 tablespoons butter

Add. Bake in 350 F. oven 20 to 30 minutes,
or until tender.

Duncan Hines, Bowling Green, Kentucky

389. Baked Stuffed Onions (Serves 6)

INGREDIENTS

DIRECTIONS

6 large white onions

Remove the outside skins and cook in boiling salted water for 20 minutes until slightly tender. Drain and cool. Cut a thin slice from the root end and discard. Remove the centers, leaving a shell approximately 3/8 to 1/2 inch thick. Set the shells to one side. Chop the removed centers.

1/2 lb. ground veal
1/2 lb. ground chuck beef
1 teaspoon salt
1/4 teaspoon black pepper

Combine with the chopped centers and mix well. Stuff the onion shells with this mixture. Place in buttered baking dish.

1 cup tomato juice
1/4 teaspoon salt
1/2 bay leaf

If any of the filling is left over after stuffing the onions, combine with the tomato juice, salt, and bay leaf. Pour over the onions.

1/2 cup buttered bread crumbs

Top onions with crumbs. Bake in oven 350 F. for 1 1/2 hours or until onions are tender and crumbs are brown.

Mrs. Duncan Hines, Bowling Green, Kentucky

390. Perfect French Fried Onions

INGREDIENTS

DIRECTIONS

large mild onions
Bermuda or white

With sharp knife, cut into 1/4 inch slices.

3 eggs
2 cups sweet milk
flour in shallow pan

Beat eggs thoroughly and add milk. Pour into shallow pan. Drop onion rings in pan and swish around to make sure that each is wet. Lift out rings, shake over pan to drain. Then drop into pan of flour. Make sure each ring is coated with flour. Place in wire French frying basket. Don't handle too many onion rings at a time—flour will get pasty and rings won't fry crisp and separate. Shake off excess flour.

deep hot fat

Have fat 450°. Place basket with onion rings in fat and give a very light stir with a two-tined fork to separate rings as they fry. Adjust heat to keep fat at 450°. When brown and crisp, pour out on paper to drain. Sprinkle with salt.

This recipe is printed here by special permission of Better Homes and Gardens Magazine.

Johnny and Kay's, Des Moines, Iowa

391. Cucumber Sauté

(Serves 4)

INGREDIENTS

2 or 3 cucumbers
salt and pepper
flour
3 tablespoons butter
sprig of fresh dill or
½ teaspoon dill seed
¼ cup sour cream

DIRECTIONS

Cut cucumbers into thick slices. Season and dredge with flour. Saute in butter until delicately browned. Sprinkle with dill seeds. Add sour cream and let cook up once. Serve at once.

Mrs. Duncan Hines, Bowling Green, Kentucky

392. Scalloped Okra

(Serves 6)

INGREDIENTS

6 strips bacon

DIRECTIONS

Fry until crisp. Remove and drain. Break in small pieces.

2 medium-sized onions
2 green peppers
1 clove garlic

Chop vegetables finely. Add to bacon drippings and saute until tender.

6 cups okra

Wash and chop in small pieces. Add to above and saute until golden brown.

4 medium-sized
tomatoes

1 tablespoon parsley—
minced

Peel and chop fine. Add to above and cook covered over low heat for 20 minutes. Just before removing from heat add bacon and parsley.

Sunset Farm, Whittier, North Carolina

393. French Fried Parsnips

(Serves 6)

INGREDIENTS

1 lb. fresh parsnips

DIRECTIONS

Peel parsnips, cut each lengthwise in 4 or 6 pieces as you would for French fried potatoes. Boil for 15-20 minutes or until about ¾ cooked. Drain water and chill.

2 whole eggs
4 oz. cream
1 cup flour
2 cups bread crumbs
salt and pepper

Beat eggs well and add cream. Season flour Roll parsnips in flour, dip into egg wash then place in bread crumbs, patting crumbs on firmly.

½ lb. butter

Melt butter until hot in shallow skillet. Place parsnips in skillet side by side, but not over lapping. Fry until golden brown and serve at once.

Hotel Cleveland, Cleveland, Ohio

394. Mushrooms Chantilly (Serves 5 to 6)

INGREDIENTS

DIRECTIONS

1 lb. fresh mushrooms

Wash carefully, but do not allow to soak in water. Cut in 1-inch chunks. Stems may also be used, if they are tender and not dry.

3 tablespoons butter
1 teaspoon salt

Saute slowly for 15 minutes, or until done. Stir occasionally to prevent sticking. Add salt about middle of cooking. Mushrooms vary in moisture so if there is too much juice when they are done, remove cover and cook until moisture has evaporated.

SAUCE:

1 tablespoon butter
1½ tablespoons flour

Melt butter and add flour and cook until smooth.

1 cup milk
1 cup heavy cream

Bring to boiling point and add to base, stirring quickly to keep from lumping. Bring to boil once and remove from fire in 1 or 2 minutes. Combine mushrooms and sauce and let come to boiling point. Set aside for 1 or 2 hours before serving.

6 tablespoons sherry wine

When ready to serve, reheat and add sherry. Do not cook after the sherry is added. May be served on sauteed or broiled eggplant, broiled tomatoes, toasted English muffins, or as a sauce for steaks or chops.

From One of America's Finest Restaurants

395. Mushrooms in Cream (Serves 4)

INGREDIENTS

DIRECTIONS

½ lb. butter
8 small green onions
2 lbs. large fresh mushrooms

Melt butter in large iron skillet. Dice onions finely and brown in butter. Wipe mushrooms clean but do not peel. Stir into skillet and simmer all together for about 7 minutes.

1 cup heavy cream
½ cup sherry
¼ cup brandy

Add cream, sherry and brandy to mushrooms and cook for 20 minutes over low heat. Serve on toast. May also be served on a thin slice of baked ham which has been slightly warmed in a little butter.

Mrs. Duncan Hines, Bowling Green, Kentucky

396. Cream Potatoes (Serves 4)

INGREDIENTS

2 cups potatoes
1 cup cream
salt
freshly ground white
pepper

DIRECTIONS

Dice potatoes finely. Place in top of double boiler over hot water. Pour cream over potatoes and season to taste. Cover and cook for two hours, stirring occasionally.

Mrs. Charles Smith, Ithaca, New York

397. Mashed Potatoes

INGREDIENTS

6 medium Idahos
more or less as
occasion requires

DIRECTIONS

Peel and slice rather thin. Boil in salt water until very well done. Drain and return to stove until all water has dried out. Put in mixer to mash until all lumps are out. Add more salt to taste, turn mixer to highest speed, add milk and whip until fluffy. Serve at once.

Colonial Tea Room, Kinsman, Ohio

398. Potato Sticks (Serves 6 to 8)

INGREDIENTS

4 large Idaho potatoes

DIRECTIONS

Peel and cook in small amount of boiling salted water until tender. Drain and whip until fluffy.

¼ cup hot milk
2 tablespoons butter

Melt butter in hot milk and beat into potatoes slowly.

2 beaten egg yokes
2 teaspoons grated
onion
¼ cup finely minced
parsley
1 teaspoon salt
¼ teaspoon white pepper

Stir egg yolks, onions, parsley and seasonings into potatoes. Spread mixture evenly in 8-inch square cake pan. Cover with waxed paper and chill overnight in refrigerator.

2 whole eggs—beaten
bread crumbs

Cut potatoes into 24 even sections, scoop out of pan one at a time and roll between hands into finger shapes. Roll in fine bread crumbs, then in beaten eggs and again in crumbs. Fry in deep hot fat, 365°, about 2 minutes or until lightly browned.

Mrs. Duncan Hines, Bowling Green, Kentucky

399. Champs Elysees Potatoes

(Serves 8)

IDEAL POTATOES (See note below)

INGREDIENTS	DIRECTIONS
8 medium large Irish potatoes	Peel and slice and then cut into strips about the thickness of a wooden match. Length is of no importance.
8 fresh mushrooms	Slice finely and pan fry these lightly in butter.
½ cup cooking oil	Grease skillet.
	Arrange one layer of raw potatoes to cover the bottom of skillet. Spread a few mushrooms over the potatoes, then add another layer of potatoes, then mushrooms. Altogether you will have 4 layers of potatoes and 3 layers of mushrooms.
salt and pepper	Season to taste with salt and pepper each layer as you put it into the skillet. Put skillet on medium heat on top of stove and cover. Cook ten minutes then remove cover and add a little more oil. Step up heat and continue cooking five minutes on each side (turning potatoes) until potatoes are nice and brown. Drain oil out of skillet and finish potatoes with a nice chunk of butter. Sprinkle a little chopped parsley over them before serving.

(NOTE) *IDEAL POTATOES are the same as above only instead of mushrooms between each layer, use some good grated cheese.*

Mario Piccardi, Chicago, Illinois

400. French Fried Potatoes

INGREDIENTS	DIRECTIONS
Use fancy Idaho potatoes	Peel and soak in water overnight. Cut in French-fry shape.
	Fry in pure leaf lard, moving them up from lower temperature lard to higher temperature lard for browning.
	Salt the potatoes immediately after taking them from the last fry kettle.

Phil Johnson, Northbrook, Illinois

French fried potatoes should be fried once, just before serving, to prevent their being soft, soggy and too greasy.

401. Souffle Potatoes (Serves 4)

INGREDIENTS

6 to 8 potatoes

DIRECTIONS

Peel carefully and cut each potato crosswise in slices about ⅛ inch thick, making sure they are as uniform in thickness as possible. Cut the ends so as to make them oval shaped. Soak a few minutes in ice water, while you are heating a kettle of lard to about 360 degrees, no higher. Remove from water and dry each slice thoroughly and drop a few slices at a time into the fat and shake and keep separate in kettle. Remove them just before they start to brown. (THIS IS IMPORTANT.) Drain on a towel and allow to cool.

Now heat the fat good and hot 400-450 F. and again put the potatoes in the hot fat and shake kettle. Do not crowd potatoes together. The thin slices will puff up into miniature footballs, hollow inside with crisp delicious shells. Remove when golden brown, salt and serve piping hot.

(Note: Potatoes must be oldish and of even texture. New potatoes will not puff).

La Louisiane, San Antonia, Texas

402. Baked Potatoes with Ham (Serves 4)

INGREDIENTS

2 large Idaho potatoes

DIRECTIONS

Scrub thoroughly, grease well and bake about 1 hour in 350° oven or until done. Split potatoes lengthwise and scoop out contents.

1 cup cooked diced ham
½ cup white sauce
½ teaspoon paprika
½ teaspoon hickory-smoked salt
½ teaspoon black pepper
1 teaspoon mustard

Mix all ingredients in double boiler until well blended. Add scooped out potato and mix well. Fill potato shells with mixture, return to oven and brown lightly under broiler.

Duncan Hines, Bowling Green, Kentucky

Mashed potatoes will be more appetizing if after boiling you drain and dry them over a gentle flame, add a bit of baking powder in scalded cream or milk to insure their being fluffy when properly beaten.

Irish, sweet potatoes and apples, when peeled, cored and sliced will not turn black if immediately placed in cold salt water.

403. French Fried Sweet Potatoes

INGREDIENTS

Sweet potatoes

DIRECTIONS

Peel and cut in ¼ in. strips. Fry in deep fat 390° for 5 minutes or until brown. When brown, take out of fat, drain and sprinkle lightly with sugar or salt.

Mrs. Elsie Smythe, Bowling Green, Kentucky

404. Skillet Potatoes   (Serves 8)

INGREDIENTS

8 large potatoes

½ cup olive oil

DIRECTIONS

Peel and slice in oblong pieces about ¼ inch thick.

Cover bottom of skillet with about 1 inch of oil. Place layer of potatoes, then salt and pepper and continue this until potatoes are used up. Put skillet on hot fire and cook 35 minutes with a cover on. When ready to serve, drain off excess oil, and turn upside down on a plate.

Shef's Farm House, Seattle, Washington

405. Baked Potatoes

INGREDIENTS

Smooth, medium-sized Idaho potatoes

DIRECTIONS

Select even, tan-colored which indicates they are well matured, no greenish color. Wash and scrub. Dry. Cut a slice off of each end so that the steam may escape during baking. Rub with olive oil or shortening. Bake in 350° oven 1 hour or until done. Break open and lay in plenty of butter.

Duncan Hines, Bowling Green, Kentucky

406. Baked Potatoes with Sour Cream   (Serves 2)

INGREDIENTS

2 medium Idaho potatoes
⅛ lb. butter
½ cup sour cream
2 teaspoons chopped chives
salt and freshly ground black pepper to taste

DIRECTIONS

Bake potatoes until done. Remove top, scoop out meat into double boiler over briskly boiling water. Add the butter, cream, chives and seasoning. Whip together until potatoes are fluffy. Fill the shells and serve at once.

Mrs. Robert Stephens, Los Angeles, California

407. Candied Sweet Potatoes with Bananas

(Serves 6 to 8)

INGREDIENTS

6 medium yams

½ cup water or ¼ cup water and ¼ cup fruit juice—orange or pineapple
¾ cup brown sugar
½ teaspoon salt
½ teaspoon mace
½ teaspoon cinnamon
2 tablespoons butter

2 bananas

DIRECTIONS

Select slender ones so that when sliced they will not be large in diameter. Parboil and then let get cold before peeling.

Peel sweet potatoes and slice in ½-inch slices. Mix sugar and liquid with spices, salt and butter. Cook together until sugar dissolves, stirring while cooking. Continue cooking until syrup thickens slightly.

Peel bananas and slice to conform to yams. In a buttered casserole or baking pan arrange slices of sweet potatoes with a slice of banana on each. Pour syrup over all and bake in a moderately hot oven, 375° for about 15 minutes or until the potatoes and bananas are hot and the syrup is bubbly.

Mrs. Duncan Hines, Bowling Green, Kentucky

408. Candied Yams Drambuie

(Serves 4)

INGREDIENTS

4 medium-sized yams

8 teaspoons honey
8 teaspoons brown sugar
8 slices butter

1½ ozs. Drambuie

DIRECTIONS

Scrub yams and boil in skins until beginning to get tender. Drain and let get cold. This can be done ahead of time if desired. Peel yams and slice in half lengthwise.

Butter a large shallow baking dish and place yam halves therein. On each half dribble 1 teaspoon honey, on that 1 teaspoon brown sugar and top with a slice of butter, not too thick.

Spoon the Drambuie over the yams so that each half will have an equal amount and bake in 350° oven for 15 to 20 minutes or until yams are thoroughly done. You might like to baste yams once or twice with juice in bottom of pan during the cooking time.

Mrs. Duncan Hines, Bowling Green, Kentucky

Potatoes and rice contain practically the same substances. To serve both at the same meal would be like serving both tea and coffee to each person.

409. Sweet Potato Puffs   (Serves 8 to 10)

INGREDIENTS

DIRECTIONS

4 good-sized sweet
potatoes

Wash and boil until tender. Peel and mash.

4 tablespoons butter
4 tablespoons brown
sugar
4 tablespoons heavy
cream

Add to potatoes and whip until fluffy.

8-10 marshmallows
1 cup corn flakes

Form balls and place 1 marshmallow in center
of each ball. Roll in corn flakes. Bake in hot
oven, 375°, for 15 minutes.

Sunset Farm, Whittier, North Carolina

410. Creamed Spinach   (Serves 3 to 4)

INGREDIENTS

DIRECTIONS

1 pkg. frozen spinach
1 small onion
⅓ cube butter
⅓ cup thick cream
salt and pepper
1 tablespoon lemon
juice

Chop onion fine. Cook spinach and onion a
little underdone. Drain well and put in Waring blender. Heat cream and add to spinach
in blender, add butter and seasonings. Beat in
blender for 1 minute to puree. Remove and
serve immediately.

Mrs. Duncan Hines, Bowling Green, Kentucky

411. Spinach Ring   (Serves 6)

INGREDIENTS

DIRECTIONS

4 quarts spinach

Cook, drain, and chop fine.

2 eggs

Beat up together.

1 tablespoon cornstarch
1 tablespoon butter
1 tablespoon sugar
salt and pepper to
taste

Mix in with eggs, and add to spinach.

1 cup whipped cream

Add to mixture and put in mold. Steam at
about 350° F. for 1 hour or more.

Mrs. W. B. Taylor, Bowling Green, Kentucky

*The use of baking soda to produce a bright green color in
vegetables should be avoided, or you may do away with their
valuable vitamins.*

*Make your soups a little ahead of time, so that you can skim
off any fat that may accumulate on the surface.*

412. Wilted Spinach

(Serves 4)

INGREDIENTS

DIRECTIONS

1 lb. spinach 1 onion chopped fine	Wash spinach thoroughly and cut in small pieces. Mix onion in with the spinach.
3 slices bacon	Cut in small pieces and fry until brown and crispy.
3 tablespoons vinegar ¼ teaspoon salt pepper to taste	Put in with the bacon and heat. Pour over spinach and serve immediately.

Waverly Guest House, Hendersonville, North Carolina

413. Baked Stuffed Tomatoes

(Serves 4)

INGREDIENTS

DIRECTIONS

6 slices bacon ½ cup onions ½ cup green peppers	Chop bacon, onions and peppers finely and fry out in heavy skillet until golden brown. Remove from fire.
1 cup grated American cheese 1 tablespoon prepared mustard	Stir into above until well blended.
4 medium-sized tomatoes cracked crumbs butter	Wash and core tomatoes. Scoop out seeds and pulp. Fill with above mixture, cover with cracker crumbs, dot with butter and place in a lightly greased casserole. Bake in 375° oven for 15 minutes or until crumbs are brown and tomato skin is crinkly.

Mrs. Duncan Hines, Bowling Green, Kentucky

414. Baked Tomatoes

(Serves 4)

INGREDIENTS

DIRECTIONS

1 No. 2½ can tomatoes	Drain off juice.
1 cup toasted bread ½ cup sugar 1 teaspoon salt 3 tablespoons butter	Mix into tomato pulp.
¼ cup bread crumbs	Pour into buttered baking pan and cover with bread crumbs. Bake in 300 F. oven for about 30 minutes.

Valley View Inn, Hot Springs, Virginia

415. Broiled Tomatoes   (Serves 4)

INGREDIENTS

4 ripe tomatoes

1 teaspoon butter
1 teaspoon dry mus-
   tard
salt and pepper

DIRECTIONS

Wash and slice off top of stem end. Place in baking pan with sliced end up.

Put 1/4 teaspoon butter and 1/4 teaspoon mustard on top of each tomato. Salt and pepper. Bake in 375° oven for 20 minutes.

Sunset Farm, Whittier, North Carolina

416. Tomato Pudding   (Serves 6)

INGREDIENTS

4 cups cubed dry bread
1 cup melted butter

2 cups canned tomato
   puree
1/2 cup water
1 cup light brown
   sugar
1/2 teaspoon salt
1 tsp. curry powder

DIRECTIONS

Put bread cubes in a baking dish and pour butter over them.

Let simmer together for five minutes and then mix with buttered bread cubes above.

Set baking dish in a pan of hot water and bake 45 to 50 minutes at 375 degrees or until top is well browned. This may be used as an adjunct to a regular dinner or as a dessert.

Duncan Hines Test Kitchen, Ithaca, New York

417. Fried Tomatoes   (Serves 6 to 8)

INGREDIENTS

2 tablespoons butter

6 to 8 tomatoes

1/2 cup flour
salt and pepper to
taste

1 cup milk

DIRECTIONS

Place in pan and let melt.

Slice in thick slices.

Dust tomato slices and fry in the butter.

Just before taking tomatoes out of pan, pour milk over them and let them boil up.

Mr. Fred Waring, New York, New York

The dishes most popular are not those complicated with a vast number of ingredients. Instead, those remembered with pleasure and desired often are the simple, easily prepared recipes.

418. Vegetables en Casserole (Serves 8)

INGREDIENTS

1 cup raw rice
1 small turnip thinly sliced
1 cup peas
1 cup tomatoes
1 sliced onion
4 medium-sized potatoes thinly sliced
1 teaspoon salt
⅛ teaspoon pepper
⅛ teaspoon allspice
4 cups chicken stock

DIRECTIONS

Wash rice well. Put rice and vegetables in layers in large casserole. Season and pour over stock. Cover tightly and cook in preheated oven 350° for about 3 hours, or until rice is tender.

Vera Kirkpatrick, San Mateo, California

419. Care of Fresh Vegetables

Wash clean . . . . keep crisp.

Use your green vegetables as soon as you can after they come from market or garden.

If you must keep them a day or two, store them in a cool place away from dust and flies.

Just before using, wash them quickly and thoroughly but never let them soak in water. You lose food value that way.

To get rid of sand and grit, lift the vegetable from the pan of water, rather than pouring the water off.

Salad greens keep crisp and crunchy if washed, wrapped in a clean cloth, and kept covered in a cold place.

420. Rice and Cheese Puffs (Serves 6)

INGREDIENTS

2 cups cooked rice
1 egg
2 tablespoons flour
½ teaspoon salt
¼ teaspoon pepper

sharp yellow cheese
⅓ cup bread crumbs

DIRECTIONS

Cook rice long enough ahead so that it is cold. Add the opposite ingredients, mix well and chill.

Shape rice mixture into balls around ½-inch cube of cheese or add ¼ lb. grated cheese to the mixture. Roll into a ball 1½ to 2 inches in diameter. Roll in bread crumbs and fry in hot fat, until crisp.

Alcove Restaurant, Mount Vernon, Ohio

421. American Rice

INGREDIENTS

2 cups dry rice

DIRECTIONS

Wash rice in colander until it is absolutely clear. (This may take 10 times.) Then wash 5 times more.

Have a large kettle filled with boiling water and add rice slowly so that the water never stops rolling. After all the rice is in, let boil 10 minutes. Then take out a kernel and bite. If the rice bites smooth, take off fire and put into a sieve. Set the pot back on the fire and put in the sieve with the rice in it and let dry out in the hot air coming up from the pot. Now, it is ready to serve.

Dr. T. J. LcBlanc, Cincinnati, Ohio

422. Green Rice   (Serves 4 to 6)

INGREDIENTS

2 tablespoons butter
2 tablespoons finely chopped onion
¼ teaspoon minced garlic
2 cups boiled rice

½ cup ground or finely chopped parsley
1¼ cups sweet milk

2 eggs
1 teaspoon salt
1 cup grated cheddar cheese

DIRECTIONS

Saute chopped onion and garlic in butter until lightly browned. Add to cooked rice.

Add to above mixture.

Beat eggs slightly blending in the salt and cheese. Add to above and pour into buttered baking dish. Bake in pan of hot water in 350° oven for about 40 minutes or until the mixture is firm.

The Country Kitchen, Litteton, Colorado

RULES FOR GOOD COOKING

Here are the rules for cooking and serving most vegetables to make the most of what Mother Nature put into them:

Use little water slightly salted . . . cook a short time . . . and never add soda to cooking water. Soda destroys vitamins.

Have the water boiling when you put green vegetables on to cook.

Leaving off the lid helps to keep the green color. With leafy greens, use a lid at the start until they are wilted.

Serve all the juice with the cooked vegetable or use it in soup or sauce.

That's being thrifty with the vitamins.

423. Wild Rice Croquettes

INGREDIENTS

½ lb. wild rice
2 cups chicken broth

3 tablespoons white
   bread crumbs
1 egg
¼ cup butter—
   melted
   salt and pepper

2 tablespoons flour
1 egg—whipped
4 tablespoons brown
   bread crumbs

DIRECTIONS

Cook the rice in chicken broth in double boiler for 45-50 minutes until fluffy.

Put rice in pan with bread crumbs, egg, butter, and season to taste. Work until pasty, then form small balls.

Roll balls in flour, then in egg, then in bread crumbs. Fry in deep fat, 400°, for 2-3 minutes to a golden brown. Serve with game.

Bismarck Hotel, Chicago, Illinois

424. Wild Rice Southern

INGREDIENTS

1 cup wild rice

¼ lb. butter
6 shallots or 3 small
   onions—chopped
1 clove garlic—minced
2 oz. ham—minced
   salt and pepper to
   taste
   Pinch sage
   Pinch thyme

DIRECTIONS

Pick over and wash rice. Cook in double boiler until tender. Wash with cold water and drain well.

Melt butter in large skillet, add ham, shallots, and garlic. Saute gently for 5 minutes. Add rice and seasoning and saute 5 more minutes, stirring constantly.

G. H. Mulder, Executive Chef, Chicago Athletic Club, Chicago, Illinois

For satisfying results in anything you cook, take precautions from beginning to end. Follow recipes carefully, use exact level measurements, and know your oven temperature. Don't proceed by guess.

Every good cook should have an oven thermometer and test the stove front and back, top and bottom, to see that the oven heats evenly. If it varies, call man from whom you purchased oven to make needed adjustments.

425. Hominy au Gratin   (Serves 4 to 6)

INGREDIENTS

DIRECTIONS

½ lb. grated mild cheese
1½ cups seasoned white sauce
2 teaspoons sugar
½ teaspoon Worcestershire Sauce

Reserve 4 tablespoons of the grated cheese for topping. Blend remainder of cheese and other ingredients in double boiler until smooth.

1 No. 2½ can hominy

paprika

Drain hominy and place in buttered casserole. Pour over it the above mixture. Cover with grated cheese and a dash of paprika. Bake 30 minutes in 375 degree oven.

Duncan Hines Test Kitchen, Ithaca, New York

426. Hominy and Chicken Casserole   (Serves 6)

INGREDIENTS

DIRECTIONS

½ lb. cooked chicken diced
1 No. 2½ can hominy —drained

Place a layer of hominy in heavily buttered casserole, then layer of chicken until dish is nearly filled.

1 No. 1 can condensed mushroom soup
4 tablespoons milk
¼ teaspoon salt
pepper to taste

Heat and blend together. Pour over the above mixture.

¼ cup bread crumbs
1 tablespoon butter
paprika

Sprinkle on top of ingredients, dot with butter and dash of paprika. Bake in 375 F. oven for 30 minutes.

(Cooked diced lean pork may be substituted for the chicken.)

Duncan Hines Test Kitchen, Ithaca, New York

427. Poppy Seed Noodles   (Serves 4)

INGREDIENTS

DIRECTIONS

1 8-oz. pkg. broad noodles
3 qts. water
2 teaspoons salt

Bring water to boil, add salt and noodles a few at a time and let cook for 9 minutes, stir and cook 3 minutes longer, or until tender. Drain.

½ cup butter
¾ cup almonds slivered
2 teaspoons poppy seed

Melt butter in saucepan, add almonds, and brown over low heat. Add cooked noodles and poppy seed. Stir well and serve hot.

Dupuis Tavern, Port Angeles, Washington

428. Green Noodles

(Serves 8 to 10)

INGREDIENTS

DIRECTIONS

1 tablespoon olive oil
1 lb. beef—ground
½ lb. pork—ground
1 clove garlic—chopped
½ cup chopped onions
2 teaspoons salt
1 teaspoon tabasco

Cook opposite ingredients in iron skillet until nicely brown.

1 No. 2 can tomatoes
1 6 oz. can tomato paste
pinch basil
pinch thyme
2 tablespoons Burgundy

Add to the above mixture, cover and let simmer from 2 to 3 hours, stirring occasionally.

1 12 oz. package of green noodles
2 quarts unsalted water grated Parmesan cheese

Drop noodles into boiling water and let cook about 10 minutes. Drain, put in large casserole, cover with sauce and place under broiler for several minutes. Serve with grated Parmesan cheese.

Studio Inn, Painesville, Ohio

429. Gnocchi a la Romano

(Serves 6 to 8)

INGREDIENTS

DIRECTIONS

1½ cups cream of wheat
1 quart boiling milk

Stir and cook for 20 minutes.

4 egg yolks

Stir in quickly.

4 tablespoons Parmesan cheese

Add and stir thoroughly.

Butter a large platter and spread mixture to about 1 inch thickness. Flatten with the hand dipped in cold water.

butter
Parmesan cheese

When time to serve, cut in circles about 1 inch in diameter and place in casserole with pieces of butter. Sprinkle top with Parmesan cheese and bake for 15 minutes. Serve with spaghetti sauce.

Giovanni's, New York, New York

Good digestion follows slow eating. This, combined with balanced meals, will improve the health of our nation.

430. Lasagna Pasticciapo   (Serves 6)

INGREDIENTS

DIRECTIONS

1 lb. fresh homemade
noodles 1" wide and
2½" long

Boil in salt water for 12 minutes then drain.

1 cup mushroom sauce
1 cup spaghetti meat
sauce
1 cup white cream
sauce

In buttered casserole, place a layer of noodles,
layer of mushroom sauce, another layer of
noodles and layer of spaghetti meat sauce, then
another layer of noodles and layer of white
cream sauce.

Top with Parmesan
cheese and do not be
stingy with the cheese

Bake in 325° oven for 15 minutes, until it gets
nice golden brown on top.

Duncan Hines, Bowling Green, Kentucky

431. Macaroni Loaf   (Serves 6)

INGREDIENTS

DIRECTIONS

1 cup macaroni–broken

Blanch macaroni.

1 cup cream
½ cup butter

Heat.

3 eggs–beaten

Add to cream mixture.

1 cup soft bread crumbs
2 tablespoons chopped
parsley
1 teaspoon chopped
onion

Add to above mixture, and then stir in macaroni.

½ cup grated cheese
1 can (small) pimentos
1 teaspoon salt

Turn into a buttered mold and bake in 350 F.
oven for 1 hour.

SAUCE:

1 lb. fresh mushrooms
2 tablespoons butter

Saute mushrooms.

2 tablespoons butter
3 tablespoons flour
2 cups cream
salt to taste

Make a cream sauce.

Add mushrooms and pour over macaroni loaf

Mrs. W. B. Taylor, Bowling Green, Kentucky

*You may be surprised to know how many good starch dishes
may be prepared quickly and in many different styles by
promptly using any leftover rice, macaroni or spaghetti. If
you want to keep any of these from boiling over just add a teaspoonful of butter, cooking oil or olive oil, and you might remember to save the water which is drained off of these. It
might make excellent soup if meat stock, vegetables or bouillon
cubes are added later.*

432. Barbecue Sauce

(Makes 1 quart)

INGREDIENTS

1 cup Duncan Hines Barbecue Sauce
3 bay leaves
¼ cup mild vinegar
¼ cup lime or lemon juice
½ cup butter
1 teaspoon English mustard
1 teaspoon hickory smoked salt
1 teaspoon chili pepper
1 cup ketchup
1 teaspoon black pepper freshly ground
1 tablespoon Worcestershire sauce
1 clove garlic (whole)
1 onion (whole)

DIRECTIONS

Boil all together for 5 minutes. Thin with tomato juice if too thick.

Leave whole onion and garlic clove in container of sauce until used.

Mrs. R. A. Stephens, Los Angeles, California

433. Cheese Sauce

(Makes about 1 pint)

INGREDIENTS

½ cup butter
3 tablespoons flour
½ tablespoon prepared mustard
1½ cups milk

½ lb. grated cheese
½ teaspoon salt
1 dash red pepper
1 dash paprika
1 tablespoon onion juice
1 tablespoon Worcestershire sauce

1 tablespoon chopped pimento

½ cup tomatoes

½ cup chopped mushrooms

DIRECTIONS

Blend butter, flour and mustard together in a sauce pan.
Add milk and place on an asbestos mat, or low heat, stirring constantly.

Add these ingredients, when the mixture is rather warm. It will thicken gradually. When thick, remove from the heat.

This is a perfect sauce for cauliflower.

Added for au gratin potatoes.

Added for shrimp creole.

Added for crab meat au gratin.

Charlot C. Moore, Henderson, Kentucky

> *Don't forget to add salt to water before boiling rice, macaroni, etc.*

434. Hollandaise Sauce (Serves 6)

INGREDIENTS

DIRECTIONS

3 tablespoons butter
½ teaspoon cornstarch
¼ teaspoon salt

Cream together. Place in double boiler over warm (not boiling) water.

2 egg yolks

Add to mixture, one at a time.

2 tablespoons lemon juice
½ cup boiling water

Blend together and stir into mixture. Keep stirring. When the water in the bottom of double boiler starts to boil, cook 5 to 8 minutes. Let cook until consistency of boiled custard. This recipe will not curdle if directions are closely followed.

Shadow Hill Tea Room, Hernando, Mississippi

435. Hollandaise Sauce—Infallible (Serves 6 to 8)

INGREDIENTS

DIRECTIONS

4 egg yolks
½ teaspoon salt
⅛ teaspoon cayenne pepper (or less)

Beat egg yolks in electric mixer until quite thick and lemon colored. Add salt and cayenne.

1 cup hot melted butter
2 tablespoons lemon juice

Add 1/3 of butter slowly to above, beating constantly. When well blended, beat in rest of the butter alternately with the lemon juice a little at a time. Sauce may be made ahead of time and kept in refrigerator. When ready to serve, place container in *lukewarm* water and stir until softened.

Duncan Hines Test Kitchen, Ithaca, New York

436. Sauce Bearnaise

Follow instructions for Hollandaise Sauce—Infallible using tarragon vinegar instead of lemon juice and add

2 teaspoons minced parsley
1 teaspoon grated onion
½ teaspoon grated horseradish (optional)

Duncan Hines Test Kitchen, Ithaca, New York

> *Hollandaise sauce should be served immediately after it is made. Never let it stand in a warm place for any length of time, as warm egg yolks are the fastest breeder of bacteria among all of our foods. If it is necessary to make the sauce ahead of time, refrigerate it, then warm in double boiler just before using.*

437. Mint Sauce Gallois

INGREDIENTS

1 cup brown sugar
1 tablespoon vinegar
2 tablespoons lemon
  juice

mint leaves

DIRECTIONS

Boil to syrup and cool.

Chop fine and add to syrup.

Mr. John Gallois, San Francisco, California

438. Mustard Sauce   (Makes about 1 quart)

INGREDIENTS

1 pint heavy cream

½ cup sugar
4 tablespoons dry
  mustard (dissolve
  with a little cream)

5 egg yolks–well
  beaten
½ teaspoon salt

1 cup vinegar

DIRECTIONS

Heat.

Add to hot cream.

Stir into mixture and cook for about 3 minutes.

Add to the above. May be served either hot or cold.

The Derings, Green Lake, Wisconsin

439. Steak Sauce (London Style)   (Serves 4)

INGREDIENTS

¼ lb. butter
⅛ teaspoon black pep-
  per
2 tablespoons mild
  prepared mustard

4 tablespoons Escoffier
  Provençale sauce

¼ lemon–juice

DIRECTIONS

Melt butter, stir in pepper and mustard making a smooth paste.

Add to the above and stir.

Cut the steak in pieces to serve. Add the juice from the steak to the sauce and let it come just to a boiling point.

Add to sauce and serve piping hot on plate, alongside the steak.

Mario Piccardi, Chicago, Illinois

440. Cocktail Sauce for Sea Food   (Serves 10 to 12)

INGREDIENTS	DIRECTIONS
¼ cup malt vinegar ⅛ teaspoon salt	Mix together.
½ teaspoon Worcester- shire sauce	Stir into mixture.
½ teaspoon Tabasco ¼ cup grated horse- radish	Mix well into the above.
⅜ cup chili sauce ⅜ cup catsup	Stir into the ingredients.

Duncan Hines, Bowling Green, Kentucky

441. Cocktail Sauce for Shrimp   (Serves 6)

INGREDIENTS	DIRECTIONS
1 cup tomato catsup 2 tablespoons vinegar a few drops Tabasco sauce 1 tablespoon horse-radish ½ cup mayonnaise 1 teaspoon lemon juice 1 teaspoon Worcester- shire sauce	Mix all these ingredients together and chill.

Tarpon Inn, Port Aransas, Texas

*Don't forget that it is the flavor of a dish which causes you to
remember it with pleasure for a long time.*

442. Hot Sauce for Shrimp   (1½ pints)

INGREDIENTS	DIRECTIONS
1 can tomato soup 4 tablespoons prepared mustard 2 tablespoons horse- radish 1½ tablespoons onion salt ¾ cup mayonnaise ⅛ teaspoon cayenne pepper	Mix all ingredients together in order given. Stir well. If too thick, a teaspoon or two of French dressing may be added.

Studio Inn, Painesville, Ohio

443. Roux

This is a combination of flour and butter which is used as a foundation for sauces, soup, etc. It is simple to make—either light in color or dark brown —but it requires very careful attention.

Use equal parts of flour and butter, cook slowly over very low heat and stir constantly to make sure of perfect blending of both ingredients. The length of time the roux is cooked determines the color—the longer the time, the browner the roux. It can be kept by storing in a tightly covered container in a cool, dry place.

444. Sauce Smitane   (Serves 6)

INGREDIENTS

DIRECTIONS

2 tablespoons butter 1 medium-sized onion chopped	Place butter and onions in sauce pan and let saute until onions are tender but not brown.
1 heaping teaspoon flour	Stir flour into above and let cook a minute, stirring constantly.
1 pint sour cream salt and pepper to taste juice of ½ lemon	Add to above, bring to boil, then simmer, stirring occasionally, for 15 minutes. Strain through fine strainer. Add more salt and pepper if desired.

This is a wonderful sauce to serve with breast of guinea hen, breast of chicken, pheasant, quail, and wild rice.

Restaurant Voisin, New York, New York

445. Tomato Sauce   (Serves 6)

INGREDIENTS

DIRECTIONS

5 onions–sliced 2 tablespoons butter 1 bottle chili sauce 1 chili sauce bottle of water	Put in a heavy stew pan and simmer slowly for 1 hour, or longer if you want it thicker.
2/3 cup chicken soup	When nearly done add to mixture.

Hartwell Farm, Lincoln, Massachusetts

To be successful in any business, you must enjoy what you are doing. This applies to the culinary side of life as well. The best cooks are those who love to cook.

446. Steak Sauce   (1 pint)

INGREDIENTS

1 cup tomato catsup
1 cup chili sauce
1 tablespoon onion—
  finely chopped
1 tablespoon green
  pepper-finely
  chopped
1 tablespoon celery—
  finely chopped
1 tablespoon Worces-
  tershire sauce
1 tablespoon A-1 sauce

DIRECTIONS

Use only catsup and chili sauce of the very
highest quality. Mix ingredients together in
the order given. Put in jar and place in refrigerator. Use as desired.

Green Gables, Phoenix, Arizona

447. Steak Sauce

INGREDIENTS

2 tablespoons butter
juice from broiled
  steak
salt
black pepper

DIRECTIONS

Melt in sauce pan over low flame, and let
brown slightly. Add the juice from the broiled
steak, salt and pepper to taste. Cook gently
until thoroughly blended and pour over steak.

Mario Piccardi, Chicago, Illinois

448. White Sauce   (Makes about 1½ cups)

INGREDIENTS

2 tablespoons butter
2 slices of onion
3 tablespoons flour
1 cup chicken broth or
  1 can chicken
  bouillon
1 teaspoon parsley
1 inch of celery stalk
  salt and white pepper
⅛ cup cream

DIRECTIONS

Saute onion slightly in butter, add flour and
when well blended, add broth slowly, stirring
to prevent lumping. Chop celery and parsley
and add to sauce. Season to taste and simmer
for 5 minutes. Add cream and let boil up
twice. Strain and serve.
This may be used anywhere a white sauce is
indicated.

Mrs. Duncan Hines, Bowling Green, Kentucky

*Fine herbs are added to soups and sauces at the last minute, so
that their delicate oils do not evaporate.*

449. Spaghetti Sauce (Serves 10 to 12)

INGREDIENTS

DIRECTIONS

1 lb. ground beef
¼ cup olive oil
salt and pepper to
taste

Be sure that the beef is finely ground. Cook in olive oil until brown. Add seasoning.

1 medium onion
½ carrot
2 6-inch stalks celery

Chop vegetables finely, add to above and cook gently until golden brown.

3 sage leaves
1 tablespoon parsley
3 sweet basil leaves
1 clove garlic
1 piece lemon rind

Chop sage, parsley, basil, and garlic very fine. Lemon rind should be about ¼ inch wide and 2 inches long. Add to above and stir well.

¼ cup dried mush-
rooms
1 cup warm water

Wash mushrooms and soak in water until soft. Remove from water and chop fine. Add to above with water in which mushrooms were soaked.

¼ teaspoon nutmeg
1 cup canned tomatoes
1 cup Italian tomato
paste

Remove seeds from tomatoes. Add to above with nutmeg and tomato paste. Stir well and bring to boil.

1 cup boiling water

Add to above. Lower heat and simmer slowly, stirring occasionally, for 2-3 hours. When done remove lemon rind and add butter. Serve over spaghetti and sprinkle with grated Parmesan cheese.

¼ cup butter

An Italian friend from San Francisco, California

Never use herbs, spices, etc. to the extent that they overpower the natural flavor of vegetables, meats, fish or fowl.

450. Tabasco Butter

As a background of flavor for sandwich fillings.

INGREDIENTS

DIRECTIONS

A few drops Tabasco
sauce
butter

Mix in soft butter (not heated).

Spread lightly on sandwich bread and use with fillings of meats, eggs, fish, sea food, poultry, game or vegetables.

Mrs. Ida Migliario, Editor, Household, Topeka, Kansas

451. Brandy Sauce   (Serves 8)

INGREDIENTS

1 cup sugar
1 tablespoon corn-
  starch
¼ teaspoon salt
1 tablespoon butter
1 cup boiling water

¼ cup or more brandy

DIRECTIONS

Mix together dry ingredients. Add butter and boiling water. Mix well and cook 6 minutes or until clear.

Add brandy after you remove sauce pan from fire.
Serve quite warm over any little plain cake or pudding.

Dolores Restaurant, Oklahoma City, Oklahoma

452. Butterscotch Ice Cream Sauce   (Makes 1 quart+)

INGREDIENTS

1¾ cups syrup (white)
2 cups sugar
1 cup butter
1 cup cream

1 cup cream

1 teaspoon vanilla

DIRECTIONS

Cook together until it reaches the soft ball stage.

Add to above and cook until the candy thermometer says 218 F.

Add to mixture. Delicious either hot or cold. Serve with roasted buttered and salted pecans.

The Farm Kitchen, Baraboo, Wisconsin

453. Chocolate Sherry Sauce   (Makes 1 pint+)

INGREDIENTS

4 squares unsweetened
  chocolate
2 cups powdered sugar
¾ cup cream
1 tablespoon butter

¼ cup sherry

DIRECTIONS

Melt chocolate in top of double boiler, add sugar, cream and butter. Stir well and cook 7 minutes. Let cool.

Cool sauce and add sherry. Serve in parfait glasses over vanilla ice cream.

For a glamorous dessert, place a square of angel food cake on dessert plate. Put on cake a scoop of vanilla ice cream, pour sauce on ice cream and top with a red cherry. This is called "Angel Food Sherry Delight."

Old Southern Tea Room, Vicksburg, Mississippi

454. Chocolate Sauce for Ice Cream (No sugar needed)

INGREDIENTS

½ lb. marshmallows

2 squares unsweetened
  chocolate
2 squares bitter choco-
  late
2 squares sweet choco-
  late
½ cup cream

DIRECTIONS

Cut into small pieces.

Shave the chocolate.
Place all ingredients in a double boiler and
let stand over boiling water until dissolved.
Stir often. Serve on ice cream. Will keep well
in covered jar in refrigerator.

Mrs. Elsie Smythe, Bowling Green, Kentucky

455. O'Brien's Fudge Sauce (Makes almost 2 quarts)

INGREDIENTS

1 lb. sugar
1½ cups plus 2 table-
  spoons heavy cream

1 lb. unsweetened
  chocolate
3 tablespoons butter

DIRECTIONS

Cook cream and sugar in double boiler for
½ hour.

In another double boiler, melt chocolate. Add
to above and stir in butter. Cook in double
boiler for another 15 minutes. Store in covered
jar and use as needed.

Can be served hot as "Hot Fudge Sundae" or cold as "Frozen Fudge
Sundae."

O'Brien's, Waverly, New York

456. Pineapple-Marshmallow Sauce (Makes 2 cups)

INGREDIENTS

24 marshmallows
1 8 oz. can crushed
  pineapple
1 tablespoon maras-
  chino juice
1 tablespoon chopped
  cherries

DIRECTIONS

Melt marshmallows. Add 2 tablespoons pineapple juice. Stir until creamy. Add drained
pineapple, cherry juice and cherries. Let cool
and serve on cake.

Jersey Dell Tea Room, Spirit Lake, Iowa

*You only get out of a meal what you put into its planning,
preparation, and loving care in the cooking.*

457. Sauce for Mince Pie   (Serves 6)

INGREDIENTS	DIRECTIONS
3 tablespoons butter 2 teaspoons sugar	Melt and mix well.
1 tablespoon lemon juice ¼ cup hot water 2 oz. rum 2 oz. brandy 1 pinch nutmeg	Add to above and when hot, pour over slices of pie.

Mario Piccardi, Chicago, Illinois

In making sauces, it is important not to make them too thick or too thin. You must try and try again to approximate perfection. If too thin, add a mixture of flour and cold water, if too thick, more liquid. But by all means avoid lumps.

458. Hard Sauce   (Serves 8-10)

INGREDIENTS	DIRECTIONS
½ cup butter 1½ cups powdered sugar	Cream butter, and add sugar gradually, beating well. The longer the beating, the creamier the sauce will be.

Variations may be made in this sauce by adding 2 tablespoons of brandy. Cointreau, Grand Marnier, or any other flavoring desired. If vanilla is used, ½ teaspoon should be sufficient.

Hard sauce is really an uncooked sauce as given above. However, below is a cooked hard sauce which you might like. It is used in the same manner as the first recipe; that is, over plum puddings, gingerbread, and the like.

COOKED HARD SAUCE:

INGREDIENTS	DIRECTIONS
1 lb. brown sugar ½ lb. butter ½ teaspoon nutmeg	Cook together in double boiler until smooth, stirring constantly. Take from heat.
2 egg yolks	Beat egg yolks well and add to above.
½ cup whiskey	Add to above. You may use more or less of the whiskey as you desire.

This may be stored in a covered jar in the refrigerator and used as needed.

Mrs. Duncan Hines, Bowling Green, Kentucky

459. Baked Eggs au Gratin

(Serves 1)

INGREDIENTS

DIRECTIONS

2 hard boiled eggs

Cut lengthwise and remove yolks. Mash the yolks.

2 fresh mushrooms–chopped
2 tablespoons chopped onion
2 tablespoons butter
salt and pepper to taste

Saute and let cool. Add to egg yolks. Fill the whites with this mixture. Place in casserole side by side and cover with a rich cream sauce.

1 tablespoon grated American cheese

Sprinkle top with grated cheese and bake in 350 F. oven for 30 minutes.

From a friend in Cincinnati, Ohio

460. Bogberry Omelet

(Serves 2)

INGREDIENTS

DIRECTIONS

1 egg
3 egg yolks

Beat together for 1 minute.

½ teaspoon salt
2 tablespoons butter

Add salt and make thin unfolded omelet.

3 egg whites–beaten
2 tablespoons butter

Place in center of omelet and gently fold half over. Place in 200 F. oven and bake 8 minutes. (Too hot an oven will ruin the omelet.)

2 slices ham–broiled or fried
2 tablespoons Bogberry jelly

Garnish with ham and jelly and serve with sweet potatoes.

2 candied sweet potatoes

Stirrup-Cup Castle, Norwalk, Connecticut

Do not attempt to serve poached eggs unless you know they are strictly fresh.

Whether you cook eggs in water, pan, double boiler, or in the oven, moderate heat prevents toughness.

Never wash eggs until ready for use. Many of the better chefs believe they should be taken from the refrigerator and let come to room temperature before using.

461. Egg Cutlets (Serves 2)

INGREDIENTS | DIRECTIONS

3 tablespoons butter
3 tablespoons flour
1 cup stock or milk

Melt butter, add flour, blend. Add liquid to make smooth thick sauce. Cook slowly.

4 eggs

Boil until hard, chop fine and put through a sieve.

½ cup smoked ham

Cut in small pieces, add to eggs and sauce. Let cool. Make small cutlets and place in refrigerator. Just before serving, dip in bread crumbs and beaten egg and fry in deep fat 3 or 4 minutes.

Serve with Bechamel, tomato or cheese sauce.

Mrs. T. G. Hazard, Jr., Narragansett, Rhode Island

462. Nut and Mushroom Omelet (Serves 4)

INGREDIENTS | DIRECTIONS

6 eggs

Beat well.

1 teaspoon salt
¼ teaspoon pepper
½ cup cream

Add to eggs and beat again.

10 tablespoons nuts

Chop fine and add to the above. Turn into hot buttered fry pan and reduce heat.

¾ lb. mushrooms

Broil and place on half the omelet and fold other half over.

4 cups buttered new cooked peas

Place omelet on platter and surround with peas.

Sundal Guest House, West Lebanon, Maine

463. Eggs a la Gallois (Serves 6)

INGREDIENTS | DIRECTIONS

1 doz. eggs

Break into *cold* frying pan.

4 drops water
¼ lb. butter
3 doz. small croutons previously diced and browned in butter

Put in pan with eggs.

Add to above.

⅛ lb. bacon, diced and previously fried in another pan small amount of diced truffles if available before scrambling

Stick fork into butter and place eggs over very slow heat, stir slowly with fork in butter. Stir continuously for about 10 minutes, stirring always in the same direction, until eggs are *scrambled soft.* Do not allow to stick. Remove pan from fire and remove eggs from pan with spoon. Place in hot earthenware dish, serve at once.

Mr. John Gallois, San Francisco, California

464. Fried Eggs

This is the way I cook the eggs.

Take a sauce pan and into it put butter or bacon drippings so that when melted there will be about a quarter of an inch of fat in the bottom. Have the fat warm, but *not* hot. Break into the sauce pan as many eggs as it will hold, two, four, six, or whatever your requirements will be. When the eggs are in the pan, baste the yellows constantly with the warm fat until a film forms over them. The reason for the low heat is so that the whites will not become frizzled and tough before the yolks are done. When they are done, they look like poached eggs, and are they good! If you want to dress them up a bit, sprinkle a little paprika over them.

If you are fortunate enough to have real country ham steaks to fry, cook the pieces so that the fat will brown the bottom of the frying pan. If you want to, you can even put in extra bits of fat and let them frizzle to a crisp. This will aid in making your fat brown. Now, break your eggs into the skillet but be sure that it is not too hot. Cook for a few minutes until whites solidify underneath, and then turn them over with a spatula and let cook a few more minutes. Here, too, the fat should not be so hot as to frizzle the whites before the yolks are done. The result will be beautifully browned eggs, with a flavor that you will never forget.

Of course, if you do not have butter, bacon drippings, or fried ham fat, then you will have to make do with just any kind of fat, but they just won't be the same, I promise you.

Duncan Hines, Bowling Green, Kentucky

465. Oeufs a la Russe (Eggs Russian Style)
(Serves 4)

INGREDIENTS	DIRECTIONS
4 teaspoons caviar 4 artichoke hearts–cooked	Place caviar on artichoke hearts and heat in oven.
4 poached eggs Hollandaise sauce	Place poached egg on each artichoke heart and cover with Hollandaise sauce.
4 slices of truffles	Tip with slice of truffle and serve.

Antoine's Restaurant, New Orleans, Louisiana

No one yet has made one egg do the work of two.

As soon as eggs are boiled hard, place in cold water. This prevents discoloring. Peel under cold running water.

466. Omelette

INGREDIENTS

DIRECTIONS

2 tablespoons flour–
mixed with a little
water

2 tablespoons butter
salt and pepper to
taste
1 cup milk

Blend and cook until quite thick. Allow to
cool.

4 egg yolks–beaten

Add to the above and stir thoroughly.

4 egg whites–beaten

Fold into mixture. Pour into hot well-buttered
large frying pan and set over heat until the mixture
sets. Place in 400 F. to 450 F. oven until straw tests
done. Remove from oven and run spatula around the
entire pan loosening omelette, then make an incision on
opposite side of the omelette and slide the spatula beneath one side and slide it over on other half at the
same time sliding omelette out on dish. Garnish with
crisp bacon or parsley or Spanish sauce. To make a
larger omelette use 6 eggs and make a little more sauce.

Mrs. Edmund H. Singmaster, Philadelphia, Pennsylvania

*In poaching eggs, stir water in one direction before sliding the
eggs in from a saucer. This will prevent the whites spreading.*

467. Poached Eggs, Caviar

INGREDIENTS

DIRECTIONS

1 piece buttered toast
1 slice nearly ripe
tomato
1 poached egg
½ teaspoon caviar
1 filet anchovy
sprig parsley

Cut a large round out of the piece of toast.
On it place the slice of tomato. On the tomato place a poached egg. Garnish with caviar,
top with anchovy filet and parsley.

(A thin slice of ham may be put under tomato slice)

A. Lee Read, Los Angeles, California

Hard boiled eggs may be started in cold water but a good soft
boiled egg is put in just as the water starts to boil and should
be timed accurately, removed from the heat promptly and
not allowed to remain in the hot water where it will continue
to cook. A few tests will soon teach you how to get soft boiled
eggs just right every time.

468. Poached Eggs in Red Wine (Serves 2)

INGREDIENTS

1 pt. red burgundy
    wine
1 sliced onion
1 carrot sliced
    lump of sugar
    pinch of salt
    pinch of thyme leaves
    or 1 bay leaf

4 eggs
    marrow

DIRECTIONS

Put wine into a deep pan. Add onion, carrots, sugar, salt, and thyme. Let it boil for 10 minutes. Strain the vegetables out.

Poach eggs in boiling wine. Remove and thicken the sauce with a little cornstarch.

Place eggs on a toasted English muffin, pour sauce over and on top place very nice slices of marrow. Just allow half a minute under the broiler.

Antoine Gilly, La Cremaillere a la Campagne, Banksville, New York

469. Poached Eggs Belle Othero or Eggs Suzette
(Serves 2)

INGREDIENTS

2 baked potatoes

4 eggs
    salt and pepper to
    taste

4 tablespoons
    Hollandaise sauce
1 tablespoon grated
    Parmesan cheese

DIRECTIONS

Make an oval incision about 3 inches long and scoop out about ½ the potato.
Break two eggs in each potato and season.

Blend together and pour over eggs and put potatoes in 325-350 F. oven for about 8 minutes.

Mario Piccardi, Chicago, Illinois

470. Scrambled Eggs and Mushrooms (Serves 1)

INGREDIENTS

3 eggs—for each person
3 teaspoons hard butter

3 strips of bacon

½ small can mushrooms

2 teaspoons chopped
    onion
    salt and pepper to
    taste

DIRECTIONS

Whip eggs and put in small pieces of butter.

Cut in small pieces and fry crisp. Remove bacon and leave drippings in pan.

Cook mushrooms in bacon drippings with cover on pan for 15 minutes. Remove cover and brown.

Mix with eggs and bacon and add to pan containing mushrooms. Stir while cooking. Do not cook too long, and eat at once.

Carder's Restaurant, Chicago, Illinois

471. Scrambled Eggs
(Serves 3)

INGREDIENTS

DIRECTIONS

2 tablespoons butter
6 tablespoons cream

Melt butter in double boiler and add cream.

6 eggs

Break in the eggs and when they become hot, start breaking them up.

salt and pepper to taste

Add seasoning and let cook until they are the consistency you like—either soft or hard scrambled.

McDonald Tea Room, Gallatin, Missouri

You may buy eggs for quality and size, but the first requisite is freshness. There are many misconceptions about the superiority of white eggs over brown ones. Color, however, is not important and you may be surprised to learn that in some sections of the country brown eggs bring a higher price. Regardless of where your grocer keeps his eggs, store yours in the refrigerator, take them out as you need them and don't buy too many at one time. It is best to figure on buying not more than a week's supply. Do not wash eggs before storing in your refrigerator.

472. Welsh Rabbit
(Serves 6)

INGREDIENTS

DIRECTIONS

1 tablespoon butter

Melt in double boiler.

1½ tablespoons flour
½ teaspoon cayenne
½ teaspoon salt

Mix dry ingredients together and add to melted butter. Stir.

2 lbs. sharp American cheese

Cut cheese up into small pieces and add gradually to above mixture until all cheese has been used and is beginning to melt.

1 cup milk (sweet)

Heat milk slightly and add to above, stirring in thoroughly.

2 eggs
1 tablespoon Worcestershire sauce

Beat eggs together and add the Worcestershire to the eggs. Gradually stir this mixture into the above, and cook until smooth. Serve on thin toast or crisp crackers.

(The success of your rabbit, as a general rule, depends upon the quality of the cheese used. Poor quality cheese sometimes will make the rabbit stringy instead of smooth and creamy as it should be. Be sure to use a rich, well-aged cheese.)

Mrs. Duncan Hines, Bowling Green, Kentucky

473. Swiss Cheese Fondue (Serves 1)

INGREDIENTS

4 oz. Gruyere cheese
4 oz. Emmenthaler cheese
½ cup dry white wine
1½ oz. Kirschwasser

1 teaspoon cornstarch
1 teaspoon Kirschwasser
salt and freshly ground black pepper to taste

DIRECTIONS

Rub heavy saucepan or chafing dish with a clove of garlic. Cut cheese into small pieces and place in saucepan. Add wine and Kirschwasser. Cook over low heat, stirring constantly until it starts to bubble.

When fondue starts to bubble, add cornstarch which has been dissolved in Kirschwasser. Season to taste and let cook until fairly thick. Do not over cook and stir constantly. Serve at once with chunks of rye bread.

Restaurant Stadt-Und Rathauskeller, Lucerne, Switzerland

Some people shy away from cheese while others will buy some of every variety they can find. The eating of cheese and cheese dishes is a custom which could well be restored to the American table and now that all of the famous old world varieties have been practically duplicated or improved upon by American cheese makers there is no reason to do without your favorite.

474. Armenian Fritters

INGREDIENTS

2 eggs–beaten
1 pint milk
½ cup sugar
1 tablespoon olive oil

3 cups flour
2 tablespoons baking powder
1 teaspoon vanilla

bananas, apples, pineapple, pears, peaches, oranges, or any fresh fruit

DIRECTIONS

Beat eggs, add sugar, milk and oil. Stir well.

Sift flour and baking powder together. Add to egg mixture and beat until smooth.

Fill frying pan half full of peanut oil or frying fat and heat until very hot, about 375°.

Dip fruit in batter and fry in hot fat or oil until brown.

Remove carefully so as not to break crust and drain. Serve plain as vegetable or with whipped cream as dessert.

Omar Khayyam's, San Francisco, California

Place fresh eggs on the lower shelf of refrigerator.

*Fry eggs in warm—not hot—skillet.
Scramble eggs in hot skillet.*

475. Squash Fritters

INGREDIENTS | DIRECTIONS

1 lb. Hubbard squash
½ teaspoon salt

Cover with water and boil until tender. Put through a sieve.

4 cups flour
1 tablespoon baking powder

Sift into the pulp.

1 cup milk

Blend into the mixture. Set in a warm place for 15 minutes. Cut dough in 1-inch strips and twist into cruller or pretzel shapes. Brown in deep hot fat and serve with maple syrup.

Food Magician, Los Angeles, California

476. Beet Relish   (Makes about 4 pints)

INGREDIENTS | DIRECTIONS

1 teaspoon salt
¼ teaspoon pepper
¾ cup sugar
½ tablespoon flour

Mix thoroughly.

½ cup vinegar

Add to dry ingredients and cook in double boiler until thick.

4 cups cooked beets— diced small
2 cups celery–chopped
½ cup onion–chopped

Mix thoroughly with above and cool.

The Old House, Lexington, Massachusetts

477. Brandied Peaches

INGREDIENTS | DIRECTIONS

4 lbs. sugar
2 cups water

Make syrup of sugar and water.

8 lbs. peaches

Peel peaches and put in cold water to prevent discoloring. Add a few at a time to the syrup and let simmer until tender. Do not let get too soft, or they will break. Place on plate to cool.

1 pint or more brandy

Take syrup from fire and add 1 pint of brandy to every quart of syrup and stir until cool. Put cooled peaches in jars (sterilized) and pour syrup over them. Seal jars tightly.

Mrs. Thomas A. Hannon, Chicago, Illinois

478. Crab Apple Relish

INGREDIENTS

DIRECTIONS

6 pints crab apples (measure after cored)

Core and put through grinder. Not too fine.

3 oranges

Put through grinder and mix in with apples.

6 pints sugar
1 lb. seedless raisins
1 teaspoon cloves
1 teaspoon cinnamon
1 pint vinegar

Add to above and let stand overnight. Then cook until consistency of marmalade. Seal while hot.

Hyannis House, Epworth, Iowa

479. Cranberry Relish   (About 16 Servings)

INGREDIENTS

DIRECTIONS

1 quart raw cranberries

Grind through meat chopper.

2 oranges–pulp and juice
1 orange rind–chopped
1 lemon–juice
1⅔ cups sugar

Mix with cranberries and let stand 24 hours before using. Will keep in jar in refrigerator for weeks.

Althaea, Lewisburg, West Virginia

480. Aunt Delia's Piccallili

INGREDIENTS

DIRECTIONS

1 peck green tomatoes
1 cup salt

Chop tomatoes, sprinkle with salt and let stand overnight. In the morning, drain.

3 quarts vinegar
5 cups sugar

Let come to a boil.

1 tablespoon mustard seed
2 tablespoons cassia
1 tablespoon ground cloves
½ tablespoon allspice
2 large sticks horse-radish

Add to hot vinegar and boil for 5 minutes.

3 peppers
3 onions

Chop and add to tomatoes. Mix in with vinegar and boil slowly for 1 hour.

Peckett's on Sugar Hill, Franconia, New Hampshire

481. Sawyer Tavern Relish

(Makes 1 pint)

INGREDIENTS	DIRECTIONS
1 tablespoon flour 1 tablespoon sugar	Combine.
1 egg–beaten	Add to above and mix well.
½ cup milk	Stir in milk gradually and cook in double boiler 7 to 10 minutes, or until thick.
2 tablespoons vinegar 1 tablespoon butter-melted	Remove from fire and stir in vinegar and butter.
1 pkg. cream cheese	Pour hot dressing over cheese and mix.
2 hard cooked eggs 1 tablespoon onion 1 green pepper 1 pimento speck red pepper salt and pepper to taste	Chop eggs, onion, green pepper and pimento. Add to mixture and season to taste with red pepper, salt and freshly ground black pepper. This relish can be used to stuff tomatoes for a salad, as a sandwich filling, or served as a relish.

Sawyer Tavern, Keene, New Hampshire

482. Tomato Relish

INGREDIENTS	DIRECTIONS
1 peck tomatoes (not too ripe–do not peel) 6 onions 6 red peppers (remove seeds)	Grind through meat chopper. Squeeze and remove what juice you can from the tomatoes.
1 quart vinegar 3 lbs. brown sugar 2 tablespoons white mustard seed 1 tablespoon cinnamon ⅞ cup salt	Boil and let cool. Mix with above ingredients and put in jars and seal.

Mrs. Voijt Frank Mashek, Chicago, Illinois

Do not store canned foods in a damp place.

Your opportunity to avoid dyspepsia and other stomach ailments will be greatly enhanced if you follow these two simple rules—Eat slowly. Eat less.

483. Cranberry Jelly

INGREDIENTS

2 cups cranberries
¾ cup boiling water

¾ cup sugar

DIRECTIONS

Wash thoroughly.
Pour over cranberries and cook for 5 minutes.

Add to the above and cook for 5 more minutes. Strain and mold. This is a never-fail method.

Mrs. C. H. Welch, Tucson, Arizona

484. Cranberry Sauce

INGREDIENTS

1½ cups water
1 cup sugar

2 cups cranberries

DIRECTIONS

Put sugar and water in a sauce pan and stir until sugar is partially dissolved. Put over heat and bring to a boil. Let boil for about 10 minutes.

Wash thoroughly. Drop into syrup and let boil until the berries pop.

Duncan Hines, Bowling Green, Kentucky

485. Cranberry Mold   (Serves 12-14)

INGREDIENTS

2 packages lemon
  gelatin
1 cup hot water
1 cup cold water

1 quart raw cranberries
1 whole orange
2 cups sugar

DIRECTIONS

Dissolve gelatin in hot water, add cold water and allow to stand until it begins to set.

Put cranberries and the orange (including peeling) through coarse grinder. Add sugar and allow to stand until sugar is dissolved. Mix with gelatin and pour into ring mold or individual molds and put in refrigerator to chill.

Whitcomb Sulphur Springs Hotel, St. Joseph, Michigan

The right food—
   Builds and repairs your body
   Keeps it in good running order
   Gives you energy for work and play
   Helps prolong your prime of life
   Is a basis for good health.
                    —Anon.

486. Dill Pickles

INGREDIENTS

18 cups water
2 cups salt–do not use
iodized salt

6 cups vinegar

cucumbers
dill to taste

DIRECTIONS

Make a brine and boil for 5 minutes. Cool.

To every 3 cups of brine, add 1 cup of vinegar.

Pack cucumbers and dill into jars, pour on the brine and seal. If cucumbers are not absolutely fresh, soak in ice water for 2 hours.

Mrs. Voijt F. Mashek, Chicago, Illinois

487. Jiffy Crisp Sweet Pickles   (Makes 10 gal.)

INGREDIENTS

5 gal. jar sour pickles

30 lbs. sugar

1 teaspoon allspice
1 teaspoon cloves

DIRECTIONS

Drain off the vinegar and slice in thin slices.

Have two 5-gallon stone crocks. Put sugar in bottom, two or three rows of pickles. Sprinkle with sugar, and repeat process until you have 2½ gallons of sliced pickles in each crock.

Add same amount to each 5-gallon crock. In a few days, gently stir. Set aside for ten days. They are delicious.

Shadow Hill Tea Room, Hernando, Mississippi

488. Mustard Pickles   (Makes 8 pints)

INGREDIENTS

25 cucumbers
5 onions
4 sweet red peppers
6 tablespoons salt

½ cup flour
3 cups sugar
1½ teaspoons dry
mustard
½ teaspoon turmeric
1 quart vinegar
2 bunches celery

DIRECTIONS

Peel and dice cucumbers. Peel and chop onions and red peppers. Mix together, add salt, cover with water and let stand overnight in stone jar.

Drain vegetables thoroughly. Clean and chop celery and add to above. Combine dry ingredients with vinegar in large kettle and stir until smooth. Add vegetables and cook 15 minutes, stirring to prevent burning. Pour into hot sterilized jars and seal.

O'Brien's, Waverly, New York

489. Pottsfield Pickle (Makes 4 quarts)

INGREDIENTS

3 pints green tomatoes
3 pints ripe tomatoes
1 quart onions
3 red peppers
3 green peppers
1 bunch celery
1 cabbage
½ cup salt

3 pints vinegar
3 pints sugar
½ cup white mustard
seed
½ teaspoon cinnamon
1 teaspoon ground
cloves
¼ cup mixed spices
(tied in bag)

DIRECTIONS

Chop coarsely or put through a meat grinder.
Add salt and let stand overnight. Drain well.

Add these ingredients to drained vegetables
and cook slowly for 1 hour.

Bottle in jars and seal tightly.

Sawyer Tavern, Keene, New Hampshire

490. Sliced Cucumber Pickles

INGREDIENTS

2 quarts boiling water
1 cup salt
1 peck cucumbers–
sliced

1 gallon boiling water
1 tablespoon alum

4 quarts vinegar
6 lbs. brown sugar
4 sticks cinnamon
2 tablespoons allspice
2 tablespoons whole
cloves
4 tablespoons white
mustard seed
4 tablespoons celery
seed
4 tablespoons mixed
spices
6 pieces horse-radish
6 cloves of garlic

DIRECTIONS

Pour mixture of boiling water and salt over
the cucumbers and let stand 3 days. Pour off
the brine and let come to boiling point. Pour
over cucumbers again and let stand 3 days.
Pour off brine again and let come to boiling
point and pour over cucumbers and let stand
3 days. This makes a total of 9 days in brine.
Drain.

Pour this mixture over cucumbers and let
stand 6 hours. Drain and place cucumbers
in stone jar.

Heat these ingredients and pour over cucumbers.

Drain each day, reheat and pour over cucumbers for nine days.

Virginia Duvall Greenhow, Frankfort, Kentucky

491. Sweet Watermelon Pickle (Makes 4 quarts)

INGREDIENTS

7 lbs. watermelon rind

7 cups sugar
2 cups white vinegar

½ teaspoon oil of cinnamon
½ teaspoon oil of cloves
(these oils keep the rind clear and transparent)

DIRECTIONS

Trim off the green, cut in 1-inch cubes and soak in strong salt water overnight. Pour off salt water and boil in fresh water until tender, but not soft.

Make a syrup, add rind and cook 10 minutes. Take from heat, cover and let stand overnight. Drain off the syrup, bring to a boil and pour over rind. Continue this process for 5 nights.

Add to ingredients the fifth morning, bring to boil and cook 10 minutes. Pack in hot sterile jars.

Kellogg's Pan-Tree, Canandaigua, New York

492. Gooseberry Jam (Makes 13 pints)

INGREDIENTS

8 lbs. gooseberries
7 lbs. sugar

DIRECTIONS

Snip blossom end from the gooseberries and mix with the sugar. Let stand for 12 hours.

Boil in an open kettle for 20 minutes after it comes to a good rolling boil. Stir constantly. Skim if necessary. Pour into sterilized jars and seal tightly.

Hartwell Farm, Lincoln, Massachusetts

493. Melon and Walnut Conserve (Makes 3 pints)

INGREDIENTS

2 pints diced peaches
2 pints diced cantaloupe
4 lemons
6 cups sugar

1⅛ cup English walnuts

DIRECTIONS

Combine peaches, cantaloupe and sugar, add juice and grated rinds of lemons. Cook slowly until thick and clear.

Blanch and chop walnuts, add to mixture and pour into sterilized jars and seal while hot.

Paint Pony Lodge, Show Low, Arizona

494. Orange Marmalade

INGREDIENTS

12 oranges–not too
    ripe, but firm
6 lemons

sugar

DIRECTIONS

Remove ends and slice. Take out seeds.
Measure fruit and add half as much water.
Let stand overnight. Then boil fruit in same
water until tender. Remove from heat and
weigh. To each pound of fruit and liquid, add
1 lb. sugar. Boil until it jellies, which should
be about 20 minutes.

Mission Inn, Riverside, California

495. Peach Conserve

INGREDIENTS

12 peaches–peeled and
    sliced
1 lb. seedless grapes–
    cut in half
1 lb. red plums, stoned
    and cut fine
2 oranges, unpeeled—
    cut fine
3½ lbs. sugar
12 kernels of peach pits
    –chopped

DIRECTIONS

Mix all ingredients and cook slowly over
low heat until thick. Seal in jelly glasses.

Marjorie Mills, Boston, Massachusetts

496. Rhubarb Conserve   (Makes 5 or 6 pints)

INGREDIENTS

6 cups diced rhubarb
1 cup raisins–chopped
1 cup crushed canned
    pineapple
1 cup orange juice
½ cup grated orange
    rind
1 lemon–juice and
    grated rind
4 cups sugar
1 teaspoon salt

1 cup broken nut meats

DIRECTIONS

Mix all together and let come to a boil. Cook
slowly for 4 or 5 hours until it becomes very
thick.

Add to mixture about 30 minutes before it is
done. Seal in hot jars.

Old Hundred, Southbury, Connecticut

497. Spiced Blackberries

INGREDIENTS	DIRECTIONS
4 cups brown sugar 2 cups vinegar	Boil together for 5 minutes.
5 lbs. blackberries	Add to the syrup.
2 sticks cinnamon 1 tablespoon whole cloves ½ tablespoon whole allspice	Tie spices in a bag and let mixture simmer for 20 to 25 minutes, until it has cooked down thick. Remove spice bag and pour berries into clean sterilized jars. Seal at once.

Pauline Johnson, Berkeley, California

498. Strawberry Jam

INGREDIENTS	DIRECTIONS
1 quart strawberries	Pour boiling water over berries to cover and let stand 3 minutes. Drain.
1 cup sugar	Add to berries and boil 5 minutes. Remove from heat.
2 cups sugar	Add to berries and boil 20 minutes. Remove and pour the berries in earthenware crock and let stand 24 hours, stirring occasionally. Pour into glasses and paraffin.

Headley Inn, Zanesville, Ohio

499. Strawberry Preserves

INGREDIENTS	DIRECTIONS
1 qt. strawberries	Wash and drain on cloth until thoroughly dry. Put in kettle.
2 tablespoons vinegar	Add to berries and, when they begin to bubble, cook 2 minutes.
4 cups sugar	Add to berries and, when they begin to bubble again, cook 4 minutes. If you like the syrup thick, remove berries and cook down the juice for another 10 or 15 minutes. Pour into large flat pan and let cool for 24 hours. Seal in hot jars.

Dolores Restaurant and Drive-In, Oklahoma City, Oklahoma

Few are the cooks who can view their results impersonally.

500. Homemade Tomato Juice

INGREDIENTS

15 lbs. ripe tomatoes
1 onion–sliced

4 tablespoons brown
    sugar
4 tablespoons salt
3 tablespoons celery
    salt
1 teaspoon red pepper

DIRECTIONS

Do not peel tomatoes. Cook thoroughly. Strain.

Add to strained juice and boil 8 to 10 minutes. Bottle in hot sterilized bottles or jars and seal at once. Keeps indefinitely.

Serve ice cold with sprig of crisp parsley.

Mrs. Wm. Guy Ruggles, Ridgeway, Wisconsin

501. Tutti-Frutti

INGREDIENTS

1 quart brandy

1 quart strawberries
1 quart pineapple
    (peeled and sliced)
1 quart cherries
1 quart currants
1 quart raspberries
1 quart gooseberries
1 quart apricots
    (peeled and sliced)
1 quart peaches
    (peeled and sliced)
32 cups of sugar

DIRECTIONS

Place brandy in large stone crock with a cover to it.

Add fruit as they come in season with an equal amount of sugar to the brandy. Stir mixture every day until the last of the fruit has been added.

Cover well and store in a cool place. Will keep indefinitely.

To be served as sauce for ice cream, puddings, or with meat course.

Mrs. Thomas A. Hannon, Chicago, Illinois

502. De Luxe Salted Peanuts

INGREDIENTS

1 lb. raw peanuts in
    shell

1 teaspoon butter

1 teaspoon salt

DIRECTIONS

Shell and scald with boiling water. Remove red skin and let dry thoroughly. (May take overnight.) Put in 350 F. hot oven and keep shaking until browned.

Glaze nuts with butter. Do not use too much butter in glazing, but just enough so that the salt will stick. Sift on the salt.

Mrs. Edmund H. Singmaster, Philadelphia, Pennsylvania

503. Apricot Upside-Down Cake

(Makes one 10-inch cake)

INGREDIENTS

DIRECTIONS

6 tablespoons butter
¾ cup brown sugar
  cooked dried apricots

I use a heavy iron skillet, but a 10-inch square cake pan will do. Melt butter in bottom of pan, sprinkle over with sugar, and arrange on sugar enough apricots to cover bottom of pan, about 2 cups full.

⅓ cup butter
1 cup sugar plus
  2 tablespoons
1 egg

Cream butter, add sugar and beat until fluffy. Beat egg and add to butter and sugar.

2 cups cake flour
2 teaspoons baking
  powder
½ teaspoon salt
¾ cup milk
1 teaspoon vanilla

Sift dry ingredients together and add to butter and sugar alternately with milk, starting and ending with flour. Add vanilla and pour batter over apricots in pan. Bake in 350° oven for about 35 to 40 minutes or until cake tests done. Turn out on large round cake plate.

For a really de luxe cake, add ½ cup English walnut meats to the apricots. When cake is done, sprinkle top liberally with freshly grated coconut. Serve with whipped cream or make a sauce from the juice drained from apricots.

Mrs. Duncan Hines, Bowling Green, Kentucky

503A. Boiled White Icing

(For two 9-inch layers)

INGREDIENTS

DIRECTIONS

2¾ cups sugar
 2 tablespoons corn
   syrup
 1 teaspoon vinegar
 1 cup water

Combine in saucepan, stir until sugar is dissolved. Let come to a boil and cook to 238° temperature.

3 egg whites
¼ cup sugar
¼ teaspoon cream of
  tartar
  pinch salt

Beat egg whites frothy. Slowly beat in dry ingredients and beat until egg whites are stiff and dry. When syrup comes to temperature, slowly pour ⅓ of syrup over egg whites, beating all the while. Return syrup to heat, and let come to temperature again. Pour another ⅓ of syrup over whites. Return syrup to heat, let come to boil again and cook for a few minutes more. Beat into egg whites and then beat icing until cold, when it should be ready to spread on cake. If directions are followed carefully, this a fool proof recipe.

Mrs. Duncan Hines, Bowling Green, Kentucky

504. Angel Food Cake with Eggnog Filling (Serves 16)

INGREDIENTS

DIRECTIONS

1½ cups egg whites (approx. 12 eggs)
1 teaspoon cream of tartar
pinch salt

Whip whites with wire whisk, add cream of tartar and salt. Beat until stiff but not dry.

1 cup sifted cake flour
1½ cups less 2 tablespoons sifted sugar

Sift flour and sugar together several times. Fold small amount at a time into egg whites with a spoon.

½ teaspoon almond extract
1 teaspoon vanilla
1 tablespoon strained lemon juice

Add flavorings, pour into a 9- or 10-inch tube pan and bake at 325° for about an hour. Remove from oven, invert pan and let stand until cold. Remove from pan and slice in four layers crosswise.

EGGNOG FILLING:

½ lb. butter
1 lb. powdered sugar sifted

Cream butter, add sugar gradually to butter and whip until creamy.

5 egg yolks

Beat yolks, add to above and mix well.

½ cup bourbon whiskey
¼ lb. chopped toasted almonds
¼ lb. macaroon crumbs

Fold bourbon, almonds and crumbs into the above. Mix well and spread between the layers of cake.

1 pint cream
2 tablespoons sugar
2 tablespoons whiskey

Whip cream, add sugar and whiskey gradually. Frost outside of cake with the whipped cream.

¼ lb. toasted almonds
¼ lb. macaroon crumbs
red cherries and green leaves

Chop almonds finely or grind coarsely. Mix with crumbs and cover outside of cake. Decorate with cherries and green leaves.

Mrs. Gordon Pilkington, St. Louis, Missouri

Since there is no leavening in Angel Cakes, a light, tender cake depends upon how much you beat the egg whites, the lightness with which you fold in the flour and sugar mixtures and the temperature at which you bake the cake.

505. Fresh Coconut Angel Cake

(Makes one 10-inch tube cake)

INGREDIENTS	DIRECTIONS
12 egg whites 1 teaspoon salt	Beat together until foamy.
1 teaspoon cream of tartar	Add to eggs and beat until stiff, but moist.
1 cup pastry flour 1 cup sugar	Sift together three or four times and carefully fold into the beaten eggs. Pour into a tin free of grease and bake in 300 F. oven for 50 minutes. Turn off oven and let cake remain for another ten minutes.

FROSTING:

2 cups sugar 1 cup water	Boil until it forms a soft ball when dropped in cold water.
3 egg whites	Whip until stiff. Slowly add the sugar syrup and whip until cold. Spread over cake.
1 coconut—grated	Sprinkle top generously with fresh grated coconut.

The White Turkey Town House, New York, New York

506. Pound Cake

(Makes 1 loaf)

INGREDIENTS	DIRECTIONS
½ lb. butter	Cream until fluffy. Beat like the D—1.
1¾ cups sugar	Add to creamed butter. Cream until fluffy and light.
5 whole eggs	Drop in one whole egg at a time while beating until you have dropped in five.
2 cups flour measured after two siftings vanilla mace	Stop the beater and *fold* in flour. Do not beat as that makes it tough. Flavor with a little vanilla and mace. Bake in loaf pan about 45 minutes at 300°. Turn oven up to 325° for browning. Leave at 325° for fifteen minutes or until brown.

The old-fashioned recipe called for brandy, nutmeg, and mace instead of vanilla. Do you have the brandy?

Mrs. H. H. Baird, Bowling Green, Kentucky

> **Strictly fresh eggs or fish do not float on top when placed in water.**

507. Luncheon Cake

(Makes 2 loaves)

INGREDIENTS

1 lb. butter
1 lb. sugar

10 eggs

1¼ lbs. all purpose flour
1½ lbs. raisins
½ lb. mixed candied
    fruit peel

DIRECTIONS

Cream butter until fluffy, add sugar and beat 5 minutes.

Break eggs in two at a time until six are in, beating each two for 5 minutes, then 1 at a time, beating each 5 minutes.

Add flour and fruit which has been lightly floured with some of the flour. Pour into 2 greased loaf pans, 9x5x3. Bake for 1½ hours in the 300° oven or until done.

Mrs. H. V. Cameron, Chatham, Ontario, Canada

508. Applesauce Cake

(Makes one 10-inch square)

INGREDIENTS

1½ cups brown sugar
¾ cup butter

1½ cups apple sauce
3 teaspoons soda

3 cups flour
1 teaspoon cinnamon
½ teaspoon cloves
1 cup raisins
1 cup nuts

DIRECTIONS

Cream together until smooth.

Dissolve soda in apple sauce and add to above.

Sift flour, measure and sift again with spices added. Add raisins and nuts to flour and stir into batter. Blend well and pour into greased lined 10-inch cake pan. Bake in 350° oven for about 40 to 50 minutes or until cake leaves sides of pan. Let cool and ice with boiled white icing.

Mrs. Duncan Hines, Bowling Green, Kentucky

509. Aunt Susan's Clabber Cake

(Serves 16)

INGREDIENTS

½ lb. butter
2 cups sugar

2 eggs—beaten

2 cups clabber
3½ cups cake flour
2 teaspoons soda
3⅓ tablespoons cocoa

DIRECTIONS

Cream together.

Add to the above.

Add to the mixture. Stir well. Pour into greased and floured pan. Bake in 350° oven for 45 minutes.

The Anna Maude, Oklahoma City, Oklahoma

510. Black Walnut Cake   (Makes one 9-inch tube cake)

INGREDIENTS

DIRECTIONS

½ cup butter
1½ cups sugar

Cream butter and add sugar gradually until light and fluffy.

2 cups cake flour
½ teaspoon salt
4 teaspoons baking powder
1 cup milk

Sift flour, measure, add salt and baking powder, and sift again. Add to butter and sugar alternately with milk, beating hard after each addition.

1 cup black walnuts
1 teaspoon vanilla

Grind walnuts finely and add to batter along with vanilla.

4 egg whites
¼ teaspoon cream of tartar

Beat egg whites until foamy, add cream of tartar and beat again until stiff, fold into batter. Pour into a 9-inch tube pan which has been well greased and floured on the bottom. Bake in a moderate oven, 325°, for 15 minutes. Turn up heat to 350° and bake 30 to 40 minutes longer, or until top springs back when lightly pressed. Turn out on cake rack and let cool.

FROSTING:

1 stick butter
1 box powdered sugar
⅔ cup cream
1 teaspoon vanilla
pinch salt
⅓ cup ground walnuts

Whip butter until light and fluffy. Sift sugar and work into butter. Stir in cream to spreading consistency, add salt and vanilla. Ice cake and sprinkle top and sides with additional ground walnuts.

Mrs. Duncan Hines, Bowling Green, Kentucky

510A. Sea Foam Icing   (For two 9-inch layers)

INGREDIENTS

DIRECTIONS

3 cups brown sugar
3 tablespoons corn syrup
1 tablespoon vinegar
dash salt
¾ cup water

Combine in saucepan, stir well and let come to a boil. Cook to 238° temperature.

3 egg whites
¼ teaspoon cream of tartar

Beat egg whites frothy, add cream of tartar and beat until stiff and dry. Follow the directions for Recipe 503A. No sugar is added to egg whites in this recipe.

Mrs. Duncan Hines, Bowling Green, Kentucky

511. Blackberry Jam Cake

(Serves 15 to 20)

INGREDIENTS

DIRECTIONS

1 cup butter
2 cups sugar

Cream butter and gradually add the sugar.

3 cups flour
2 teaspoons cinnamon
1 teaspoon nutmeg
1 teaspoon cloves
1 teaspoon allspice
1 cup buttermilk
1 teaspoon soda
4 egg yolks–beaten

Dissolve soda in buttermilk and add eggs, then stir into butter and sugar alternately with flour mixture beginning with dry ingredients. Sift flour and measure. Add spices and sift again.

1 teaspoon vanilla
1 cup blackberry jam

Add to mixture.

4 egg whites–beaten
    stiff

Fold into mixture. Bake in large pan with tube in center at 300 F. for 15 minutes, then at 350 F. for 15 minutes and then 360 F. for 30 minutes. Test with wire tester before removing from oven.

Headley Inn, Zanesville, Ohio

512. Burnt Sugar Cake

(Makes two 9-inch layers)

INGREDIENTS

DIRECTIONS

1 cup butter
2 cups sugar

Cream together.

¾ cup milk
4 tablespoons brown
    sugar syrup

Make syrup by melting granulated sugar in an iron skillet— (may be made up in quantity and kept on hand). Combine.

3 cups cake flour

Add to butter alternately with milk mixture.

4 eggs

Add eggs one at a time to mixture, beating well each time.

1 tablespoon baking
    powder
1 teaspoon vanilla

Add last. Pour into greased and floured pans. Bake at 350 degrees for 40 minutes.

The Anna Maude, Oklahoma City, Oklahoma

> *I believe there isn't any profession that requires more artistry, talent and experience than the careful preparation and cooking of good food.*

513. Cheese Cake

(Serves 6 to 8)

INGREDIENTS

DIRECTIONS

1/4 lb. graham crackers
2 tablespoons sugar
1 1/2 teaspoons cinnamon
6 tablespoons melted
butter

Roll crackers very fine. Add other ingredients,
mixing well. Line 10-inch spring-form pan.

1 1/2 lbs. cream cheese
1 cup sugar
3 eggs
1/2 teaspoon vanilla

Place cheese in electric beater and beat well.
Add sugar gradually and then eggs one at a
time. Vanilla last. Pour into pan and bake
20 minutes at 375°.

1 pt. sour cream
3 tablespoons sugar
1/2 teaspoon vanilla

Whip cream lightly, add sugar and vanilla.
Pour carefully over baked pie. Bake in 500°
oven for 5 minutes. Cool and place in
refrigerator.

Hody's, Los Angeles, California

514. Lindy's Cheesecake

(Serves 12)

INGREDIENTS

DIRECTIONS

1 cup sifted flour
1/4 cup sugar
1 teaspoon grated
lemon rind
1 egg yolk
1/2 cup butter
1/4 teaspoon vanilla

Combine dry ingredients including lemon
rind in bowl. Make well in center. Add egg,
butter and vanilla, work together quickly
until well blended. Add a little cold water if
necessary to make hold together. Wrap in
waxed paper and chill thoroughly in refrigerator for about 1 hour. Roll out 1/8 inch thick
and place over greased bottom of 9-inch
spring form pan.
Trim off extra dough. Bake in hot oven, 400°
for 15 to 20 minutes or until a light gold color.
Cool. Butter sides of pan and place over base.
Roll remaining dough 1/8 inch thick and line
sides of pan. Fill with following mixture:

2 1/2 lbs. cream cheese
1 3/4 cups sugar
3 tablespoons flour
1 1/2 teaspoons grated
orange rind
1 1/2 teaspoons grated
lemon rind
1/4 teaspoon vanilla
5 eggs
2 egg yolks
1/4 cup heavy cream

Put cheese in electric mixer and beat at second speed. Add sugar gradually then remainder of ingredients in order given. Eggs
should be added one at a time. When thoroughly blended and smooth, pour into lined
pan above and place in pre-heated oven 550°,
and bake from 12-15 minutes. Reduce heat
to 200° and continue baking for 1 hour. Cool
before cutting.

Lindy's, New York, New York

515. Jerry's Chocolate Cake

(Makes 2 9-inch layers)

INGREDIENTS

¾ cup butter
2¼ cups sugar
3 eggs

3 cups cake flour
½ teaspoon salt
1½ cups buttermilk

3 squares chocolate
1 teaspoon vanilla
1½ tablespoons vinegar
1½ teaspoons soda

DIRECTIONS

Cream butter and sugar together until fluffy. Add eggs one at a time.

Sift flour, measure, add salt and sift again. Add to mixture with buttermilk starting with dry ingredients and ending with dry.

Melt chocolate and stir into above mixture with vanilla. Dissolve soda in vinegar and stir in by hand. Pour batter into greased and floured 9-inch cake pans. Bake in 375° oven for about 30 to 40 minutes or until done.

FROSTING:

2 unbeaten egg whites
1½ cups sugar
few grains salt
⅛ cup cold water
2 teaspoons corn syrup
⅛ to ¼ teaspoon cream of tartar

1 teaspoon vanilla

Combine all ingredients and beat at medium speed for 1 minute. Cook and beat for 7 minutes over boiling water.

Add to above and beat until creamy and ready to spread on cake.

Mrs. Joseph Weaver, Jr., Minneapolis, Minnesota

516. 8 Yolk Fudge Cake

(Makes three 9-inch layers)

INGREDIENTS

2 cups sugar—sifted
¾ cup butter

8 egg yolks

2 squares bitter chocolate

2½ cups flour
¾ teaspoon soda
2 teaspoons baking powder
¼ teaspoon salt
1¼ cups buttermilk
1 teaspoon vanilla

DIRECTIONS

Cream until light and fine grained.

Beat until thick and lemon colored and add to above.

Melt and add to mixture.

Sift dry ingredients four times, add to above mixture alternately with buttermilk. Stir in vanilla. Pour into three layer pans. Bake in 350 F. oven for 30 minutes.

Violet Bray Berry, Berkeley, California

517. Chocolate Fudge Upside Down Cake

(Makes one 9-inch square)

INGREDIENTS	DIRECTIONS
¾ cup sugar 1 tablespoon butter	Cream together.
½ cup milk	Add to the above and stir.
1 cup flour ¼ teaspoon salt 1 teaspoon baking powder 1½ tablespoons cocoa	Sift together and add to mixture. Stir well and put in 9-inch buttered and floured pan.
½ cup walnuts—chopped	Sprinkle with nuts.
½ cup sugar ½ cup brown sugar ¼ cup cocoa	Mix well together and spread over top.
1¼ cups boiling water	Pour over the top of all. Bake in 350 F. oven for 30 minutes. Let cool in pan.

Cathryn's, Portland, Oregon

518. Hoagy Cake

(Makes one 10-inch square)

INGREDIENTS	DIRECTIONS
1¼ cups sugar ½ cup butter 2 eggs	Cream butter and sugar, add well-beaten eggs.
1¼ cups buttermilk 1 teaspoon soda ½ teaspoon salt 1 teaspoon baking powder 2 cups sifted cake flour	Combine soda, baking powder and salt with flour and add alternately with buttermilk to above.
grated rind of 2 oranges ½ cup chopped nuts	Add to above, pour into 10-inch cake pan and bake in 350° oven for 45 minutes or until done.

SAUCE:

1 cup sugar juice of 2 oranges juice of 1 lemon	Combine sugar with juice of oranges and lemon and cook for 5 minutes. While cake is still in pan, pour sauce over cake, cut and serve immediately.

Dunton's Cafeteria, Dallas, Texas

> *Things that do not mix—alcohol and gasoline, cigarettes and tablecloths.*

519. Chocolate Cake Supreme   (Makes two 9-inch layers)

INGREDIENTS	DIRECTIONS
½ cup butter 2 cups sugar	Cream together until you have a fluffy mass.
4 squares bitter chocolate	Melt in double boiler and add to above.
2 egg yolks 1 teaspoon vanilla	Beat egg yolks, add vanilla to beaten yolks and add to above.
2½ cups cake flour 2 teaspoons baking powder ½ teaspoon salt	Sift together three times.
1½ cups sweet milk	Add alternately with flour mixture.
2 egg whites	Beat stiff and fold into mixture. Place in 2 9-inch cake pans which have been greased, paper lined, and lightly greased again. Bake in 350° oven for about 30 minutes or until done.

FROSTING:

2 eggs 2 lbs. powdered sugar sifted	Beat the eggs well and gradually work in the sugar.
½ lb. butter 4 squares bitter chocolate 2 teaspoons lemon juice 2 teaspoons vanilla 2 cups chopped nuts 3 tablespoons cream	Melt together butter and chocolate. Add to above. Add lemon juice and vanilla and mix well. Add cream and mix. Fold in nuts and spread on cake.

Mrs. Duncan Hines, Bowling Green, Kentucky

You cannot expect perfect results in making cakes unless you are certain that the ingredients are of top quality—strictly fresh.

Part of the success in your cake making lies in using the proper size pan. Never try to crowd a 9-inch cake into an 8-inch pan or you will have cake batter all over the bottom of your oven. If you try to put an 8-inch cake into a 9-inch pan, the result will be a product which is thin and tough. Cake tins cost so little that you should have a set of each size in your kitchen if you wish to be a successful cake maker.

520. Fudge Squares

(Serves 6)

INGREDIENTS	DIRECTIONS
½ cup butter 2 oz. bitter chocolate or ⅓ cup cocoa plus 1 tablespoon butter	Melt butter and chocolate.
½ cup cake flour 1¼ cups sugar ⅛ teaspoon salt	Sift twice and add to above.
3 eggs—beaten 1 teaspoon vanilla ¾ cup chopped nuts (walnuts or pecans)	Stir into mixture and bake in 350 F. to 375 F. oven for 25 minutes.

Duncan Hines, Bowling Green, Kentucky

521. Lane Cake

(Makes two 10-inch layers)

INGREDIENTS	DIRECTIONS
1 cup butter 2 cups sugar	Cream together until very light.
3¼ cups flour 3 teaspoons baking powder	Sift together 4 times.
1 cup milk	Add to creamed mixture, alternately with the flour.
8 egg whites—beaten 1 tablespoon vanilla	Add vanilla to egg whites and fold into mixture. Bake in two layers or one tube pan in 350 F. oven for 40 to 50 minutes, or until cake springs to touch. Test with straw.

LANE CAKE FILLING:

½ cup butter 1 cup sugar	Cream together.
7 egg yolks—beaten	Add egg yolks and cook in double boiler, stirring constantly until smooth and thick. Remove from fire.
1 cup raisins—chopped 1 cup nut meats—chopped 1 teaspoon vanilla	Add to mixture while it is still hot.
1 wineglass brandy	Add to mixture and spread over the cake.

This is a rich but distinguished cake.

Dr. T. J. LeBlanc, Cincinnati, Ohio

522. Christmas Nut Cake

(Makes one 10-inch tube cake)

INGREDIENTS	DIRECTIONS
½ lb. butter ½ lb. sugar	Cream together in electric mixer.
5 egg yolks	Add to above one at a time. Remove from mixer.
¼ cup sour cream ¼ teaspoon soda	Dissolve soda in cream and add to above, stirring lightly.
½ lb. flour ½ whole nutmeg grated ⅓ cup whiskey	Sift flour and nutmeg together. Add to above alternately with whiskey.
¾ lb. raisins ½ lb. pecans or hickory nuts 1 pkg. candied red cherries ⅛ lb. citron	Chop fruit and nuts and flour well with extra flour. Add to above folding in gently.
5 egg whites	Beat whites stiff and fold into above. Pour in greased tube pan with paper in bottom.

Place in 300° oven. Put pan of water on lower level and bake for 2 hours or until done. This cake cannot be kept for any length of time, but must be eaten within a week.

Mrs. Duncan Hines, Bowling Green, Kentucky

523. White Cake Supreme

(Makes two thick 9-inch layers)

INGREDIENTS	DIRECTIONS
1 cup butter 2 cups sugar	Whip butter in electric mixer until creamy. Add sugar gradually and blend until very light and creamy.
3½ cups cake flour 4 teaspoons baking powder ½ teaspoon salt 1 cup milk 1 teaspoon vanilla	Sift flour and measure. Add baking powder and salt and sift together 2 or 3 times. Stir into butter and sugar mixture alternately with milk, starting and ending with dry ingredients. Beat batter until smooth. Add vanilla and remove from beater.
8 egg whites	Beat until stiff and fairly dry. Fold into batter, and place in two greased, paper-lined cake

pans. Bake in 350° oven for 40 minutes or until it tests done. Frost with your favorite frosting. This can also be baked in 3 8-inch pans at 350° for about 25 to 30 minutes.

Mrs. Duncan Hines, Bowling Green, Kentucky

524. Orange Cake (Makes two 9-inch layers)

INGREDIENTS	DIRECTIONS
1 tablespoon grated orange rind ¼ cup orange juice strained	Put rind in juice and let stand while making the cake. Save the pulp for filling.
¾ cup butter 1½ cups sugar	Cream butter, add sugar gradually and cream thoroughly.
3 egg yolks	Beat egg yolks and add to mixture.
2¼ cups cake flour 3½ teaspoons baking powder ½ teaspoon salt	Sift flour, measure and add baking powder and salt.
¾ cup water	Add water to the orange juice and add alternately with the dry ingredients.
3 egg whites—beaten	Fold into mixture. Pour into well greased layer pans and bake in 350 F. oven for 30 to 35 minutes.

CLEAR ORANGE FILLING:

2 tablespoons butter 4 tablespoons cornstarch 2 tablespoons grated orange rind 1 cup sugar ½ teaspoon salt 1½ teaspoons lemon juice 1 cup orange juice and pulp	Mix all together and cook in double boiler 5 minutes. Spread between layers and on top and sides of cake.

Francis E. Fowler, Jr., Los Angeles, California

525. Orange Layer Cake

Use your favorite yellow cake recipe, but when mixing dough, substitute ¼ of the amount of liquid stipulated with orange juice. Cool and ice.

ORANGE BUTTER CREAM ICING

INGREDIENTS	DIRECTIONS
¼ cup butter 2 cups powdered sugar 1 egg beaten 1 cup orange marmalade ¼ teaspoon salt	Cream together butter and sugar. Stir in egg. Fold in marmalade and salt. If the marmalade is thin, reduce the amount to ¾ cup and it may be necessary to add a little more sugar.

Damon's, Cleveland, Ohio

526. Prune Layer Cake

(Serves 10 to 12)

INGREDIENTS

⅓ cup butter
1¼ cups sugar

2 egg yolks—beaten
1 egg—beaten
5 tablespoons milk

1¼ cups stewed prunes—
    chopped
1 teaspoon lemon juice

1½ cups flour
½ teaspoon baking
    soda
1½ teaspoons baking
    powder
¼ teaspoon salt
1 teaspoon cinnamon
1 teaspoon cloves
1 teaspoon nutmeg

DIRECTIONS

Cream together.

Add to above mixture, and stir well.

Add to mixture and stir.

Sift together and add to mixture and stir lightly.

Put batter in two cake pans and bake in 375 F. oven for 25 to 30 minutes, lowering temperature gradually until it is properly baked.

Cover with boiled white icing. This delicious cake remains fresh for some time.

Mrs. Alonzo Newton Benn, Chicago, Illinois

527. Chocolate Sponge Cake

(Makes three 8-inch layers or two 10-inch layers)

INGREDIENTS

¼ lb. or 4 squares
    bitter chocolate
1 cup milk

5 egg yolks
2 cups sugar

1¼ cups flour
1 teaspoon baking
    powder
    pinch salt
1 teaspoon vanilla
5 egg whites

DIRECTIONS

Shave the chocolate and add to milk. Cook over a low heat, stirring constantly until thick. Let stand until cool.

Beat egg yolks and add sugar gradually. Add chocolate and milk mixture.

Sift flour, measure and add baking powder and salt. Sift again and stir into above. Add vanilla. Blend well.
Beat the egg whites stiff and fold into cake mixture. Place in greased and floured pans and bake in 350° oven until a straw or cake tester pulls out clean. Do not overbake or cake will be dry. Ice with caramel or chocolate icing.

Mrs. Elsie Smythe, Bowling Green, Kentucky

In making cakes, have ingredients at room temperature.

528. Cherry Sponge (Serves 4)

INGREDIENTS

DIRECTIONS

3 egg yolks—beaten
3 tablespoons sugar

Beat into yolks until smooth and lemon colored.

3 egg whites—beaten

Put on top of yolks.

3 teaspoons flour

Sift over the egg whites. Fold in lightly.

Put mixture in an 8-inch square or round cake pan 1½ inches deep.

1½ cups sweet black cherries

Wash and dry. Drop into the egg batter so they are distributed evenly over the surface.

Bake in 320 F. oven for 10 to 15 minutes until lightly browned. Let cool, slice, and then dust with powdered sugar and serve.

Mrs. A. E. R. Peterka, Cleveland, Ohio

529. Fairy Loaf Cake (Makes one 9- or 10-inch tube cake)

INGREDIENTS

DIRECTIONS

8 egg yolks
1¼ cups sugar
½ cup salad oil

Beat egg yolks until fluffy. Add sugar gradually and beat thoroughly. Add oil and beat until fluffy.

2¾ cups sifted cake flour
3 teaspoons baking powder
½ teaspoon salt
1 cup water
1½ teaspoon vanilla or 1 teaspoon vanilla and ½ teaspoon lemon or what you will

Sift flour and baking powder and salt. Add to first mixture alternately with water and flavoring, beating carefully. The batter will be thin. Bake in a 9- or 10-inch tube pan or in a large sheet pan at 350° for 35 to 50 minutes. This is a good cake to cut into pieces and frost for petit fours. It is also good sliced in 3 layers and iced between the layers and on top. I sometimes color the water with burnt sugar and have a caramel cake.

Dorothy C. Raymond, The Spokesman-Review, Spokane, Washington

---

Do not attempt to make good coffee unless your utensil has been scoured and is absolutely clean and be sure to use the correct grind of fresh coffee and do not buy too much coffee at one time. Coffee should be drunk within 10 minutes after being brewed.

530. Sponge Cake

INGREDIENTS

DIRECTIONS

12 egg yolks—beaten
½ cup sugar

Beat in sugar with egg yolks, a teaspoon at a time.

1 lemon—juice
1 cup flour—sift 4 times

Alternately add juice and flour to above until it becomes a smooth dough.

12 egg whites—beaten
1 pinch of salt
½ cup sugar

Slowly beat sugar and salt into the egg whites. Cut into the batter.

1 teaspoon vanilla

Add to mixture. Pour batter into an ungreased 10-inch tube pan. Bake in 325 F. oven for 1 hour and 15 minutes. (This delicious sponge cake we use to make "Ice-Cream Sandwiches." One slice of cake, coffee ice cream with butterscotch sauce. It's "Yummy.")

(This delicious sponge cake we use to make "Ice-Cream Sandwiches." One slice of cake, coffee ice cream with butterscotch sauce. It's "Yummy.")

Duncan Hines, Bowling Green, Kentucky

531. Sultana Cake

INGREDIENTS

DIRECTIONS

1 lb. butter
1 lb. sugar

Cream together.

8 eggs

Mix into the above.

1½ cups milk

Slowly add to the mixture.

8 cups cake flour
3 teaspoons baking powder

Sift and add to mixture.

1 lb. sultana raisins
¼ lb. orange peel
orange and lemon extract to flavor

Add to mixture. Bake in 350 F. oven for 1 hour, or more.

Mrs. David Donald, Pittsfield, Massachusetts

532. Devils Food Cake   (Makes two 9-inch layers)

INGREDIENTS

DIRECTIONS

2 cups sugar
2 tablespoons
shortening
3 eggs
¼ teaspoon salt
2 teaspoons vanilla

Cream together butter and sugar until fluffy. Beat eggs and stir into creamed mixture with salt and vanilla.

1 cup buttermilk

Add to the above.

3 cups cake flour
2 teaspoons of soda

Sift together and add to mixture.

4 squares unsweetened
chocolate
1 cup sweet milk

Heat milk and chocolate in double boiler until chocolate is dissolved. Stir into cake batter, place in two 9-inch pans which have been greased and lined with paper and bake in 325° F. to 350° F. oven for 1 hour.

Buckley Tea Room, Walworth, Wisconsin

533. Ice Box Fruit Cake   (Makes 7 small pans)

INGREDIENTS

DIRECTIONS

3 lbs. seeded raisins
2 lbs. pitted dates
2 lbs. figs
2 lbs. pecan meats
50 candied cherries
(red and green)
½ lb. candied
pineapple
¼ lb. citron peel
¼ lb. orange peel
¼ lb. lemon peel

Cut in small pieces and put into a mixing bowl.

1 teaspoon salt
1 teaspoon cloves
1 tablespoon nutmeg
1 tablespoon cinnamon

Blend together and add to the above mixture.

1 cup sugar
1 orange—juice and
grated rind
½ cup of other fruit
juice or
brandy may be
added

Dissolve sugar in orange juice and add to the above mixture. Mix well.

Line pans with waxed paper and press mixture into them. Place in refrigerator with pressure for 10 days.

Mrs. B. McIntyre, Cincinnati, Ohio

534. Patio Ice Cream Cake (Serves 6-8)

INGREDIENTS

DIRECTIONS

2 eggs
1 cup sugar
½ cup milk
1 teaspoon butter

Beat eggs well, add sugar. Use an electric beater if possible. Bring milk just to a boil, add butter, and add to egg mixture.

1 cup flour
1½ teaspoon baking powder
½ teaspoon salt
½ teaspoon vanilla

Sift dry ingredients together, add to egg mixture gradually. Add vanilla. Bake in 350° oven for 20 minutes or until done.

PATIO CARAMEL SAUCE:

1 cup brown sugar
1 cup brown corn syrup

Boil together for 5 minutes.

¼ cup white sugar
¼ cup butter

Caramelize sugar, add to syrup, add butter and boil a few minutes longer.

½ cup coffee cream
pinch salt
1 teaspoon vanilla
slivered toasted almonds
vanilla ice cream
whipped cream

Remove from heat and stir in cream, salt and vanilla. When ready to serve, cut cake in large squares—split each square and place vanilla ice cream between layers. Put whipped cream over top, and drip caramel sauce over all. Sprinkle with toasted almonds.

Terrace Patio, Ft. Lauderdale, Florida

535. Orange Muffins (Makes 12 muffins)

INGREDIENTS

DIRECTIONS

2 tablespoons shortening
1 cup sugar

Blend together.

2 eggs—beaten lightly
juice of 2 oranges

Add to mixture.

3 cups flour
1 tablespoon baking powder
½ teaspoon salt

Sift together and stir into mixture. Leave a little of the flour to stir in later.

½ cup milk

Add to mixture.

rinds of 2 oranges— grated

Add to mixture with the balance of the flour. Pour into muffin pan and bake in 350° F. oven for 30 minutes.

Mission Inn, Riverside, California

536. Poppy Seed Cake (Makes three 9-inch layers)

INGREDIENTS	DIRECTIONS
1 cup poppy seed ¾ cup scalding milk	Soak overnight.
1½ cups sugar ¾ cup butter ¾ cup cold milk	Cream butter and sugar together. Stir in milk.
3 teaspoons baking powder 3 cups flour	Sift together three times and blend all ingredients together.
4 egg whites—beaten	Fold into mixture. Bake in three layers in 9-inch cake tins in 350 F. oven for 25 to 30 minutes.

FILLING:

2 egg yolks 1 lemon—juice 1 cup sugar 2 tablespoons corn-starch 1 cup scalding water 1 pinch salt	Cook until thick and fill each layer with lemon filling.
½ cup chopped nuts	Sprinkle with nuts and top with icing.

ICING:

2 egg whites 1 cup sugar 4 tablespoons cold water	Mix together and cook in double boiler until thick. Beat constantly with an egg beater while cooking. Put on cake while hot.

Lake Breeze Resort, Three Lakes, Wisconsin

537. Date and Nut Confection (Serves 4 to 6)

INGREDIENTS	DIRECTIONS
1 cup pitted dates—diced ½ cup black walnuts—broken 1 cup granulated sugar 1 teaspoon baking powder pinch of salt	Mix together thoroughly.
4 egg whites—beaten	Fold into above mixture and bake in buttered tin in 300 F. oven for 20 minutes. When cool, serve with whipped cream.

Gurney's Inn, Montauk, Long Island, New York

538. Hart's Old Fashioned Spice Cake

(Makes one 12x7½-inch cake)

INGREDIENTS

2 cups brown sugar
1½ cup shortening—
    butter preferred

3 eggs or 5 yolks
1 teaspoon allspice
1 teaspoon cinnamon
1 teaspoon cloves

2 cups pastry flour
1 teaspoon soda
½ teaspoon salt
1 cup sour cream

DIRECTIONS

Cream butter and sugar together until thoroughly blended.

If whole eggs are used, separate. Beat yolks well. Add yolks and spices to mixture and beat well.

Sift flour and measure. Add soda and salt to flour and sift into mixture alternately with cream. Stir lightly to blend well. If whole eggs are used, beat egg whites stiff and fold into batter. Pour into greased lined and floured cake pan and bake in 350° oven for 50 minutes until cake starts to shrink from sides of pan. Let cool for a few minutes and turn out on cake rack.

OLD FASHIONED SOUR CREAM FROSTING:

1 cup heavy sour cream
1½ cups white sugar

Mix together sugar and cream and put on low heat to boil. Let cool slowly, stirring occasionally. Takes about ½ hour. Drop a little into a cup of cold water. When it forms a soft ball it is done.

½ teaspoon soda
1 teaspoon vanilla
    pinch of salt
1 tablespoon butter

Add soda to sugar and cream mixture, put back on stove on high heat and cook for 1 minute, stirring rapidly to prevent sticking. It should be a nice caramel color. Remove from stove, add vanilla, salt and butter.

2 tablespoons sweet
    cream

Stir frosting well and let cool slightly, then beat, adding cream to right consistency to spread. Should spread like butter. This will keep for a week if kept under lock and key.

Hart's Old Tyme Coffee House, Moose Lake, Minnesota

Apple pie without rat cheese is minus the "umpth."

539. Spiced Layer Cake with Seafoam Frosting
(Makes two 8-inch layers)

INGREDIENTS | DIRECTIONS

⅛ cup butter
1 cup sugar

Cream butter thoroughly. Add sugar gradually and cream until light and fluffy.

1 egg
1 egg yolk

Add to butter mixture and beat well.

2 tablespoons molasses

Add and mix thoroughly.

2 cups flour—sift once and measure
2 teaspoons baking powder
¼ teaspoon salt
¼ teaspoon ginger
¼ teaspoon mace
¼ teaspoon allspice
¼ teaspoon nutmeg
¾ teaspoon cloves
¾ teaspoon cinnamon
¾ cup milk

Sift dry ingredients together three times. Add to creamed mixture alternately with milk, beating after each addition until smooth.

Bake in greased layer pans in 375° F. oven for about 25 minutes, or until done.

SEAFOAM FROSTING:

1½ cups brown sugar
½ cup water
¼ teaspoon cream of tartar

Blend together, bring to a boil and cook to 242°.

4 egg whites—beaten

Slowly add the above syrup to eggs, beating all the time.

Williamsburg Inn, Williamsburg, Virginia

540. Sunshine Cake
(Makes one 10-inch tube cake)

INGREDIENTS | DIRECTIONS

1 cup flour
1 teaspoon baking powder
1½ teaspoons cornstarch
½ teaspoon salt

Sift three times.

4 egg yolks—beaten
½ cup sugar

Beat together.

2 tablespoons flour
3 tablespoons cold water
1 teaspoon vanilla

Add to egg mixture and stir into dry ingredients.

4 egg whites—beaten
½ cup sugar

Fold into mixture and pour into angel food cake pan. Bake in 300 F. oven for 45 minutes, then in 350 F. oven for 15 minutes. Invert pan until the cake is cold.

Sawyer Tavern, Keene, New Hampshire

541. Gumdrop Fruit Cake

(Makes 2 or 3 small loaves)

INGREDIENTS	DIRECTIONS
1 cup butter 2 cups sugar	Cream together.
2 eggs—beaten	Add to the above.
4 cups flour 1 teaspoon cinnamon ¼ teaspoon nutmeg ¼ teaspoon cloves ¼ teaspoon salt	Sift flour, measure, add spices and salt and sift again. Put a little aside to mix with raisins, nuts and gumdrops. Add the remainder to the above alternately with:
1½ cups sieved apple-sauce	To be added to mixture alternately with the flour.
1 teaspoon soda 1 tablespoon hot water	Dissolve and stir into mixture.
1 teaspoon vanilla	Add to mixture.
1 to 2 lbs. gumdrops 1 lb. white raisins	(Do not use any black gumdrops.) Cut in pieces with scissors.
1 cup pecans	Fry in a little butter and add to gumdrops and raisins. Mix in the flour and add to

the mixture. Line two or three small loaf pans with greased parchment or heavy paper and bake in 300 to 325 F. oven for 2 hours. If oven glass or casseroles are used, do not line with paper, but bake at a lower temperature of 275 to 300 degrees.

Dolores Restaurant and Drive-In, Oklahoma City, Oklahoma

542. Hazel Nut Cake

(Makes two 9-inch layers)

INGREDIENTS	DIRECTIONS
1 cup butter 2 cups sugar	Cream butter and add sugar gradually, beat until fluffy.
3 cups flour pinch salt 2 teaspoons baking powder 1 cup milk	Sift flour, measure and sift twice more. Third sifting add salt and baking powder. Add to butter and sugar mixture, first flour, then milk, until all of each has been beaten into batter.
6 egg whites 1½ cups hazel nuts 1 teaspoon cinnamon ½ teaspoon cloves	Beat egg whites stiffly. Fold into batter. Chop or grind hazel nuts and add to batter along with spices. Pour batter into 2 greased and lined cake pans and bake in 375° oven for 35 to 45 minutes or until done. Turn out on

racks and let cool. When cool, ice with butter icing. Sprinkle additional ground hazel nuts on icing between layers and on top of cake.

Mrs. Duncan Hines, Bowling Green, Kentucky

543. Some Reasons for Cake Failures

FALLING

  Too much shortening
  Too much sugar
  Too short baking time
  Too low oven
  Too much leavening

DRYNESS

  Too much flour
  Too little shortening
  Too much leavening
  Too long baking time
  Too low oven

COARSE GRAIN

  Too little creaming
  Egg whites not thoroughly combined
  Too much leavening
  Too little flour

UNEVEN SURFACE

  Oven shelf not level
  Uneven oven heat
  Pans too close to oven sides

MOIST, STICKY CRUST

  Too much sugar

CRUMBLING

  Too much shortening
  Too much flour
  Too much air incorporated
  Too much leavening

UNDERSIZE

  Unequal ingredient temperature
  Undermixed (particularly not creamed long enough)
  Too little leavening
  Too large pan
  Too hot oven

HEAVY

  Too slowly mixed, after adding milk
  Too much shortening
  Too slowly or too quickly baked

SPLIT TOP

  Too much flour
  Too hot an oven

HEAVY LAYERED BOTTOM

  Undermixed
  Too much liquid

544. Torte

(Serves about 12)

INGREDIENTS

DIRECTIONS

6 egg whites
1½ cups sugar

Beat egg whites stiff, adding sugar gradually.

1½ teaspoons vinegar
1 teaspoon vanilla
¼ teaspoon almond
   extract

Add to the above. Drop on brown paper placed on cookie sheet, using a spoon that holds about 2 tablespoonsful. After they are placed on the sheet, make an indentation with the back of the spoon. Bake in 300 F. oven for 45 minutes, then raise the temperature to 325 F. for 15 minutes. Remove from paper, using a spatula. If they stick, reheat the sheet and try again.

1 quart strawberries
½ cup sugar—superfine

Do not crush the berries. Add sugar and fill each indentation with berries.

1 cup whipping cream
   —whipped

Top each meringue with whipped cream. If berries are not used peaches may be upturned and filled with a soft custard.

CUSTARD:

3 cups milk and ½ cup
   sugar, or
2 cups milk and 1 cup
   peach juice and ⅓
   cup sugar

Scald.

6 egg yolks—beaten
⅓ cup sugar
1 teaspoon salt
⅛ teaspoon almond
   flavoring

Put in double boiler and pour hot milk over. Cook slowly until mixture coats a spoon. Stir while cooking. Cool.

Valley Green Lodge, Orick, California

545. Butter Cookies

(Makes 50 to 60)

INGREDIENTS

DIRECTIONS

1 lb. butter
1 cup sugar

Cream together.

6 cups flour
1 pinch of salt

Sift and add to mixture. Roll out thin, cut and bake in 375 F. oven 10 to 12 minutes.

Mr. Francis E. Fowler, Jr., Los Angeles, California

Egg whites beat best at room temperature.

546. Betty Cass' Brown Sugar Cookies

INGREDIENTS

2 cups brown sugar
½ cup shortening
½ cup butter
2 eggs
2 cups flour
1 teaspoon baking
   powder
2 teaspoons vanilla
1 cup chopped pecans

DIRECTIONS

Mix in the order given and drop by a teaspoon
on buttered baking sheet. Press pecan half in
each one. Bake in 350 F. oven for 15 minutes.

Mrs. R. T. Cooksey, Madison, Wisconsin

547. Brownies   (Makes 1 pan 12x12 inches)

INGREDIENTS

2 squares bitter
   chocolate
½ cup butter

1 cup sugar
2 eggs

1 teaspoon vanilla
1 cup nuts—broken

¾ cup flour
½ teaspoon baking
   powder
½ teaspoon salt

DIRECTIONS

Melt together over hot water.

Add to above and beat thoroughly.

Add to mixture.

Sift together and add to mixture. Stir in thoroughly. Pour into a greased and floured baking pan and bake in 350 F. oven for 25 to 30
minutes. When cool, cut into squares. These
may be iced before serving.

The Old House, Lexington, Massachusetts

548. Brownies   (Makes one pan 12x12 inches)

INGREDIENTS

1 cup sugar
½ cup melted butter
2 squares chocolate
2 eggs
1 teaspoon salt

½ cup flour
1 cup walnuts—
   chopped

1 teaspoon vanilla

DIRECTIONS

Blend together.

Stir into mixture.

Add to mixture. Pour into a shallow tin and
bake in 350 F. oven for 20 minutes.

The Krebs, Skaneateles, New York

549. Carmens

(Makes 1 cookie sheet)

INGREDIENTS

DIRECTIONS

1 cup butter
2 cups brown sugar—
   sifted

Cream together until light.

4 egg yolks—beaten
2 egg whites—beaten

Add to the above.

1 cup milk
1 teaspoon vinegar
1 teaspoon soda

Mix these together.

2¼ cups pastry flour
1 teaspoon cinnamon
½ teaspoon cloves
1 teaspoon allspice

Sift together. Alternately add a little of the milk mixture, then the flour mixture to the butter and eggs. Mix well.

1 teaspoon vanilla

Fold into the mixture and spread on cookie sheet about ⅜-inch thick.

3 egg whites—beaten
   stiff
1 cup brown sugar
½ cup chopped nuts

Make a meringue and spread over the dough. Bake about 40 minutes in 350 F. oven. Cut in small pieces. These are very delicate and should be carefully handled.

Rock Hill Inn, Cape Cottage, Maine

550. Cherry Nut Cookies

(Makes 60 cookies)

INGREDIENTS

DIRECTIONS

1⅓ cups butter
2 cups brown sugar

Cream together.

4 cups flour
1 teaspoon soda
1 teaspoon salt

Sift these ingredients and mix and add a portion to the above.

3 eggs

Add the eggs and continue mixing. (If an electric mixer is used, the bowl and beater should be scraped down thoroughly.) Add nearly all the remaining flour.

1⅓ cups nuts
   (pecans or walnuts)
1⅓ cups candied cherries
1⅓ cups dates

Chop and dredge with the remaining flour and add to the mixture. Drop cookies on a greased and floured sheet pan and bake about 15 minutes in 375-400 F. oven until brown. This dough can be kept in refrigerator and baked as needed.

Richards Treat Cafeteria, Minneapolis, Minnesota

In making a puree, pass the food through a fine sieve.

551. Chocolate Drop Cookies with Icing

(Makes 36 cookies)

INGREDIENTS	DIRECTIONS
½ cup butter 1 cup brown sugar	Cream together.
1 egg—beaten	Add to the above.
2 cups flour ½ teaspoon salt ½ teaspoon soda	Sift flour, measure, add salt and soda and sift again.
¾ cup milk	Add to mixture, alternately with flour, beginning with dry ingredients.
2 squares unsweetened chocolate—melted ½ cup nuts—chopped 1 teaspoon vanilla	Blend together and add to the mixture. Drop on greased pans and bake in 400 F. oven for 15 minutes.

ICING:

2 tablespoons butter 2 squares chocolate	Melt together in double boiler.
4 tablespoons cream 2 cups powdered sugar 1 pinch salt	Blend all these ingredients and add chocolate and butter mixture. Beat until smooth.
1 egg—beaten	Fold into mixture and spread on cookies.

Grace Peterson Adams, Chicago, Illinois

In order to insure perfect cakes, be sure that your oven temperature is correct.

552. French Cookies (Tulles)

(Makes 40)

INGREDIENTS	DIRECTIONS
4 egg whites—beaten 1 cup sugar 1 teaspoon vanilla	Beat together.
1 cup almonds	Blanch and grind fine. Add to the above
¼ lb. butter—melted	Add to mixture.
1 cup flour	Stir in slowly. Drop by teaspoonful on a buttered pan. Bake in 350 F. oven for 15 minutes. Let cool on rack before putting them away.

Villa LaFayette, Mountain View, California

553. Bourbon Balls

INGREDIENTS

1 cup vanilla wafer or graham cracker crumbs
1 cup pecans
¼ cup bourbon whiskey
1½ tablespoons white corn syrup
4 tablespoons cocoa
1 cup powdered sugar

DIRECTIONS

Roll wafers or crackers into fine crumbs. Chop pecans. Mix whiskey and corn syrup with crumbs, nuts and cocoa. Form into small balls or flat patties. Roll in powdered sugar and place in refrigerator until ready to serve.

Mrs. Duncan Hines, Bowling Green, Kentucky

554. Christmas Wine Cakes

(Makes about 30 standard size cup cakes)

INGREDIENTS

2 cups sugar
1 cup butter
2 eggs

3½ cups flour
½ teaspoon salt
1 teaspoon soda
1 teaspoon cinnamon
1 teaspoon cloves

2 cups unsweetened applesauce

1 cup chopped fruit cake mix
1 cup raisins
1 cup nuts

DIRECTIONS

Cream butter and sugar until fluffy. Add eggs and beat well.

Sift flour and measure. Retain ½ cup to flour fruits and nuts. To remaining flour add other ingredients and sift again. Stir into creamed mixture.

Heat to boiling point and add to above.

Combine opposite ingredients and flour well with reserved flour. Stir into batter and mix well. Spoon batter into muffin pans lined with paper cup linings. Fill ⅔ full. Bake for 30 minutes in 350° oven.

WINE SAUCE:

3 cups sugar
½ teaspoon salt
6 tablespoons cornstarch
6 cups currant or claret wine
few drops red coloring

Mix together sugar, salt and cornstarch. Stir in wine, mix well and cook over low heat until thick and clear. Add few drops of red coloring to make ruby red. Serve hot over warm cakes.

Dupuis Tavern, Port Angeles, Washington

555. Date and Nut Cakes

(Makes 20 cakes)

INGREDIENTS	DIRECTIONS
1 package of dates, cut fine 2 cups boiling water	Pour water over dates.
2 tablespoons butter 1 teaspoon soda	Add to dates.
2 eggs—beaten 2 cups sugar 3 cups flour	Blend these ingredients and add to above mixture. Stir well.
1 cup walnuts—broken 1 teaspoon vanilla	Fold into mixture and pour into greased muffin tins. Bake in 350 F. oven for 30 minutes.

Ireland's Rustic Lodge, Gold Beach, Oregon

556. Ginger Crisps

(Makes 36 cookies)

INGREDIENTS	DIRECTIONS
1 cup shortening	Cream until soft and waxy.
1 cup granulated sugar	Add gradually to above and cream until fluffy.
2 eggs—beaten	Stir in eggs.
½ cup molasses	Add molasses and beat until well blended.
4½ cups flour 3 teaspoons ginger 1 teaspoon soda 1 teaspoon salt	Sift together and add to the mixture. Mold into roll and place in refrigerator until thoroughly set. Slice as thin as desired. Bake in a 325 F. oven on a lightly greased cookie sheet until the cookies are brown.

Miss Katharine L. Little, Chicago, Illinois

557. Ginger Snaps

(Makes about 30)

INGREDIENTS	DIRECTIONS
½ cup butter 1 cup sugar ½ cup lard	Cream.
2 eggs—beaten	Stir into the above.
½ cup molasses	Add to above and mix well.
4½ cups flour 3 teaspoons ginger 1 teaspoon salt 1 teaspoon soda	Sift together and stir into the above. Let stand in refrigerator overnight. Roll out thin and cut with round cookie cutter. Bake in 400 F. oven for 15 to 20 minutes.

Rider Tavern, Painesville, Ohio

558. Nut Macaroons

(Makes 6 or 7 dozen)

INGREDIENTS

2 cups powdered sugar
—sifted
½ cup flour—sifted
1 teaspoon baking
powder
5 egg whites
1 lb. chopped nuts

DIRECTIONS

Blend dry ingredients. Stir egg whites into the dry ingredients without beating. Add the nuts. Drop from a teaspoon onto a greased cookie sheet. Bake in 300 F. oven 15 minutes or until set. Do not bake too hard or they won't be good.

McDonald Tea Room, Gallatin, Missouri

559. Ice Box Nut Cookies

(Makes 5 or 6 dozen)

INGREDIENTS

2 cups brown sugar
1 cup butter
2 eggs
1 teaspoon soda
1 teaspoon water
3¾ cups all-purpose flour
1 teaspoon salt

1 teaspoon vanilla
1 cup chopped nuts

DIRECTIONS

Cream butter, add sugar and beat until creamy. Beat eggs and add.
Dissolve soda in water and add to sugar mixture. Sift salt with flour twice and mix all well.

Add vanilla and nuts. Line loaf pan with waxed paper, pack in cooky mixture. Chill overnight in refrigerator. Next day slice thin and bake in 325° F. oven for 10 to 15 minutes. This will keep several days in the refrigerator.

The Maine Maid, Jericho, Long Island, New York

560. Jackson Cookies

(Makes 40 to 50 cookies)

INGREDIENTS

1 cup butter
1½ cups sugar

3 eggs—beaten

¼ cup milk
½ teaspoon soda
1 pinch of salt

2 cups flour
1 teaspoon nutmeg
1 teaspoon cinnamon

1½ cups raisins
½ cup chopped pecans
or walnuts

DIRECTIONS

Cream together.

Add to above.

Stir into mixture.

Blend and add to mixture.

Mix well and stir into mixture. Spread on shallow well-greased pans and bake in 375 F. oven for 10 to 12 minutes. Remove from oven and cut into squares.

Mrs. Mathew Jackson, Chicago, Illinois

561. Little Apple Cakes (Makes 1 doz. large or 18 small)

INGREDIENTS	DIRECTIONS
½ cup lard 1 cup sugar	Cream together.
1 egg—beaten	Add to above.
2 cups flour ½ teaspoon soda 1 teaspoon salt 2 teaspoons baking powder ½ teaspoon cinnamon ½ teaspoon cloves ½ teaspoon nutmeg ½ cup nuts—broken 1 cup chopped apples ½ cup chopped dates 1 teaspoon vanilla ½ cup cold coffee	Stir all these ingredients into the above mixture, in their order, and bake in Gem tins in 350 F. oven from 30-40 minutes.

Mrs. Mathew Jackson, Chicago, Illinois

562. Oat Cakes (Makes about 36)

INGREDIENTS	DIRECTIONS
3 cups quick cooking oats	Put through a meat chopper.
½ cup corn meal ½ cup butter or shortening 1 cup flour 3 teaspoons sugar 1 teaspoon salt ½ teaspoon soda 1 teaspoon baking powder	Add to the above and mix thoroughly.
⅔ cup hot water	Add to mixture. Roll thin, cut and bake on a lightly greased cookie sheet in a 350 F. oven for 30 to 40 minutes.

Mrs. David Donald, Pittsfield, Massachusetts

After a cake has cooked, keep it fresh and moist by storing it in a container which has a tight fitting cover.

563. Orange Cookies

(Makes 36)

INGREDIENTS

½ cup butter
1 cup sugar
1 orange rind—grated
1 egg—beaten
½ cup orange juice
3 cups flour
4 teaspoons baking
powder

DIRECTIONS

Mix in the order given. More flour may be required.

Roll into a sheet, cut in rounds, dredge with sugar and bake in 350 F. oven for about 20 minutes, or until brown.

This recipe makes soft cookies, if crisp ones are desired, use ¼ cup of orange juice.

Villa LaFayette, Mountain View, California

564. Orange Tea Cakes

(Makes about 40)

INGREDIENTS

1¼ cups almonds—
chopped about the
size of rice kernels
½ lb. orange peel—
chopped
2 cups cake flour
2½ cups powdered sugar

1 pint heavy cream
a few drops orange
coloring

DIRECTIONS

Place in a mixing bowl. Blend all ingredients.

Mix into ingredients and put into pastry bag with a No. 5 or No. 6 tube. Lay out in little mounds on a heavily greased pan. Bake in 340 F. oven. Do not allow to get brown, as they should retain their orange color. Ice the bottoms with temperate sweet chocolate.

Chalet Suzanne, Lake Wales, Florida

565. Pecan Drop Cakes

(Makes about 30)

INGREDIENTS

1 egg white—beaten
1 cup brown sugar

1 cup pecans (whole or
broken)

DIRECTIONS

Beat sugar into egg white.

Add nuts and drop from a spoon onto a buttered cookie sheet.

Bake in 300 F. oven for 40 minutes. Should be a light brown when done.

Mrs. George P. Meier, Indianapolis, Indiana

566. Quick Brown Sugar Drop Cookies

(Makes 7 dozen)

INGREDIENTS

DIRECTIONS

1 lb. butter
2 cups brown sugar
2 egg yolks
3½ cups flour
2 teaspoons vanilla

Mix all together.

1 cup chopped nuts

Drop mixture from the end of a teaspoon into the nuts. Place on baking sheet and bake in 400 F. to 450 oven for 10 minutes.

The Hearthstone, Winnetka, Illinois

567. Pecan Puffs

(Makes about 2 dozen)

INGREDIENTS

DIRECTIONS

½ cup butter

Beat until soft.

2 tablespoons sugar
1 teaspoon vanilla

Blend until creamy.

1 cup pecans—put through a meat grinder
1 cup cake flour—sifted powdered sugar

Mix pecans and flour these together and stir into the butter mixture. Roll into small balls and place on greased baking sheet. Bake in 300 F. oven for 45 minutes. While hot, roll in powdered sugar and when cooled, roll again in powdered sugar.

Mrs. Louie M. Weathers, Elkton, Kentucky

568. Salted Peanut Cookies

(Makes about 5 dozen)

INGREDIENTS

DIRECTIONS

1 cup butter—melted
2 cups brown sugar

Blend together.

2 eggs

Beat well and add to above.

2 cups flour
1 teaspoon baking powder
1 teaspoon soda
1 teaspoon salt

Sift together and add to mixture.

2 cups oats
1 cup cornflakes
1 cup whole salted peanuts

Stir into mixture and drop from a teaspoon onto a lightly greased cookie sheet. Bake in 350-degree oven for 15 to 20 minutes.

The Ruttger's Lodge, Deerwood, Minnesota

569. Pecan Cookie Balls

(Makes approximately 10 or 12 doz. cookies)

INGREDIENTS

1 cup butter
1 teaspoon salt
2 teaspoons vanilla
½ cup powdered sugar

2 cup sifted flour
2 cups finely chopped pecans

DIRECTIONS

Blend butter with salt and vanilla. Add sugar gradualy. Cream well.

Sift in flour, add chopped nuts. Shape dough into little balls slightly larger than a marble. Place on greased cookie sheet and bake about 15 minutes in moderate oven 350°. Remove from pan and quickly but carefully roll the hot cookies in sifted powdered sugar. This forms a frosting-like coating over the cookies. Cool, then roll again in powdered sugar. Store in an air tight container. (Takes about 2 cups powdered sugar for coating.)

Mrs. Alfred North, Philadelphia, Pennsylvania

570. Rocks

(Makes about 48 medium sized cookies)

INGREDIENTS

1 cup butter
1 cup white sugar

4 egg yolks

2¼ cups flour
1 teaspoon cinnamon
1 teaspoon cloves
1 cup black walnut meats
1½ cup raisins

1 level teaspoon soda
1½ tablespoons boiling water

4 egg whites

DIRECTIONS

Cream butter and add sugar gradually, beating until fluffy.

Beat egg yolks and add to butter and sugar.

Sift flour, measure, add spices and sift again into batter. Add walnuts and raisins and stir, mixing well.

Dissolve soda in water and add to batter, mixing well.

Beat egg whites until stiff and fold into batter. Drop by teaspoonsfuls onto greased cookie sheet and bake in 375° oven for 15 minutes or until done and nicely browned.

Mrs. J. C. Bristow, Richmond, Virginia

571. Baba au Rhum (Serves 6)

INGREDIENTS

DIRECTIONS

- 2 egg whites
- 2 egg yolks
- 1 cup sugar

Beat egg whites stiff. Beat egg yolks until light and add to whites and beat together. Add sugar slowly and beat with spoon for 5 minutes.

- 1 cup flour
- 1 teaspoon baking powder
- pinch salt
- ½ cup hot milk
- 1 tablespoon butter
- ½ teaspoon lemon extract
- ½ teaspoon vanilla

Sift dry ingredients together and add to egg mixture. Melt butter in hot milk and beat into mixture. Add flavoring. Pour into Mary Ann pan and bake in 360° oven for 25-30 minutes. Makes 6 Mary Anns.

BUTTERED RUM SAUCE: (Makes 3 cups)

- 2 cups sugar
- 1 cup cold water
- 1 tablespoon butter
- ⅓ cup rum
- Vanilla ice cream

Boil sugar and water for 2 minutes. Remove from heat and add butter. Cool and add rum. Soak the cake in rum sauce, then place in serving dish. Fill center with vanilla ice cream and garnish with whipped cream, serve at once. This is one of my favorite desserts.

The Toll House, Whitman, Massachusetts

572. Vanilla Cookies (Makes 3 or 4 dozen)

INGREDIENTS

DIRECTIONS

- 8 teaspoons butter
- 8 teaspoons lard

Cream together.

- 1 cup sugar
- 1 egg—well beaten
- ¼ cup milk

Add to creamed mixture.

- 2 cups flour
- 2 teaspoons baking powder
- ½ teaspoon salt

Sift dry ingredients and add to mixture.

- 2 teaspoons vanilla

Add to mixture. Roll thin and cut with cutter. Bake on a lightly greased cookie sheet in a 375° F. oven for 6 minutes.

Peckett's on Sugar Hill, Franconia, New Hampshire

Save the juices from canned pineapple, peaches and other fruits. Put them in glass bottles, set them away in the refrigerator and use these juices in your breakfast fruit cup or add a little lemon to make some refreshing hot weather "ades." Such glass bottles also come in handy for storing vegetable stock or meat stock in the refrigerator for later use in soups or gravies.

573. Cake Doughnuts   (Makes 35 doughnuts)

INGREDIENTS

DIRECTIONS

1½ cups brown sugar
2 eggs

Beat whole eggs until they are light and stir into sugar.

4 tablespoons melted butter
1 cup whole milk

Stir into above.

4 cups sifted flour
4 teaspoons baking powder
½ teaspoon cinnamon
½ teaspoon salt

Add baking powder, cinnamon and salt to flour and sift again. Add to above, stirring only enough to get ingredients thoroughly blended. Place in refrigerator to chill, at least 24 hours if possible. (This prevents the doughnuts from soaking up the fat when fried).

Roll out a little of the dough at a time on floured board, cut with doughnut cutter. Fry in deep hot fat about 365° until brown on one side. Turn over and brown on other side. Drain and roll in powdered sugar. This dough may be kept at least a week in a covered dish in the refrigerator. Break off and cook only enough of the dough at a time to fill your requirements, as freshly cooked doughnuts are better than those left standing overnight.

Mrs. Duncan Hines, Bowling Green, Kentucky

574. Histulas (Little Fruit Doughnuts)
(Makes 4 or 5 dozen)

INGREDIENTS

DIRECTIONS

½ cup sugar
2 egg yolks, beaten

Combine sugar and egg yolks.

½ cup sour milk
½ teaspoon soda

Mix milk and soda and add to egg mixture.

2 cups sifted flour
¼ teaspoon salt

Sift flour, measure, then sift with salt. Add to above.

½ cup pecans
¼ cup raisins
¼ cup dates
1 orange rind—grated

Pecans, raisins, and dates should be finely chopped. Add to above with orange rind.

2 tablespoons orange juice

Add the orange juice. Drop from teaspoon into deep hot fat, 325°, and fry until light brown. Turn while cooking. Remove from fat and drain on absorbent paper. Sprinkle with sugar. (Histulas should be quite small, only slightly larger than the hole in an ordinary doughnut. It helps to drop the amount spooned out of the dough briefly into flour. Then each ball can be molded by hand. The coating of flour keeps the grease from soaking in.)

Belle Anderson Ebner, Wabasha, Minnesota

575. Doughnuts

INGREDIENTS

DIRECTIONS

½ lb. butter
¾ lb. white sugar

Cream butter and add sugar gradually.

6 egg yolks
1 cup milk

Beat egg yolks and add with milk to above mixture, beat well.

6 cups flour
1 tablespoon baking powder

Sift flour and baking powder together. Add to the above and mix well.

1 wine glass brandy
6 egg whites—stiffly beaten

Add to the above mixture. Cut doughnuts and let stand from 5 to 15 minutes before frying. Fry in 370° fat until brown on one side, turn and brown on the other. Remove and drain on paper towels. Frost with icing or sprinkle with fruit sugar.

These doughnuts will be just as good tomorrow as today. May also be warmed by running into a hot oven for a few minutes.

Helen Gougeon, Weekend Magazine, Montreal, P. Q. Canada

576. Paint Pony Ginger Cookies (Makes approx. 8 dozen)

INGREDIENTS

DIRECTIONS

1½ cups shortening
2 cups granulated sugar
2 eggs

Cream shortening and add sugar. Stir eggs into mixture one at a time.

½ cup molasses

Stir into above.

4 cups flour
2 teaspoons salt
2 teaspoons cinnamon
2 teaspoons nutmeg
2 teaspoons ginger
2 teaspoons cloves
4 teaspoons soda
1½ cups chopped glacé fruit

Sift flour and measure. Add soda, spices and salt to flour and sift again. Stir into above mixture until well blended. Add fruit with last addition of flour so that it will be floured as it is being stirred into batter. Shape dough into balls about 1 inch in diameter. Roll in extra granulated sugar. Put on greased cookie sheet and bake at 375° for 10 to 20 minutes until done.

Paint Pony Lodge, Show Low, Arizona

Any fifteen year old girl can make delicious cookies if she follows the rule. Use only good ingredients—exact measurements, careful handling, correct temperatures and baking time.

Underbaking a cake will cause it to sink in the middle or to have heavy moist streaks. Overbaking it causes it to have a hard brown crust and it will be dried out.

577. Apple Pie

INGREDIENTS

1 cup of sugar
2 tablespoons flour
½ grated nutmeg
½ cup orange juice
3 tablespoons light corn
  syrup
⅓ cup melted butter

winesap apples cut
into thin slices
(enough to fill a pie
pan)

DIRECTIONS

Mix all together.

Add to the above and thoroughly mix together. Butter a pie pan heavily before putting in the pastry, then fill with the apple mixture and make strips for the top. Preheat oven. Bake at 400 F. for 15 minutes, then reduce oven to 250 F. and bake for 35 to 40 minutes.

Duncan Hines, Bowling Green, Kentucky

Here are our two favorite versions of the No. 1 American dessert. You pays your money and you takes your choice.

578. Apple Pie

INGREDIENTS

1¼ cups flour
2 tablespoons poultry
  fat
2 tablespoons butter
3¾ tablespoons ice water
  pinch salt

1 stick butter
1 cup sugar
1 heaping tablespoon
  flour
  winesap apples

DIRECTIONS

Sift flour and salt. Cut in butter and poultry fat, add ice water and mix gently. Roll out thin and line pie pan which has been heavily buttered. Left over pastry used for strips to cover top of pie.

Slice half of the stick of butter over the crust in the pie tin. Mix together sugar and flour and put half over butter. Peel and chop enough apples to fill pie tin heaped up. Cover with remainder of sugar and flour mixture. Top with strips of crust and slice remainder of butter over top. Place in 450° F. preheated oven for 10 minutes, lower heat to 350° F. and bake for 25 to 30 minutes or until done and pastry is brown on top.

Mrs. Duncan Hines, Bowling Green, Kentucky

579. Apple Dumplings (Serves 6)

INGREDIENTS

2 cups cake flour
2 teaspoons baking powder
½ teaspoon salt

⅔ cup shortening

⅓ cup milk, or perhaps ½ cup

6 to 8 tart apples

½ teaspoon cinnamon
¼ teaspoon nutmeg
¾ cup brown sugar

6 tablespoons butter

½ cup brown sugar
½ cup granulated sugar
2 cups water
½ cup butter

DIRECTIONS

Mix and sift dry ingredients.

Work shortening in lightly with the tips of fingers.

Make hole in flour and add milk gradually while mixing lightly. Knead lightly into a ball and roll into a rectangular-shaped piece of dough about ¼ inch thick and cut into six pieces.

Peel and slice apples and divide between six squares of dough.

Mix these ingredients and add to the apples.

Dot each square with a tablespoon of butter and bring up the corners of the dough and pinch together to make dumpling.

Make a syrup of these ingredients and while hot, set in dumplings, and bake in 350 F. to 375 F. oven for 1 hour, or until apples are done. Dumplings are best when made of quick cooking apples, though winter apples may be used if slowly cooked.

Richards Treat Cafeteria, Minneapolis, Minnesota

My favorite pie is apple. Instead of putting ice cream on it, try a thin slice of ham. You'll be surprised.

580. Taffy Tarts (Makes 8 tarts)

INGREDIENTS

pie pastry

¼ cup butter
1 cup brown sugar
1 egg
½ cup currants
3 tablespoons evaporated milk
¼ teaspoon vanilla

DIRECTIONS

Make your favorite pastry. Fit into greased muffin tins.

Cream butter, add sugar and blend well. Beat egg slightly and stir in. Add milk, currants and vanilla. Pour into pastry lined tins and bake in 350° oven for 30 minutes.

Duncan Hines, Bowling Green, Kentucky

581. Fresh Apple Cobbler with Hot Rum Sauce

(Serves 6 to 8)

INGREDIENTS

2½ cups sliced cooked
   apples
1 cup sugar
½ cup butter
1 teaspoon cinnamon

   pie crust

HOT RUM SAUCE:

2 cups juice from
   cooked apples
2 cups sugar
4 tablespoons Cuban
   rum

DIRECTIONS

Stir sugar into apples. Fill a greased deep dish pie pan or casserole ⅔ full. Dot with butter and sprinkle cinnamon over the surface.

Roll out very thin, cut into strips and criss cross over surface, bake in 450° oven until apples are glazed.

Simmer juice and sugar until thick or consistency of light syrup. When ready to serve, add ½ tablespoon rum to each 2 tablespoons hot apple syrup and pour over each serving of hot cobbler.

Mrs. Duncan Hines, Bowling Green, Kentucky

582. Apricot and Peach Turnovers

(Makes 8)

INGREDIENTS

½ lb. dried apricots
½ lb. dried peaches
1½ cups water

1 cup sugar
⅓ cup butter
½ grated nutmeg
1 tablespoon flour

1 recipe of pastry

DIRECTIONS

Cook until the consistency of mush.

Add to the above.

Cut pastry into saucer-shaped rounds and put in ample filling. Fold over and seal the edges. With a fork, prick the top so the steam can escape.

Place on a baking sheet and bake in 350 F. oven for 15 minutes, then lower to 300 F. and bake until a golden brown and the crust seems crisp on both sides.

Duncan Hines, Bowling Green, Kentucky

583. Apricot Cream Pie   (Makes one 9-inch pie)

INGREDIENTS

DIRECTIONS

¾ cup sugar
3½ cups milk

Put in double boiler and bring to scalding point.

4 tablespoons corn-
starch
½ cup cold milk

Dissolve and add to above.
Cook until mixture thickens.

2 egg yolks beaten
slightly

Add a small amount of the above hot mixture to the eggs, mix and pour back into
the double boiler. Cook until thick.

½ teaspoon salt
1 teaspoon vanilla
1½ tablespoons butter

Add to above and blend well.

1 cup cooked apricots
1 baked 9-inch pie
shell

Cut apricots in pieces and add to above. Stir
well. Cool. Put in baked pie shell and cover
with meringue.

APRICOT MERINGUE:

6 egg whites
¾ cup sugar

Whip until stiff and dry, add sugar gradually.

¾ cup cooked apricots

Drain well and add to above. Spread on pie
and serve. DO NOT BROWN IN OVEN.

Mills Restaurants of Ohio (Cincinnati, Columbus and Cleveland)

584. Butterscotch Chiffon Pie   (Makes one 9-inch pie)

INGREDIENTS

DIRECTIONS

¾ cup brown sugar
4 egg yolks
½ teaspoon salt
½ cup milk

Cook in double boiler until thick.

1 tablespoon gelatin
¼ cup cold water

Dissolve and add to the above mixture. Let
cool.

4 egg whites—beaten
stiff
¼ cup sugar

Beat well and fold into the above mixture.
Place in 9-inch baked pie shell and cover with
whipped cream.

The Normandy Farm, Rockville, Maryland

*Cheese with pie is not new but you may be surprised to find
how good it tastes with fresh peaches, apples or other fruit.*

585. Black Bottom Pie

(Makes one 9-inch pie)

INGREDIENTS

DIRECTIONS

CRUST

14 crisp ginger snaps
5 tablespoons melted
   butter

Roll snaps out fine. Add butter to cookie crumbs and pat evenly into a 9-inch pan. Bake 10 minutes in 300 F. oven. Allow to cool.

FILLING

2 cups milk—scalded
4 egg yolks—beaten

Add eggs slowly to hot milk.

½ cup sugar
1¼ tablespoons corn-
    starch

Combine and stir into above. Cook in double boiler for 20 minutes, stirring occasionally until it generously coats a spoon. Remove and take out 1 cup.

1½ squares chocolate

Add to the cup of custard and beat well.

1 teaspoon vanilla

As custard cools, add vanilla, pour into pie crust and chill.

1 tablespoon gelatin
4 tablespoons cold
  water

Blend thoroughly and add to remaining hot custard. Let cool, but not thick.

4 egg whites
½ cup sugar
¼ teaspoon cream tartar
2 tablespoons rum

Beat into a meringue and fold into custard. Add rum. As soon as chocolate custard has set, add this. Chill again until it sets.

1 cup whipped cream

Spread on top of pie.

½ square chocolate

Shave and sprinkle over pie and serve.

Dolores Restaurant, Oklahoma City, Oklahoma

586. Black Walnut Pie

(Makes one 9-inch pie)

INGREDIENTS

DIRECTIONS

¼ lb. butter
1 cup sugar
1 cup dark corn syrup
3 eggs
1 teaspoon cinnamon
¼ cup black walnut
  meats
2 tablespoons boiling
  water
1 unbaked pie shell

Melt butter, add sugar and syrup and stir to dissolve. Beat eggs and add to mixture. Put walnut meats in cloth and beat to pulp. Add to mixture with cinnamon and stir in water. Bake in uncooked pie shell in 350° F. oven for 50 minutes.

Kelley's Inn and Tea Room, Franklin, North Carolina

587. Blueberry Pie

(Makes one 9-inch pie)

INGREDIENTS

1 quart blueberries
1¼ cups sugar
4 tablespoons melted butter

DIRECTIONS

Bake in double crust. Do not add thickening agents. Serve runny in a fairly deep dish. Line pie tin with pastry. Combine berries, sugar and butter, pour into shell. Bake in 375° oven 40 to 60 minutes or until crust is golden brown.

Lowell Inn, Stillwater, Minnesota

588. Chess Pie

(Makes one 8-inch pie)

INGREDIENTS

3 eggs

DIRECTIONS

Beat lightly.

1 cup sugar
¼ teaspoon salt
¼ teaspoon nutmeg

Mix dry ingredients together and add slowly to eggs, beating all the while.

½ cup butter

Melt and add to above.

¼ tablespoon tart jelly

Stir into above, mixing well. Pour into unbaked pie crust and place in 350° oven for 10 minutes and then reduce heat to 300° for 20 minutes or until it sets.

Mrs. Earle Forbes, Versailles, Kentucky

589. Chess Pie

(Makes one 9-inch pie)

INGREDIENTS

½ cup butter
1½ cups sugar

DIRECTIONS

Melt butter, stir and add sugar slowly. Remove from heat.

1½ teaspoons vinegar
1½ teaspoons cornmeal

Dilute vinegar if very strong. Add to above with cornmeal. Cool slightly.

3 eggs

Beat slightly and add to above. Pour into an unbaked pastry shell and bake for 10 minutes at 425°. Then lower to 300° and bake for 1 hour. Take from oven when pie shakes slightly.

Mrs. Rhea G. Price, Bowling Green, Kentucky

590. Cavalier Pie Supreme

(Makes two 8-inch pies)

INGREDIENTS

DIRECTIONS

2 tablespoons gelatin
½ cup cold water
1½ cups hot water

Soak gelatin in ½ cup cold water for 5 minutes. Dissolve in hot water and let cool.

1 qt. whipping cream
6 egg yolks
1 cup powdered sugar
pinch salt
1 teaspoon vanilla

Whip cream until thick. Beat egg yolks and add to cream, and whip again for 1 minute. Add gelatine and whip well again. Pour into baked pie shell, and put into refrigerator to congeal.

1 pt. whipping cream
⅓ cup powdered sugar
½ teaspoon vanilla

Whip cream until thick. Add sugar and vanilla and whip until stiff. Spread over pie.

4 oz. bitter-sweet
chocolate

Grate chocolate and spread over pie and return to refrigerator until ready to serve.

Beach Plaza Hotel, Virginia Beach, Virginia

591. Frozen Chocolate Peppermint Pie

(Makes one 12-inch pie)

INGREDIENTS

DIRECTIONS

4 egg whites
½ teaspoon cream of tartar
1 cup sugar

Beat egg whites until frothy. Add cream of tartar. Beat until whites are stiff. Add sugar slowly a tablespoon at a time beating until mixture is thick and glossy. Line a deep 12-inch pie pan with meringue and bake in preheated 300° oven for 50-60 minutes. Cool.

2¾ cups whipping cream
2 cups fudge sauce
½ teaspoon oil of peppermint

Whip cream until stiff. Slowly add fudge sauce and oil of peppermint.

1 qt. vanilla ice cream

Soften a bit in electric beater. Spoon into cooled meringue shell. Do not let ice cream get too soft—just enough to manage. Pour over this the chocolate whipped cream mixture. Freeze until firm.

If you do not have a 12-inch pan, use 2 9-inch pie pans.

Belle Anderson Ebner, Wabasha, Minnesota

In making cakes or pies, always have your oven preheated to the temperature called for in the recipe. To be sure that your oven is the proper temperature, check with an oven thermometer.

592. Chocolate Angel Pie

(Makes one 9-inch pie)

INGREDIENTS

2 egg whites
½ cup sugar
⅛ teaspoon cream of tartar
½ cup nuts—chopped

DIRECTIONS

Sift together sugar and cream of tartar. Beat eggs until stiff but not dry. Add sugar while beating and continue beating until smooth and glossy. Line greased pie pan with meringue. Sprinkle with chopped nuts. Bake in 275° oven for 1 hour until delicate brown. Cool thoroughly.

¾ cup semi-sweet chocolate bits
3 tablespoons hot water
1 teaspoon vanilla
1 cup heavy cream—whipped

Melt chocolate in double boiler, stir in water and let cook until thick. Add vanilla and fold into whipped cream. Fill shell and chill in refrigerator 3 to 4 hours.

Royce Cafe, Edmond, Oklahoma

593. Bittersweet Mint Pie

(Makes one 9-inch pie)

INGREDIENTS

1 baked 9-inch pie shell

½ cup cold milk
1 tablespoon unflavored gelatin

DIRECTIONS

Sift gelatin over cold milk and let soak.

1½ cups milk
¾ cup sugar
1 tablespoon cornstarch
3 egg yolks

Scald milk. Combine sugar and cornstarch, add some of the hot milk to dissolve. Beat egg yolks, stir carefully into sugar and milk and when combined, stir into rest of hot milk. Cook in double boiler over hot water until mixture coats spoon. Add softened gelatin and stir to dissolve. Chill until fairly firm.

2 squares unsweetened chocolate
3 egg whites
½ cup cream
¼ cup green Creme de Menthe
3-4 drops green coloring

Melt chocolate over hot water. Let cool slightly. Beat egg whites until stiff. Whip cream but not too stiff. When custard is chilled, beat until smooth and fluffy, then beat in egg whites. When thoroughly blended, fold in whipped cream. Divide into two equal portions, approximately 2 cups each. Add melted chocolate to one portion. Mix well and pour into bottom of pie shell. To the other half add Creme de Menthe and coloring. Blend well and pour on top of chocolate in pie shell. Chill until firm.

½ cup cream
grated chocolate

When ready to serve, whip cream, spread over pie and sprinkle on small amount of grated chocolate.

Mrs. Merritt Agard, Taughannock Farms, Inn, Ithaca, New York

594. Christmas Pie

(Makes one 9-inch pie)

INGREDIENTS

DIRECTIONS

CRUST:

1½ cups ground Brazil
    nuts
  3 tablespoons sugar

Mix nuts and sugar thoroughly, pack evenly on bottom and sides of pie pan and bake in 400° oven for 8 minutes or until lightly browned. Watch carefully as it scorches easily.

FILLING:

  1 envelope gelatin
    unflavored
  ¼ cup cold water

Soak gelatin in cold water until dissolved.

  3 egg yolks
  ¼ cup sugar
  ⅛ teaspoon salt
1½ cups scalded milk

Beat egg yolks with fork and add sugar gradually. Then stir in carefully and gradually the milk. Place in double boiler and cook over boiling water until it coats a metal spoon. Remove at once and stir in gelatin. Cool, then chill custard until it mounds when dropped from a spoon. Beat with an egg beater until smooth.

  ½ cup glaced cherries
  2 tablespoons light rum
  3 egg whites
  ¼ cup sugar

Stir in cheeries which have been sliced thin. Beat in carefully the rum. Beat egg whites until stiff, add gradually the sugar and beat until stiff and dry. Fold into the custard. Pour into the cooled baked Brazil nut crust. Place in refrigerator until the following day or for at least four hours until firm.

  ½ pint whipped cream
  sliced Brazil nuts

Whip ½ pint or more of cream and spread over the pie. Top with sliced Brazil nuts.

Brevard Hotel, Cocoa, Florida

Pie is as American as the Fourth of July. It is part of our background and our history. It may have originated in the Old Countries, but we have staked out a claim on it by constant usage and improvement. Everyone has his favorite pie, but Apple Pie is probably THE favorite American Dessert.

595. Coconut Cream Pie   (Makes one 10-inch pie)

INGREDIENTS | DIRECTIONS

1 cup milk
1⅓ cups sugar
pinch salt

Bring to a boil.

2 egg yolks—beaten
2 tablespoons corn-
starch
1 tablespoon milk

Blend cornstarch and milk and mix with eggs. Add to hot milk above and cook slightly.

2½ teaspoons gelatin
1 tablespoon milk

Dissolve gelatin in milk and pour hot mixture over it. Let set until firm. Put in electric beater and beat well.

½ cup coconut
1 cup whipped cream
1 teaspoon vanilla

Add to above mixture and put in refrigerator for 10 minutes.

2 egg whites—beaten

Fold in stiff egg whites, pour in baked pastry shell, cover with whipped cream and sprinkle with coconut.

El Encanto Tea Shop, Los Angeles, California

596. Continental Cream Pie   (Makes one 9-inch pie)

INGREDIENTS | DIRECTIONS

14 ginger cookies or
graham crackers

Roll fine.

5 tablespoons butter—
melted

Mix well with above. Pat evenly in a 9-inch spring form pan. Bake in 300 F. oven for 10 minutes.

FILLING:

4 egg yolks—beaten
2 cups milk—scalded

Slowly add milk to eggs.

1½ tablespoons corn-
starch
½ cup sugar

Combine and stir into the above. Cook over simmering water for 20 minutes, or until custard generously coats spoon. Remove from the fire.

1 tablespoon gelatin
4 tablespoons cold
water

Soak. Add to the custard while it is still hot. Let cool.

4 egg whites—beaten
½ cup sugar
candied fruit

Beat egg whites very stiff, gradually beat in sugar and add to custard while it is still soft and smooth. Fill the pie crust and set it in the refrigerator. Sprinkle with candied fruit.

2 tablespoons brandy

Added to the custard makes a "special" Continental Cream Pie.

Hilton Hotel, El Paso, Texas

597. Custard Pie

(Makes one 9-inch pie)

INGREDIENTS

DIRECTIONS

1 unbaked pie shell

3 eggs—beaten lightly
2½ cups milk
1 cup sugar
1 pinch salt
2 tablespoons melted
    butter

Mix together and put in unbaked pie shell. Sprinkle top with grapenuts or graham cracker crumbs. Do not stir. Bake in 400 F. oven for 12 to 15 minutes. Then reduce heat to 300 F. and cook until custard is set in the center of the pie.

Stone's Restaurant, Marshalltown, Iowa

598. Eggnog Pie

(Makes two 9-inch pies)

INGREDIENTS

DIRECTIONS

3 tablespoons gelatin
2 tablespoons cold
    water
2 cups boiling hot water

Dissolve in cold water, then add hot water. Allow to cool and begin to set before proceeding with the following.

8 egg whites—beaten
    stiff
2½ cups sugar
4 oz. rum

Add to egg whites the sugar and rum and then mix with gelatin, beating until smooth and glossy.

1 pint whipped cream

Fold in whipped cream and pour into previously baked pie shells. Place in a cool place and allow to set. Top with additional whipped cream.

Santa Maria Inn, Santa Maria, California

599. Eggnog Pie

(Makes one 9-inch pie)

INGREDIENTS

DIRECTIONS

1 tablespoon gelatin
¼ cup cold water

Soak gelatin in cold water for five minutes.

4 egg yolks—beaten
½ cup sugar
½ teaspoon salt
½ cup hot water

Put ingredients in double boiler and cook until custard consistency. Add gelatin, stir and dissolve. Let cool.

4 egg whites—beaten
¼ cup sugar
3 teaspoons rum

Fold in egg whites, sugar and rum and fill baked pie shell. Place in refrigerator to set. Serve with thin layer of whipped cream over top and grated nutmeg.

The Carr House, Wolfeboro, New Hampshire

Healthful food is the basis for body building, wholesome disposition, energy, and a longer and healthier life.

600. Date and Nut Pie

(Serves 5)

INGREDIENTS

12 dates
1 cup pecans
12 premium crackers
1 cup sugar
½ teaspoon baking
   powder

3 egg whites
1 teaspoon almond
   extract

DIRECTIONS

Chop dates and nuts fine. Roll crackers fine.
Combine baking powder with sugar. Combine
all of the ingredients and mix well.

Beat egg whites until stiff and add extract,
fold into above mixture. Pour into an 8-inch
greased pie pan. Bake 30 minutes in a 350
degree oven or until light brown. Cool before
cutting and serve with whipped cream if
desired.

Villula Tea Garden, Seale, Alabama

601. English Toffee Pie

(Makes two 9-inch pies)

INGREDIENTS

2 uncooked pie shells

3 cups heavy sour cream
2½ cups sugar
1 teaspoon cloves

3 eggs
2 egg yolks

3 cups seedless raisins
¾ cups English walnuts
¾ cups blanched
   almonds
1 teaspoon vanilla
¼ cup sherry

DIRECTIONS

Use deep pie pan.

Combine.

Beat together whole eggs and egg yolks and
add to above.

Chop walnuts and quarter almonds. Stir into
above with raisins, vanilla and sherry. Pour
into pie shells and bake in 400° oven for 15
minutes. Reduce to 350° and bake 35 to 40
minutes or until a silver knife inserted in
center comes out clean. Can be served with
vanilla ice cream.

(As a variation hazel nuts may be used also. In that case use ½ cup each
of almonds, walnuts and hazel nuts.)

Pendarvis House, Mineral Point, Wisconsin

*An amateur cook should not attempt a dish with a vast number
of ingredients but should start out simply.*

602. Graham Cracker Pie

(Makes two 9-inch pies)

INGREDIENTS

40 graham crackers—
    crushed
1 tablespoon cinnamon
½ cup sugar
½ cup softened butter

FILLING:

1 quart milk

8 egg yolks—beaten
4 tablespoons cornstarch
2 teaspoons vanilla
1 pinch of salt
2 tablespoons melted
    butter
½ cup sugar

8 egg whites
½ teaspoon cream of
    tartar
1 cup sugar
¼ teaspoon salt
1 teaspoon vanilla

DIRECTIONS

Mix ingredients and press in pie pan. Add the filling.

Heat.

Mix this filling, add the heated milk and cook until thick. Then fill the pie shells.

Preheat oven to 425°F. Beat egg whites with cream of tartar until frothy. Then add the sugar very gradually. Beat until stiff and glossy. Pile meringue onto pie, making sure to seal onto the edge of the crust. Bake in preheated 425° oven for 4 minutes, or until golden brown. Cool.

Sanders Cafe, Corbin, Kentucky

603. Heavenly Pie

(Makes one 9-inch pie)

INGREDIENTS

3 egg whites—beaten
½ cup sugar

⅓ cup confectioners
    sugar

1 cup whipping cream

DIRECTIONS

Beat egg whites stiff and dry. Add sugar gradually.

Fold into mixture. Bake in ungreased 9-inch glass pie plate in 275 F. to 325 F. oven for 1 hour. About 2 hours before serving, crush the top slightly.

Whip and spread over the pie. Place in the refrigerator until ready to serve. Shred bitter chocolate over the top.

The Weathervane, Middlebury, Vermont

604.   Filling for Small Pastries, Tarts, etc.

INGREDIENTS	DIRECTIONS
¼ lb. butter ¾ lb. lump sugar	Melt together.
2 lemons—grated rind 2 lemons—juice	Add to above.
6 egg yolks—beaten 4 egg whites—beaten	Add to mixture and stir until it thickens. Pour into baked tart shells.

Columbia Gorge Hotel, Hood River, Oregon

605.   French Cream Coconut Pie   (Serves 6 to 8)

INGREDIENTS	DIRECTIONS
1 pint milk 1 cup sugar	Scald.
4½ tablespoons cornstarch 5 egg yolks ⅔ cup milk	Mix together and add slowly to above, stirring constantly until mixture thickens. Remove from fire.
4⅝ tablespoons butter 1 pinch salt	Add to above mixture and stir until butter is dissolved.
1 tablespoon vanilla	Stir into mixture, and pour immediately into 9-inch baked pie shell.
½ can coconut or ½ fresh coconut—grated	Put on top of filling.
½ pint whipping cream—whipped	Put on top of coconut.

To vary this pie, stir into finished cream filling 3½ squares unsweetened melted chocolate, or top with fresh fruit such as red raspberries, before topping with whipped cream. Place in refrigerator before serving.

Duncan Hines, Bowling Green, Kentucky

Every kitchen should have a good knife sharpener.

When guests are invited to my home for seven o'clock dinner, we begin the meal promptly at seven-thirty whether all have arrived or not. There is no reasonable excuse for thoughtless guests to spoil a good dinner for those who arrive at the appointed hour.

606. Hazelnut Pie

(Makes one 9-inch pie)

INGREDIENTS

3 eggs
½ cup sugar
¼ teaspoon salt
1 cup dark corn syrup
½ teaspoon vanilla
1 cup toasted chopped
  hazelnuts

DIRECTIONS

Beat eggs slightly and add other ingredients in order. Mix well. Line pie tin with plain pastry, pour in filling and bake 45 minutes in 300° oven. Serve with whipped cream.

1 cup golden table syrup instead of dark corn syrup makes a maple flavored pie.

Plentywood Farm, Bensenville, Illinois

607. Jefferson Davis Pie

(Makes two 9-inch pies)

INGREDIENTS

3 cups sugar
1 cup butter

4 eggs—beaten lightly

1 cup milk

1 tablespoon flour
¼ teaspoon salt
1 teaspoon vanilla

DIRECTIONS

Cream together.

Add to the above.

Stir into mixture.

Blend into mixture. Then beat all the above like the devil. Line 2 pie pans that have first been well butterd, with pie crust. Pour in the filling and bake in 450 F. oven for 10 minutes, then reduce heat to 350 F. for another 30 to 35 minutes.

Mrs. McKenzie Moss, Bowling Green, Kentucky

608. Lemon Chiffon Pie

(Makes one 9-inch pie)

INGREDIENTS

4 egg yolks—beaten
½ cup sugar
½ cup lemon juice
1 lemon rind—grated
1 pinch salt

1 tablespoon gelatin
¼ cup cold water

4 egg whites—beaten
½ cup sugar

DIRECTIONS

Cook in double boiler, stirring constantly until consistency of custard.

Soak until gelatin is dissolved. Then add to hot custard.

Beat sugar into egg whites. Fold hot custard into egg whites carefully. Put in baked pie shell and chill 3 hours.

Stone's Restaurant, Marshalltown, Iowa

Add a bit of lemon juice to make meringue cut cleaner.

609. Grandma Obrecht's Lemon Pie

(Makes one 9-inch pie)

INGREDIENTS

1½ cups sugar
5 tablespoons corn-
starch
½ teaspoon salt

1½ cups boiling water

2 teaspoons butter
4 egg yolks, slightly
beaten

½ cup lemon juice
rind of 1 lemon—
grated

DIRECTIONS

Mix together.

Add to above, cook over direct heat, stirring constantly until mixture boils. Then place in double boiler, cover and cook until thick.

Remove above from fire, add butter and egg yolks, return to fire and cook two minutes.

Add lemon juice and rind to above. Cook until thick. Pour into baked pie shell.

MERINGUE:

4 egg whites
8 tablespoons
granulated sugar
¼ teaspoon cream of
tartar

Beat egg whites very stiff, add sugar and cream of tartar gradually. Beat until well blended. Spread over pie, sprinkle with a little sugar before baking. Bake in pre-heated 350° oven until brown.

Lowell Inn, Stillwater, Minnesota

It has been suggested that the above lemon pie filling would be delicious used as a filling for a sponge cake baked in a tube pan. Slice cake crosswise in 3 layers, fill with lemon filling and frost with whipped cream. It is yummy!

610. Kentucky Lemon Pie

(Makes one 9-inch pie)

INGREDIENTS

5 eggs
1½ cups syrup
juice of 2 lemons
grated rind of 1
lemon
1 cup sugar
¼ cup butter—melted

DIRECTIONS

Beat eggs well. Add syrup then other ingredients in order and beat together until well mixed. Pour into unbaked pie shell and bake on lower shelf of 375° oven for 10 minutes. Remove to middle shelf and reduce heat to 350° for 30 to 40 minutes.

Boone Tavern, Berea, Kentucky

611. Lemon Fluff Pie

(Makes one 8-inch pie)

INGREDIENTS

1 baked pie shell

4 egg yolks
¾ cup sugar
juice of 2 lemons
rind of 1 lemon—
grated

2 egg whites
1 teaspoon sugar

2 egg whites
¼ cup sugar

DIRECTIONS

Make your favorite pastry, bake and cool.

Beat egg yolks and gradually add sugar. Add lemon juice and rind and cook in double boiler for about 12 minutes. Stir constantly. If it gets lumpy beat with egg beater and remove from heat.

Beat egg whites until stiff and add sugar. Fold into above mixture and pour into pie shell.

Beat egg whites until stiff and add sugar gradually. Cover pie with meringue and brown in 400 degree oven for about 5 minutes.

Stoddard's Atop Butler Hall, New York City

612. Frosted Lime Pie

(Makes 6 individual pies or one 10-inch pie)

INGREDIENTS

1½ cups hot water
1¼ cups sugar

7 tablespoons corn-starch
7 tablespoons cold water (or ½ scant cup)

2 large egg yolks (or 3 small ones)

⅓ to ½ cup fresh lime juice depending on strength and taste
1 teaspoon grated lime rind
1 tablespoon butter
a few drops of green coloring

MERINGUE:
¼ lb. marshmallows
2 large egg whites or 3 small ones
¼ cup sugar
1 tablespoon lime juice

DIRECTIONS

Put in top of double boiler and bring to a boil over direct heat.

Mix to a thin paste and add to the above and cook over hot water until thick and smooth, stirring frequently.

Beat slightly and add to above. Cook a few minutes longer. Remove from fire.

Mix and add to the above. Chill slightly and pour in baked pie shells, top with meringue

Melt marshmallows in double boiler. Beat egg whites stiff and combine with sugar, lime juice and marshmallows. Pile gently on top of the pie filling. These may be browned slightly under the broiler, but are nicest chilled and garnished with sprigs of fresh mint leaves dipped in egg white and bar sugar.

Vera Kirkpatrick, San Mateo, California

613. Lime Pie

(Makes one 9-inch pie)

INGREDIENTS	DIRECTIONS
2 tablespoons sugar 3 egg yolks	Beat together.
1 can condensed milk	Beat into the egg mixture.
½ cup lime juice	Add to mixture and stir thoroughly. DO NOT COOK.
1 baked pie shell	Pour mixture into pie shell.
3 egg whites 3 tablespoons sugar	Whip up egg whites, adding the sugar gradually. Spread over the pie and put in 350 F. oven a few minutes to brown the top

Brown's, Fort Lauderdale, Florida

614. Pie Crust for two nine-inch double crust pies (Three to One Formula)

Three parts of flour to one of shortening by volume.

INGREDIENTS	DIRECTIONS
1⅓ cups (⅔ lbs.) shortening	Carefully combine, using pastry blender, one half of the shortening with the flour to a corn meal consistency. Add remaining shortening and blend to the size of large peas. All flour must be completely absorbed in the shortening.
4 cups (1 qt.) all purpose flour (sifted)	If pastry flour is used, either the shortening may be slightly reduced, or the flour increased. This blended shortening and flour may be prepared the day before and set in the refrigerator.
To 12 tablespoons cold water, add 2 teaspoons salt	Add cold water, a little at a time while stirring until dough forms a loose ball in the bowl. Cut dough in four equal parts for four crusts. We use pastry canvas and rolling pin cover which have been permeated with the same type of

flour used in the dough. Lightly roll out dough to ⅛ inch thickness. Use trimmings in lower crust only which can be rolled a little thicker than the top crust. Place pie tin on dough and trim allowing ½ inch around the tin. Bake in 450° oven till brown. Check oven temperature often with oven thermometer. Well browned pie tins or Pyrex give good results. Do not use new pie tins.

Lowell Inn, Stillwater, Minnesota

> *Dinners are cooked in the kitchen, served in the dining room, but digested at home.*

615. Pastry Shells

(Makes 6 individual shells)

INGREDIENTS

½ cup lightly salted butter

1 cup sifted pastry or all purpose flour
5 teaspoons cold water

DIRECTIONS

Cream butter as for cake (do not melt by heat).

Next add flour and cold water. Mix lightly. Roll out as pie crust. Cut to fit individual pastry shell pans. Bake at 450 degrees 8-10 minutes. For meats, chicken, and sea food filling.

Lowell Inn, Stillwater, Minnesota

616. Macaroon Pie

(Makes one 9-inch pie)

INGREDIENTS

12 crackers
1 cup sugar
1 teaspoon baking powder

½ cup nut meats
12 to 15 dates

3 egg whites
1 teaspoon almond flavoring
whipped cream

DIRECTIONS

Roll crackers fine. Mix the opposite ingredients together.

Chop nuts and dates. Add to above and mix.

Beat egg whites until stiff. Add almond flavoring and fold into date and nut mixture. Pour into greased 9-inch pie pan and bake for 30 minutes at 350 degrees. Serve with whipped cream.

Royce Cafe, Edmond, Oklahoma

617. Maid of the Mist Pie

(Makes one 9-inch pie)

INGREDIENTS
CRUST:

14 graham crackers
¼ cup butter

FILLING:

3 egg yolks
1 cup sugar
juice of two large lemons

3 egg whites

½ pt. whipping cream

DIRECTIONS

Crush with rolling pin. Blend butter with crumbs and pat into pie pan.

Beat sugar and eggs well together, add lemon juice, place in double boiler and cook to custard consistency.

Beat very stiff, fold into custard, blend thoroughly, put into crust and bake in very moderate oven, about 325 F., until set.

Whip until stiff, cover pie when cool, just before serving.

Chanticleer Lodge, Lookout Mountain, Tennessee

618. Pecan Tart

(Makes 18)

INGREDIENTS

DIRECTIONS

4 eggs—beaten lightly
1 cup sugar
1¼ cups syrup
1¼ cups pecans—chopped
1½ tablespoons vanilla
1½ tablespoons butter

Stir together lightly and put into patty shell. Bake in 250 F. oven for 30 minutes.

1 cup whipping cream
—whipped

Before serving, top each tart with whipped cream.

Stoddard's Atop Butler Hall, New York, New York

619. Pecan Pie

(Makes one 9-inch pie)

INGREDIENTS

DIRECTIONS

3 eggs

Beat well.

1 cup sugar
1 cup white corn syrup
¼ lb. butter—melted
1 teaspoon vanilla
1 cup chopped pecans

Add ingredients in order given to eggs. Pour in uncooked pie shell and cook in pre-heated oven, 350°, for 30-45 minutes.

New Perry Hotel, Perry, Georgia

620. Nell Palmer's Pecan Pie

(Makes one 9-inch pie)

INGREDIENTS

DIRECTIONS

3 eggs

Beat until light.

¾ cup sugar
¼ lb. butter—melted
1 cup dark corn syrup

Slowly beat into the eggs.

Pour into uncooked pie shell and bake slowly in 300 F. oven for 40 minutes.

1 cup pecan halves

Completely cover the pie with whole pecan halves and return to a 350 F. oven and bake for another 10 to 15 minutes. May be served with whipped cream.

Lowell Inn, Stillwater, Minnesota

When cooked dishes call for milk there is little difference in the raw or pasteurized product. For drinking purposes, however, it is always safer and healthier to insist on pasteurized milk; and the new methods of irradiation for vitamin D homogenizing, which distribute the cream evenly throughout, are further improvements well worth noting.

621. Open Fresh Strawberry Pie (Makes one 9-inch pie)

INGREDIENTS | DIRECTIONS

1 cup flour
½ cup shortening

Blend completely. Makes rich crust.

½ teaspoon salt
1 tablespoon cold water

Mix together and add to above mixture. Roll out and bake in 425 F. oven for 15 minutes.

FILLING:

1 cup crushed fresh
strawberries
1 cup sugar
1 tablespoon cornstarch

Boil until transparent.

fresh strawberries—
enough to fill the pie

Put strawberries in pie shell and pour over hot berry syrup and chill. Raspberries may be substituted for strawberries.

Lowell Inn, Stillwater, Minnesota

622. Plum Rolls (Serves 8 to 10)

INGREDIENTS | DIRECTIONS

1 No. 2½ can prune
plums or 1 quart
canned damsons

Drain plums thoroughly, remove pits, and cut into coarse pieces. If you use canned damsons, add sugar to taste to sweeten.

4 tablespoons sugar
2 tablespoons butter
1 teaspoon Angostura
bitters

Add to juice strained from plums, place in baking pan and bring to boil on high heat.

2 cups flour
½ teaspoon salt
3 teaspoons baking
powder
2 tablespoons sugar

Sift dry ingredients together.

4 tablespoons butter

Cut butter into dry ingredients as in any pastry.

1 egg
½ cup milk

Beat egg thoroughly, combine with milk, and add to above to make soft dough. Place on floured board and roll to ½-inch thickness. Spread with chopped plums and roll up. Slice roll crosswise into 1½-inch lengths and place, cut side down, in hot syrup. Bake in 350°oven for about 30 minutes or until pastry is done.

Mrs. Duncan Hines, Bowling Green, Kentucky

All fresh fruits should be washed before using.

623. Frozen Praline Pie

(Makes one deep 10-inch pie)

INGREDIENTS

DIRECTIONS

MERINGUE SHELL:

4 egg whites
1 cup sugar
½ teaspoon cream of tartar

Beat egg whites until frothy, add cream of tartar. Beat until stiff and dry. Add sugar slowly and stir until mixture is glossy. Put in 10 inch spring form pan on bottom and around sides to form pie shell. Bake in 300° oven for 50 to 60 minutes. Cool.

FILLING:

Make the Butterscotch Sauce, Recipe No. 452.

2 qts. vanilla ice cream
1 cup pecan halves
1 cup ground pecans

When sauce and meringue are cool, soften 1 qt. ice cream in mixer until sufficiently soft to spoon into shell. Put in freezer and let get firm. Pour over ice cream a thick layer of sauce and cover with pecan halves. Let get firm again. Soften the other quart of ice cream and put on top. Let this get firm, then top with thick layer of sauce and cover entirely with ground pecans. Cover tightly with aluminum foil and return to freezer. Serve in wedges with a spoonful of sauce on top.

Belle Anderson Ebner, Wabasha, Minnesota

624. Pumpkin Pie

(Makes two 9-inch pies)

INGREDIENTS

DIRECTIONS

3½ cups canned pumpkin
1 teaspoon cinnamon
½ teaspoon ginger
1 teaspoon nutmeg
1 teaspoon salt
1 cup sugar

Mix together.

4 eggs—beaten
4 tablespoons butter

Melt butter and add with eggs to above.

2 cups rich milk

Scald and stir into mixture. Line a buttered pie pan with pastry and brush over with slightly beaten egg white before putting in the filling. Bake in 425° F. oven for 15 minutes, then reduce to 350° F. and bake 30 minutes or until filling is firm and crust well browned.

Duncan Hines Test Kitchen, Ithaca, New York

First roll lemons and oranges if you want to extract juice more easily.

I like all food that smells good, looks good, tastes good and is good for me. This eliminates ground hog, coons, possum, gophers, snakes and such.

625. Pumpkin Chiffon Pie

(Makes one 10-inch pie)

INGREDIENTS

DIRECTIONS

1 cup brown sugar
3 egg yolks
1¼ cups pumpkin
2 teaspoons cinnamon
½ teaspoon ginger
¼ teaspoon allspice
½ teaspoon salt

Put in double boiler and cook until it begins to thicken.

1 tablespoon gelatin
¼ cup cold water

Soak gelatin in water for 5 minutes. Add to hot mixture and stir until thoroughly dissolved. Cool.

3 egg whites—beaten
2 tablespoons sugar
1 baked 10-inch pie shell

Beat sugar into whites and fold into mixture. Pour into baked pie shell and chill. Serve garnished with whipped cream.

The Dinner Bell, Oakland, California

626. Rhubarb Pie

(Makes one 9-inch pie)

INGREDIENTS

DIRECTIONS

CRUST:

1 cup flour
1 teaspoon baking powder
¼ teaspoon salt
⅓ cup shortening
water

Sift dry ingredients together. Work in shortening quickly with fingers until of crumb consistency. Add just enough cold water to make stiff dough. Roll out and line 9" pie pan.

FILLING:

4 cups rhubarb

Cut in ½" pieces. Place in uncooked pastry shell.

1½ cups sugar
½ cup flour

Mix together and sprinkle over rhubarb.

2 eggs

Beat whole eggs well and put by spoonfulls over rhubarb.

2 tablespoons butter

Break in small pieces and sprinkle over pie. Strip pie with thin strips of pastry. Bake in oven 350° until done.

Sunset Farm, Whittier, North Carolina

Use your oven to full advantage when you have a baking job to do. Fill the extra space with apples, sweet potatoes, Irish potatoes, prepared squash, eggplant or other things which might be available. Even if you do not eat them at the same meal, many of these may be set away for lunch or dinner the next day.

627. Raspberry Pie

(Makes one 9-inch pie)

INGREDIENTS | DIRECTIONS

2 cups frozen
raspberries

Defrost and drain juice.

¼ cup cold water
2 tablespoons butter
½ cup sugar
1 teaspoon lemon juice
pinch salt

Combine berry juice with cold water and other ingredients and place over heat.

3 tablespoons
cornstarch
¼ cup cold water
1 baked 9-inch pie
shell

Dissolve cornstarch with cold water and add to above. Cook until thick, stirring constantly. Remove from fire, add berries, let cool. Pour into 9-inch baked pie shell. Serve with whipped cream.

John Ebersole's Restaurant, White Plains, New York

628. Sour Cream Raisin Pie

(Makes one 10-inch pie)

INGREDIENTS | DIRECTIONS

1 10-inch baked pastry
shell

Prepare.

FILLING:

½ cup seedless raisins
½ cup nut meats

Chop raisins and nuts and mix together.

1 cup sugar
2½ tablespoons flour
1 teaspoon cinnamon
¼ teaspoon ground
cloves

Mix together dry ingredients and add to raisins and nuts.

1½ cups sour cream

Pour over above mixture and stir all together thoroughly. Place in double boiler and bring to a boil.

3 egg yolks

Beat egg yolks together and add gradually to above mixture, stirring constantly to prevent lumping. Cook all together until thick. Let cool and pour into pastry shell.

3 egg whites
6 tablespoons sugar

Beat the egg whites together and add the sugar gradually. Top the pie with the meringue and brown in a slow oven.

The Blue Gentian, Saranac Lake, New York

629. Rum Cream Pie

(Makes one 9-inch pie)

INGREDIENTS

6 egg yolks
1 cup sugar

1 tablespoon gelatin
½ cup cold water

1 pint heavy cream
½ cup Jamaica rum

DIRECTIONS

Beat eggs until light. Add sugar slowly to yolks.

Soak gelatin in cold water, put gelatin and water over low heat and let come to a boil. Pour it over the sugar and egg mixture, stirring briskly.

Whip cream until it is stiff. Fold into above mixture. Add rum, stir well, cool but do not let set. Pour into a crumb shell or a cooked pastry shell, sprinkle generously with shaved bitter sweet chocolate. You should use a deep spring form pan for this rather than a regular pie tin as this makes a very thick pie.

The Smorgasbord, Stow, Ohio

630. Spiced Nut Pie

(Makes one 9-inch pie)

INGREDIENTS

3 egg yolks
½ cup sugar
¼ lb. butter

1 cup mixed nuts—
   pecans and walnuts
1 cup steamed seedless
   raisins
½ teaspoon cinnamon
½ teaspoon cloves
1 teaspoon nutmeg
¼ teaspoon salt
2 tablespoons cider
   vinegar

3 egg whites
½ cup sugar

DIRECTIONS

Cream together egg yolks, butter and sugar.

Mix and add all to above.

Beat egg whites stiff and slowly beat sugar into whites. Fold into above.

Bake in moderate oven 350° in uncooked pastry shell about 40 minutes.

McLester Hotel, Tuscaloosa, Alabama

Far too many people do not know how to cut lemons properly for juice in iced tea, on fish, etc. Too often it is a thin, round, half slice good only for messing up your fingers. I like lemons quartered lengthwise, with the membranous core and seeds removed before serving.

631.   Sunny Silver Pie

(Makes one 9-inch pie)

INGREDIENTS	DIRECTIONS
4 egg yolks 2 or 3 tablespoons lemon juice rind of 1 lemon—grated ⅛ teaspoon salt ½ cup sugar	Cook in double boiler until thick, stirring constantly. Remove from fire.
1½ teaspoons gelatin ⅓ cup cold water	Soak gelatin in cold water about 5 minutes, and add to the above.
4 egg whites—beaten ½ cup sugar	Beat together well. Fold into the above mixture.
1 baked pie shell	Place in baked pie shell and set in refrigerator for 2 or 3 hours.
1 cup whipping cream	Whip and spread on top of pie.

High Hampton, Cashiers, North Carolina

Have you ever eaten a cold baked apple? Then try one with a little cinnamon, nutmeg and warm milk. You may bake these while using the oven for something else, letting them cool and then storing them in the refrigerator for later use. Stale bread may be toasted at the same time and will add flavor as well as proteins along with your baked apple and warm milk.

632.   Treasure Chest Pie

(Makes one 9-inch pie)

INGREDIENTS	DIRECTIONS
½ cup butter 1 cup sugar	Cream together.
3 egg yolks—beaten 1 egg white—beaten	Stir into mixture until it foams.
½ cup cooked raisins ½ cup mincemeat ½ cup walnuts—broken ½ cup pecans—broken 2 tablespoons orange juice 1 teaspoon vanilla ½ teaspoon salt 2 tablespoons Apple Jack brandy	Add to mixture and pour into pie shell *uncooked.* (Make a rich flaky crust, but do not bake it first.) Put a criss-cross crust on top and bake in 400 F. oven for 12 to 15 minutes until the filling sets and then cover the pie with an inverted pie pan, lower the temperature to 350 F. and bake until the top crust becomes brown and the filling is well set. May be served with whipped cream, but that is not necessary.

Duncan Hines, Bowling Green, Kentucky

633. Alsatian Pudding

(Serves 8 to 10)

INGREDIENTS

DIRECTIONS

½ lb. butter
2½ cups powdered
sugar

Cream together butter and sugar until *very* light and fluffy.

8 egg yolks

Add to the above and beat well.

½ cup strong cold coffee

Add very slowly to the above.

1 dozen ladyfingers—
split
rum

Line an oblong pan with waxed paper and place a layer of split ladyfingers on bottom and sprinkle with rum. Next a layer of creamed mixture. Another layer of ladyfingers and sprinkle with rum and so on until mixture is used ending with a layer of ladyfingers. Put into refrigerator overnight.

shredded, toasted
almonds

Just before time to serve, turn out of pan, slice and sprinkle each slice with almonds.

Mrs. Bland Farnsworth, Bowling Green, Kentucky

634. Apple Pudding

(Serves 12-14)

INGREDIENTS

DIRECTIONS

4 lbs. winesap apples
2 cups granulated
sugar

Peel apples and slice thin. Place in bottom of buttered baking pan (8x14-inch). Sprinkle with sugar.

2 cups brown sugar
¾ lb. butter
2 cups flour

Cream butter and sugar together in mixer. Stir in flour. Pat out dough and cut in cookie shapes. Place close together all over top of apples. Bake until golden brown in preheated oven, 350°, for 45-50 minutes. Serve warm with cream or ice cream.

The Ardzli Restaurant, Springfield, Ohio

635. "My Weakness"

(Serves 1)

INGREDIENTS

DIRECTIONS

3 Parker House rolls-
hot from the oven
6 pats of butter
6 teaspoons sugar

Split each roll in half, spread on each 1 pat of butter and 1 teaspoon sugar.

Elmer D. Becker, Chicago, Illinois

636. Baked Indian Pudding
(Serves 8)

INGREDIENTS	DIRECTIONS
3 cups milk	Scald the milk.
3 tablespoons Indian meal ⅓ cup molasses	Mix together and stir into hot milk and cook until it thickens. Stir constantly to prevent scorching. Remove from fire.
½ cup sugar 1 egg—beaten 1 tablespoon butter ½ teaspoon ginger ½ teaspoon cinnamon ¼ teaspoon salt	Add to mixture and mix thoroughly. Pour into a buttered baking dish and put in 300 F. oven.
1 cup milk	In ½ hour pour the milk over above mixture and continue baking for 2 hours.

The Toll House, Whitman, Massachusetts

637. Old Fashioned Indian Pudding
(Serves 8)

INGREDIENTS	DIRECTIONS
4 cups milk	Scald in double boiler.
5 tablespoons Indian meal	Gradually add meal to the above and cook 15 minutes, stirring constantly.
2 tablespoons butter 1 teaspoon salt ½ teaspoon ginger ½ teaspoon cinnamon 1 cup molasses 2 eggs—well beaten	Add these ingredients to the mixture.
1 cup sweet apples— sliced very thin	Stir into mixture and turn into buttered baking dish.
1 cup cold milk	Pour over all and bake in 325 F. oven for 1 hour. Serve with vanilla ice cream.

The Carr House, Wolfeboro, New Hampshire

While non-union pay, there is one job that outstrips all others in the number of people who work at it and the hours worked—the housewife. I suggest that we men give them a satisfying increase in pay.

638.   Chocolate Bread Pudding

(Serves 8)

INGREDIENTS	DIRECTIONS
2 tablespoons butter 4 squares unsweetened chocolate	Melt in double boiler.
½ cup sugar ¼ teaspoon salt	Add to the above.
4 egg yolks—beaten ½ cup milk	Add to mixture and cook until slightly thickened.
2 cups fresh bread crumbs 1 teaspoon vanilla ½ cup nut meats.	Add to the above and mix thoroughly.
4 egg whites—beaten	Fold into mixture. Turn into mold; filling about ⅔ full. Steam for 25 minutes. Serve with butter sauce or whipped cream, either hot or cold.

Robert G. Brehmer, Jr., Fond du Lac, Wisconsin

639.   Chocolate Pudding

(Serves 6 to 8)

INGREDIENTS	DIRECTIONS
1 pint milk	Heat in double boiler.
4 tablespoons cornstarch 3 tablespoons cold milk	Stir together into smooth paste and add to milk. Cook until smooth.
4 oz. of unsweetened chocolate or 4 tablespoons cocoa ½ cup sugar	Add to mixture. Take from the fire.
4 egg whites—beaten	Fold into mixture and set away to harden.

CUSTARD SAUCE:

INGREDIENTS	DIRECTIONS
4 egg yolks—beaten 4 tablespoons sugar	Beat together.
1 pint scalding milk	Add to egg mixture and cook as you would a soft custard.
1 teaspoon of vanilla	Add to mixture and pour over the pudding.

Mrs. Belle A. Marquis, Mansfield, Ohio

Better that grease clog the sink than your stomach.

640. Chocolate Steam Pudding

(Serves 6 to 8)

INGREDIENTS	DIRECTIONS
3 tablespoons butter ⅔ cup sugar 1 egg—beaten	Cream and blend together.
2¼ cups flour 4½ teaspoons baking powder ½ teaspoon salt	Sift together and mix into the above.
1 cup milk	Add to mixture.
2½ squares unsweetened chocolate	Melt and add to mixture. Turn into molds filling no more than half full. Steam 2 hours and serve with sauce.

SAUCE:

¼ cup butter	Work until very soft.
1 cup powdered sugar	Gradually add to the butter.
½ teaspoon vanilla 1 pinch of salt	Add to mixture.
¼ cup whipping cream	Whip and fold into the sauce.

The Hearthstone, Winnetka, Illinois

641. Chocolate Souffle

(Serves 4 to 6)

INGREDIENTS	DIRECTIONS
2 tablespoons butter 2 tablespoons flour	Blend together.
¾ cup milk	Gradually add to the above. Cook until it reaches the boiling point.
1½ squares chocolate—melted ⅓ cup sugar 2 tablespoons hot water	Mix together and add to the mixture and stir until smooth.
3 egg yolks—beaten	Add to mixture. Let cool.
3 egg whites—beaten ½ teaspoon vanilla	Fold into mixture. Turn into baking dish and bake in 350 F. oven for 25 minutes, or until done. Serve hot with hard sauce.

Mrs. W. B. Taylor, Bowling Green, Kentucky

Your hostess may say, "It is perfectly all right," when you are thirty minutes late for dinner, but it comes not from the heart. Next time you may not be invited.

642. Cottage Pudding with Strawberry Sauce

(Serves 6 to 7)

INGREDIENTS	DIRECTIONS
2 cups of flour 2½ teaspoons baking powder ½ teaspoon salt	Sift all together.
1 egg—beaten ¾ cup sugar 3 tablespoons melted butter 1 cup milk	Mix together, and stir in the flour. Bake in a shallow pan in 375 F. oven for 30 to 40 minutes.

SAUCE:

1 tablespoon butter 1½ cups powdered sugar	Cream together.
1 egg white—beaten	Mix into the above.
1 pint strawberries—mashed, or any other fruit	Add the fruit just before serving. It is well to have a generous serving of the sauce, and if so, double the quantities.

Mr. H. M. Carruth, Cleveland, Ohio

643. Date Souffle

(Serves 8)

INGREDIENTS	DIRECTIONS
2 tablespoons butter 3 tablespoons sugar	Cream together
3 egg yolks	Beat and add to above.
2 tablespoons flour ¾ cup milk	Add to the above, alternately with milk.
3 egg whites—beaten 1 teaspoon salt	Beat together and fold into mixture.
1 package dates—chopped (14 oz.)	Fold into mixture and pour into a 1½ or 2 quart greased casserole. Set in pan of hot water and bake in 350 F. oven for 35 minutes. Serve with orange sauce.

ORANGE SAUCE:

1 cup sugar 1 cup orange juice 1 orange rind—grated 1 lemon—juice 1 teaspoon cornstarch 1 tablespoon butter 1 egg yolk	Mix together and cook in a double boiler, until it coats a spoon.

The Hearthstone, Winnetka, Illinois

644. Gooseberry Mousse or Pudding (Serves 6)

INGREDIENTS

DIRECTIONS

1 quart gooseberries
½ lb. sugar
½ pint water

Cook slowly until tender enough to put through a sieve.

1 tablespoon brandy
a little green coloring

Add brandy and coloring. Let cool.

1 pint whipping cream
—whipped

Fold whipped cream into mixture. If made into a mousse, put in refrigerator trays and freeze.

Any fresh fruit, minus the coloring may also be used.

Duncan Hines, Bowling Green, Kentucky

645. Grated Sweet Potato Pudding (Serves 12)

INGREDIENTS

DIRECTIONS

½ cup sugar
½ cup butter
½ cup chopped nuts

Cream butter, sugar, and nuts.

3 eggs

Add eggs one at a time and beat well.

4 cups grated sweet
potato (raw)
1 cup corn syrup,
light or dark
2 cups sweet milk
1 teaspoon each salt,
nutmeg, cinnamon,
and cloves

Add grated potato, milk, syrup and spices and bake 2 hours in moderate oven in well buttered iron skillet.

When brown crust forms on top stir down and let brown again. Serve plain or with whipped cream, either hot or cold.

If pudding gets too dry while baking, add another cup milk, stir lightly and let brown again.

This pudding makes a delicious cold weather dessert and is handed down from the old days of Dutch oven baking.

Mayfair Hotel, Searcy, Arkansas

Some say that raw endive, celery, carrot and parsley mixture strengthens the eyes.

Away from home, in recent years I have stuck to ham and eggs when in doubt, as it would require a very poor cook to spoil good ham, and the best chef cannot rejuvenate an old egg.

646. Indian Tapioca Pudding

(Serves 6 to 8)

INGREDIENTS	DIRECTIONS
2 cups milk	Scald.
2 tablespoons tapioca 2 tablespoons Indian meal ⅔ cup molasses ⅓ cup sugar	Mix and stir into the hot milk. Cook 20 minutes, stirring constantly until it thickens. Remove from the fire.
3 tablespoons butter 1 egg 1 teaspoon salt 1 teaspoon cinnamon 1 teaspoon ginger 2 cups cold milk	Add to the above mixture, stir and pour into greased baking dish. Set in pan of hot water and bake 4 hours in 350 F. oven.
1 cup cold milk	Add milk about 1 hour before serving, but do not stir. Serve with whipped cream or hard sauce.

Mrs. Locke's Dining Porches, Fryeburg, Maine

647. Macaroon Charlotte Russe with Butterscotch Sauce

(Serves 15)

INGREDIENTS	DIRECTIONS
1 pint whipping cream ½ tablespoon almond extract ½ tablespoon vanilla	Whip cream and blend in flavor.
½ lb. macaroons—crumbled	Fold into the above.
5 oz. egg whites—beaten ⅟₁₆ teaspoon salt	Beat together and fold into mixture.
sponge cake may be used in place of lady fingers if cut the same shape.	Arrange lady fingers as desired in glasses in which the Charlotte Russe is to be served and fill with creamy mixture. Place in refrigerator until ready to serve. Serve with butterscotch sauce.

BUTTERSCOTCH SAUCE:

1 lb. brown sugar 1 can evaporated milk (14½ oz. size) 4 tablespoons butter	Put all ingredients in a double boiler and cook until it coats the spoon. This sauce is very necessary as its richness complements the Charlotte Russe.

Jane Davies Restaurant, New York, New York

648. Tapioca Cream Pudding (Serves 6 to 8)

INGREDIENTS | DIRECTIONS

½ cup pearl tapioca
½ cup water

Soak tapioca in water at least 12 hours.

1 quart sweet milk

Heat milk in double boiler and add tapioca to hot milk. Cook 1 hour until tapioca is clear. Stir occassionally.

½ cup granulated sugar

Add to milk and tapioca and cook an hour.

3 egg yolks
1½ tablespoons sugar

Beat egg yolks and sugar in mixer until thick and lemon colored. Add a little of the hot mixture to the yolks. Stir yolks into milk and tapioca and mix well. Return to double boiler and cook until eggs are done, approximately 20 minutes.

¼ teaspoon vanilla
⅛ teaspoon salt

Stir in vanilla and salt. Let cool, stirring occasionally until lukewarm.

Grace E. Smith's Restaurant, Toledo, Ohio

649. Raisin Puffs (Serves 8 to 10)

INGREDIENTS | DIRECTIONS

½ cup butter
1 cup sugar

Cream together.

2 eggs—beaten

Add to above.

2 cups flour
2 teaspoons baking powder
1 cup milk

Sift dry ingredients together and add to mixture, alternately with milk.

1 cup raisins—cut up

Flour raisins and add to mixture. Steam in cups ¾ of hour. Serve with whipped cream.

Sawyer Tavern, Keene, New Hampshire

When tapicoa puddings are sticky, they have been cooked too long. Cook tapioca only until it is clear.

650. Lemon Pudding (Serves 6)

INGREDIENTS | DIRECTIONS

1 cup sugar
2 tablespoons butter

Cream.

2 egg yolks
2 tablespoons flour
1 lemon—juice and rind grated

Add to above and stir well.

1 cup milk

Add to mixture.

2 egg whites—beaten

Fold into mixture. Pour into greased casserole. Place in water, bake in 300° oven until done, but do not let it bake stiff on the bottom. Preferably served hot—but it may be served cold with whipped cream.

Mrs. W. B. Taylor, Bowling Green, Kentucky

651. Macaroon Pudding (Serves 6 to 8)

INGREDIENTS | DIRECTIONS

4 egg yolks—beaten
½ cup sugar

Mix together.

1 tablespoon gelatin
1 cup milk

Soak gelatin in milk for 5 minutes. Stir into egg yolks and let come just to the boiling point. Let cool.

4 egg whites
vanilla to taste

Beat egg whites stiff and flavor to taste. Fold into custard.

12 almond macaroons
1 cup whipped cream

Break macaroons into small pieces and fill a large mold or individual molds. Pour the custard over the pieces and put in refrigerator until it sets. Serve with whipped cream. Sprinkle with glazed cherries and chopped nuts. If a circle mold is used, fill the center with whipped cream.

Miss Katharine L. Little, Chicago, Illinois

652. Raisin Pudding (Serves 6 to 8)

INGREDIENTS | DIRECTIONS

1 cup sugar
1 cup flour
2 teaspoons baking powder
½ cup sweet milk
1 cup raisins

Mix together in order given and pour into greased baking dish.

1¼ cups brown sugar
2 cups hot water
1 tablespoon butter

Dissolve sugar in hot water and add butter. Stir until melted. Pour over above and bake in 350° oven for 45 minutes.

Mrs. K's Toll House Tavern, Silver Spring, Maryland

653. Maple Rag-a-Muffin Dessert   (Serves 6)

INGREDIENTS

1½ cups flour
½ teaspoon salt
3 teaspoons baking
   powder
¼ teaspoon cream of
   tartar
4 tablespoons shorten-
   ing
⅛ to ½ cup milk
   butter
1½ cups maple syrup

¼ cup chopped nuts
½ cup whipping cream
   or
1 pint vanilla ice cream

DIRECTIONS

Sift dry ingredients. Cut in shortening and add
milk to make a soft dough. Roll out on a
lightly floured board and cut 12 small biscuits.
Place in well greased pan and dot generously
with butter. Heat syrup and pour over biscuits.
Bake 15 minutes in a 450° oven.

Serve warm with whipped cream or a small
scoop of ice cream. Garnish with nuts.

Twist-o' Hill Lodge, Williston, Vermont

654. Blueberry Pudding   (Serves 8)

INGREDIENTS

1 qt. blueberries
1 cup sugar
4 tablespoons arrowroot
   or cornstarch
   juice of 1 lemon

½ cup sugar
4 tablespoons butter
¼ teaspoon salt
1 egg
½ cup milk
1½ cups sifted flour
2 teaspoons baking
   powder
1 teaspoon vanilla

DIRECTIONS

Wash berries and drain. Mix sugar and arrowroot and add to berries. Place in greased casserole, and sprinkle with lemon juice.

Cream together butter and sugar. Add salt.
Beat the egg and add it. Add milk and mix
well. Stir in flour briskly and spoon over berries. Bake in 425° oven for about 20 to 25 minutes. Serve warm with vanilla ice cream.

You may use frozen blueberries if you wish. If so it will take two packages
for the recipe. Let defrost for about 10 or 15 minutes.

Mrs. Duncan Hines, Bowling Green, Kentucky

The smell of good food is more important than the taste.

655.   Orange Souffle

INGREDIENTS

DIRECTIONS

6 egg whites
6 tablespoons sugar

Beat eggs stiff and beat in sugar gradually.

4 tablespoons orange
  marmalade
1 teaspoon orange
  extract

Mix into the above. Put in a double boiler that holds 3 quarts. Cook slowly for 1 hour. Turn out on a round platter. (It should stand up like a man's silk hat.) Pour sauce around it and serve.

SAUCE:

6 egg yolks—beaten
1 cup sugar
1 pinch of salt

Beat together until smooth.

1 pint whipped cream
2 tablespoons Curaçoa

Add to the sauce just before serving.

candied kumquats—
  sliced

Decorate each portion.

Chalet Suzanne, Lake Wales, Florida

Whatever you eat, if not digested it does not nourish.

656.   Persimmon Pudding

INGREDIENTS

DIRECTIONS

1 cup persimmon pulp
1 tablespoon butter
1 cup sugar
2 teaspoons soda
½ cup milk
1 cup flour
1 teaspoon vanilla
1½ teaspoons baking
  powder
1 pinch of salt

Mix together, turn into molds filling about ⅔ full and steam for 3 hours.

Serve with sauce.

SAUCE:

2 egg yolks—beaten
1 cup sugar

Beat together.

½ cup sherry wine

Add to eggs.

½ pint whipping cream
  —whipped

Add to mixture just before serving.

Mammoth Cave Hotel, Mammoth Cave, Kentucky

657. Ozark Bakeless Pudding

(Serves 6)

INGREDIENTS | DIRECTIONS

½ cup butter
1 cup sugar
2 eggs
1 cup chopped nuts
1 small can crushed
 pineapple—drained
½ lb. graham crackers

Cream butter and sugar. Add well beaten eggs, nuts and pineapple. Crush the graham crackers and in a dish place a thick layer of crackers, then the mixture and top with remainder of crackers. Let set for 12 hours in refrigerator and serve with whipped cream. (Peaches may be substituted for the pineapple.)

Hotel Taneycomo, Rockaway Beach, Missouri

658. Plum Pudding

(Serves 6 to 8)

INGREDIENTS | DIRECTIONS

½ lb. citron
¼ lb. candied lemon and
 orange peel
1 lb. raisins
1 lb. currants

Chop fruits.

1 lb. suet
¼ teaspoon cloves
⅓ teaspoon cinnamon
¼ teaspoon allspice

Put suet through food chopper. Mix all these ingredients together.

6 eggs beaten
2 cups sugar

Mix together and stir into above.

1 cup sherry wine
2 cups flour
2 teaspoons baking
 powder

Thicken the wine with flour and baking powder and pour over fruit mixture. Dip a cloth in hot water and line with flour. Pour in the pudding and tie. Have the water boiling and keep boiling for 6 hours. Keep the pudding covered with water during this process.

Mrs. Charles Normand, Belton, Texas

659. Pudding Saxon

(Serves 8)

INGREDIENTS | DIRECTIONS

2 cups sugar
4 eggs—beaten
3 oz. citron peel—
 chopped
6 oz. raisins
1 pint milk
8 slices bread—diced
1 orange rind—grated
3 oz. melted butter

Mix and blend.

Pour into a greased mold and set in hot water. Bake in 375 F. oven for 30 minutes. Serve hot.

This is a man's dessert.

The Viking Norwegian Restaurant, Santa Barbara, California

660. Pumpkin Pudding (Serves 6)

INGREDIENTS

DIRECTIONS

1 cup sugar
½ cup butter

Cream together.

5½ cups pumpkin

Add to above.

6 egg yolks—beaten
4 egg whites—beaten

Stir into above.

1 pint milk
3 teaspoons cinnamon
¼ teaspoon salt
2 teaspoons ginger
¼ teaspoon nutmeg
1 teaspoon lemon extract

Add to the above and mix thoroughly. Pour into buttered baking dish, set in pan of hot water. Bake 45 minutes in 375 F. oven.

2 egg whites
¼ cup sugar

Beat stiff into a meringue. Spread over pudding and bake until meringue is brown. Chill. Serve with chilled cream.

Duncan Hines Test Kitchen, Ithaca, New York

661. Brown's Rice Pudding (Serves 4)

INGREDIENTS

DIRECTIONS

¼ cup raw rice
1 qt. whole milk
¼ cup sugar
½ teaspoon vanilla
pinch of salt
pinch of cinnamon
½ cup raisins

Wash rice thoroughly and place in earthenware casserole. Add milk, sugar, salt, cinnamon and vanilla. Cook in 250° oven for 3½ hours stirring frequently. Then add raisins, more if you like, and cook half an hour longer.
Raisins will curdle milk if added before pudding is almost done.

Brown's Restaurant, Ft. Lauderdale, Florida

662. Stephanie Pudding (Serves 4)

INGREDIENTS

DIRECTIONS

1 tablespoon gelatin
¼ cup cold water

Soak.

1 cup grape or
loganberry juice—hot

Dissolve gelatin with hot juice.

½ cup sugar
¼ cup lemon juice

Add to dissolved gelatin and strain. Set in a cool place. Stir mixture occasionally and when thick whisk until frothy.

3 egg whites—beaten

Add to above mixture and beat until stiff enough to hold its own shape. Serve cold with boiled custard sauce.

Marjorie Mills, Boston, Massachusetts

663. Riz a L'Imperatrice
(Serves 10 to 12)

INGREDIENTS

DIRECTIONS

⅓ cup—chopped citron
⅓ cup candied lemon peel—chopped
⅓ cup candied orange peel—chopped
3 oz. Kirschwasser

Combine fruits and marinate in Kirschwasser while making the pudding. Stir occasionally.

2 cups milk
1 tablespoon vanilla or one 1-inch stick vanilla

Add vanilla to milk and heat in top of double boiler.

½ cup water
½ cup sugar
¾ cup rice

Combine water and sugar in sauce pan and let come to a boil. Wash and drain rice and drop into boiling syrup. Cook 5 minutes stirring constantly. Drop the rice mixture by spoonfuls into the above hot milk and let cook until almost all of the liquid is absorbed. Stir occasionally (liquid absorbed in about 1 hour). Remove piece of vanilla.

2 tablespoons unflavored gelatin
½ cup cold water
1 pint heavy cream

Soak gelatin in cold water about 5 minutes and add to above mixture, stir to dissolve. Let set until cool. Whip cream until stiff and add fruits and Kirschwasser. Add whipped cream and fruits to rice mixture and pack into a two-quart oiled mold. Let stand over night or until well set. Unmold and serve with a strawberry or raspberry sauce, made from simmering 1 package of frozen fruit with ½ cup sugar.

Grand Hotel Victoria-Jungfrau, Interlaken, Switzerland

664. Fresh Fruit Trifle
(Serves 8)

INGREDIENTS

DIRECTIONS

24 almond macaroons
¾ cup sherry wine

Dip macaroons in wine and place in a flat serving dish.

6 egg yolks—beaten
1 cup sugar
⅛ teaspoon salt

Beat eggs 5 minutes in electric beater or with rotary beater for 15 minutes, adding sugar and beating a little longer. Add the balance of sherry and salt. Place in double boiler and cook until it thickens, stirring constantly. Pour this mixture over the macaroons and allow to cool.

Any fresh fruit, or whipped cream and almonds

Just before serving cover with fresh sliced peaches, figs, or strawberries. Or with whipped cream and blanched almonds.

Peter Pan Lodge, Carmel, California

665. Angel Food Mold

(Serves 6 to 8)

INGREDIENTS

DIRECTIONS

1 envelope gelatin
½ cup cold milk

Soak gelatin in cold water about 5 minutes.

2 cups milk
2 egg yolks
1 cup sugar

Cook in double boiler, pour over gelatin and milk, stir to dissolve. Let cool.

1 teaspoon vanilla
2 egg whites—beaten
1 pint of whipping
cream—whipped

Add to cooled mixture.

Bits of angel food
cake

Put bits of angel food in mold and pour mixture over them.

Serve with whipped cream into which cut and sugared strawberries have been added.

Mrs. Voijt Frank Mashek, Chicago, Illinois

666. Baked Apple Sunshine

(Serves 12)

INGREDIENTS

DIRECTIONS

12 red cooking apples
1 pkg. dry mincemeat

Wash and core apples. Peel half way down from top. Fill centers with mincemeat. Place in baking pan.

1½ cups sugar
2 cups water

Mix together and boil for 5 minutes. Pour over apples and bake in 400° oven for 45 minutes, basting occasionally.

½ cup sugar

Sprinkle over apples and glaze quickly under broiler. Lift into serving dishes.

1½ cups orange juice
little grated orange
rind (Cranberry
juice or lemon juice
is also good.)

Drain juice from apples, add orange juice and rind and boil 10 minutes. Pour over apples, chill and serve with cream.

Dupuis Tavern, Port Angeles, Washington

There are four basic principles that should not be overlooked in cooking any dish—proper and accurate measurements, proper cooking temperature, proper length of cooking time and proper time of serving.

667. Arabian Nights Baked Apples   (Serves 8)

INGREDIENTS

8 large red tart apples
Brown sugar
Red color
Piece of orange peel

DIRECTIONS

Core and remove peeling down ¼ way from stem end. Place in kettle on rack and add ¾ cup hot water. Stuff cavities with sugar and color peeled part with a drop or two of red color. Put orange peel in water, put on lid and cook slowly until tender. Remove and let cool.

½ cup finely chopped dates
½ cup finely chopped figs
¼ teaspoon cloves
½ teaspoon cinnamon
2 teaspoons Jamaica rum

Mix all well together. Stuff cavities of apples, place in greased baking dish. Dust heavily with brown sugar which has been mixed with cinnamon and cloves. Brown in 375° oven until sugar caramelizes.

Chas. H. Baker, Jr., Coconut Grove, Florida. Author of "A Gentleman's Companion," books of exotic recipes.

668. Bananas Foster   (Serves 1)

INGREDIENTS

1 banana
2 pats butter
2 teaspoons brown sugar
1 teaspoon cinnamon

DIRECTIONS

Melt butter in Crepe Suzette pan of chafing dish. Peel banana and cut in half lengthwise and again crosswise so that there will be four pieces. Add to melted butter and sprinkle with brown sugar. Sprinkle with about 1 teaspoon cinnamon. Cook until banana is tender and falling apart, turning carefully several times while cooking.

1 teaspoon banana liqueur
1 oz. rum—Baccardi

When banana is tender, pour the banana liqueur and rum over it, flame and serve at once over vanilla ice cream.

Owen Brennan's Restaurant, New Orleans, Louisiana

To get better flavor and natural sweetness from cooked fruits serve while hot.

669.   Killarney Cherries

INGREDIENTS

DIRECTIONS

1 lb. ox-heart cherries
1 pint claret
1 cup sugar
1 stick cinnamon bark
12 whole cloves

Let come to boil, cover, then reduce heat and simmer 12 to15 minutes. Drain the cherries and chill. Cook juice until it reduces to about one-third.

2 tablespoons red currant jelly

Add to sauce, melt and chill.

3 tablespoons cherry brandy

Put in sauce just before serving.

1½ cups whipped cream
1 tablespoon Kirschwasser
1 tablespoon sugar

Serve cherries in silver dishes, set in bed of ice. Pour over sauce and top with whipped cream. Should be very cold.

Chas. H. Baker, Jr., Coconut Grove, Florida. Author of two books of exotic recipes, "A Gentleman's Companion."

670.   Coconut Bavarian Cream

INGREDIENTS

DIRECTIONS

1 pint coffee cream

Let come to a boil.

2 tablespoons gelatin
1 cup sugar
pinch salt

Dissolve gelatin in small amount of cold water. Add sugar and gelatin to cream and let cool.

1 teaspoon almond flavor
2 cups shredded coconut
1½ pint whipped cream

Add to above and chill in ring mold. When ready to serve, turn out on platter, top with more shredded coconut and serve with caramel sauce.

CARAMEL SAUCE:

1 tablespoon butter
1 lb. brown sugar
1 cup coffee cream
2 egg yolks
dash salt
1 teaspoon vanilla

Combine butter and sugar in double boiler. Add beaten egg yolks, cream and salt. When smooth and thick, let cool. Add vanilla.

Dolores Stephens Boyle, Oklahoma City, Oklahoma

Do not pare apples, pears, bananas, etc., before you are ready to serve or use. Otherwise they may discolor unless put in a dish and sprinkled with lemon juice.

671. Baked Pineapple Hawaiian
(Serves 4)

INGREDIENTS	DIRECTIONS
1 large pineapple	Cut off the top down the fruit 1½ inches. Reserve this for use later. Cut out the heart with a curved grapefruit knife, but do not dig through the shell. Dice the fruit, discarding the pithy section.
½ cup sugar	Coat the fruit and put back in the shell. Add the juice.
4 tablespoons Cognac	Pour over the fruit.
1 teaspoon cinnamon	Dust the fruit. Put the top back on and skewer in place. Bake in 350 F. oven 30 to 40 minutes until the fruit is tender. Serve on a silver platter.
1 tablespoon brandy	Light and bring to the table blazing.

Chas. H. Baker, Jr., Coconut Grove, Florida. Author of "A Gentleman's Companion," two volumes of exotic recipes.

672. Baked Prunes with Orange Slices
(Serves 6)

INGREDIENTS	DIRECTIONS
2 cups prunes—large size 2 cups water 1 stick cinnamon	Rinse prunes and place in a casserole, add water and cinnamon. Cover tightly and bake in 350° oven for 1 hour.
½ cup ganulated sugar 1 orange	Sprinkle sugar over prunes. Slice orange thinly and place on top of prunes. Cover and continue baking for 1 hour.

Mrs. Duncan Hines, Bowling Green, Kentucky

The guest helper in your kitchen usually succeeds in spoiling your good efforts.

For better health—eat more vegetables

673. Oranges a la Mirliton

(Serves 24)

INGREDIENTS	DIRECTIONS
24 oranges	Peel and save some of the skins. Quarter the oranges and slice the skins very thin and about two inches long. Julienne.
1 quart simple syrup	Have enough liquid to cover the oranges. Bring to a boil and add the oranges, together with the skins that have been julienned in thick syrup. Bring to a boil and remove from fire.
2 tablespoons Grenadine	Add to make a rosy red color. When thoroughly cooled, set in refrigerator to chill.
1 teaspoon Kirsch, Cointreau or any orange cordial	When ready to serve, add to each portion.

Le Mirliton, New York City

674. Peaches Flambees Royale

(Serves 4)

INGREDIENTS	DIRECTIONS
4 peaches 1 pint cold water ½ cup sugar ¼ stick cinnamon 1 lemon peel—whole	Cook peaches in this mixture with skins on. Let water come to boiling point and boil for 15 minutes, keeping the pot covered all the time. Take out the peaches, skin, cut them in half and remove pits. Place them in a chafing dish.
½ cup strawberries or raspberries—crushed ½ cup syrup (that the peaches were cooked in)	Put in chafing dish with the peaches and let get hot.
4 oz. brandy 2 oz. of Curaçao 3 or 4 small pieces of orange peel	Add to the above, and set aflame.
4 scoops of vanilla ice cream	Put in individual dishes and pour the flaming ingredients over all.

Mario Piccardi, Chicago, Illinois

Raw fruits and vegetables should be eaten with the skins as much as possible.

675. Fried Peaches

INGREDIENTS	DIRECTIONS
1 tablespoon butter	Place in frying pan and let melt.
6 to 8 peaches—peeled	Place whole peaches in pan.
1 cup brown sugar	Put over peaches and let simmer for 30 minutes. Keep turning the peaches.
½ cup cream	Just before serving, pour over peaches and let it boil up. Serve hot.

Fred Waring, New York City

676. Peaches Supreme

INGREDIENTS	DIRECTIONS
8 or 10 peaches—halved 1 vanilla bean ½ cup sugar ½ cup water	Cook just enough to tenderize peaches. Set aside to chill.
1 quart raspberries—fresh	Mash into a puree. Chill.

MAKE A BLACK CURRANT MOUSSE

| |
|---|---
1 cup black currant jam or fresh currants —strained
½ cup powdered sugar | Combine.
2 cups whipping cream —whipped
1 teaspoon vanilla | Fold into mixture and freeze in refrigerator tray, 2 hours.
2 tablespoons Cassis Liqueur
1 pint whipping cream —whipped
3 tablespoons currant jam | Just before serving, blend this mixture. Put the mousse on a platter, cover with brandy mixture. Put peaches on top and all around and pour puree over all.
½ lb. almonds—chopped | Top with nuts. Serve at once and have all mixtures ice cold.

Mrs. C. H. Welch, Tucson, Arizona

FOOD VALUE PLUS

Do you eat at least one green vegetable every day . . . more if possible? That's what the guide to good diet, drawn up by the Nation's nutrition experts, says each of us needs. For green vegetables are rich in many of the food values we need to help keep us healthy.

677. Peanut Brittle Delight

(Serves 6 to 8)

INGREDIENTS

- 2 cups peanut brittle
- 2 cups marshmallows
- 1½ cups whipping cream
- ½ teaspoon vanilla
- ½ cup sugar
- 1 cup peanuts

DIRECTIONS

Crush very fine.
Quarter.
Whip cream, add sugar and vanilla. Fold peanut brittle and marshmallows into whipped cream. Let stand two hours before serving. Serve in sherbet glasses. Garnish with peanuts.

Hotel Roanoke, Roanoke, Virginia

678. Pineapple Delight

(Serves 6)

INGREDIENTS

- 1 large ripe pineapple
- 1 pint fresh strawberries
- 1 large banana
- ½ cup creme de menthe

DIRECTIONS

Cut off the top of the pineapple, retaining the tips and all to use as a lid. Scoop out the meat of the pineapple, leaving only the rind with a thin inside layer of fruit pulp. Cut the scooped out fruit into small cubes. Put into a bowl with the strawberries which have been capped and washed. Chill. Just before serving quarter the banana and cube. Mix with other fruits and put all the fruit into the pineapple shell. Pour the creme de menthe over the fruit in the shell. Replace top. Serve from the pineapple into dessert dishes.

(Pineapple and strawberries may be sprinkled with sugar before chilling if desired.)

Mrs. Wallace Rigby, Larchmont, New York

679. Strawberries a la Tsarina

(Serves 2)

INGREDIENTS

- 2 cups stemmed strawberries
- 2 tablespoons powdered sugar

DIRECTIONS

Toss and put in bowl. Chill.

- 2 tablespoons port wine
- 2 tablespoons orange curaçao
- 2 tablespoons cognac

Blend and pour over berries.

- 1 cup whipped cream
- 1 teaspoon curaçao

Put berries in individual dishes, cover with cream and serve.

Chas. H. Baker, Jr., Coconut Grove, Florida. Author of those exotic recipe books, "A Gentleman's Companion."

680. Hedelmakeitto (Cold Fruit Soup)   (Serves 6)

INGREDIENTS | DIRECTIONS

½ lb. prunes
½ lb. apricots and pears (dried)
½ cup sugar

Wash in warm water and let soak overnight with the sugar added to 1½ quarts water.

3 fresh apples
1 cinnamon bark

Add to the above and boil. Strain the fruit.

1 to 2 tablespoons potato starch

Mix with the cold water and thicken the fruit juice. Boil again for a few minutes and add the fruit. Serve cold.

Mrs. Kuusamo, New York, New York

681. Strawberries Biltmore   (Makes 1 quart)

INGREDIENTS | DIRECTIONS

1 quart strawberries

Stem and clean and wash thoroughly. Drain on napkin.

rum—enough to cover berries
¼ lb. powdered sugar

Add to berries and let stand for 2 hours before serving. Not too long, however, as the berries will become soggy. Drain and serve very cold.

SAUCE:

1 pint vanilla ice cream
2 oz. Kirschwasser

Mix and stir well.

1 cup whipping cream —whipped
½ cup sugar

Fold into the above mixture and chill. Serve over the strawberries in glass compote.

Biltmore Hotel, Los Angeles, California

682. The Wonder Dessert   (Serves 5)

INGREDIENTS | DIRECTIONS

1 cup oranges

Cut in small pieces and squeeze out some of the juice. This is important or the dessert will be soft and run.

1 cup walnuts

Break in pieces not too small.

1 cup fresh marshmallows
¼ cup sugar

Cut with scissors and add sugar to prevent them from sticking together.

1 pint whipping cream —whipped
¼ teaspoon vanilla

If possible whip with an electric whipper to make stiff. Add vanilla and mix in other ingredients. Serve in fruit cup, piled high. Will keep for a few hours in refrigerator, but is better if served at once.

O. B. Wright, Long Beach, California

683.   Strawberry Lindomar
(Serves 8 to 10)

INGREDIENTS

15 marshmallows
½ pint crushed straw-
    berries

1 cup cream

½ pint sliced straw-
    berries
2 oz. sauterne

DIRECTIONS

Quarter marshmallows and melt in double
boiler with the crushed strawberries. Cool.

Whip cream and combine with above mixture.
Put in refrigerator tray and let freeze.

Pour sauterne over sliced strawberries just before serving and pour over frozen mixture as a
sundae.

Lindomar Hotel, Pacific Palisades, California

---

*When an unbaked pie crust is to be filled with a very moist
filling, it is best to brush its surface with a small amount
of lightly beaten egg white, and then to chill the crust. This
precaution will prevent the moisture of the filling from pene-
trating into the lower crust.*

*Pie a la mode is all right if it is good pie and the ice cream
is top-grade vanilla—but heaven forbid using chocolate.*

---

684.   Chocolate Ice Cream
(Serves 15)

INGREDIENTS

2 eggs—beaten
1 cup sugar
1 tablespoon flour

1 quart milk
3 squares unsweetened
    chocolate—melted

1½ cups sugar

1 teaspoon vanilla
1 pinch of salt
1 quart cream

DIRECTIONS

Cream together.

Scald milk and mix a little with the chocolate,
making a smooth paste. Add the balance of the
milk, and pour over the egg mixture. Cook
in double boiler, stirring until a custard.

Add to custard and cool.

Add to mixture. Put in freezer and freeze.

The Santa Fe Inn, Santa Fe, New Mexico

---

*If you freeze fresh fruit, may I suggest that you defrost them
about halfway when ready to serve. If you defrost them completely, they become soft and flabby and lose some of their flavor.*

685. Frozen Eggnog

(Makes 2 quarts)

INGREDIENTS	DIRECTIONS
5 egg yolks—beaten 1¾ cups sugar	Beat together until light and creamy.
¾ cup Bourbon nutmeg to taste	Add to mixture.
5 egg whites—beaten	Fold into mixture.
1 pint whipping cream —whipped	Add to mixture. Put in freezer and freeze. Pack until ready to serve. This can also be made in refrigerator trays.

Shadow Hill Tea Room, Hernando, Mississippi

686. Coffee Ice Cream

(Serves 18)

INGREDIENTS	DIRECTIONS
1 quart heavy cream 4 oz. coffee—ground	Boil together and let stand in closed jar for about 15 minutes.
1 quart heavy cream 2½ cups granulated sugar	Let come to boil.
10 egg yolks—beaten	Stir slowly into the cream and sugar mixture. Strain the coffee solution and add to the cream mixture.
Freeze for about 15 minutes.

Waldorf-Astoria Hotel, New York, New York

687. Fresh Peach Ice Cream

(Makes 3 quarts)

INGREDIENTS	DIRECTIONS
1 quart peaches— peeled and crushed	Stew the stones and skins slowly in a little water for 10 minutes.
1¼ cups sugar	Strain the above mixture into the sugar. Mix carefully, and add to the crushed peaches.
1 quart heavy cream	Mix with the peaches and freeze in electric freezer using 4 measures of ice to 1 of salt. When frozen, remove to an ice cream cabinet.

Hartwell Farm, Lincoln, Massachusetts

688. Lemon Ice Cream

(Makes 3 gallons)

INGREDIENTS

DIRECTIONS

5 teaspoons lemon
  extract
10 lemons—juice
10 cups sugar

Combine and let stand for 1 hour.

2 quarts whipping
  cream—whipped
5 quarts milk

Add to the above mixture and pour into
freezer and freeze.

Headley Inn, Zanesville, Ohio

689. Black Raspberry Ice

(Makes about 3 quarts)

INGREDIENTS

DIRECTIONS

2 quarts black
  raspberries
5 cups sugar
  juice of 6 lemons
3 cups hot water

Run raspberries through colander, then
squeeze through coarsely woven cloth, ex-
tracting every possible bit of pulp but no
seeds. Mix sugar and hot water, stir, and bring
to boil. Boil for 15 minutes. Combine lemon
juice, raspberries and syrup. Cool and freeze.

Virginia McDonald's Tea Room, Gallatin, Missouri

690. Three Fruit Ice

(Makes 2 quarts)

INGREDIENTS

DIRECTIONS

2 cups sugar
3 cups water

Heat water and dissolve sugar in water. Let
cool.

3 bananas
1 cup lemon juice
1 cup orange juice

Slice bananas thin and make puree by pass-
ing through sieve. Add to above with juices.
Freeze in refrigerator. If an old-fashioned
freezer is used, it is not necessary to puree the
bananas but chop fine.

Mrs. Wallace J. Rigby, Larchmont, New York

Butter keeps best in a covered dish.

*Keep your milk and cream in refrigerator with bottles securely
capped.*

691. Sherry Almond Ice Cream   (Serves 8)

INGREDIENTS	DIRECTIONS
1 tablespoon gelatin ¼ cup cold water	Soak gelatin in cold water about five minutes.
1 cup boiling water 1¼ cups sugar	Add to gelatin and stir well until dissolved. Cool. When it begins to set, beat with an egg beater until frothy.
6 egg whites—beaten	Fold into mixture.
⅓ cup sherry ½ teaspoon almond extract	Add to mixture.
1 cup almonds—chopped	Fill ring mold with alternate layers of mixture and nuts. Put in freezer and let set for 2 hours or until frozen through.
SAUCE:
6 egg yolks—beaten 1 pint milk	Cook in double boiler until it coats a spoon.
¼ cup sugar ⅛ teaspoon salt ½ teaspoon vanilla	Add to mixture and let cool.
3 tablespoons sherry	Add to cooled mixture.
½ pint whipping cream —whipped	Just before serving, fold into mixture, and fill the center of the mold.

Duncan Hines, Bowling Green, Kentucky

692. Macaroon Ice Cream   (Makes 3 pints)

INGREDIENTS	DIRECTIONS
24 stale macaroons	Roll to a crumb.
1 quart whipping cream	Scald and whip.
½ pint sherry wine 1 cup sugar	Dissolve the sugar in wine. Combine the two liquids.
1 cup shredded almonds	Add to combined liquids. Fold in crumbs and put in freezer. Freeze for at least 4 hours.

Duncan Hines, Bowling Green, Kentucky

The proper care in the preparation of food is of prime importance in the results achieved by a good cook.

693. Vanilla Ice Cream

(Makes 3 quarts)

INGREDIENTS	DIRECTIONS
3 pts. cream	Scald in double boiler.
1¼ cups sugar	Add to hot cream and stir to dissolve sugar.
8 egg yolks	Beat until thick and creamy. Add sugar and cream mixture gradually, beating well to make custard.
¼ teaspoon salt 1 teaspoon vanilla ⅛ teaspoon almond flavor	Stir into above. Let cool. Freeze, using 2 parts cracked ice to 1 part rock salt.

Forestwood Lodge, Grantsburg, Wisconsin

694. Spiced Iced Coffee

(Serves 6)

INGREDIENTS	DIRECTIONS
Make coffee as usual, only a little stronger	Strain and cool.
1 stick cinnamon 2 whole cloves 6 teaspoons sugar cream to taste	Add cinnamon, cloves, sugar, and cream. Strain while filling glasses.
½ cup whipping cream —whipped	Serve with a lot of cracked ice and top with dab of whipped cream.

Crestmont Inn, Eagles Mere, Pennsylvania

Try a drop of vanilla in your iced coffee.

695. Cafe Diablo

(Serves 6)

INGREDIENTS	DIRECTIONS
6 demitasses of coffee	Make in coffee-maker.
6 whole cloves ½ stick cinnamon 2 bay leaves 1 lemon peel 1 orange peel ¼ cup whole roasted coffee beans 6 lumps of sugar 2 oz. Jamaica rum 4 oz. brandy	Mix in deep chafing dish and set liquor afire. Keep stirring with a ladle and very slowly add the coffee, stirring all the time to keep the flame burning. Serve in demitasse cups, using ladle and a spoon to remove coffee beans.

Mario Piccardi, Chicago, Illinois

696. Apricot Rickey   (1 drink)

INGREDIENTS   DIRECTIONS

½ lime   Add ice and seltzer water.
2 tablespoons apricot
  syrup

Conrad Hilton Hotel, Chicago, Illinois

697. Fruit Punch   (1 gallon)

INGREDIENTS   DIRECTIONS

1 quart lemon juice   Mix all together and add a little seltzer water.
⅔ quart orange juice
1 pint pineapple juice
1 pint white grape
  juice
  grenadine to taste
  fruits in season

Conrad Hilton Hotel, Chicago, Illinois

698. Grenadine Rickey   (1 drink)

INGREDIENTS   DIRECTIONS

½ lime   Add ice and seltzer water.
2 tablespoons Grena-
  dine syrup

Conrad Hilton Hotel, Chicago, Illinois

699. Loganberry Punch   (1 gallon)

INGREDIENTS   DIRECTIONS

1 quart lemon juice   Mix all together and add a little seltzer water.
1 quart loganberry
  juice
⅔ quart orange juice
  loganberry syrup to
  taste
  fruit in season

Conrad Hilton Hotel, Chicago, Illinois

700. Hot Brick   (1 drink)

INGREDIENTS   DIRECTIONS

1 teaspoon butter   Put in glass and stir until butter is melted
1 teaspoon sugar   and sugar dissolved.
½ glass boiling water

1½ jiggers Bourbon   Add and stir. Drink while hot.
   whiskey

Col. C. H. Welch, Tucson, Arizona

701. Duncan Hines Mint Julep

(Serves 1)

INGREDIENTS

2 jiggers Bourbon whiskey
1 tablespoon whole mint leaves (do not crush)
1½ teaspoons simple syrup (more if you like it sweeter)

6 or 8 mint leaves cracked ice (not shaved)

3 springs of mint leaves
½ teaspoon powdered sugar

DIRECTIONS

Let stand for about 2 hours, then remove the mint leaves. Simple syrup is made by slowly cooking cane sugar and water until it becomes syrupy. If you prefer, honey may be used instead to sweeten liquor. Rim the julep cups with a piece of lime or lemon, dip in powdered sugar and set in refrigerator to frost.

Fill julep cups half full with cracked ice. Pour in the sweetened liquor and fill the cup with ice.

Put on top and sprinkle mint sprigs with powdered sugar for decoration and serve.

Duncan Hines, Bowling Green, Kentucky

702. Old English Raspberry Vinegar

INGREDIENTS

1 lb. ripe raspberries

1 qt. white wine vinegar. (This can be made by exposing any good white domestic wine to the air and adding 1 tablespoon vinegar.)

1 lb. ripe raspberries—crushed

1 lb. ripe raspberries—crushed

1 lb. lump sugar for each pint of juice

DIRECTIONS

Crush in a bowl.

Pour over the berries and let stand overnight. Then strain through a cloth.

Strain the above mixture through a cloth over this second pound of crushed berries and let stand overnight.

Strain as above over this third pound of crushed berries and let stand overnight.

Put sugar into stone crock and strain the entire mixture onto it. Do not squeeze the bag. Stir until sugar is dissolved. Put the crock in a pan of water and let simmer slowly. Skim now and then until it gets clear and there is no more scum. Cool and bottle. A teaspoon or so diluted in water with cracked ice, makes a delightful non-alcoholic cooler.

Chas. H. Baker, Jr., Coconut Grove, Florida. Author of "A Gentleman's Companion," books of exotic recipes.

703. Mid-Ocean Fizz

(Serves 1)

INGREDIENTS

1 jigger gin
½ jigger Cognac
½ jigger French dry
   vermouth
2 dashes orange bitters

DIRECTIONS

Shake well with cracked ice. Fill glass with chilled club soda and top with a twist of green lime peel.

Chas. H. Baker, Jr., Coconut Grove, Florida. Author of "A Gentleman's Companion," books of exotic recipes.

704. New Orleans Ramos Gin Fizz

(Serves 1)

INGREDIENTS

a dash of orange-
   flower water
½ jigger lemon juice
½ tablespoon simple
   syrup
2½ ounces dry gin
2 ounces cream
½ the white of one egg

DIRECTIONS

Plenty of ice and much shaking.

Duncan Hines, Bowling Green, Kentucky

705. Champagne Cocktail

(Serves 1)

INGREDIENTS

cracked ice

1 lump sugar

2 jiggers Cognac

1 pint Champagne

2 tablespoons Green
   Chartreuse

DIRECTIONS

Crack fine and fill a large glass.

Saturate with Angostura Bitters and put on top of ice.

Pour over the sugar and ice.

Pour over all.

Float on top.

This cocktail is fit for the gods. After two, I am sure you will agree.

Chas. H. Baker, Jr., Coconut Grove, Florida. Author of "A Gentleman's Companion," books of exotic recipes.

Hot sugar syrup is an excellent sweetening for beverages.

706. Omar's Delight

(Serves 1)

INGREDIENTS | DIRECTIONS

1 jigger Southern Comfort
½ lime—juice
⅓ oz. lemon juice
1 dash Curaçoa
½ teaspoon sugar

Frappe thoroughly.

Omar Khayyam's, San Francisco, California

707. Scarlett O'Hara Cocktail

(Serves 1)

INGREDIENTS | DIRECTIONS

⅔ jigger Southern Comfort
⅓ jigger cranberry juice
¼ lime—juice
2 cubes ice

Stir with ice, strain and serve.

Francis E. Fowler, Jr., Los Angeles, California

708. Tom Collins

(Serves 1)

INGREDIENTS | DIRECTIONS

½ lemon—juice
1 tablespoon bar sugar

Muddle.

2 oz. gin

Add to the above. Use a tall glass. Put in a couple of ice cubes.

1 split soda

Add soda. Stir well and relax.

The Blackstone, Chicago, Illinois

709. A Favorite "Old Fashioned" Cocktail

(Serves 1)

INGREDIENTS | DIRECTIONS

1 lump sugar
1 teaspoon cold water
1 dash Angostura Bitters

Muddle in a glass until dissolved.

1 cube of ice

Put into the glass.

1½ jiggers Southern Comfort

Pour over the ice and stir.

½ slice orange
1 maraschino cherry

Hang orange over side of glass, add cherry and serve.

Duncan Hines, Bowling Green, Kentucky

710. Duncan Hines Eggnog

(Serves 20)

INGREDIENTS	DIRECTIONS
36 strictly fresh egg yolks	Beat well.
1½ lbs. granulated sugar	Slowly beat into the eggs.
2 pints Jamaica rum	Add slowly, very slowly to eggs.
2 qts. milk	Stir into the above.
2 qts. heavy cream	
4 qts. Bourbon whiskey	Slowly add to mixture.
36 egg whites beaten stiff	Fold into eggnog. Pour into cups and top with grated nutmeg. (The flavor will be better if it stands in a cold place for about 6 hours.)

Duncan Hines, Bowling Green, Kentucky

711. Wild Moose Milk—A Different Eggnog

(Makes about 6 quarts)

INGREDIENTS	DIRECTIONS
1 quart milk	While liquid is slowly heating, add the sugar and stir until dissolved.
1 quart cream	
6 cups sugar	
9 nutmegs whole—cracked	Put in bag and add to mixture. Bring to boiling point, but do not boil.
2 or 3 sticks cinnamon	
3 dozen strictly fresh eggs	Break 6 eggs at a time and remove egg germ. (The germ is apt to make the mixture stringy, if not removed.) Beat eggs until thoroughly mixed, but do not beat until foamy. Do not try to beat all the eggs at one time. Put beaten eggs in a pitcher and add drop by drop to hot milk mixture, stirring all the while. The addition of the eggs is very important and cannot be hurried or the mixture will become lumpy. This process will take about three or four hours and when done the mixture will be a smooth custard. Remove from fire and allow to cool.
1 bottle rum (1/5 size)	Stir into mixture and put in bottles. Cork tightly and keep in cool place. Keeps indefinitely.
2 bottles brandy (1/5 size)	

When serving, the eggnog can be thinned with milk, cream, or water. Can be served either hot or cold.

Col. C. H. Welch, Tucson, Arizona

712. A Word About Coffee Making

Americans drink more than a hundred billion cups of coffee each year, and consumption is still increasing steadily. It is probably the number two beverage throughout the world, being second only to water. In the United States we have many different methods of preparing coffee, and some people have developed special techniques of their own to produce coffee unlike anything else wrung from a coffee bean.

Buy a good brand of coffee and the right grind for whatever brewing method you wish to use. Fresh coffee makes the best coffee, so do not store your supply too long.

Use cold water and never, never start with hot or tepid water if you want the best flavor from your coffee. For medium coffee use 1½ to 2 tablespoons of coffee per cup and vary the measurements either way to make it stronger or weaker. Serve as soon as possible.

I have found some of the new automatic coffee makers to be very good. The higher cost of these units over the conventional type of pots is off-set by the pleasure you get from a better cup of coffee.

If you have any left over coffee in the summer time, pour it into an ice cube tray and freeze it. Then you will have coffee cubes for your iced coffee.

713. Tea Made in the Sun for Iced Tea

I think you will enjoy the subtle flavor of tea made in the sun. In a quart bottle, place four teaspoons of tea, fill with cold water, cover with aluminum foil and place in sun in window or outside where the sun can shine on it. Length of time required to brew depends upon how hot the sun is, from 1½ to 3 hours. When sufficiently dark in color, strain, fill glasses with ice and pour in the tea. This amount will make four large glasses. You can vary the amount of the tea to accord with your personal taste. If you need more than four glasses of tea, add one teaspoon for each additional glass. After straining, dilute with water to desired strength. Tea made this way will have no bitter taste, since the tea was not put into hot water, the acrid oils were not extracted. If not all of the tea is used at noon, it will still be good for dinner.
Duncan Hines, Bowling Green, Kentucky

SEASONING FOODS

by a top chef or a housewife in the kitchen is far better than a person trying to do this with salt and pepper, etc., at the table.

BUYING MEATS

There is a wide variation in the quality of meats. Prime grades are found in comparatively few markets and not in many eating places because, first, there is not a sufficient amount of prime quality to supply the demand and also the price is necessarily high.

Normally the amount of beef coming into packing plants will not grade more than 8 per cent prime. At other seasons of the year, the amount will drop to 2 per cent or lower.

The next best grades are known as U. S. Choice No. 1, No. 2, No. 3, and these three additional grades amount to about 19 or 20 per cent of the total. Below these four grades, the quality rapidly drops and finally there is approximately 49 per cent which consists of old cows, bulls, low grade yearlings, etc.

In selecting your meat purchases, the first consideration should be to buy only U. S. Government inspected meats and then select the best grades your pocketbook will permit.

Buying fine beef is principally a matter of looking for certain definite characteristics. Good cuts of beef are plump—well filled out, with a thick smooth covering of white fat. The color of top grade beef is bright red, and the lean is streaked throughout with pure white fat. This latter quality, typical of all of the finest beef, is called "marbling." To make it easier for you to be sure of excellent beef, the packers brand their names *on the top grades.*

Good lamb is always in season, offering a multitude of piquant meat dishes to enliven the weekly menu. All lamb cuts are richly flavorful, and all lamb cuts are tender because lamb is young meat. Breeders have done much to improve the year 'round quality of lamb, so now you can always buy tender, delicious lamb.

Veal is a delicately flavored meat which may be served in an infinite number of ways. There are many unusual veal dishes, often served with tasty cheese or mushroom sauces. But equally delicious are flavorful roasts served with simple meat gravies.

Grades of pork do not vary greatly, and the pork you buy these days will be uniformly good in quality. To get the best flavor and true tenderness, pork should always be well-done. Roasts should be cooked at a moderate temperature to keep in the juices and to prevent the hardening of the surface meat.

Equally important, of course, is the reputation of the seller.

714.

THE ART OF CARVING
IN THE HOME

CORRECT carving is an art, which, when mastered is
an accomplishment that adds greatly to the charm
and grace of dining. It brings both genuine pleasure to the
carver and an abundance of praise from the assembled
guests.

In carving, as in everything else, there is a right and a
wrong way to do it, and invariably, the right way is the best
and easiest.

Do not take your carving duties as another one of those
unnecessary evils—a task that must be performed regardless of results. Carving technique is not difficult, but requires a knowledge of how and where to cut.

The best flavor of meats and fowl is emphasized when it
is carved and served in an appetizing manner.

How distressing it is, when guests see a host hack and
slash across one bone after another and bespatter the table
with odds and ends. Such performance always dampens
the appetite of those present. But what a pleasing contrast
it is to watch a carver, who dissects the joints smoothly without slashing up and down the bone, wondering if he will
ever hit the joint. When one carves with ease and grace,
producing smoothly cut pieces, it immediately brings forth
enthusiastic and favorable comment.

Avoid doing what one novice carver did to a roast of
beef. He judged his slices by his own appetite and cut
them so thick there was not enough meat to serve all those
present. Was he embarrassed? It is doubtful whether he
has offered to carve since.

The other extreme is a person carving slices so thin you

suspect he wanted the roast to last until next payday.

Carving should be done at the table always, except when there are many guests present, which makes this impractical. Thus carving is done in the kitchen.

Standing to carve is not necessary and certainly is not a graceful poise, as carving does not require unusual strength. The chair should be high enough so that the carver can do the job with ease and comfort.

No matter how good a story-teller you are, save them until after the carving is done, because slow carving takes the zest out of an otherwise fine dinner. While the carving is being done, let someone else tell the stories.

Knowledge, thoughtful practice, and always a sharp knife (which should be sharp when it is placed on the dinner table) are the essentials for good carving. Above all, do not hack, slash, or saw. Use a swinging, smooth stroke and cut across the grain whenever possible. If you cut parallel with the grain, the meat will be tougher. Also be sure that you inquire of your guests if they prefer rare, medium, or well done, light or dark meat, the oyster of a fowl, etc. Do not serve all the most delectable cuts to one or two persons.

After starting to slice, do not change the angle of your knife, or you will get a jagged slice instead of a nice, smooth one.

You should make a mental note of how many guests you have at your table, and for the first serving, cut no more than is needed, as the second helping should be as savory as the first. However, keep an eye on your guests' plates and be ready to carve and serve second helpings promptly when desired.

And then there are some men with robust appetites who cut hunks or slabs of meat or fowl when serving the ladies. Occasionally, you may encounter a woman who will hold her own in matching your eating capacity, but remember, it is better form to serve the ladies smaller slices. They will accept a second helping, if desired, just as readily as we men. No one relishes mountains of food on a plate.

After you have mastered the art of carving, then strive for speed.

Guests should appear unconscious of the efforts of the carver. The thoughtful hostess will engage the attention of the others so there will not be a pall of silence over the assembled guests as the carving is being done.

The method of carving in public eating places is necessarily quite different from carving in the home.

TO THE LADIES

In days gone by, so history records, ladies of royalty and others took weekly lessons from a Master Carver and became experts in the art of carving.

Later on, correct carving in the home became practically a lost art, but today, in America, many women are taking an active interest in carving; and what a thrill it is to watch a woman do an efficient and dainty job of it. It does not mean that their slices are skimpy, but as stated before, heavy pressure or great strength is not required. Men be careful, or the first thing you know, you will be relegated to the kitchen to become experts in the realm of dishwashing. If so, learn to do a clean job of it.

Before meats or fowl are arranged on the platter, see that any skewers, thread, cord, toothpicks, steel pins, etc., used for trussing are removed, excepting those used on rolled roasts, etc., that are necessary to hold the meat together while being carved.

Clean-cut slicing is impossible if the meat or fowl is over-cooked. The most attractive slices are the ones cut just the right thickness for the particular kind of meat that is being carved. Too thin slicing is ungenerous and too thick slicing lacks appetite appeal

All too often, the meat or fowl is placed on the table in the wrong position, making it impractical for the carver. In one home, to help overcome this unfortunate handicap, a chart was drawn showing the correct position in which a roast, etc., should be placed on the table. This chart was hung in the kitchen so the maid or anyone else could offer no excuse for placing the platter on the table in the wrong position.

The platter holding the roast, etc., should be of ample size, with enough margin around the meat — say 2 inches to 4 inches.

When a large roast or turkey is carved, there should also be a small extra platter (pre-heated) on which to place drumsticks, wings, etc. Place the brown or most appetizing side of the meat top side up on this platter.

Many carvers forget to serve parsley, watercress, etc., and serving more than just a bit is a hindrance. Do not put too many garnishes or vegetables on the platter when a roast is served, as you may see some of it scattered over the table. Remember, the carver needs plenty of room on the platter to do the right kind of job.

Very often the carver's end of the table is cluttered up with water glasses, candlesticks, flower vases, and other do-dads, so that there is not sufficient room for him to maneuver efficiently or gracefully. Be sure there is plenty of elbow room at this end of the table.

The carving directions given are for right-handed people. Left-handed folks will naturally adjust the position of the roast, etc., to suit their particular needs.

Spoons for serving gravy, dressing, etc., are very often overlooked when placing the carving set on the table. These are always necessary.

The illustrations that follow are of cuts of meats that are most frequently served in American homes, and the majority of these illustrations clearly show the principal bone structure of the various cuts of meats. If you will keep their location in mind, it will greatly aid you in your carving efforts.

While the art of carving cannot be mastered overnight, nevertheless it is not difficult to learn, and the reward of your efforts is the feeling of self-satisfaction, plus the praise of your guests which is a pleasure in itself, well worth striving for.

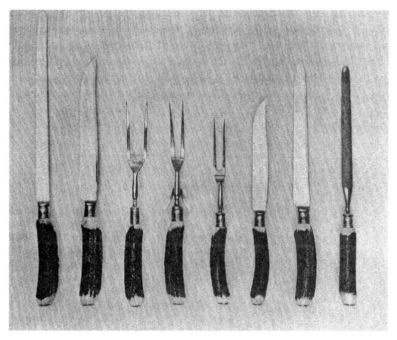

I enjoy using cutlery as illustrated above.

CARVING SETS

When buying a carving set, select one with steel that will satisfactorily hold an edge. The length of knives to be used for various cuts of meats and fowl is largely a matter of personal preference.

For broiled steaks or small game, a 5½-inch to 6-inch blade is used. The same type knife is also used for other broiled or fried meats.

For a roast of beef and a leg of lamb, veal, etc., or for general carving, a knife with an 8-inch blade may be used. For turkey or large roasts, use an 8½-inch to 10-inch blade.

All knives should be sharp when they are brought to the table, as no one can carve satisfactorily without having a sharp knife.

The carving set should be kept separate from the rest of the cutlery as a matter of precaution in protecting the carving edge of the knives. It is a wise practice to wash the carving set separately and place the knife blades in leather cases to avoid dulling the edges by running against the steel or fork, which usually happens if loosely laid away. For fish, use a silver knife with a broad 8-inch blade having a dull edge, and a wide fork. Fish does not stick to a silver knife.

HOW TO USE THE STEEL

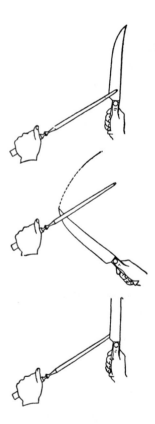

The steel is used to put a keen or sharp edge on the knife and there is a technique in handling it. The steel should be held firmly in the left hand, thumb parallel with fingers across and on top of handle. (See illustration.) Hold the point of the steel upward and slightly away from your body. Hold the knife in the right hand, as shown, place the heel of the blade (where the blade enters the handle) against the point of the steel on the side farthest from your body. With a quick swinging motion of the wrist and forearm, bring the blade down and across the steel toward the left hand, and continue this motion until the point of the blade has passed over the steel. Then the knife is again brought into position, but this time on the side of the steel nearest your body, and with the same motion, is drawn across the steel. This brings both sides of the blade in contact with the steel. As a rule, a half dozen strokes on each side will be sufficient. Do not bear too heavily on the knife, nor hold it at too great an angle. The edge of the knife should make about a 25-degree angle with the steel. The same steel may be used for short and long knives.

A PORTERHOUSE STEAK

The first step is to separate the meat from the bone as shown in illustration (on next page). The carver holds the steak steady by inserting the fork to the left of the large muscle and with the point of the steak knife severs the meat from around the bone, making the cut as close to the bone as possible. The bone should be removed to one side of the platter, so it will not interfere with making the slices.

With the fork still in position, and with the knife at right angles to the original position of the bone, the carver cuts slices about one inch in width, beginning at the bone end as illustrated (on next page). In this way the tenderloin and the large muscle are cut at the same time. It may be necessary, however, to cut thinner slices from this tenderloin section in order to serve each person a portion. (See drawing.) A slice of the tenderloin and wide muscle should be served each person.

In carving steaks, cut slices at an angle to hold in the juices

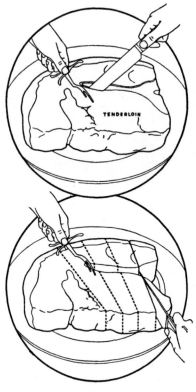

and prevent the meat from drying out too quickly.

Unless the number of persons to be served makes it necessary, the flank end of the steak is not carved, but may be used in some attractive left-over dish at another meal. If it is to be served, it should be cut across the width. Thus the fibers that run lengthwise in this part of the steak are shortened and make a more desirable serving.

SIRLOIN AND OTHER STEAKS

Carving a sirloin steak is essentially the same as carving a porterhouse steak. The bone is removed by cutting down close to it with the point of the knife. The steak is then cut into slices about one inch in width, cutting them on an angle to hold in the juices and prevent the meat from drying out too quickly. In carving any steak, the width of the slice is usually determined by the number of persons to be served. In sirloin steaks, the direction of the muscles changes, and the angle of the blade should be increased to cut the fibers as short as possible.

Carving a pin-bone sirloin steak is much easier if the pin bone is removed by the butcher and the flank end ground and inserted in the cavity left by removal of the bone. This not only makes carving easier, but it solves the problem of the flank end, because grinding this portion cuts the connective tissues and the flank end is made just as tender as the rest of the steak.

ROUND STEAK

As a rule, the butcher cuts round steak much thinner than porterhouse or sirloin steaks, and in carving round steak much wider portions are served. The individual portions usually are cut about 2 inches wide and 3 inches to 4 inches long. The natural divisions between the muscles may serve as a guide in carving round steak.

SWISS STEAK

A swiss steak, being thicker than round steak, individual servings are carved thinner than a round steak.

BEEF TENDERLOIN

Being boneless, beef tenderloin presents no problem in carving, except to cut even slices.

The carver holds the meat with the fork grasped in his left hand. Beginning at the large end, the tenderloin is cut across in slices a little less than $\frac{1}{2}$ inch in thickness.

BEEF BRISKET

Place boned beef brisket on the platter with the flat side down and with the largest end to the right of the carver. The general direction of the muscle fibers is parallel to the length of the platter. With the fork inserted in the thick part of the brisket, the carver begins at the small end and cuts straight down to the platter, making slices not more than $\frac{1}{8}$ inch in thickness. These slices are cut across the grain of the meat.

BEEF TONGUE

The tongue should be trimmed, removing the skin, etc., before bringing it to the table. It should be placed on the platter with the large end to the right and the rounded side away from the carver. The fork is inserted in the thick part, and thin slices are cut straight down across the grain. About $2\frac{1}{2}$ inches of the tip end should be severed and sliced lengthwise, so as to get the greatest number of good-sized slices.

ROASTING

In spite of the ideas prevalent in the minds of many experienced cooks, the following rules for roasting meats have been formulated as a result of scientific experimental studies.

1. A moderately low oven temperature should be used.

2. Searing does not keep in juices and, therefore, is unnecessary.

3. The roast should be placed in the pan fat side up, thus it often eliminates basting.

4. A roast may be salted before or after cooking.

5. A roast should never be covered.

6. Water should not be added.

7. Flouring a roast is unnecessary.

8. A meat thermometer is the most accurate means of telling when a roast is rare, medium, or well done.

The rules of roasting given above apply to beef, veal, pork, and lamb; but, naturally, there are certain variations in roasting the different kinds of meat.

A good carver keeps his eyes on whatever is being carved.

Better use a wooden carving board rather than a slippery china or silver platter.

The temper of a host is often judged by his carving.

STANDING RIB ROAST

Have the backbone separated from the ribs at the market, as this facilitates removing the backbone easily after roasting. With the backbone removed in the kitchen, carving is much easier because it leaves only the rib bones from which the slices must be cut.

The roast is placed before the carver with the cut surface up and the rib side to his left. The carver firmly inserts the fork, with the guard up, between the two top ribs; beginning at the outside right edge at the large end of the roast, the knife is drawn through the roast to the rib side as shown in top drawing. A slice about ⅜ inch thick makes an attractive serving. It may be somewhat thicker or thinner according to personal preference.

The slice is loosened by cutting along the rib bone with the tip of the knife as shown in middle drawing.

As each slice is cut, it is steadied with the fork and lifted on the blade of the knife (as shown in bottom drawing) to one side of the platter, or if the platter is not large enough, to another hot smaller platter placed near the carver to receive the slices as they are made.

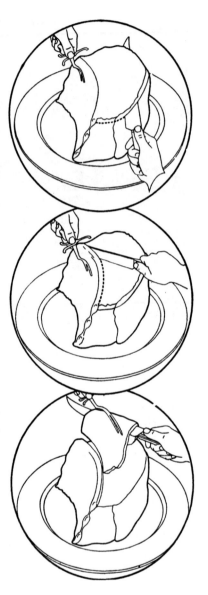

ROLLED RIB ROAST

In carving a rolled rib roast, the important consideration is to make even slices which are uniform in thickness. To accomplish this, care should be taken not to alter the angle of the knife when making the slices.

The rolled rib roast is held together by cords, which obviously cannot be removed in the kitchen. If they were, the roast would fall apart. Good carving of a rolled rib roast, therefore, necessitates the cutting and disposition of cords in a neat manner. Only one cord is severed at a time as it is reached in making the slices. The cord is cut with the point of the knife, loosened with the fork, and removed to one side of the platter.

The roast is placed on the platter with the smaller cut side up and the larger side down so it will rest firmly. The carver holds the roast steady by inserting the fork at the extreme left 1 inch or 2 inches below the top of the roast as illustrated. The guard on the fork should be up as it is in all cases when the carver is cutting toward his left hand. As the slices are made, the carving fork is taken out and moved downward from time to time as necessary.

In making the slice, the carver draws the knife from right to left through the roast. The thickness of the slice depends on personal preference and will vary from ⅛ inch for a thin slice to ⅜ inch for a thick slice. As each slice is carved, it is lifted on the blade of the knife and steadied with the fork as it is placed on one side of the platter, or to another hot platter provided for this purpose, or on the dinner plate.

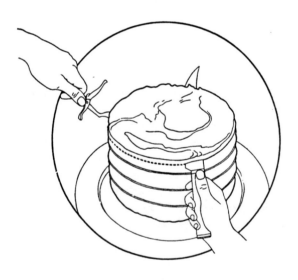

BLADE POT ROAST

A blade pot roast contains at least a portion of one rib and a part of the blade bone. In the relatively long cooking period, the connective tissue, which binds the bones to the muscles, is softened to such an extent that these bones are loosened and may be slipped out easily, in which case it is just as well to remove them in the kitchen before the roast is brought to the table for carving. The carver then has only the task of making attractive servings from a boneless piece of meat. The chief problem in carving a blade pot roast, whether the bone is in or not, is to make attractive slices across the grain of the meat. There are several muscles, the fibers of which run in different directions, and because of this, and because the bones may be in the roast, it is not possible to carve a slice parallel to the cut surface, such as one does in carving a rib roast. A very satisfactory method of carving a blade pot roast is illustrated on next page.

Holding the pot roast firmly with the fork inserted into the left, and following the natural dividing line between muscles, the carver removes a small section of the pot roast, separating the meat from the blade bone (if it has not been removed in the kitchen). The first drawing shows the carver cutting one section by running the knife along the division between two muscles and between the muscle and the bone. Next, the carver inserts the fork in the piece just separated; and, with the knife on the top surface, he turns the meat so that the surface, which was in a horizontal position, is now in a vertical position, as shown in the second drawing. The grain of the meat is now parallel with the platter, and the carver can easily cut slices across the grain. With the fork inserted in this smaller portion of the roast (shown in the third drawing), the carver cuts slices down to the platter.

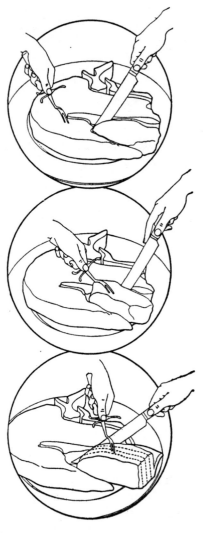

These slices should be cut ¼ inch to ⅜ inch in thickness. When one section of the pot roast is carved in this fashion, another section is carved in the same manner.

ROAST LOIN OF PORK

It is much easier to carve a roast loin of pork if the backbone has been separated from the ribs. This is done by the butcher sawing across the ribs close to and parallel to the backbone. The backbone becomes loosened during the roasting and is removed by cutting close to the backbone and parallel to the ribs as shown on the drawing. (On next page.)

The roast is placed on the platter so that the rib ends are up and the platter is placed before the carver so that the rib side is toward him. There are two good reasons for placing the roast before the carver in this fashion. First, the guests at the table see the more attractive side of the roast, and, second, it is much easier for the carver to follow the direction of the rib bones, which are his guide in making the slices, as all of the rib bones may not be absolutely perpendicular to the platter.

In carving a roast loin of pork, it should be borne in mind that the servings are more tempting if the slices are cut fairly thin. A fork is inserted between the ribs to hold the roast firmly. The carver then draws the knife as close as possible to the left side of the first rib. In making the second slice, the knife is drawn as close as possible to the right side of the second rib. The third slice will be cut close to the left side of the second rib. Proceed in the same manner until there are enough slices to serve everyone at the table. One serving will contain a rib bone and the next will be boneless. It is not necessary to lift the slices to one side of the platter; instead they are allowed to fall back as they are cut off.

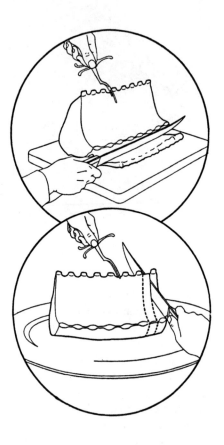

If personal preference indicates serving thicker slices than those previously outlined, then the cut is made between each two pairs of ribs; thus each serving contains a rib.

With a large roast loin of pork, it may be possible to cut two boneless slices between each two ribs.

CROWN ROAST OF LAMB OR PORK

A crown roast of lamb or pork which has been prepared properly at the market is very easy to carve. In fact, the carver proceeds in much the same manner as in carving a pork loin roast.

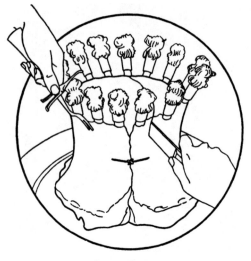

Crown Roast

The carver steadies the crown roast by inserting the fork to the left between the ribs. He then makes the slices by cutting through the center between each two ribs.

One chop and a portion of dressing or vegetables that may be used to fill the center of the crown are served to each person.

A crown roast of lamb or pork is suitable for special occasions, and it lends itself to many garnishes and may be served with a number of different accompaniments.

BONED AND ROLLED SHOULDER ROASTS

Veal and lamb shoulders are boned and rolled for roasts and are placed on the platter with the cut surface at right angles to the platter. The carver makes the slices by cutting from the top of the roast down to the platter and allowing each slice to fall back as it is made. Boned and stuffed shoulder roasts are carved in the same manner, i.e., down through the meat and the dressing to the platter. These rolled shoulder roasts are held together with cords or skewers, which are removed by the carver as required.

ROAST (*left*) LEG OF LAMB

Strange as it may seem, few carving instructions have ever taken into consideration the fact that both right and left legs must be carved, yet with the shank end always to the left of the carver, it is obvious that there will be a difference in the position of the cushion as it lies upon the platter. If a left leg, the cushion will be toward, and the thin side away from, the carver, as shown in illustration above. If a right leg, the reverse is true. Behind the leg bone in both a right or left leg is a large meaty section known as the cushion. It is from this section that the most desirable servings are obtained. In front of the leg bone in either leg is the thinner section.

Drawings show a right leg.

Understanding the location of the bones will be a great help to the carver in making the most desirable servings. The two lower drawings indicate the bone structure and the lines on the chart represent the direction the knife will follow in making the slices. Note the relation of these lines (slices) to the bones.

If a large (right) leg, illustrated at right, the carver first inserts the fork firmly in the large end of the leg and carves two or three lengthwise slices from the thin side by turning the platter as shown in top drawing. This makes a flat surface on which the roast is then turned upright and rests firmly on this cut surface while the cushion is carved, as shown on two lower drawings. If it is a large left leg, the thin section will be away from the carver, in which case simply turn the platter in order to make these first few slices to form the base upon which the roast will rest while continuing the carving.

With the fork inserted in the left of the roast, and beginning at the shank end of the leg, the carver makes the first slice down to the leg bone and continues to make slices until the aitch bone is reached, if that many slices are required. These slices should be ⅛ inch to ¼ inch in thickness to make the most attractive servings. With the fork still in place the carver runs the knife parallel to the leg bone, right to left, in order to free the slices all at one time. These slices should be served on very hot plates with a little of the natural (mint-flavored) gravy.

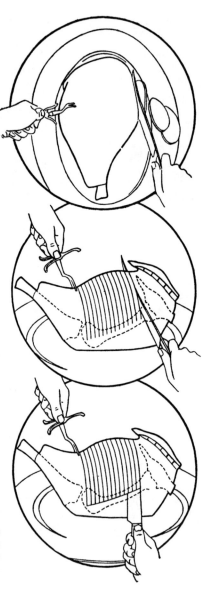

A WHOLE HAM

There are many ways of carving hams; and while the method illustrated in the four drawings may appear to some as a decided departure from established procedure, it is not a departure from principles and has been carefully worked out to find the easiest way to secure the maximum number of servings, uniform in size and attractive in appearance.

Carving a whole ham presents some of the same problems encountered in carving a leg of lamb. It has the same bone and muscle structure, and right and left legs should also be considered. Since a baked ham is usually decorated in some way, it should be placed on the platter with the fat side up. The shank end should be to the carver's left, the same as a leg of lamb. If a right ham, the thin side of the ham will be nearest the carver, and if a left ham, be away from him. (The photograph shows a left ham, and the drawings show a right ham.)

In carving a right ham (see drawing), the first two or three slices are cut parallel to the length of the ham from the thin side, which is nearest the carver. The purpose of making these first few slices is to form a base upon which the ham may more firmly rest upright while the carving is being done. Next turn the ham so it rests upright on this flat-cut surface (see the two center drawings for bone structure of a ham). Hold the ham firmly with the fork and cut a small wedge-shaped piece near the shank end (note drawing); this facilitates making the slices and releasing them from the bone after they are made (note drawing). The carver then proceeds to cut thin vertical slices down to the leg bone until the aitch bone is reached. With the fork still in place to steady the ham, the slices are released from the bone by running the knife along the leg bone at right angles to the slices. If, after carving one side, more servings are desired, the ham is turned back to its original position on the platter with the fat side up, and slices are again cut at right angles to the bone. These slices are not as wide as those from the cushion section, but they do make attractive servings for second helpings.

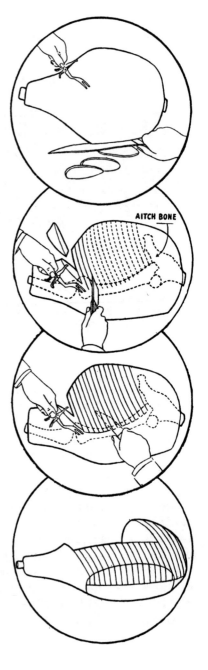

AITCH BONE

The method of carving a left ham is the same as for a right one, except that the first few slices will be removed from the side farthest from the carver. If desired, the carver may swing the platter around to carve the first few slices from the thin side.

I have seen hams carved in many different ways, and a common practice has been to lay the ham flat on the platter, fat side up, hock end to the carver's left and the butt end to the right. With the fork firmly inserted into the meat about 2½ inches to the right of the small end, make the first cut a "V" about 3 inches right of the hock, then slice straight through the ham down to the bone. After cutting as many slices as needed for the first servings make a horizontal cut from right to left along the top of the bone to loosen all slices at one time. Lift all the slices at once and place them on a service platter. If, after cutting slices across to the aitch bone, it is necessary to carve more slices, turn the ham over and proceed to carve the remaining side in the same way.

Some carvers remove the aitch bone in the butt end and stand it upright on a flat platter or in a round deep dish, holding it by the shank end in a vertical position.

CARVING A HALF HAM

The shank end of a half ham is not as difficult to carve as the butt end, because the bone is round and the carver can see it from the face side. Beginning at the face of the ham (cut surface), slices are cut down to the bone; then the knife is run parallel to the bone to free the slices. After the top side is carved, the ham is turned over and the other side is carved in the same way.

Carving a butt end will be much easier if the aitch bone is removed before carving. The face of the ham should be toward the carver's right, fat side up. Beginning at the top, thin slices are cut from the face of the ham down to the leg bone, and removed by cutting along the bone at right angles to the slices.

In carving a half ham, it is easier to carve only two or three slices at a time and remove them, rather than to make all the slices and attempt to separate them from the bone at one time.

SHRINKAGE OF MEAT DURING COOKING

The question of shrinkage in meat during cooking is one of considerable practical importance, because shrinkage affects appearance, palatability, nutritive value, and the number of servings. It is important, therefore, that shrinkage in cooking be kept as low as possible—consistent with an attractive and palatable product. Shrinkage is the difference between the weight of the meat before it is cooked and its weight after cooking. Losses which occur during cooking are of two kinds: (1) Evaporation loss and (2) drippings loss.

CARE OF MEAT IN THE HOME

When meat is received from the market, it should be unwrapped and wiped or scraped off—but never washed—and stored immediately in the coldest part of the refrigerator. The meat should be placed on a clean, dry plate or shallow dish, uncovered or lightly covered. The reason for not closely covering meat stored in the refrigerator is that a little drying of the surface is desirable, because it retards bacterial growth. The meat may be lightly covered by placing a piece of waxed paper loosely over the top. Cooked meats should be covered because the surface has been dried out during cooking and further drying in the refrigerator is undesirable.

Smoked meats, such as ham and bacon, should be kept in a dark, cold place. When preparing bacon, only the amount required should be removed from the refrigerator. If the package or container is taken out and allowed to stand at room temperature while the meal is prepared, moisture will condense on it and lessen the keeping qualities of the bacon.

The packer and the retailer keep meat under the best possible storage conditions, so that it will reach the consumer in the best possible condition. But from the time of delivery until the meat is cooked, keeping meat under proper storage becomes the homemaker's responsibility.

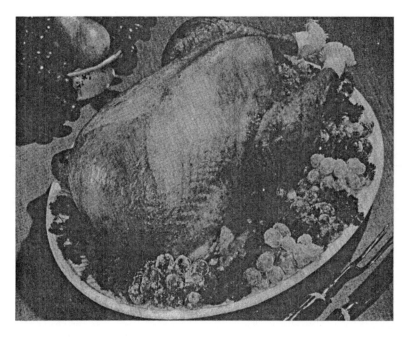

A TURKEY

Again I emphasize the importance of having anything you carve placed in the correct position on the table. The turkey legs should be placed to the carver's right and the neck to his left. Usually the turkey comes to the table lying flat on its back.

In general, the muscles run lengthwise of the bird. Before starting to carve, tilt it a bit forward so the legs and wings are in a more accessible position to sever. Then remove the leg (both drumstick and thigh in one piece). To do this, only three cuts are necessary. Meanwhile the bird is held firmly by placing the fork astride the keel or breast bone. Make the first cut in front of the thigh and cut deep to the pinion or joint which holds it to the backbone. Second, cut back of the thigh to the pinion joint. These two cuts practically make a V. Third, cut the skin between the leg and body so it will not tear as the thigh is removed. All three cuts are shown in the top drawing (next page). Finally, grasp the frilled drumstick in your fingers, turn it toward you and the entire leg should easily and quickly pull cleanly away from the socket joint. Of course, if the turkey is not thoroughly cooked, it may be necessary to force the leg away from the body with the knife to dislocate the joint. Lay the entire leg (drumstick and thigh) on the hot side platter. To separate the leg (drumstick) from the thigh, lay the browned side down, because the inside permits the joint to be more clearly seen and is an easier way to sever with one clean cut through the joint as shown on the drawing. If an attempt is made to sever this joint by cutting from the outside, you may be a bit embarrassed, because the joint is not so readily visible from that side. After the drumstick and thigh have been severed, place them upright on the

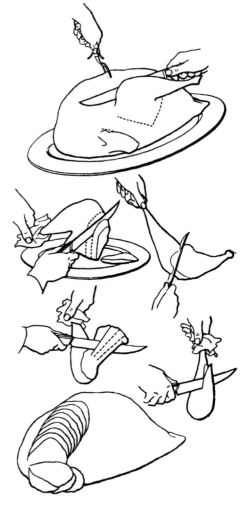

platter, so the brown side is on top, which is more appetizing to your guests.

Next, remove the wing. Here some carvers encounter difficulties because they fail to observe the fact that the joint that holds the wing to the shoulder is much closer to the body than the joint that holds the thigh to the backbone. Therefore, in removing the wing, first make one cut on the outside a little in front of the shoulder joint. The second cut forms another V as shown on the top drawing. Then cut under the wing to sever it from the body, and as the joint is approached, turn the knife inward toward the front of the shoulder and cut deep enough so the blade will strike between the joint. Now place the fork under the end of the wing and push out and forward. It should disjoint easily. Place the wing on the side platter and, again, it is easy to sever the upper and lower part when cut from the inside. (The tips of the wings should be removed before roasting, there is little meat on them to eat, and they are good for flavoring soups and gravies.)

A small piece of dark meat, the "oyster," is a choice morsel which lies in the cavity in the back, or on each side of the backbone just above the thigh, ahead of the tail. From the drumstick, slice the dark meat in 1/4-inch slices. These slices are made by holding the end of the drumstick upright in the left hand and cutting from the inside down through the ligaments as shown on drawing. In slicing the thigh, hold it flat on the small platter with the fork and cut in 1/4-inch slices. These lengthwise sections are then cut across the grain at a 45-degree angle into two, three, or four pieces, depending on the size of the bird. Do not stop to do a clean job of the bone.

Some carvers leave the drumstick and thigh in one piece. To carve in this manner, hold the drumstick as shown on drawing, slice the meat first from the thigh and then from the drumstick. It does not matter much which method you follow, but be sure to cut attractive-looking slices.

Some carvers place the dark meat at one end of the small platter and the white meat at the other end.

In carving the breast or white meat, hold the fork in the left hand and insert it firmly astride the keel or breast bone, just beyond its highest point. Another way is to insert the fork through the rib section. Some people carve the breast parallel to the breast bone, but many prefer the method shown on drawing, which is my favorite, because I can carve more uniform and appetizing slices by using this angle across the grain. Whether to carve enough white meat to serve all plates, or to cut the breast as each plate is served, depends on the preference of the carver, but in any case you should follow the method that will insure hot meat for all and be in keeping with the type of dinner service. Usually cutting slices as each plate is served is the better procedure.

Another method of carving a turkey is to remove only the drumstick portion of the leg, removing the wing as before, then tip the bird on its side, so the breast portion is away from the carver. This brings the thigh (still attached to the body) uppermost. Carve the dark meat from the thigh by slicing parallel to the bone, first on one side, then on the other side. This technique yields thick or thin slices as may be desired. The thigh is easily held in position with the fork placed astride the thigh bone.

Some carvers slice the breast upwards, but the majority prefer to carve the breast as outlined on the drawing.

A spoon is used for serving the dressing from the vent end, which usually has sufficient opening without further cutting. The vent end is more convenient for getting at the dressing until the bird needs turning around to carve the remaining side. Then, if need be, remove the dressing from the neck region, by cutting a section of skin and folding it back.

In serving, first place the dressing on the plate and on top of it, or to one side, the dark meat, and on top of the dark meat place slices of white meat. As some people prefer giblet gravy over the meat and dressing, others like it on the meat, and others on the dressing only, and some dislike it altogether, I believe the best procedure is to have the gravy served by someone else, or passed.

CAPON OR ROAST CHICKEN

A capon or chicken is carved in practically the same manner as a turkey. The principal difference is in the smaller size of pieces served. However, some carvers, after removing the leg, thigh, and wing, prefer to have the position of the bird at right angles with the breast facing the carver.

The drumstick and thigh cannot be cut into as many pieces as a turkey and very often these pieces are served as full portions.

The back is smaller than a turkey, and for that reason the oyster may be too small to offer.

Broiled or fried chicken is usually served as it is cut for cooking.

These, or any other water fowl, are carved somewhat differently from a turkey or chicken, because the shape of the body is different. The greater portion of the meat is on the breast, consequently some carvers prefer slicing the breast before removing the legs or wings.

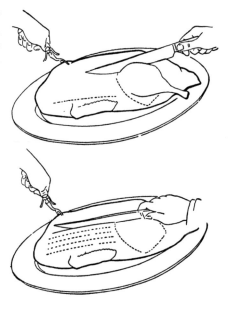

Although some epicures consider the wings a choice part, there is little meat on them, and many carvers make a cut parallel with the breast, just above the wing joint (see drawing), and do not remove or serve the wings.

The position of the bird on the table is the same as for a turkey or chicken.

To remove the leg and thigh in one piece, make a V cut, the same as for carving a turkey, but remember, the thigh joint lies closer to the backbone and is more difficult to remove from a small water fowl than from a chicken or turkey. You may need to use the knife blade to pry the thigh away from the back to dislocate the socket joint.

To carve the breast, leave the wing intact, insert the knife just above the wing joint parallel to the keel or breast bone, and push the knife straight down. As it hits the breast bone, turn the blade slightly to loosen the meat from the bone. Hold the bird by inserting the fork prongs deep and piercing the breast bone; one prong on each side. Do not carve the slices too thick. An average duck should yield four slices on each side of the breast, a larger duck, five or six slices. Some carvers prefer placing the duck or goose with the breast facing them, but, again, the position is a matter of personal preference.

LARGE FISH

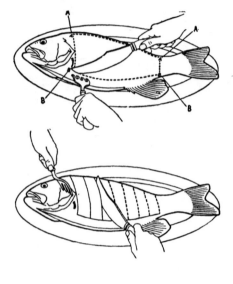

Place the whole fish on a platter, tail to the right and the backbone away from the carver. Use a broad 8-inch silver (not steel) blade knife with a blunt edge and a wide fork. Hold the fish firmly by placing the fork in the head, as shown on drawing. Sink the blade of the knife deep to the middle from "A" to "A" and from "B" to "B," also cut from "A" to "B" near the head and tail (see drawing), then cut in 1-inch to 1½-inch slices as indicated. Use the same procedure for carving the other side of the fish.

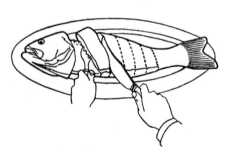

SMALL PAN FISH

When serving small pan fish, first cut from "A" to "A" and from "B" to "B," also from "A" to "B" along the lines as shown on drawing. Then lift the entire filet away from the bone structure by first loosening and lifting along the top line "A" to "A" and then down to the bottom line "B" to "B." Each side or filet is served as one portion.

Thanks to the National Live Stock and Meat Board, Chicago, for their aid in compiling these carving instructions.

Acknowledgments

I want to thank Cora Jane Spiller, Duncan Hines's great-niece, for providing me with many aspects of the information found in these pages concerning the individuals who contributed these recipes. She has always made herself available whenever I've needed some help in tracking down some arcane matter pertaining to Duncan Hines, and I want to record my sincere thanks here.

I also want to thank Ashley Runyon, my editor, for guiding this book from start to finish, as well as the entire production staff at the University Press of Kentucky for doing a fine job.

Index

CPSIA information can be obtained at www.ICGtesting.com
Printed in the USA
BVOW02s0619280314

348991BV00001B/1/P